MAKING SENSE OF SENTENCING

Edited by Julian V. Roberts and David P. Cole

On 3 September 1996, Bill C-14 was proclaimed in force, initiating one significant step in the reform of sentencing and parole in Canada. This is the first book that, in addition to providing an overview of the law, effectively presents an analysis of the legal reforms and their ramifications in this controversial area.

The commissioned essays in this collection cover such crucial issues as options and alternatives in sentencing, patterns revealed by recent statistics, sentencing of minority groups, Bill C-41 and its effects, conditional sentencing, and the structure and relationship between parole and sentencing. An introduction and a concluding chapter draw the essays together resulting in a timely, comprehensive, and extremely readable work on this critical topic.

Broad in scope and perspective, this major new socio-legal study of the law of sentencing will be illuminating to students, members of the legal profession, and the general reader.

JULIAN V. ROBERTS is Professor of Criminology at the University of Ottawa and editor of the *Canadian Journal of Criminology*. He previously worked for the Department of Justice Canada and the Canadian Sentencing Commission.

DAVID P. COLE is a Provincial Court Judge in Scarborough, Ontario, and is co-author of *Release from Imprisonment: The Law of Sentencing*. He was co-chair of the Commission on Systemic Racism in the Ontario Criminal Justice System.

Making Sense of Sentencing

EDITED BY
JULIAN V. ROBERTS AND DAVID P. COLE

UNIVERSITY OF TORONTO PRESS
Toronto Buffalo London

Toronto Buffalo London
Printed in Canada

ISBN 0-8020-0686-8 (cloth)
ISBN 0-8020-7644-0 (paper)

Printed on acid-free paper

Canadian Cataloguing in Publication Data

Main entry under title:

Making sense of sentencing

Includes bibliographical references and index.
ISBN 0-8020-0686-8 (bound) ISBN 0-8020-7644-0 (pbk.)

1. Sentences (Criminal procedure) – Canada. I. Roberts, Julian V.
II. Cole, David P., 1948– .

KE9355.M34 1998 345.71'0772 C98-932131-2
KF9685.M34 1998

University of Toronto Press acknowledges the financial assistance to its publishing program of the Canada Council for the Arts and the Ontario Arts Council.

Contents

Foreword

The very existence of the volume you hold in your hands is evidence of audacity, of real courage on the part of those who conceived and executed it. Their task – making sense of sentencing – is daunting. Given the shifting, ambiguous, and contradictory purposes and objects of our sentencing system, it must be conceded that it is unlikely to be fully achieved, at least in our lifetime. But the dread importance of sentencing and the amount of human endeavour put into this painful and capricious exercise makes it important to comprehend what we can and to do what we can to make things better.

Not all of the decisions that affect sentence fall within the scope of these studies. Indeed, many of the most important ones lie outside it. Decisions regarding sentence are often made in other contexts, for example, in plea and sentence bargaining between counsel or, even earlier, at the stage of prosecutorial discretion exercised by police, by responses to budget constraints, or in the mist-shrouded process of setting enforcement priorities. Those decisions are hidden and largely undefined: an unwatched exercise of very broad discretion.

Sentences imposed reflect competing exercises of power by different participants in the criminal justice system, even in the absence of sentencing 'guidelines.' Indeed, even within the accountable and visible parts of the sentencing structure, the pushes and pulls of the system itself are often changing, reflecting a pecking order in which Crown attorneys filch power from judges, and, in turn, judges snatch power from parole boards.

In a sense, these changes can be considered minor, for one phenomenon overwhelms them all: we, as a society, remain addicted to punishment. The individuals who influence punishment decisions may change, but this peculiar and singularly ungratifying public addiction remains constant.

Today the talk and techniques of sentencing have changed, and to give proper credit, broadened. But we have seen no decrease in the use of imprisonment as a sanction. Rather, the simple days when probation or a fine were the alternatives to imprisonment have yielded to a sentencing vocabulary of greater sophistication and complexity but little real improvement. All these changes have been effected in the name of progress, under the rubric of flexibility, with solemn assurance that the use of alternatives will benefit the offender as well as society. But this is rarely true.

For example, all too often diversion programs camouflage a new refusal by the Crown to simply withdraw charges that formerly would never have been considered worth a trial, unless the accused agrees to enter into a series of sometimes difficult obligations. All too often these new obligations are ones which, though simple on paper, cannot be fulfilled by the legions of the inept, the handicapped, the resentful, and the poor who comprise our offender population. The criminal law is applied with disproportionate efficiency to those who have inadequate social abilities, skills, and opportunities. Thus the new flexibility of the criminal justice system becomes a trap for its users. In this way, use of the conditional sentence may well lead to an increase in overall imprisonment because its conditions will not be kept. More and more people are under some form of strict control within the criminal justice system – whether by imprisonment or by supervision in the community.

This volume, despite my enduring pessimism, is an intellectual confection, providing a taste of some of the most important thinking of our generation on these intractable problems. There is wonderful analysis throughout. The essays reflect the luxury of careful thought by people with a close and passionate involvement in the criminal justice system.

Our sentencing regime has created huge expectations and delivered the most modest of results. But this volume discloses that if we put our minds to it, we can, oh, so easily, imagine ways of doing it better.

CLAYTON C. RUBY

Acknowledgments

The editors would like to thank Virgil Duff for his support and advice during the planning phase of this book. As well, we are grateful to Anne Forte and the staff of the University of Toronto Press for bringing the project to fruition. A special debt is due to Allyson May for her excellent work in copy-editing the text. We also express our gratitude to the Department of Justice, Canada, for making a number of copies of the volume available to interested parties across Canada. Finally, we take this opportunity to thank the individual contributing authors who worked on this project without renumeration, for the sole purpose of increasing public and professional awareness of the sentencing process and sentencing reform in this country.

JULIAN V. ROBERTS AND DAVID P. COLE
15 October 1998

MAKING SENSE OF SENTENCING

1

Introduction to Sentencing and Parole

JULIAN V. ROBERTS AND DAVID P. COLE

Introduction

Five young people were accused of killing a man in Toronto's High Park. Witnesses stated that they had heard the teenagers say that they were going to the park to 'get some money from a queer' or to 'beat up a faggot.' The victim, a teacher from the neighbourhood public school, was found dead in his car shortly after midnight. A post-mortem showed that death was caused by cranial injuries inflicted during the course of a severe beating. The five individuals were arrested a week later and charged with second degree murder. The trial judge described the incident as an 'execution.' The accused pleaded guilty to the lesser charge of manslaughter, the unintentional taking of human life, which carries a maximum penalty of life imprisonment.

What is the appropriate sentencing response to such an atrocious crime? Should the accused be punished severely, despite their age, on account of the seriousness of the offence? Or, given the fact that they are first-time offenders, should the judge impose a sentence that will promote their rehabilitation? What kinds of mitigating and aggravating factors should be considered? Must a severe sentence be imposed in order to send a message to other offenders? What role should the family of the victim play in determining the sentence imposed? Is imprisonment necessary, and if so, for how long? If the offenders are incarcerated, what factors should determine whether, and when, they should be granted early release from prison?

Sentencing and the parole system are criticized by many but understood by few. This lack of understanding may seem strange; after all, the process appears straightforward enough. When an accused person has been found guilty, or pleads guilty to a criminal offence, a conviction is recorded. A hearing follows (immediately in some cases, later in others), during which a judge decides what kind of penalty to impose. While the process may seem straightforward, the sentencing decision is one of the most difficult facing a judge, for two principal reasons. First, the consequences are high: the sentence may result in the deprivation of a person's liberty for a substantial period of time. And second, there are many conflicting pressures upon the sentencing judge. In this book we examine both the process by which offenders are sentenced and the mechanisms by which prisoners obtain early release from prison (parole). The meaning of a sentence of imprisonment cannot be fully understood unless and until we also understand the process of early release, which permits prisoners to leave the institutions to which they were sent, in order to serve some portion of their sentences in the community. We attempt to make sense of what is, to many observers, a complex and baffling system, one which contains many contradictions.

Defining Sentencing

In its report published in 1987, the Canadian Sentencing Commission proposed the following definition: 'Sentencing is the judicial determination of a legal sanction to be imposed on a person found guilty of an offence' (Canadian Sentencing Commission 1987, 153). This definition contains all the traditional elements, namely, that the sanction must be legal, it must be imposed by a judge, and it can only follow a criminal conviction. But it masks the complexities of the sentencing process, which are the focus of this volume.

The Complexity of Sentencing: Determining the Purpose, the Sanction, the Quantum

Consider some decisions taken earlier in the criminal justice process. Someone reports to the police that he or she has been assaulted. The victim provides an identification of the assailant. The most important decision confronting the police officer is whether to lay a criminal charge. First, however, the officer will attempt to establish whether an offence has in fact been committed (or attempted). A number of factors may be taken into account, but the task is clear to the officer. The same is true at later stages of the system. At trial, for instance, a judge or a jury will have to decide whether the Crown has proved its case beyond a reasonable doubt. If this threshold of proof has not been reached, the accused must be acquitted. The evidence may frequently be complex – and the testimony at times contradictory – but the nature of the decision is straightforward. The sentencing judge, however, is faced with a more complex task. At the sentencing hearing there will be submissions both from the Crown and defence counsel, which may represent the convicted offender in very different ways. Having heard this testimony, the judge will have to consider the purpose of sentencing both in general and in this particular case. What is the sentence supposed to achieve?

The Purposes of Sentencing

Why do we punish offenders? No single objective exists: there are many reasons for sentencing people convicted of crimes. While most (although not necessarily all) people would agree that offenders should be punished in some way, there is far less consensus about the purpose of punishment. The principal justifications fall into one of two categories. One purpose is the attempt to reduce the level of crime in society by deterring others from committing offences. Advocates of general deterrence (see below) hope to prevent offending by inspiring fear in other, potential offenders.

Sentencing purposes of this kind are called reductivist, because they aim to reduce crime rates by preventing crimes that might otherwise have been committed. These sentencing goals are amenable to research: we can establish whether they work, and to what extent. The other general category of sentencing purposes has effects that cannot be measured empirically. An example of this category would be the goal of retribution. Proponents of punishment for punishment's sake argue that punishing offenders is necessary, even if there is no discernible effect on the crime rate.

Past or Future Crimes?

Another way of classifying sentencing objectives concerns the object of inquiry at the time of sentencing. In some cases the focus is on an offender's criminal conduct, which lies in the past. The severity of the sentence to be imposed is determined not by gauging the offender's risk for reoffending but by measuring the seriousness of the crime for which he or she has been convicted. The 'just deserts' sentencing perspective (see below) falls into this camp. But sometimes the focus is on the future, with the probability of whether the individual will commit further offences. The answer to the question of how likely the offender is to reoffend determines the kind of sanction and the severity of sanction that is imposed. Offenders with a high risk (or, more accurately, those who are perceived to have a high risk) of reoffending receive the harshest punishments, particularly if this risk involves crimes of violence.

There is an ethical aspect to this choice between punishing past or future offending. Advocates of desert-based sentencing would argue that it is unethical or unfair to punish someone for our perception of how likely it is that he or she will reoffend. We may believe that a particular bank robber constitutes a high risk for recidivism, and accordingly sentence him to a lengthy custodial term. But what if our belief is wrong? What if, despite all our predictive tools, he is an exceptional case and would never have offended again? Then we would have incarcerated him unnecessarily. Desert advocates would say that it is more equitable to punish an individual for what he or she has done (that is, the crime of conviction), than for what that person might do, or, more accurately, for what we *think* he or she might do in the future.

General Deterrence

There are two kinds of deterrence: general and specific. Both attempt to prevent crime by threatening punishment. General deterrence aims to discourage other potential offenders from offending. Thus a judge may impose a stiff sentence in a case of impaired driving to 'send a message' to others that they will be punished if they drink and drive. The idea is to warn other members of society who are contemplating, or who might contemplate, committing a crime of the consequences. The threat of punishment is supposed to make them think twice before offending. The aim is crime prevention and the mechanism is fear of future punishment. Note that we say fear of 'punishment,' and not fear of arrest, conviction, or any of the other possible consequences of committing a crime. However, being charged with a crime and eventually finding yourself as an accused in court would be for many people a humiliating experience, and may in itself serve as a deterrent. This is particularly true for people who find themselves in court for the first time.

The efficacy of general deterrence as a crime control mechanism has been in question for some time. Research has generally shown that it is not particularly effective. One impediment is the fact that the general public, including potential offenders, seldom hear about sentences imposed for deterrent purposes. Potential offenders cannot be deterred if they are unaware of the penalties for particular crimes. Reviews of the voluminous research on deterrence have generally concluded that there is little empirical support for the proposition that increasing the severity of penalties will act to deter potential offenders. Criminologist Douglas Cousineau, who reviewed this literature for the Canadian Sentencing Commission, concluded: 'Drawing upon some nine bodies of research addressing the deterrence question, we contend that there is little or no evidence to sustain an empirically justified belief in the deterrent efficacy of legal sanctions' (Cousineau 1988, vi).

This conclusion will surprise many people, because the deterrence mechanism seems intuitively plausible. After all, we see people being deterred from various forms of lawbreaking all the time. People refrain from double-parking, from speeding, from cheating on their income tax returns, and so on because they are afraid of being caught and punished. It is perhaps because deterrence has such intuitive appeal that it has been cited so frequently in sentencing decisions. Unfortunately, the extension of the principle of deterrence breaks down at the level of more serious transgressions proscribed and punished by the criminal law. Recent decisions by appellate courts across the country have acknowledged the limitations of deterrence as a sentencing purpose or suggested that a deterrent effect can be achieved by sanctions other than imprisonment.[1]

Specific or Individual Deterrence

Individual deterrence focuses on the offender being sentenced. The idea is to make the individual refrain from further offending through fear of the consequences of a reconviction. Thus a critical statistic for individual deterrence advocates is whether the individual commits further crimes. Individual deterrence is often invoked to justify the imposition of a harsher penalty on a repeat offender, on the grounds that that offender 'did not learn his lesson the first time.' Offenders with previous convictions that resulted in a period of probation may well be sentenced to a term of custody on any subsequent conviction, the argument being that the custodial term will achieve what probation failed to do: deter the offender. Many people assume that there is a link between the severity of a punishment and the extent to which it can deter criminal behaviour. Here, too, the literature confounds common wisdom. Although it is a hard question upon which to conduct research, it appears that a harsh punishment (imprisonment) is no more effective a deterrent than a milder punishment (probation). Careful research has compared the recidivism rates of offenders sentenced to prison or probation. (Statistical techniques were employed to control for differences between the two populations of offenders.) The results indicated that the recidivism rates were about the same, although, according to deterrence theory, people sentenced to prison should be less likely to reoffend than people placed on probation. One of the most important and well-controlled studies was conducted by the Rand Corporation in the United States (see Petersilia, Turner, and Peterson 1986). Researchers compared the recidivism rates of people sentenced to probation and others sentenced to prison. The two samples were comparable in terms of background variables that might be related to recidivism (such as criminal history, seriousness of the crime committed, and so on). Contrary to deterrence theory, the probationers had lower, not higher recidivism rates than the individuals who had been sent to prison. Other studies (e.g., Bottomley and Pease 1986) have demonstrated the same pattern of results.[2]

A proposition that has found widespread support in the literature is that it is not the severity of the sanction that deters offenders, but the certainty of being punished. This is logical: if the probability of being apprehended and punished is close to zero, the severity of the penalty is irrelevant. On the other hand, if you know that you are going to be caught and punished, whether the penalty is three months in prison or a year will not make much difference to your decision to commit a crime.

Attrition in the Criminal Process

A major obstacle to preventing crime by sentencing offenders is the degree of attrition. In other words, the number of crimes committed is much higher than the number of cases in which a sentence is finally imposed. The reality is that most cases drop out before a sentencing hearing takes place: only a minority of crimes are reported to the police; some of these will be discarded as 'unfounded'; and of those that do result in the laying of a criminal charge, only a fraction will result in a conviction. Data from Canada (Dutton 1987; Roberts 1995b) and the United Kingdom (Ashworth 1995) indicate that only 2–5 per cent of crimes result in a conviction and, consequently, in a sentencing hearing. For example, research by Dutton (1987) on wife assault revealed that only 1 case in approximately 175 results in the imposition of a sanction. Changes in sentencing policy, including increasing the severity of sanctions imposed, will therefore have little appreciable impact on the crime rate.

An analogy may help to illustrate the problem. Imagine a disease for which a treatment exists that cures approximately one-third of patients treated (approximately one-third of offenders in Canada reoffend). Imagine further that only 2–5 percent of all persons stricken with the disease actually report to a medical setting and are subsequently treated. Under these conditions, the overall prevalence of the disease in the population cannot be affected by the treatment. The same logic applies to the prevalence of criminality. Even if *all* convicted offenders were incarcerated (at present approximately one-quarter of all sentences result in a period of custody), the overall crime rate would not change appreciably. Ashworth summarizes the problem well when he writes, 'It should therefore be clear that, if criminal justice policy expects sentencing to perform a major preventive function, it is looking in the wrong direction ... any assumption that crime will go down if sentences go up and vice versa, seems wildly unrealistic' (Ashworth 1995, 26).

Incapacitation

Some argue that punishment serves a disabling function; that is, the purpose is to prevent crime simply by removing the offender from society. If an offender is given a five-year prison term, then for the duration of the time he or she spends in prison that offender will not be free to commit further crimes against the public. Advocates of this justification for punishment argue that it is the only way to respond to people convicted of serious crimes of violence. Incapacitation is assumed to do little or nothing for the offender; it is directed exclusively toward the interests of society.

Most of the research on incapacitation is American. Nevertheless, the results are applicable to Canada. The general finding is that hoping to reduce the crime rate by detaining large numbers of offenders for long periods is exactly that, a hope. Predicting which offenders are likely to reoffend turns out to be very difficult and the system ends up incarcerating (incapacitating) large numbers of offenders, many of whom would not have reoffended. Implementing an effective incapacitation strategy (one that would result in significant reductions in the crime rates for specific offences) is impossible until we are able to predict who is going to reoffend with a higher degree of accuracy. (The exception to this would appear to be violent recidivists, who present a poor prognosis for rehabilitation.) Canadian judges have tended to steer clear of incapacitation as a sentencing purpose.

Rehabilitation

There is far more support among members of the judiciary for rehabilitation. When a judge imposes a sentence for the purpose of rehabilitation, the aim is to restore the offender to the community by changing him or her from an 'offender' into a law-abiding citizen. This goal can be accomplished in a number of ways and the means include treatment programs of various kinds. There is general agreement now, recognized by Parliament, that for many offenders, imprisonment is not an appropriate route to rehabilitation. Although a number of rehabilitation programs are offered in Canada's penal institutions, the carceral milieu is sufficiently harmful that judges use imprisonment to achieve other sentencing goals and attempt to rehabilitate offenders by means of a noncustodial sanction, such as probation. Considerable research has been conducted on the effectiveness of different treatment strategies, much of it Canadian (e.g., Gendreau and Goggin 1997).

Just Deserts and the Principle of Proportionality

According to the just deserts perspective, when a judge imposes a sentence, it is an expression of censure or blame. The individual offender has transgressed and the punishment imposed expresses blame for the transgression. When people commit crimes, the criminal justice system holds them responsible and censures them through the sentencing process. Judicial censure appeals to the offender's sense of morality; according to this sentencing philosophy, we are effectively asking offenders to be responsible and to recognize the immorality of criminal behaviour.

Central to the just deserts perspective is the notion of proportionality. The degree of censure, that is, the amount of punishment, must reflect the degree of harm committed. According to this principle, the severity of any punishment should be directly proportional to the seriousness of the crime committed.[3] The principle of proportionality in sentencing lies at the heart of everyday notions of justice. Most people believe that the severity of the penalty should reflect the seriousness of the crime committed. In fact, one of the reasons that proportionality is so important to the sentencing process in Canada (and elsewhere) is that it underlies popular conceptions of rewards as well as punishments.[4] When an offender convicted of sexual assault receives what appears to be a very lenient sentence in light of the seriousness of the crime – say a term of probation – our sense of injustice is aroused. Why? Because the penalty does not reflect the degree of harm inflicted. This is another way of saying it is not a proportional sentence. The same feeling of injustice is also aroused when an offender convicted of a trivial offence receives a severe sentence. A couple of years ago, a man in Quebec was sentenced to twenty-nine months in prison for failing to pay a fine. This sentence disturbed many people for the same reason: the severity of the sentence was disproportionate to the seriousness of the crime for which it was imposed.

Punishment

The issue of punishment has always been central to society. Punishment pervades our everyday experiences to an even greater extent than deterrence. We punish recalcitrant children, uncomprehending animals, countries that violate international codes of conduct, and, from time to time, we even punish ourselves through some form of self-abnegation. There are direct analogies between the punishing function of the criminal justice system and the structure of many of the world's religions. The Catholic church, for example, incorporates concepts of sin, punishment, and expiation through confession and the concept of penance, which are analogous to crime, punishment, and pardoning in the criminal justice system.

Denunciation

This purpose of sentencing is related to censure. As the Canadian Sentencing Commission noted: 'Denunciation is essentially a communication process which uses the medium of language to express condemnation' (Canadian Sentencing Commission 1987, 142). The idea is that a sentence imposed on an offender influences public perceptions of the seriousness of the crime for which it was imposed. It was once said that people in the seventeenth century viewed the crime of theft as serious because a conviction for theft resulted in the infliction of a very severe penalty (death). The message of the gallows was therefore twofold. On one level it was a message of terror: commit this crime and you will receive the most serious punishment (death). On another level there was a symbolic message: theft is a very serious crime and, if you had any doubts, look what happens to people convicted of this offence. The second message is a moral one; it appeals to our perceptions of the blameworthiness of particular acts.

In a similar way, the excruciating torture and eventual death inflicted on offenders in the Roman empire who attempted to murder the emperor, or regicides in seventeenth-century England, were designed to convey a similar message. When Guy Fawkes was hung, drawn, and quartered in London in 1605 for attempting to blow up Parliament, a message was sent to other potential traitors. The infliction of bodily injury prior to (and, in the case of Oliver Cromwell, after) execution may have deterred some would-be traitors. But these extreme displays of cruelty were more likely an attempt to convey to the population that the murder of an emperor or a monarch is a crime like no other, and accordingly must be punished like no other crime.[5]

Choosing among Purposes

If judges have all these purposes from which to choose, and if different judges favour different purposes, the result may be disparity in sentencing. Variability in preferences for sentencing purposes among judges is not merely academic; it has important practical consequences for the offender. The nature of the sentencing purpose will determine the nature and severity of the sanction imposed. This has been conclusively demonstrated by American research. Robert McFatter (1978) employed a sample of judges in a sentencing simulation. He found that different judges did indeed favour different sentencing purposes for the same case, and that their preferences resulted in different sentences. In order to eliminate all other possible explanations, McFatter randomly assigned some judges to sentence from a deterrence perspective, others from a rehabilitation perspective. They were then given the same case to sentence. Results showed that the judges assigned to a deterrence-oriented perspective favoured very different sentences than judges assigned to the other sentencing purposes.

To summarize, there are many sentencing purposes and different purposes will be pursued in different cases. The task of selecting an appropriate purpose becomes even more complex when the objective to be followed may well vary from crime to crime and from offender to offender. Some offences are so serious that they require denunciation by the criminal justice system; others may not merit such a severe response. Some offenders are so dangerous that they need to be incapacitated for a considerable period of time, while other offenders convicted of crimes of comparable seriousness may not require incarceration at all. As a result, there may well be variation among judges in terms of sentencing purposes and the sentences imposed: judges may favour different sentencing purposes, which will give rise to different dispositions. The issue of sentencing disparity will be explored in greater depth later in this book.

The lesson for sentencing reform is clear. If reformers wish to reduce the amount of disparity in sentencing, judges will have to be given some guidance as to which sentencing purpose is most important. This determination is far from easy.

The Choice of Sanction

Once the judge has resolved – to his or her own satisfaction, although not necessarily to that of everyone else – the issue of what the sentence is supposed to accomplish, he or she must then proceed to the next stage and determine which of a range of possible sanctions is likely to achieve the sentencing purpose. Will a heavy fine provide sufficient deterrence, or is a period of imprisonment necessary? Will a term of probation promote the rehabilitation of the offender and, if so, what kinds of conditions should be imposed? The decision-making process does not end here. After selecting a sanction, the judge must determine the quantum. That is, how large should the fine be, or how long the period of imprisonment or probation? A judge will at this point probably consider the sanctions that have been imposed by other judges in similar cases.

In attempting to resolve all these questions, to decide upon the sentencing purpose, the nature of the sanction, and the quantum of punishment, members of the judiciary turn to a variety of sources. Some are officially acknowledged (such as previous judgments appearing in the published law reports), others are of a more tenuous nature. For example, judges may draw upon their discussions with colleagues, or their own intuition about what kinds of dispositions 'work.' They will probably also draw upon their own experiences on the bench, and upon their personal theories of sentencing. And, of course, they will also consider the recommendations of other professionals involved (such as probation officers who prepare presentence reports) and formal submissions regarding sentence from Crown and defence counsel. After considering all of this information, the judge will have to determine a sentence – within a short space of time. Many offenders are deprived of their liberty in a sentencing hearing that may last only a few minutes, at most. Clearly then, the sentencing decision is highly complex, and a 'correct' sentence, one that will meet with universal approval, may not exist.

Consequently, legislatures around the world have experienced great difficulty in attempting to reform the sentencing processes. While agreement can be achieved on some broad principles, there is no real consensus about the direction that should be taken by judges. This may well explain why the 1996 sentencing reforms in Canada did not promote one particular purpose to the exclusion of all others. As we shall see in the next two chapters, while Parliament decided to provide judges with some guidance, this involved retaining many of the traditional sentencing purposes.

A Typical Sentencing Hearing

Despite the fact that 'the sentencing process is merely a phase of the trial process,' the typical sentencing hearing bears little resemblance to the formalities of the trial or the entry of a guilty plea which precedes it. Particularly in busy provincial courts, where approximately 98 per cent of all sentences are imposed, the sentencing hearing and the imposition of the sentence usually take place immediately after the finding of guilt has been made, with little opportunity for reflection on that finding.

Most sentencing hearings are quite informal. For example, it is unusual that evidence is given under oath. Instead, counsel for the accused describes the 'offender's age, mode of life, character and personality,'[6] all in the form of assertions as to what he or she has been told by the accused, family members, associates, and employers. If documentary evidence is provided, it normally consists of character or employment letters; it is very rare that the Crown insists on formal notice of any intention to tender such materials, and it is unusual that the maker is called to provide the information under oath. Indeed, the rule in Canadian courts is that '[a] judge may take into consideration information given by counsel and act upon it unless the other side does not accept it.'[7]

Similarly informal procedures exist where the Crown wishes to prove aggravating factors. If the accused is alleged to have a criminal record, a computer printout of the record is shown to the accused; if it is admitted, the printout is immediately handed up to the judge. Again, if the Crown seeks to rely on a victim impact statement,[8] it is presented to the judge after the accused has had a brief opportunity to examine it. Only if the accused objects to the record or the victim impact statement are more formal steps taken to prove their contents.

It sometimes transpires that either counsel or the judge feels that a presentence report (PSR) would be of assistance in the sentencing process.[9] A PSR is a social history of an accused, designed to provide the sentencing court with accurate and timely information about 'the antecedents, family history, previous convictions, character of employment and other information.'[10] There are no formal rules as to when a PSR must be prepared;[11] it is solely a matter of discretion on the part of the sentencing judge. Most of the time the recommendation comes from one or both counsel. Sometimes the very nature of the offence suggests that a report is needed to provide some further background about the accused prior to sentencing. On occasion, the judge or counsel want to have some assessment of the accused's suitability for a particular rehabilitative program. A PSR may be ordered to ensure that some information about the offender is available to custodial authorities, particularly if a lengthy sentence is about to be imposed. In his text on sentencing, Ruby notes that, according to the case law: '[u]nless the information that might have been forthcoming in a pre-sentence report is made available by other appropriate means, a judge may be criticized for sentencing in an absence of sufficient information in a number of cases, especially those involving youthful and first offenders.'[12]

There is a vast body of case law considering such complex and difficult issues as the proper content of and inferences to be drawn from presentence reports, the correct interpretation to be given to the meaning of jury verdicts, the correct standard of proof to be applied to assumptions about the incidence of crime in a particular jurisdiction, and the appropriateness of taking into account other offences admitted but not formally charged. This case law has been substantially refined since the important case of *R. v. Gardiner*,[13] in which the Supreme Court of Canada held that, where contested, the standard of proof of any fact is the same as in the trial proper, namely, beyond a reasonable doubt.

Once the facts sufficient for sentencing are before the court, the judge asks counsel for the accused and the Crown if they have recommendations to make, either as to the length of sentence to be imposed or any specifics, such as terms to be included in a conditional sentence or probation order or the amount of restitution to be made to the victim. Sometimes counsel are in agreement with all or some of the elements of a sentence proposed to the judge; indeed, many accused (rightly or wrongly) give up their right to a trial in exchange for a joint 'plea bargain' being placed before the sentencing judge. The judge is not formally obligated to accept any joint recommendation proposed; however, the influential 'Martin Committee' in Ontario suggested that judges should not decline to accept such sentencing proposals unless they believe that a joint or partially joint submission 'overlooks an important fact about the crime or the accused.'[14]

The recent amendments to the Criminal Code (section 726) require the court to provide the offender with an opportunity to make a statement. Despite this legislative requirement, experience to date suggests that unless the accused is unrepresented by counsel, he or she is rarely provided with an opportunity to speak to sentence, it being assumed that counsel has advanced any submission that might be made on behalf of the accused. Similarly, the Criminal Code (section 726.2) directs that the judge is to 'state ... the reasons for [the sentence], and enter those ... reasons into the record of the proceedings.' Once again, the exigencies of busy courts mean that detailed attention is usually paid to these issues only when there is something exceptional about the case.[15] Reasons for sentence may be as summary as: 'The court accepts the terms of the plea bargain, for the reasons expressed by counsel,' or 'There seems to be nothing exceptional about the facts; the usual sentence of X is imposed.'

Conditional Release from Prison

Any book dealing with sentencing must include the process of conditional release from prison. For offenders condemned to a period of imprisonment, this is the beginning, rather than the end of the story. Let us suppose that a judge imposes a sentence of life imprisonment upon an offender. What exactly does this mean for the prisoner? How long will he or she have to spend in prison? In terms of time actually served in prison, a life sentence can mean many things. The only common element is that all life prisoners will be under some form of supervision for the rest of their lives; the warrant of the court does not expire. For those convicted of first degree murder, it means at least twenty-five years in prison;[16] inmates sentenced to life imprisonment for second degree murder must serve at least ten years in prison. Offenders sentenced to life terms for offences other than murder – such as manslaughter, robbery, or aggravated sexual assault[17] – must serve at least seven years in prison before they may apply for parole. Clearly, the phrase 'life imprisonment' is imprecise, to say the least. This complexity comes about as a result of the parole system.[18]

Lesser sentences are similarly complex. The five individuals convicted of manslaughter in the case with which we began this chapter each received nine years in prison. How long will they actually spend in prison? The answer to this question is probably: 'it depends.' If they are successful in applying for day parole, they may serve thirty months in prison and then be released to the community (provided that they abide by certain conditions and return to a halfway house each evening). They may serve three years in prison, and then receive permission to spend the remaining six years of the sentence in the community. This is known as full parole.[19] It is also possible that the prisoners will be denied release on day and full parole, in which case they will most likely leave the prison after six years, through statutory release. Finally, the prisoners may, through a combination of factors, be detained in prison for the full nine years, without any early release until the warrant expires, at which point they will leave the prison as free individuals (although now carrying the burden of a criminal record). A sentence of nine years' imprisonment can therefore mean anywhere between 30 and 108 months in custody, depending upon factors relating to the crime, the offender, his or her behaviour while serving time, and decisions taken by criminal justice personnel, such as members of the parole board.

A Typical Parole Hearing

When a prisoner enters an institution to serve a sentence, various institutional personnel are assigned to work with him or her. At the federal level these officials constitute a 'case management team.' One of the team's major duties is to generate institutional performance reports and summaries of information for the parole board. Because the typical parole board hearing will take on average about two hours (even less in provincial cases), the board members are likely to rely heavily on the views and recommendations of the case management team. (The 'concurrence rate' between the case management team recommendation and the actual National Parole Board decision is around 85 per cent.)

To be considered for parole, the prisoner must first file an application. Once this is done, a series of institutional and community reports about the parole applicant is generated. For example, if the prisoner indicates in his application that he proposes to reside at a certain address and be employed with a firm, a community assessment is conducted to confirm residence and employment. This community assessment forms part of the 'progress summary' that the case management team is required to produce for the board prior to the hearing. These documents are expected to summarize what is known of the offence, to review the offender's institutional history (including reports from staff), to report on the attitude of the police force in the proposed destination, and to outline known details of performance on previous conditional releases (including bail and probation).

Although policy varies from time to time, in virtually any case involving wilfully causing death or serious physical or psychological harm, federal and provincial parole boards will not give serious consideration to a proposal for release without assessments by psychologists and psychiatrists. Where treatment is suggested and that treatment is available within correctional facilities (however belatedly), release will not be granted until such treatment program has been completed and a positive report obtained. Current board policy is that every effort will be made to secure at least a transcript of the sentencing judge's reasons for sentence, the theory being that the transcript will contain an accurate description of the facts. If this is not available, the case management team will rely on a statement of facts provided either by Crown counsel or the investigating police force.

It is well known – and perhaps understandable – that parole applicants often seek to minimize or deny their culpability in order to attempt to make a good impression on the parole board. While board policy is that a claim of innocence will not rule out favourable consideration for conditional release, it sometimes causes considerable difficulty. In an infamous wrongful conviction case, the National Parole Board denied Donald Marshall's application for parole because he refused to admit any wrongdoing. The board was quite candid in conceding to the commissioners inquiring into Marshall's wrongful conviction that it interpreted his claim of innocence as indicating that he had not learned from the experience of being convicted and incarcerated and was therefore at risk to reoffend. Although there was considerable public criticism of the National Parole Board for this position, the board argued that in the vast majority of cases with which it deals, a continuing denial (or minimization) of guilt is usually indicative of the prisoner's refusal to acknowledge the need to change attitudes and behaviours that led directly or indirectly to the conviction for which he or she was serving a term of imprisonment.

Unlike court proceedings, parole board hearings are deliberately designed to be very informal, in order that the parole applicant may feel at ease. While facilities vary considerably across the country, several common elements serve to emphasize the informal nature of the proceeding. First, apart from the tape-recording device, there is little sense that one is speaking 'for the record.' Participants in the process are encouraged to use everyday language, which is of considerable reassurance to the less articulate prisoners, who are worried about their ability to express themselves. The air of informality is further emphasized by the fact that the board members usually open the hearing by introducing themselves and sometimes shake hands with the applicant. Finally, all participants sit around the same table. Thus the hearings are more akin to discussions rather than formal presentations.

In preparation for the hearing, all attending board members will have read at least the progress summary, reports from mental health professionals, and any submissions or support letters filed by or on behalf of the prisoner. When the files for forthcoming hearings are distributed a few days in advance by board staff, one of the members is randomly assigned to 'lead' on a case, which means that he or she will be responsible for being the principal questioner during the hearing.

The governing Regulation specifies that a parole applicant may be represented by an 'assistant.' 'Assistants' need not be legally trained; indeed, in many parts of the country, it is quite rare that a parole applicant is represented by a lawyer. Further, the role of the assistant is not like that of a lawyer speaking to sentence in court. The vast majority of parole board hearings are comprised of the parole applicant responding to questions put by the leader or other board members; the assistant's role is limited to advising the prisoner during the hearing and summing up at the end. Although the assistant is present as an advocate, since the hearing is inquisitorial, there is no one against whom the assistant can act as an adversary. No Crown attorney is present to speak on behalf of the victim or the community.

During the first stage of a parole hearing the board's hearing assistant reviews a checklist of procedural safeguards to ensure, *inter alia,* that the prisoner is aware of the purpose of the hearing and that he or she has received disclosure of the written materials to be relied upon. In the next phase the institutional head of the case management team summarizes the case.

Once the team members have presented the case, the 'leader' will commence a thorough and probing questioning of the prisoner. As the board's jurisdiction to grant release commences from the offence, much of the hearing is likely to be occupied in discussing the facts and circumstances of the crime, the applicant's criminal record, and his or her pre-incarceration lifestyle. Above all, the prisoner is expected to demonstrate in some significant way that he or she has gained some insight into the circumstances that led to the offence.

After these subjects have been reviewed in considerable detail, the leading board member will usually question the prisoner about his or her performance and behaviour while incarcerated, with a particular emphasis on participation in any kind of treatment program. For example, a prisoner who has enlisted in Alcoholics Anonymous, may be asked to detail the major recommended steps toward an alcohol-free life style and to name the officials responsible for administering the program in the institution. Unlike judges, board members are likely to have a detailed knowledge of the content of these programs, and sometimes of the personnel who administer them. While there is no guarantee that frankness will lead to success, deceit almost inevitably results in a failure of the parole application.

Once submissions from the prisoner or the assistant are completed, the board typically asks whether any participant has anything to add arising from the discussion. All parties other than the board members then retire from the hearing room to await the decision and reasons. After a few minutes they are invited to return, whereupon the leader will announce the decision and reasons.

Sentencing, Release from Prison, and the Views of the Public

Public opinion is one of the major problems associated with the sentencing process. Of all the stages of the criminal justice system, sentencing attracts the most negative ratings in opinion polls. If you were to stop people in the street and ask them whether sentences in Canada are appropriate, four out of five will respond that sentencing is too lenient (Roberts 1995c). This pattern has emerged from surveys dating back many years now (see Doob and Roberts (1983)), and is reflected in public evaluations of criminal justice professionals, which tend to be most positive for the police, and least positive for judges.[20]

A measure of the public discontent with sentencing can be found in reaction to two sentencing decisions handed down as this chapter was being written. In one, a Toronto judge handed down a sentence of two years less a day plus three years' probation in a case of sexual assault involving over twenty victims. Counsel for the defence had recommended five years; the Crown had suggested ten. The trial judge's sentence was overturned on appeal, and a sentence of five years incarceration was substituted by the Ontario Court of Appeal.[21] In the other, a judge in Montreal sentenced two offenders to serve eighteen months in the community, under supervision. They had been convicted of a group rape. Both of these decisions received widespread media attention, and although no polls were conducted or research undertaken on the issue, it seems clear that the public was highly critical of these sentencing decisions and probably generalized its criticism to apply to all judges.

Confronted with a murder victim and provided with an investigative staff, most of us would not know where (or how) to begin a homicide investigation. We would consider this a technical matter best left to the homicide squad. But provide most people with the briefest summary of the facts of a crime and they will soon tell you what kind of sentence is appropriate for the offender. And we are all quick to evaluate the sentences we hear about from other people or in the media.[22]

The sentencing and conditional release process is complicated, and many members of the public fail to understand why the system cannot be made simpler. An analogy may help to establish the point. Many people also complain about the apparently needless complexity of our taxation system. The tax return itself is intimidating; the Income Tax Act is long, complicated, and full of provisions that permit exceptions to the basic tax rates. Some people believe that you need to be a tax lawyer or an accountant to understand the system adequately; many feel that this complexity could be eliminated. They argue that a flat tax rate of, say, 30 per cent of gross income could be imposed on all taxpayers, with no exceptions. Such a proposal would result in a system that would have clarity and equity (all taxpayers would pay the same rate, regardless of the number of taxation specialists they might be able to hire). But would such a system be just? Would it permit the government to pursue progressive social goals, such as helping the needier members of society or people who have dependents?

While most Canadians assume that they have an idea of the kinds of sentences imposed in court, when their estimates of sentencing patterns are compared with actual sentencing statistics, public estimates turn out to be wide of the mark. This was demonstrated over fifteen years ago in research conducted for the federal Department of Justice. A representative sample of the public was asked to estimate the incarceration rate for a number of offences. The results indicated that most people underestimated the true severity of the courts. One reason then, why the public is so critical of sentencing patterns is that it fails to appreciate how severe judges in Canada are toward convicted offenders. However, it is important to point out that surveys that suggest that the public is always harsher than the courts may not tell the whole story.

Interesting findings emerge from research studies in which public sentencing preferences are compared to actual sentencing patterns. The most recent demonstration comes from the United Kingdom. Members of the public were given a description of a specific offender to read, and then asked to sentence the offender. The description was a summary of an actual case. It was fairly typical case of burglary, committed by an offender with a criminal record for the same offences in the past.[23] Such offenders are almost always sent to prison, here and in the United Kingdom. And this is what happened. The offender had actually been sentenced to three years in prison (which was reduced on appeal to two years). When asked to 'sentence' this offender themselves, the public in fact tended to favour a less severe disposition: *fully half of the respondents felt that the offender should not go to prison at all.* Of those respondents who felt that imprisonment was the most appropriate sanction, the average sentence length was one year (see Hough and Roberts (1998)).

If this study were the only evidence that the public is less punitive than we are frequently led to believe, it could be dismissed as an exception. But there is now a large body of evidence, much of it Canadian, which supports the conclusions drawn from this recent British study. The lesson seems clear: the public is critical of the judiciary, but at least part of this dissatisfaction can be attributed to misperceptions of current sentencing practices.

The public also appear to disapprove of the parole process (Roberts 1988a). There is nothing unique about Canada in this regard; surveys conducted in the United States, the United Kingdom, and Australia show the same result. For example, a survey conducted in Canada in 1992 found that four out of five respondents were dissatisfied with parole (Roberts and Stalans 1997). However, it is not so much the concept of parole to which people object, but rather the practice (or what they perceive the practice to be). The public appear to believe that parole boards have been getting more lenient in recent years. Here, too, many members of the public are misinformed, seeing the parole system as more lenient than it really is. As with sentencing, though, when confronted with an actual case, the public responds more positively. This emerged from a research study conducted by Cumberland and Zamble (1992).[24]

Visibility of Sentencing Decisions: The Role of the Media

Sentencing occupies an important position in the criminal justice process, in part because sentencing decisions are far more visible than decisions taken at other stages of the system, by the police or the Crown, for example. Sexual assault provides a good illustration. Suppose a person reports to the police that she or he has been sexually assaulted. Whether the police lay a charge is a critical decision, but one about which the public is unlikely to hear. The same is true for decisions taken by the Crown. Under the sexual assault provisions of the Criminal Code, there are three levels of the crime:[25] sexual assault, sexual assault with a weapon or threats to a third party, and aggravated sexual assault. In some cases it may not be clear which section is applicable. The victim may consider the assault to be a case of aggravated sexual assault (which carries a maximum penalty of life imprisonment), while the police officer may see things in a different way. The Crown may decide to lay a charge at level one (sexual assault), rather than at the highest level.

Determining the specific charge is a pivotal decision, from which many consequences flow. If the offender is charged with and subsequently convicted of sexual assault (level one), he will probably spend a couple of months in prison (or may not go to prison at all). Had he been convicted of aggravated sexual assault (level three), the sentence would probably be two years or more (see Birkenmayer and Besserer (1997)). The decision taken by the Crown counsel is thus vital to the outcome of the case, and yet, like the behaviour of the police, it is unlikely to be reported by the news media. Accordingly, the public is unlikely to hear about it. On the other hand, a great deal of scrutiny will follow the decision of a judge in a case of sexual assault. If a judge imposes a lenient sentence on an offender convicted of sexual assault, this becomes newsworthy and it will come to the attention of an already critical public.

The treatment of sentencing by the news media is important to understand, for it affects public opinion. Most people, criminal justice professionals included, acquire their information about sentencing from the media. Stories dealing with sentencing in the news media tend to be brief, focusing exclusively on the severity of the sentence and the seriousness of the crime to the exclusion of other important information (Roberts 1995c). The judge's reasons for the sentence, the purpose being served, the offender's criminal record, submissions from the Crown and defence counsel, information from the presentence report – little of this material makes its way into a newspaper report. Is it then surprising that the public has a negative view of the sentencing process?

Consequences of Imprisonment

Judges have the power to intervene in the lives of citizens to an extent largely unknown in other areas of civic life. Nowhere is the power of the state more apparent than when it deprives others of their liberty. But the consequences of imprisonment go far beyond mere physical confinement. About a hundred years ago, Oscar Wilde, who knew more about the effects of imprisonment than most, wrote that 'all sentences are sentences of death' (Wilde 1981, 654). By this he meant that all sentences of imprisonment change the individual prisoner in some permanent way. And it is hard to disagree. Lest we think that Wilde wrote of an earlier period with no relation to our own, it is important to recall the pains of incarceration to which individuals are still exposed. The silent, repetitive marching that Wilde was compelled to endure has been abolished, but solitary confinement and many similar privations persist to this day in Canada's penal institutions (Jackson 1983). People who are sentenced to prison are exposed to environmental forces that place them at risk for a wide range of negative events, including divorce, ill health, assault, homicide, and suicide. To take just one of these, research has shown that suicide rates of prisoners are many times higher than rates for comparable individuals at liberty (Burtch and Ericson 1979; Reed and Roberts 1998).

Short of execution, imprisonment is the ultimate intrusion into a person's life, and we should accordingly know a great deal about how it is being ordered, and why. Significant numbers of people are incarcerated every year in Canada, and many scholars have been asserting for some time now that we incarcerate too many people. At the time of writing, the incarceration rate in Canada is 130 per 100,000 residents (National Crime Prevention Council 1997). While this rate is not as high as the rate in the U.S. – where over one million people are now in prison – it is considerably higher than other Western, industrialized nations. The National Crime Prevention Council of Canada reviewed the research literature on incarceration and concluded that 'Canada has always had high incarceration rates compared to those of other western nations ... simply put Canada relies heavily on prisons' (2). Moreover, in light of the fact that Canada's crime rates are significantly lower than those in America, one wonders whether our high incarceration rate is in fact justified. Could justice have been equally well served if some of the offenders who were sent to prison had been given alternative, non-custodial penalties instead? Clearly, we need to know how alternatives to imprisonment can be exploited to a greater degree than at the present.

Reforming Sentencing and Parole

The final questions that we shall address in this book are what has been done and *what should be done* to reform the sentencing and parole systems in Canada. The sentencing reform bill (C-41) addressed throughout this volume is the product of nearly two decades of discussion and research in this country.[26] Although a number of commissions of inquiry published reports in the 1950s and 1960s,[27] the reform process can formally be traced back to 1984, when a royal commission was created to examine the sentencing and parole process. The Canadian Sentencing Commission was specifically directed to study the issue of sentencing guidelines.

After three years of study and consultation the commission published its report (Canadian Sentencing Commission 1987), which contained a comprehensive package of reform proposals. These included new sentencing guidelines system (which judges would have been required to follow, unless they provide reasons for their 'departure' sentence); a revision of the maximum penalty structure; a statement of the purpose and principles of sentencing; the abolition of the mandatory minimum penalties (except those prescribed for the murder offences), and the abolition of full parole (except for life-term prisoners). Most of the commission's proposals were well-received, with the important exception of the abolition of parole. The commission favoured a sentencing system in which the term of imprisonment actually served by the prisoner would bear a closer relationship to the sentence imposed in court. However, there was strong support then, and there continues to be now, for a system of discretionary release from prison. Indeed, in 1999, parole will have been a feature of the correctional system in Canada for a hundred years.

The work of the Sentencing Commission was followed the next year by the report of a parliamentary committee headed by David Daubney (Daubney Committee 1988). Unlike the Sentencing Commission, this committee held public hearings and visited a number of correctional institutions. The result was a report containing almost a hundred recommendations to reform the sentencing and parole process. Many of the recommendations of the committee echoed those of the Sentencing Commission, although there were some important differences (for example, the committee favoured a rather different statement of purpose and an advisory sentencing guideline system which would not have been binding upon judges).

Over the next few years, the federal government (which has responsibility for the Criminal Code, which regulates sentencing) used these two reports as the basis for consultations with the provinces and interest groups. Although many elements of the sentencing process were in need of reform, several issues emerged as being particularly important. First, the question of guidelines needed addressing. The challenge to reformers was to come up with a system that would provide more guidance to judges than was currently available, but without preventing them from exercising their proper discretion to impose a sanction. Many models were available for study, ranging from sentencing grids (described in Chapter 19 by Shereen Benzvy-Miller), which prescribe a fairly narrow range of sanctions for each offence, to more flexible systems in which judges are given guiding principles, but no specific sentence ranges. A second important issue involved the relationship between the sentencing and parole systems (explored in Chapter 15 by Mary Campbell). Finally, there was the question of reforming the maximum penalty structure and the proposal to create a permanent sentencing commission for Canada, to guide reform initiatives in the future.

The end result[28] of the federal government's deliberations and consultations was two significant pieces of legislation. The Corrections and Conditional Release Act was passed in 1992. Among other reforms, this statute made major changes to the way in which federal offenders (those serving two years or more) can obtain early release. Two years later, the Department of Justice introduced the sentencing reform bill (C-41), which became law in September

1996. Subsequent chapters in this book review the most important provisions of this legislation. It is important to note, however, that the reform process should not end with a single piece of legislation. Many issues remain to be addressed. To take just one example, the Criminal Code still contains a set of outdated maximum penalties which, for the most part, bear little relationship to the sentences actually imposed at the trial court level or the relative seriousness of the crimes for which they can be imposed. We can only hope, therefore, that C-41 is a step, albeit an important one, on a longer journey.

In addition to this legislative activity, there has been a wealth of scholarship on the topics of sentencing and parole in Canada since the publication of the Canadian Sentencing Commission's report in 1987 (e.g., Brodeur 1990; Cole and Manson 1990; Dumont 1994, 1990; Dozois et al. 1989; Gabor 1990; Pires 1990; Roberts and von Hirsch 1992, 1995). So this is a timely point at which to examine the sentencing process.

Outline of the Book

There are several legal texts currently available for those readers interested exclusively in the law of sentencing (e.g., Ruby 1994). The present volume is more of a hybrid. We start from the position that sentencing practice, policy, and theory can only be understood by adopting a multidisciplinary approach that draws on legal and sociological knowledge. Moreover, the reader can only obtain a true idea of sentencing after hearing from active practitioners and scholars. The contributing authors draw on both the legal perspective and the sociological tradition and are either experienced practitioners or academics active in the field. The area of sentencing and parole is sufficiently broad that we have been forced to omit some issues. Space prevents us from dealing with the sentencing of young offenders, other than to note the provisions in the Young Offenders Act that determine the sentencing and parole arrangements for young persons convicted of murder. Although there is an increasingly large literature on white-collar crime and the punishment of corporate offenders, this topic is omitted as well. Nor do we deal with punishments that are no longer legal in Canada, such as execution or flogging. There is a provision in the Criminal Code that empowers a judge to compel an individual to enter into a recognizance and abide by certain conditions which will restrict his or her freedom of action. We consider this to be a form of preventive sentencing, although it is not found within the sentencing provisions of the Code. Nevertheless, discussion of section 810.1 is beyond the scope of our inquiry.[29] We do not cover the question of sentencing according to the dangerous offender provisions. Finally, we do not discuss the complex provisions relating to the

Criminal Records Act, which regulates the means by which offenders can obtain an official pardon.

Since Parliament passed significant reform legislation in 1996, we begin, in Chapter 2, with a general overview of the sentencing reform bill (C-41), written by David Daubney and Gordon Parry. Chapter 3, written by Julian Roberts and Andrew von Hirsch, contains an evaluation of the statement of purpose and principle contained in Bill C-41, now part of the Criminal Code of Canada. It is followed by three chapters dealing with the most important (and controversial) element of the sentencing reform: the new disposition, known as a conditional sentence. In Chapter 4, Jack Gemmell explores the origin, nature, and purpose of conditional sentencing. This is followed by an exploration of some of the problems that may arise with the use of the new disposition (Chapter 5) and an update on the appellate courts' response to conditional sentences to date (Chapter 6).

Allan Edgar then reviews the sentencing options available to judges in Canada (Chapter 7). What penalties are available, and under what conditions may a judge impose them? Chapter 8 contains an overview of sentencing trends, based upon the most recent statistics available from Statistics Canada. This chapter also explores research that has examined sentencing disparity and attempts to resolve the question of whether disparity is a problem in this country. The book then turns to the sentencing of special categories of offenders. In Chapter 9, Richard Schneider addresses the problem of sentencing mentally disordered offenders. The next chapters examine, respectively, the sentencing of aboriginals (Chapter 10, written by Carole La Prairie), female offenders (Chapter 11, written by Dianne Martin) and black offenders (Chapter 12, written by Toni Williams).

Sandra Bacchus explores the critical issue of the role of the victim in sentencing (Chapter 13). In Chapter 14, Gary Trotter provides an analysis of the role of the appellate courts in the sentencing process. The book then focuses on conditional release from imprisonment. Mary Campbell discusses the origin and purpose of parole (as well as its relationship to the sentencing process) in Chapter 15, while Sandra Leonard describes the specific mechanisms by which prisoners are able to serve part of their custodial terms in the community under supervision (in Chapter 16). In Chapter 17, David Cole and Julian Roberts review the sentencing arrangements for offenders convicted of murder. This chapter includes a discussion of judicial review, the provision by which 'lifers' may have their parole eligibility dates reviewed by a jury. The parole arrangements for lifers have also recently been reformed.

Two additional chapters explore alternatives to the sentencing process. Jonathan Rudin explains the necessity of such options for the sentencing process and discusses a number of alternatives, including sentencing circles (Chapter

18). Shereen Benzvy Miller evaluates the sentencing grid system used in many American states and at the federal level (Chapter 19). The book concludes with two chapters that reflect upon progress toward sentencing reform in Canada. In Chapter 20, Jean-Paul Brodeur reviews sentencing reform proposals since the publication of the report of the Canadian Sentencing Commission in 1987. In the final chapter (21), Anthony Doob explores some common themes emerging from the contributions to this book.

At the end of the day, we hope that this volume will contribute to greater public and professional understanding of the area of the law that has the greatest impact on the life and liberty of individual citizens.

ENDNOTES

1 See *R. v. Wismayer* (1997), 115 C.C.C. (3d) 18 (Ont. C.A.); *R. v. Ursel* (1998), 117 C.C.C. (3d) 289 (B.C.C.A.); *R. v. W. (L.F.)* (1998), 119 C.C.C. (3d) 97 (Nfld. C.A.); *R. v. Parker* (1997), 116 C.C.C. (3d) 418 (N.S.C.A).

2 Dean Champion reviewed this voluminous literature and concluded that 'incarceration seems to make little difference [to recidivism]. When this factor did make a difference, it tended to increase recidivism rates' (Champion 1994, 99).

3 It is important to note that according to desert theory, an offender's criminal history also plays a role, albeit a very limited one, in determining the severity of the sentence. Thus first offenders should receive a discounted sentence, although once their first-offender 'status' has disappeared (as a result of additional convictions), the severity of subsequent sentences should not become harsher. Other sentencing purposes, such as individual deterrence, assign a much greater role to an offender's criminal history (see Roberts (1997a, 1997b), for a review of this issue).

4 That is, when people are rewarded (professionally for example) in a manner that is disproportionate to their skills, experience, or work-rate, this disturbs many people, as it appears to violate a notion of fairness.

5 Of course, the effect can work in the opposite direction. An argument made against decriminalizing certain offences is that public perceptions of the behaviour will change. For instance it was originally argued that homosexual acts and attempting suicide – both of which were formerly crimes – should not be decriminalized, as this would lead to an increase in the incidence of both behaviours.

6 *R. v. Iwaniw; R. v. Overton* (1959), 127 C.C.C. 40 (Man. C.A.).

7 C.C. Ruby, *Sentencing*, 4th ed. (Toronto: Butterworths 1994), 57.

8 See Chapter 13 by Sandra Bacchus for a discussion of the evolution of the law surrounding such statements.

9 Authority for the preparation of such reports is found in s. 735 of the Criminal Code.

10 This wording comes from the first Ontario legislation authorizing the preparation of presentence reports (Probation Act, R.S.O. 1922, c. 103, s. 3(1)). Probation

officers in Ontario became formally involved in juvenile courts in 1908 and adult courts in 1921.

11 See G. Parker, 'The Law of Probation,' 19 *Can. J. of Crim. and Corr.* 51 (1977); C.F. Dombek and Murray W. Chitra, 'The Pre-Sentence Report: An Update,' (1981) *C.L.Q.* 216.

12 Ruby, *Sentencing*, 77.

13 *R. v. Gardiner*, [1982] 2 S.C.R. 368.

14 Ontario, Ministry of the Attorney General, *Report of the Attorney General's Advisory Committee on Charge Screening, Disclosure, and Resolution Discussions*, chair G.A. Martin (Toronto: Queen's Printer 1993), 327–30.

15 If a transcript of the reasons for sentence is ordered, it is usually only to comply with s. 743.2, which directs that where an offender is sentenced to a penitentiary term, the court's reasons for so doing are to be prepared and forwarded to the penitentiary authorities for their guidance.

16 According to s. 745.6 of the Criminal Code, there is the possibility of a judicial review after fifteen years for certain life-term prisoners. This means that a jury will review a prisoner's file and decide if he or she should be eligible to apply for parole at some point before the twenty-five-year mark. This provision is described and discussed in Chapter 17 of this book.

17 Life 'maximum' sentences can be and sometimes are imposed for offences other than murder. In 1994, a judge in the Ontario Court (General Division) imposed three life sentences on a man convicted of three armed robberies.

18 The system can lead to some curious outcomes. In 1993, an offender pleaded guilty to a number of charges, including hostage taking. A twelve-year joint submission on sentence was arranged between defence and Crown counsel. However, the offender, worried that he might have to serve all twelve years, asked the judge to impose a life sentence which, in his opinion, might offer an earlier chance of release on parole.

19 In some cases, a sentencing judge can order the offender to serve half the sentence in prison before he or she becomes eligible to apply for parole. This is known as judicial determination (see Chapter 16 by Sandra Leonard in this volume).

20 Recent data are representative: almost two-thirds of the public believed that the police were doing a 'good' or 'excellent' job. Only 20 per cent of the public rated judges in this way (see Hough and Roberts (1998)).

21 *R. v. Stuckless,* [1998] O.J. No. 3177, 10 Aug. 1998.

22 This was demonstrated by systematic research. Members of the public were given very brief newspaper summaries of sentencing decisions to read. Afterwards they were asked their opinion of the sentences reported and how confident they were of their evaluations. Most people were both very critical of the dispositions reported and very confident of their opinions (see Doob and Roberts (1983)).

23 The exact description was the following: 'A man aged 23 pleaded guilty to the burglary of a cottage belonging to an elderly man whilst he was out during the day. The offender, who had previous convictions for burglary, took a video worth 150 pounds [approximately $360] and a television which he left damaged near the scene of the crime.'
24 Members of the public were asked to make a decision about an application for parole. The results indicated substantial support for the granting of parole in particular cases. A substantial majority of subjects endorsed release on parole even for a violent recidivist (see Cumberland and Zamble (1992)).
25 S. 271, 272, and 273 of the Criminal Code.
26 For a survey of recent events relating to sentencing and parole, see Roberts and von Hirsch (1992).
27 See, for example, the Fauteux Report (1956) and the Ouimet Report (1969).
28 Before these bills were introduced, a number of other legislative proposals were advanced. For example, in 1988, the solicitor general announced his intention to move the eligibility point for applications for full parole from one-third to one-half of the sentence served. Reaction to this proposal was as hostile as it was swift, and the proposal was withdrawn. The Corrections and Conditional Release Act eventually contained a modified version of the proposal.
29 This provision was invoked in the case of Wray Budreo, a notorious sex offender. The decision in that case is currently (1998) under review by the Ontario Court of Appeal.

ADDITIONAL READING

Canadian Journal of Criminology. 1990. Special Issue on Sentencing and Sentencing Reform. 32, no. 3.

Canadian Sentencing Commission. 1987. *Sentencing Reform: A Canadian Approach*. Ottawa: Supply and Services Canada.

Cole, D., and A. Manson. 1990. *Release from Imprisonment: The Law of Sentencing, Parole and Judicial Review*. Scarborough, Ont.: Carswell.

National Crime Prevention Council of Canada. 1997. *Incarceration in Canada*. Ottawa: National Crime Prevention Council.

Roberts, J.V., and A. von Hirsch. 1992. Sentencing Reform in Canada: Recent Developments. *Revue Générale de Droit* 23:319–55.

Roberts, J.V., and L. Stalans. 1997. Sentencing and Parole. In *Public Opinion, Crime, and Criminal Justice*, ch. 10. Boulder, Col.: Westview Press.

Ruby, C. 1995. *Sentencing*. 4th ed. Toronto: Butterworths.

Tonry, M. 1996. *Sentencing Matters*. New York: Oxford University Press.

von Hirsch, A. 1993. *Censure and Sanctions*. Oxford: Clarendon Press.

Walker, N. 1991. *Why Punish?* Oxford: Oxford University Press.

WEBSITES FOR RESEARCHING SENTENCING

http://www.acjnet.org
http://www.carswell.com
http://www.ussc.gov/index.html
http://gov.on.ca/MBS/english/publications/pubonweb/crimescc/ccc_0
11.html
http://www.sgc.gc.ca/public/reportshtm/corrrections/e199672.htm
http://www.sgc.gc.ga/public/reportshtm/abocor/e199410/e199410.htm
http://www.com/home/mallen/sentence.html

2

An Overview of Bill C-41 (The Sentencing Reform Act)

DAVID DAUBNEY[1] AND GORDON PARRY[2]

The Canadian Sentencing Commission was created in 1984 and published its report in 1987. This was followed in 1988 by the publication of the report of the House of Commons Standing Committee on Justice and Solicitor General (Daubney Committee). For the next several years, the federal government consulted on various reform policies. The final result of this process of consultation was Bill C-41, the first significant sentencing reform bill in decades. The bill changes the way in which judges will approach sentencing in Canada. In this chapter, two of the architects of the reform bill provide an overview of the bill's most important provisions.

Background to the Legislation

In 1979 the federal government and the provinces unanimously agreed to a comprehensive review of the Criminal Code. This exercise, known as the Criminal Law Review, led to two publications dealing with different aspects of the criminal justice system. In 1982, the Government of Canada published *The Criminal Law in Canadian Society*, which provided a basic framework of principles within which the more specific issues of criminal law could be addressed. In 1984, *Sentencing*, a White Paper, was published as a result of the work of the Sentencing Project within the overall Criminal Law Review. Early in 1984, the Trudeau government introduced Bill C-19, which included the first-ever Canadian legislative statement of the purpose and principles of sentencing. That bill died on the Order Paper.

In 1987, the Canadian Sentencing Commission, which had been established in May 1984, tabled its report in Parliament. Among its many noteworthy recommendations were the following:

- a legislative statement of the purpose and principles of sentencing;
- the creation of a permanent sentencing commission to develop presumptive sentencing guidelines;
- the abolition of full parole;
- the abolition of mandatory minimum sentences;
- the reduction of maximum sentences (to a twelve-year ceiling);
- a ranking of the seriousness of each Criminal Code offence; and
- greater use of alternatives to incarceration.

In the spring of 1987 the House of Commons Standing Committee on Justice and Solicitor General (Daubney Committee), in the midst of an emotional parliamentary debate on capital punishment, undertook a comprehensive inquiry into sentencing, conditional release, and related aspects of the federal correctional system. Following a year-long cross-Canada series of hearings, the committee tabled its report, *Taking Responsibility*, in 1988. Among its ninety-nine recommendations were the statutory enactment of a statement of purpose and principles of sentencing, the creation of advisory sentencing guidelines, and greater use of community sanctions, particularly those that involved restorative justice approaches.

In 1990, the government, by way of response to both the Sentencing Commission and 1988 Daubney Committee reports, issued a major discussion paper on sentencing and parole, *Directions for Reform: A Framework for Sentencing, Conditional Release and Corrections*. It suggested a statement of the purpose and principles that was essentially an amalgam of the commission and committee drafts, while opting for the committee's statement of the fundamental purpose of sentencing: the contribution to the maintenance of a just, peaceful, and safe society through the imposition of just sanctions. The document did not endorse sentencing guidelines, although it did suggest that a permanent sentencing commission be created.

In 1992, Justice Minister Campbell introduced Bill C-90, a major sentencing reform bill with five main components: a statement of the purpose and principles of sentencing; codified rules of evidence and procedure for sentencing hearings; a scheme of alternative measures (diversion) for adult offenders; a restructuring and consolidation of Part XXIII of the Criminal Code; and a number of technical amendments. Bill C-90 received second reading approval in principle on 7 May 1993, but died on the order paper with the dissolution of the thirty-fourth Parliament later that year.

Bill C-41

In 1994, Justice Minister Rock introduced Bill C-41, a comprehensive sentencing reform scheme dealing not only with the matters addressed in C-90 but also with intermediate sanctions.

The bill received Royal Assent on 13 July 1995, as Chapter 22 of the *Statutes of Canada*, 1995, and was proclaimed in force (except for subsection 718.3(5) and the provisions dealing with hospital orders) on 3 September 1996.

The legislation created a new Part XXIII of the Criminal Code of Canada, which contains the following main elements:

- sections enabling jurisdictions to establish alternative measures (diversion) programs;
- a statement of the purpose and principles of sentencing;
- a statutory code of procedure and evidence for sentencing hearings;
- modernized probation provisions;
- a new fine regime;
- a stand-alone restitution order;
- a new sentencing alternative, the conditional sentence of imprisonment; and
- reordered and somewhat modified provision dealing with imprisonment, life imprisonment, eligibility for parole, pardons, and disabilities.

These sentencing reforms were intended to achieve three objectives: to provide a consistent framework of policy and process in sentencing matters; to implement a system of sentencing policy and process approved by Parliament; and to increase public accessibility to the law respecting sentencing.

Alternative Measures

Section 717 of the Act authorizes alternative measures to be used 'to deal with a person alleged to have committed an offence only if not inconsistent with the protection of society' and a number of conditions are met, including that:

- the measures are part of an authorized program;
- the person considering their use is 'satisfied that they would be appropriate, having regard to the needs of the person alleged to have committed the offence and the interests of society and of the victim'; and
- the alleged offender consents to participate and accepts responsibility for the act or omission that forms the basis of the alleged offence.

It was Parliament's hope that a greater use of alternative measures would increase the opportunities for creative, individual responses to offenders alleged to have committed relatively minor crimes. Included among options offered as part of alternative measures programs are restitution, personal service work for the victim, community service work, mediation (where the victim agrees), and referral to a specialized program for counselling and treatment.

Statement of the Purpose and Principles of Sentencing

Section 718 of the Act states that:

The fundamental purpose of sentencing is to contribute, along with crime prevention initiatives, to respect for the law and the maintenance of a just, peaceful and safe society by imposing just sanctions that have one or more of the following objectives:

(a) to denounce unlawful conduct;
(b) to deter the offender and other persons from committing offences;
(c) to separate offenders from society, where necessary;
(d) to assist in rehabilitating offenders;
(e) to provide reparations for harm done to victims or the community; and
(f) to promote a sense of responsibility in offenders, and acknowledgment of the harm done to victims and to the community.

While this legislated statement of purpose[3] can be seen as codifying jurisprudence on sentencing objectives such as denunciation, specific and general deterrence, rehabilitation, and incapacitation (if needed), it also signals Parliament's interest in the restorative justice objectives of reparation for harm done to victims and the community and in promoting a sense of responsibility in offenders and acknowledgment of the harm done to victims and to the community. The language used in subsections 718(e) and (f) is drawn from that recommended in the 1988 Daubney Committee report *Taking Responsibility*, and the report of the Canadian Sentencing Commission. The Daubney Committee, in particular, was struck by the potential of the concept of offender responsibility and accountability.

Section 718.1 states that a sentence must be proportionate to the gravity of the offence and the degree of responsibility of the offender. This is described in the marginal heading as a fundamental principle. Both the Sentencing Commission and the Daubney Committee stressed the importance of proportionality, which the commission described as 'the paramount principle' governing the determination of a sentence. The proportionality principle should serve to ensure sentences that are not disproportionately lenient or harsh.

Section 718.2 sets out a number of other sentencing principles:

(a) a sentence should be increased or reduced to account for any relevant aggravating or mitigating circumstances relating to the offence or the offender, and, without limiting the generality of the foregoing,
  (i) evidence that the offence was motivated by bias, prejudice or hate based on race, national or ethnic origin, language, colour, religion, sex, age, mental or physical disability, sexual orientation, or any other similar factor, or
  (ii) evidence that the offender, in committing the offence, abused the offender's spouse or child,
  (iii) evidence that the offender, in committing the offence, abused a position of trust or authority in relation to the victim shall be deemed to be aggravating circumstances; or
  (iv) evidence that the offence was committed for the benefit of, at the direction of or in association with a criminal organization;
(b) a sentence should be similar to sentences imposed on similar offenders for similar offences committed in similar circumstances;
(c) where consecutive sentences are imposed, the combined sentence should not be unduly long or harsh;
(d) an offender should not be deprived of liberty, if less restrictive sanctions may be appropriate in the circumstances; and
(e) all available sanctions other than imprisonment that are reasonable in the circumstances should be considered for all offenders, with particular attention to the circumstances of aboriginal offenders.

Parliament has indicated how seriously it views hate-motivated crimes, abuse of positions of trust and authority, and spousal and child abuse by setting out the deemed aggravating circumstances in paragraphs 718.2(a)(i), (ii), and (iii).

Subsection 718.2(d) codifies the principle of using imprisonment with restraint and subsection 718.2(e) requires judges to canvass available noncarceral sanctions that are reasonable in the circumstances. By making particular reference to the circumstances of aboriginal offenders, Parliament has acknowledged the disproportionate involvement of aboriginal Canadians with our justice system.[4]

One contextual issue should be raised. Much of the debate during the development of the sentencing policy contained in Bill C-41 had to do with whether the objectives and principles were specific enough. The debate often broke down to two opposing camps: those who believed that numerical guidelines should be provided to constrain the judiciary in such a way that disparity and overuse of incarceration would be addressed, and those who believed that the judiciary needed flexibility to address the widely disparate types of cases that appeared before the courts and to administer true 'justice' in such dissimilar circumstances. The policy direction chosen in the bill was not to have specific numeric sentencing guidelines. This decision was based on two major findings from consultation: most judges (as represented by the judiciary during consultation) did not want guidelines – not even the 'soft' version suggested by the Canadian Sentencing Commission; and the provinces, as represented by the Crown attorneys from the provincial and territorial jurisdictions that were consulted, did not want numerical guidelines, largely due to concern about their potential impact on provincial carceral populations.

The bill established principles and broad directions that must be applied in the required reasons for sentence. This approach was based on the assumption that courts of appeal will consider the reasons in support of sentence and their relation to the statement of purpose and principles of lower courts. Over a period of time, the development of appellate jurisprudence would provide the guidelines that were being sought by those advocating numerical sentencing guidelines.

Probation

The probation provisions in Bill C-41 were designed to address several problems with the former probation regime. It was widely believed that the enforcement provisions respecting probation did not work effectively. The sanction for breach of probation was considered ineffective and was too often the subject of plea bargains; moreover, the penalty available for breach was not sufficient to encourage either Crown prosecutors or probation officers to pursue it vigorously. The conditions of probation similarly appeared outdated and ineffective, and there was confusion respecting the nomenclature employed (probation, suspended sentence). Finally, frustration was expressed that supervision was too often ineffective, due to a lack of ability to change conditions of probation to suit the case, and the overall authority of the probation officer.

The definition of probation (section 731) has not been changed; it remains the same as the old Code requirements of section 737. A new provision has been added, however, relating to offences where firearms are used. Section 100 of the Criminal Code creates prohibition orders against the possession of firearms, ammunition, or explosive devises. Such orders are imposed on offenders convicted (or discharged) in connection with offences involving violence, threats of violence, or firearms. Section 731.1 requires the court to consider the operation of section 100 before a probation order can be imposed.

Section 732.1 groups conditions of probation into mandatory conditions and optional conditions. The overall intent is to modernize probation conditions to clear up anomalies. The 'standard' conditions involve keeping the peace, appearing when required, and keeping the court or probation officer advised of changes during the period of probation.

The community service order was altered in view of research that suggested such orders in excess of 240 hours were ineffective. The overall period during which such orders may function was limited to eighteen months by the House of Commons Justice Committee during its review of C-41 to make application more administratively effective. Finally, to aid in treatment programs, particularly those related to substance abuse or family violence, where the offender agrees and a program is available, a condition may be imposed to require an offender to participate actively in a program of treatment. The court may impose other reasonable conditions 'for protecting society and for facilitating the offender's successful reintegration into the community' (paragraph 732.1(3)(h)).

The burden of proof of a breach was changed by subsection 733.1(1), which reads as follows:

> (1) An offender who is bound by a probation order and who, *without reasonable excuse*, fails or refuses to comply with that order is guilty of
> (a) an indictable offence and is liable to imprisonment for a term not exceeding two years; or
> (b) an offence punishable on summary conviction and is liable to imprisonment for a term not exceeding eighteen months, or to a fine not exceeding two thousand dollars, or both.

Fines

As a sanction, the fine is flexible and applicable to a wide variety of offences and offenders. It is the most commonly used disposition in the criminal courts, not only in Canada but also in other jurisdictions. The Canadian Sentencing Commission recommended changes to the fine system (see recommendations 12.14–12.16). The 1988 report of the Daubney Committee supported the recommendations of the Canadian Sentencing Commission respecting restitution and the use of imprisonment for fine default.

Section 734 replaces the former subsection 718(1) and removes the restriction on the imposition of a fine in the former subsection 718(2). Both the Ouimet Committee and the Law Reform Commission of Canada had recommended removal of statutory limitations on the imposition of fines. A similar proposal was found in the 1984 attempt to amend sentencing legislation (Bill C-19) and was further supported by the Canadian Sentencing Commission (recommendation 12.14). This proposal was the object of consultation with all provinces and territories and has been widely approved. The increased flexibility should make possible more appropriate sentences in cases where a fine with incarceration is deemed by sentencing judges to be an inappropriate restriction on their discretion.

The largest area of discussion during the development of the provision was the mechanism by which the court would determine if the offender could pay. Some provinces expressed the concern that probation officers would have to 'become accountants' to assess whether the offender could pay. There were also fears that courts would overload the PSR system in order to obtain information about the offender's means. The courts were worried about the impact on court dockets if the process were too elaborate.

The wording in the bill was simple: 'A court may fine an offender under this section only if the court is satisfied that the offender is able to pay the fine, or discharge it under section 736.' It is intended only that the court conduct a simple interview with the offender to make its determination. This seemed to reflect actual practice in many jurisdictions. In cases where the offender was represented, such information would be provided by the defence and subject to cross-examination by the Crown. Unless the province took advantage of its regulatory power under subsection 721(2) to specify 'the content and form of the report,' it would be possible for the court to request such information in a PSR. The intent, however, is that the process be simple. If the court is not satisfied that the offender can pay, one of the other sanctions available to the court – absolute or conditional discharge, probation, the conditional sentence (if the circumstances are appropriate), or incarceration – should be used.

Subsection 734(4) specifies that incarceration is still the ultimate sanction for non-payment. But incarceration is determined in accordance with the formula in subsection (5). This will overcome the wide disparity noted by the Canadian Sentencing Commission respecting time imposed in lieu of payment. While there was some concern that the 'formula' was too complex, this seems unfounded. The words of subsection 734(5) simply describe the following:

$$\frac{\text{outstanding amount + costs}}{8 \times \text{applicable provincial minimum wage}} = \text{number of days served}$$

There was considerable discussion about how to determine the number of days to be served in default. The Canadian Sentencing Commission proposed a table that would be annexed to the Criminal Code. This mechanism was felt to be cumbersome, however, since it could fall rapidly out of date and would be difficult to amend. The concept of a day of work at the provincial minimum wage was chosen in order to provide approximate parity between jurisdictions. While the parity is not exact, it would vary by the same factors that caused the minimum wage to vary. Also, it was assumed that by tying the time incarcerated to a day of work at the minimum wage, persons with means would choose to pay rather than be incarcerated. Finally, this formulation requires no ongoing legislative attention by the federal government. Whatever factors cause the provinces to change their minimum wage would change the calculation automatically.

Once it is decided that a fine is appropriate and that the offender can pay, the court may specify terms and conditions if the offender cannot pay immediately. These conditions include the amount to be paid, the manner ('x' instalments of 'y' dollars), the date by which all of the fine must be paid, and any other conditions that the court considers to be important. Section 734.2 will provide to the offender written documentation of the terms and conditions respecting his or her fine. The offender will be notified of the consequences of non-payment and of the means available to have the terms and conditions of the court order modified. This information will be provided in writing by the court, together with explanations of the consequences of non-payment. The overall approach is intended to be simple and inexpensive to administer.

To ease the potential administrative burden of the court, section 734.3 permits an officer of the court to be named to carry out much of the administration. This process is currently in effect in Quebec, through its program using a *percepteur d'amende*. Courts may make rules that govern the manner in which such an officer of the court operates.

Sections 734.5 and 734.6 provide new, noncarceral means of enforcement. Section 734.5 states that the jurisdiction to which the fines are owed is authorized to refuse to deliver services that would otherwise be rendered until such time as the fine is paid. The concept is simple: an offender who doesn't pay bills will not receive full service. The measures are restricted to renewing a licence, permit, or other similar instrument. Section 734.6 permits that where a fine is in default in accordance with the definition in subsection 734(3), in addition to any other method provided by law, the attorney general may file the order as a civil judgment. Civil enforcement could lead to the use of seizure of property or garnishment of wages. Section 734.7 provides that before a warrant of committal in default of payment can issue, the court must be satisfied that neither withholding of services nor civil enforcement is appropriate in the circumstances or that the offender has, without reasonable excuse, refused to pay the fine or discharge it through a fine option program.

Restitution

Sections 738 through 741.2 replace the unproclaimed sections 725–9 of the former Code. Those provisions, which dealt with restitution, had remained unproclaimed largely as a result of provincial resistance. Restitution was an important aspect of the overall policy direction to involve victims more effectively in the sentencing process. It was therefore important to deal with the impasse that had developed respecting the restitution provisions that remained unproclaimed in the Code.

In *R. v. Zelensky*[5] it was held that restitution lies within Parliament's authority, being in pith and substance part of the sentencing process. A strong attempt to fashion a regime consistent with the *Zelensky* case underlies the policy expressed in these new sections. An order for compensation should only be made with restraint and caution, and in particular, it should not be made where there is any serious contest on legal or factual issues. The process under section 738 is a summary one but it does not preclude an inquiry by the judge to establish an amount of compensation, provided that this can be done expeditiously and without turning the sentencing proceedings into the equivalent of a civil trial. Paragraph 738(1)(c) was added by the House of Commons Standing Committee on Justice and Legal Affairs to highlight the issue of spousal violence. Section 741.2 specifies that 'a civil remedy for an act or omission is not affected by reason only that an order for restitution under section 738 or 739 has been made in respect of that act or omission.' This will ensure that victims have access to civil suit for damages, notwithstanding the fact that restitution may have been ordered as part of the criminal process. A restitution order can simply be filed as a civil judgment and collected as such.

These sections, developed in close consultation with the provinces, are intended to provide effective restitution at an overall cost that is acceptable to those charged with administering the program. It will be important to conduct research at a future point to determine whether the object of providing more effective restitution has been met, whether these provisions, in common with the victim fine surcharge, have provided a better operational environment to deal with the concerns of victims and their treatment by the criminal justice system.

The Conditional Sentence of Imprisonment

Unquestionably the most novel aspect of Bill C-41 was the creation of a new sentencing option, the conditional sentence of imprisonment. The term 'conditional sentence' first appeared in Bill C-19 and was intended to replace the suspended sentence. Section 661 of Bill C-19 provided: 'Where an offender, other than a corporation, is convicted of an offence, except an offence for which a minimum punishment is prescribed by law, the court may suspend the imposition of any other sanction and direct that the offender enter into a recognizance in Form 28 without sureties to keep the peace and be of good behaviour for such period, not exceeding two years, as the court thinks fit.' The conditional sentence in Bill C-19 was essentially a peace bond for a period of up to two years and was to be distinguished from probation. It was not expressly targeted to offenders who would otherwise be imprisoned. The 'conditional sentence' in section 742.1, in contrast, has been developed as a true alternative to custody in the sense that its application is directed at offenders who would otherwise be jailed. The innovation of the conditional sentence is, in part, a response to the fact that Canada has a very high incarceration rate for non-violent offences.

The conditional sentence is a sentence of imprisonment of less than two years that the offender is allowed to serve in the community under mandatory (subsection 742.3(1)) and optional (subsection 742.3(2)) conditions. It is designed to be a noncarceral alternative for otherwise prison-bound offenders and may be ordered where:

(a) the offence is not punishable by a minimum term of imprisonment;
(b) the court imposes a sentence of less than two years; or
(c) the court is satisfied that allowing the offender to serve the sentence in the community would not endanger the safety of the community and would be consistent with the fundamental purpose and principles of sentencing set out in sections 718 to 718.2.

Judges are given a broad discretion to select among a menu of optional conditions and to impose such other reasonable conditions considered desirable 'for securing the good conduct of the offender and for preventing a repetition by the offender of the same offence or the commission of other offences' (paragraph 742.3(2)(f)).

The compulsory conditions of the conditional sentence order are set out in subsection 742.3(1) and include law-abiding behaviour, appearing before the court when required to do so, reporting to a supervisor as required, remaining within the jurisdiction of the court unless expressly given permission by the court to leave the jurisdiction, as well as notifying the court or the supervisor in advance of any change of name or address and promptly notifying the court or supervisor of any change of employment or occupation. The optional conditions set out in subsection 742.3(2) are similar to many of those available in probation orders. The court may order the offender to abstain from the consumption of alcohol or nonprescription drugs; to abstain from owning, possessing, or carrying weapons; to provide for the support or care of dependants; to perform up to 240 hours of community service work over a period not exceeding eighteen months; to attend a treatment program; and to comply with such other reasonable conditions as the court considers desirable to secure the good conduct of the offender and to prevent a repetition of the same offence or other offences by the offender. This latter provision permits the court to impose a conditional sentence even if there are concerns about recidivism, provided that the court is satisfied that this concern can be addressed by appropriate conditions in the conditional sentence order itself.

A copy of the conditional sentence order must be given to the offender, along with an explanation of the procedure for applying for changes to the optional conditions (section 742.4) and the breach procedure (section 742.6).

Unlike the case of a breach of probation, a breach of a condition of a conditional sentence order is not a new offence. An allegation of a breach must be supported by a written report of the conditional sentence supervisor (in most jurisdictions a designated probation officer) (subsection 742.6(4)). The hearing into the breach must take place within thirty days of the offender's arrest, where a warrant was issued (paragraph 742.6(3)(a)), or, where a summons was issued, within thirty days after its issuance (paragraph 742.6(3)(b)).

Where the court is satisfied on a balance of probabilities that the offender has, without reasonable excuse (the proof of which lies on the offender), breached a condition, it may do nothing (paragraph 742.6(9)(a)), modify optional conditions (paragraph 742.6(9)(b)); suspend the conditional sentence order, requiring the offender to serve part of the remaining sentence in custody (paragraph 742.6(9)(c)); or terminate the conditional sentence order and require the balance of the sentence to be served in custody (paragraph 742.6(9)(d)).

The lower standard and onus of proof emphasize the nature of the conditional sentence, i.e., that it is a sentence of imprisonment being served in the community. The court has essentially substituted the community for jail as the place where the sentence is to be served, as long as conditions set out in its order are respected. Like conditional release, it is a change in the conditions or venue of the service of the sentence and not in the sentence itself.

Subsection 742.6(1) provides for the application of the provisions of Parts XVI and XVIII of the Code with respect to compelling the appearance of an accused for a hearing on an alleged breach of a conditional sentence order.

If an offender is imprisoned for another offence, whenever committed, the running of the conditional sentence, unless otherwise ordered, is suspended during that period of imprisonment (section 742.7).

Conditional sentences are being used extensively in most parts of the country. It is too soon to provide an assessment of their effectiveness as mechanisms for community crime control. The Department of Justice has developed a comprehensive research and evaluation plan to monitor the impact of the sentencing legislation. However, early indications are that conditional sentences can satisfy sentencing principles and objectives while representing savings in economic, social, and human terms.

Procedure and Evidence

Sections 720–9 are central to the overall attempt to provide codified clarification to the procedures that apply to the sentencing process. The sections are structured to be logical and useful for both professionals and lay persons. The grouping proceeds from requiring a hearing, through presentence reports, victim impact statements, copies of reports, issues related to fact finding, consideration of other offences at sentencing, offender input, and reasons for sentence. The wording 'as soon as practicable' in section 720 is used to suggest that the proceedings should be expedited, but allowance is implicitly made for adjournments where and when necessary. It was decided not to codify the common law on adjournments. The section requires the court to hold a sentencing hearing as soon as practicable after a determination of guilt. It reflects the current law and practice and is premised on the principles of clarity and efficiency.

The codification of sentencing evidence and procedure does not imply that there need be a lengthy and formal hearing. Indeed, the word 'hearing' from the Bill C-19 version has been replaced by 'proceedings,' since it was suggested that 'hearing' connotes separateness and formality. The intent is that the process be expeditious, but permit the court to obtain more complete information.

Subsection 721(2) is an example of an approach to problem solving adopted because of disagreements during policy development. During consultation several provinces implored the federal government to specify the circumstances in which a presentence report could be requested by the courts. Their concern was that such reports were requested too frequently and their preparation took resources away from the supervision of cases in the community, a duty that was considered more in keeping with the overall function of the probation service. The judiciary and much of the defence bar, on the other hand, adamantly opposed any limitation of the ability of the court to order a PSR. The solution in the legislation was to provide provinces with legislative authority to 'make regulations respecting the types of offences for which a court may require a report, and respecting the content and form of the report.' It was assumed that any province wishing to make such regulations would consult closely with its judiciary and other interested parties and work out an appropriate arrangement in view of the situation in that jurisdiction.

The content of the presentence report (PSR) was an issue that received much attention during the development of the bill. Subsection 721(3) establishes minimum content requirements; provinces may specify additional content in accordance with the regulations mentioned above. The intent was to ensure not only that there was a minimum standard respecting content but, more particularly, that any former record of the offender was made available to the court. During consultation it was repeated on many occasions that multiple concurrent periods of probation were being awarded to offenders because the court was not aware of the offender's criminal and/or juvenile record. There appeared to be confusion about whether records from the Young Offenders Act (YOA) were appropriate for consideration if the offender appeared in court as an adult. The rest of the PSR may be tailored by the province and the court to suit requirements. The overall intention is to provide a cost-effective mechanism whereby the court will be provided with minimum content in a PSR, but also has the option to request specified information in appropriate circumstances. Provinces may eliminate from consideration some information by virtue of the regulations they may make in accordance with subsection 721(2), as discussed above.

Section 723 requires the sentencing court, before deciding the question of sentence, to call on counsel (or, where the offender is unrepresented, the offender) for submissions. This provision resembles subsection 646(2) of Bill C-19 and is consistent with recommendations of the Law Reform Commission (LRC). It is based on the principles of fairness and efficiency and seeks to ensure an adequate basis for an appropriate sentencing decision. It reflects both current practice and the common law. Counsel and the unrepresented offender are given the opportunity to make submissions. Finally, this wording does not prevent joint submissions from being made. Subsection 723(3) reflects current practice and the inherent power of judges to inquire into any matter on which the judge desires information before sentence and to call such evidence as necessary for this purpose without the consent of either the Crown or the offender.

Subsection 723(5) clarifies that hearsay evidence is admissible at sentencing hearings. This general rule is qualified by the provision that a person with personal knowledge of the matter may be called to testify where the court considers it to be in the 'interests of justice.' This test, principally directed to the accuracy of such information, imports flexibility into the procedure by allowing the court to decline further or better proof of hearsay evidence where it would not be feasible or necessary. The provision reflects the decision of the Supreme Court of Canada in *R. v. Gardiner*,[6] in which Dickson J., as he then was, remarked that the 'sentencing judge must have the fullest possible information concerning the background of the accused if he is to fit the sentence to the offender rather than to the crime' and 'hearsay evidence may be accepted where found to be credible and trustworthy.' The LRC would have preferred hearsay evidence to be accepted except in relation to aggravating facts which are in dispute.

Section 726 requires the court to ask the offender to speak to sentence. This provision differs slightly from the former section 668 of the Criminal Code in that there is a requirement to give the offender an opportunity to speak to sentence, whether or not the offender is represented, and an omission to comply with this section will affect the validity of the proceedings. This provision would have been endorsed by the LRC.

Section 726.2 requires judges to provide reasons for sentence in all cases. This provision will satisfy recommendations of the Daubney Committee, the Canadian Sentencing Commission, the Law Reform Commission, and the Council of Europe. It helps to ensure that the decision-making process is understood by those whom it affects. It should enhance public understanding, promote a more accurate appreciation of the sentencing process, and encourage the imposition of reasonable and fair sentences.

Conclusion

Bill C-41 is an attempt to achieve comprehensive sentencing reform in Canada. The policy, legal, and political processes involved in the development of this legislation led, of necessity, to a number of compromises. The approaches, however, are consistent with many of the suggestions made previously about the appropriate content for sentencing reform in this country. Of course, the legislation has been controversial. It seems likely that no legislative changes to the sentencing regime in Canada could have been undertaken in a way that was not controversial. The controversy, however, should not be the focus of future activity in this area; rather, our attention should be focused on the utility of the legislation in achieving the ends outlined in this chapter.

A major assumption for future consideration will be the degree to which the faith placed in judicial discretion and the supervisory capacity of courts of appeal has been realized. Both issues were clearly questioned by the Canadian Sentencing Commission. The resistance to numerical guidelines during the policy formulation process resulted in the approach adopted in the legislation. Future research should be attentive to the jurisprudence that develops around these reforms within the context of reducing sentencing disparity, dealing with the incarceration of low risk offenders, and the manner in which alternatives to incarceration are employed.

On a more operational level, assessment of the distinction drawn between probation and the conditional sentence will be required. The use of fines and the effectiveness of noncarceral enforcement mechanisms will also warrant scholarly examination, and the ability of the legislation to cause greater attention to be given to the plight of victims and aboriginal persons will be important in assessing the overall impact of this package of reforms. Finally, the influence of the statement of purpose and principles on sentencing practice will be one of the more important research areas when the impact of this legislation is evaluated.

We would argue that this legislation goes as far as the political and legal environment in Canada in the mid-1990s permits. Whether it is too adventurous or too timid is an issue that will be grist for the mill of the next generation of sentencing reformers.

ENDNOTES

1 David Daubney is General Counsel and head of the Sentencing Reform Team in the Department of Justice. In 1988 he was chair of the House of Commons Standing Committee that conducted a review of sentencing and parole (see Daubney Committee (1988)).

2 Gordon Parry has worked in the area of sentencing and parole for many years. He was head of the Sentencing Review Team when Bill C-41 was developed.

3 The statement of purpose differs from that set out in Bill C-90 in the following respects: (i) it contains the first ever Code reference to the contributing role of crime prevention initiatives and acknowledges that sentencing alone (and implicitly the criminal law alone), cannot maintain a just, peaceful, and safe society; (ii) the role of sentencing in contributing to *respect for the law* through the imposition of just sanctions, is articulated, echoing the recommendation of the Canadian Sentencing Commission; and (iii) the words 'where necessary' were added to the objective of separating offenders from society. This addition is not without significance when read in conjunction with the sentencing principles set out in ss. 718.2(d) and (e) and the new conditional sentence option that will be described below.

4 According to a June 1996 *Juristat* published by the Canadian Centre for Justice Statistics, less than 4 per cent of the Canadian population is aboriginal but aboriginal offenders account for 17 per cent of all provincial inmates and 13 percent of all federal inmates in custody.

5 *R. v. Gardiner*, [1982] 2 S.C.R. 368.

ADDITIONAL READING

Canadian Sentencing Commission. 1987. *Sentencing Reform: A Canadian Approach.* Ottawa: Supply and Services Canada.

House of Commons Standing Committee on Justice and Solicitor General (Daubney Committee). 1988. *Taking Responsibility. The Report of the Standing Committee on Justice and Solicitor General on its Review of Sentencing, Conditional Release and Related Aspects of Corrections.* Ottawa: Queen's Printer.

Roberts, J.V., and A. von Hirsch. 1992. Sentencing Reform in Canada: Recent Developments. *Revue Générale de Droit* 23:319–55.

3

Legislating the Purpose and Principles of Sentencing[1]

JULIAN V. ROBERTS AND ANDREW VON HIRSCH[2]

This chapter critically examines one of the key components of Bill C-41: the statement of purpose and principles of sentencing, which is now part of the Canadian Criminal Code (section 718). The statement is designed to provide judges with guidance and is modelled on, but differs in important respects from, earlier proposals made by the Canadian Sentencing Commission (1987) and the Daubney Committee (1988). The authors of this chapter review the statement in order to answer the question of whether it is likely to achieve the policy goals set for it by the federal government.

Introduction

As noted in Chapter 1, sentencing is designed to serve many purposes. How is a judge to know which purpose is appropriate in which kind of case? One of the aims of the federal government's sentencing reform initiative was to help develop a uniform approach to sentencing. One of the most important changes in the sentencing process introduced by Bill C-41 was the addition of the statement of the purpose and principles of sentencing to the Criminal Code of Canada (sections 718–718.2). An effective statement could have far-reaching symbolic and practical effects upon the sentencing system. This is particularly true in the present context, since the federal government's sentencing reform initiative no longer contains a sentencing guideline scheme.

Why Is a Statement of Purpose and Principles Necessary?

Before they can impose an appropriate sentence, judges should have an idea of the purpose (or purposes) that a particular sentence is supposed to serve. They need an answer to the age-old question, 'Why punish?' More than that, they should also have a guide to the most important principles to be followed when sentencing an offender. Until the passage of Bill C-41, this guidance came almost exclusively from the case law. But case law endorses many different purposes and principles, and judges can find support for almost every sentencing purpose in previous decisions. Many people have argued that the question of sentencing purposes should not be left entirely to the judiciary to resolve. Several groups (e.g., the Canadian Sentencing Commission) have suggested that Parliament itself should take a stand on this issue. Once the purpose(s) of punishment have been established by the elected representatives of the people, the business of sentencing specific offenders can in most cases be left to an independent judiciary. In short, we need a *legislated* statement of the purpose and principles of sentencing.

The potential benefits of a statutory statement of the purpose(s) of sentencing are clear. In the absence of such a statement, judges are free to follow their own individual sentencing philosophies, which can vary greatly from case to case and from judge to judge. Since sentencing means many things to different people, the result can be substantial variation in both the choice and application of the various sentencing purposes. This alone must contribute to the considerable variation in sentencing practices across the country, which are documented in Chapter 8 of this volume. What is needed is a clear pronouncement from Parliament that would guide both judges at the trial court level and the appellate courts across the country. It was a professed aim of Bill C-41 to provide such guidance.

Every major body of inquiry that has studied sentencing in Canada – including the Canadian Sentencing Commission, the Daubney Committee, and the Law Reform Commission of Canada – has acknowledged the necessity of a legislated statement of sentencing purpose. The federal government itself adopted this perspective in its 1990 blueprint documents for Bill C-41. In addition, a survey of the judiciary conducted by the Canadian Sentencing Commission showed the importance of a legislated statement to this constituency as well: two-thirds of the judges surveyed favoured the adoption of such a statement (Canadian Sentencing Commission 1987).

The need for a statement has also been recognized by most sentencing experts and by governments in other jurisdictions. For example, the 1991 Criminal Justice Act, applicable to England and Wales, contains a fairly clear guiding statute for sentencing.[3] Several other European countries have also adopted coherent statutory statements of the purpose of sentencing: Both Finland (1976) and Sweden (1988) adopted legislation establishing the pre-eminence of proportionality in sentencing.

The challenge to drafters of a statement of sentencing purpose and principles is to reconcile diverse and frequently conflicting sentencing aims. Though difficult, the task is by no means impossible, nor does it necessarily require promoting a single sentencing purpose at the expense of all others. Multi-purpose statements can offer guidance and affect sentencing practices at the trial court level, but they must specify the conditions under which certain aims are to be favoured over others. In this respect, a statement of purpose complements a sentencing guideline system. It can be argued that the statement of purpose is the compass, and numerical guidelines are the road map. Without the guidelines, judges may know roughly where they are going, but not necessarily how to get there; without the statement, judges would be following instructions in the absence of a clear sense of overall direction.

Previous Proposals for a Statement of Purpose

Canadian Sentencing Commission (1987)

The Canadian Sentencing Commission devoted an entire chapter (6) of its report to discussion of a statement of purpose and principles. The commission's statement is a complex document containing the following elements: an overall purpose for the criminal law, a primary purpose of sentencing, a series of sentencing principles (followed by a series of considerations for these principles) and, finally, what appear to be considerations for these considerations. According to the commission's statement, the fundamental purpose of sentencing is to preserve the authority of and promote respect for the law through the imposition of just sanctions. This fundamental purpose is followed by the fundamental principle that sentences should be proportionate to the gravity of the crime and the degree of responsibility of the offender for the offence. This in turn is followed by formal recognition of the principle of restraint, according to which a judge should select the least onerous sanction appropriate in the circumstances.

After applying these principles, judges are invited to consider denunciation, deterrence (specific and general), incapacitation, and reparation. In short, the statement ends by including many of the traditional sentencing purposes, although the term 'purpose' is not employed. A statement that endorses multiple purposes in this way must provide some clear indication of how judges are to choose between these purposes. No such guidance is given by the Sentencing Commission. In our view, judges would use the breadth of the Sentencing Commission's statement as a justification for continuing to pursue their own individual sentencing philosophies. The problem with an all-encompassing statement that appeals to all possible sentencing objectives is that no-one can disagree with it. Given the multiplicity of views, a statement of purpose that provokes no disagreement can offer no practical guidance.

Daubney Committee (1988)

The statement of purpose contained in the Daubney Committee report is essentially a re-formulation of the Sentencing Commission approach, with the added theme of accountability. Thus the purpose of sentencing in the committee's view is to 'contribute to the maintenance of a just, peaceful and safe society by holding offenders accountable for their criminal conduct through the imposition of just sanctions'. Accountability forms the core of the Daubney Committee statement, whereas it was simply one consideration for the Sentencing Commission. That distinction aside, our criticisms of the commission's statement also apply to the committee's proposal: it is long, complex, and includes almost every sentencing purpose ever proposed.

Statement of Purpose and Principles in Sections 718–718.2[4]

The statement of purpose contained in sections 718–718.2 of the Criminal Code contains four elements: (i) a fundamental purpose for sentencing, which might be termed the *raison d'etre* of the whole process; (ii) ten[5] objectives or goals, the fulfilment of which would promote the fundamental purpose of sentencing; (iii) a fundamental principle to restrain the influence of the objectives; and finally (iv) a series of what might be termed subordinate sentencing principles. The statement follows.

Statement of Purpose and Principles of Sentencing

Purpose

718. The fundamental purpose of sentencing is to contribute, along with crime prevention initiatives, to respect for the law and the maintenance of a just, peaceful and safe society by imposing just sanctions that have one or more of the following objectives:

(a) to denounce unlawful conduct;
(b) to deter the offender and other persons from committing offences;
(c) to separate offenders from society, where necessary;
(d) to assist in rehabilitating offenders;
(e) to provide reparations for harm done to victims or to the community; and
(f) to promote a sense of responsibility in offenders, and acknowledgement of the harm done to victims and to the community;

Fundamental Principle

718.1 A sentence must be proportionate to the gravity of the offence and the degree of responsibility of the offender.

Other Sentencing Principles

718.2 A court that imposes a sentence shall also take into consideration the following principles:

(a) a sentence should be increased or reduced to account for any relevant aggravating and mitigating circumstances relating to the offence or the offender; and, without limiting the generality of the foregoing,
  (i) evidence that the offence was motivated by bias, prejudice or hate based on race, national or ethnic origin, language, colour, religion, sex, age, mental or physical disability or sexual orientation or any other similar factor, or
  (ii) evidence that the offender, in committing the offence, abused the offender's spouse or child,
  (iii) evidence that the offender, in committing the offence, abused a position of trust or authority in relation to the victim shall be deemed aggravating circumstances; or
  (iv) evidence that the offence was committed for the benefit of, at the direction of or in association with a criminal organization;
(b) a sentence should be similar to sentences imposed on similar offenders for similar offences committed in similar circumstances;
(c) where consecutive sentences are imposed, the combined sentence should not be unduly long or harsh;
(d) an offender should not be deprived of liberty, if less restrictive alternatives may be appropriate in the circumstances; and
(e) all available sanctions other than imprisonment that are reasonable in the circumstances should be considered for all offenders, with particular attention to the circumstances of aboriginal offenders.

The Fundamental Purpose of Sentencing

According to section 718, the fundamental purpose of sentencing is to 'contribute, along with crime prevention initiatives, to respect for the law and the maintenance of a just, peaceful and safe society by imposing just sanctions that have one or more of the following objectives.'[6] From the very outset of the statement judges might well be confused. When determining the nature and severity of the sanction, are judges supposed to be assisting in crime prevention or imposing proportionate punishments? The difference is important. Should sentences be looking ahead, to crimes that might be prevented, or should they be looking backward at the seriousness of the crimes already committed? The fundamental purpose draws upon, although it is not exactly the same as, the Canadian Sentencing Commission's proposed statement.[7]

The language of the fundamental purpose reflects the dual nature of the whole statement, which incorporates elements of both utilitarian and retributivist traditions. By referring to 'crime prevention initiatives' the statement raises the notion that a particular sentencing policy can have a significant impact upon crime rates. This can only lead to false expectations, since shifts in sentence severity are unlikely to affect the overall crime rate. As noted earlier in this book, such a small percentage of all offenders are actually sentenced that sentencing can have little impact on the crime rate.[8] At the same time, the phrase 'just sanctions' clearly anticipates the principle of proportionality and sentencing according to a desert-based philosophy.

The Objectives of Sentencing: Rounding up the Usual Suspects

According to section 718, all 'just sanctions' must have at least one of ten sentencing objectives. The statement identifies ten objectives that the 'just sanctions' are designed to fulfil. These are the various purposes that have been advanced over the years, namely: denunciation, individual deterrence, general deterrence, incapacitation, reparation to the individual, restitution to the community, the promotion of a sense of responsibility in offenders, acknowledgment of the harm done to victims, acknowledgment of the harm to communities, and the creation of opportunities to assist in the offender's rehabilitation. Since judges may pick and choose from among this menu of sentencing purposes, the result is little more than a legislated statement of the status quo. To this extent, section 718 codifies current judicial practice.

The role of the fundamental purpose of sentencing contained in section 718 will be largely symbolic. It conveys a message that will have little practical impact in terms of sentencing practices. In contrast, the list of sentencing objectives is more instrumental than symbolic: it provides judges with a number of alternatives, all of which may lead to different dispositions. But it fails to inform judges as to the conditions under which one objective should be emphasized at the expense of the rest. No indication is provided to the sentencing judge of the circumstances in which deterrence is appropriate, or when denunciation might take precedence over restitution or reparation.

An hypothetical example illustrates the difficulties. Consider a case of domestic violence in which a judge has to sentence an offender convicted of assault. The fundamental purpose of sentencing found in section 718 prompts the judge to seek a just sentence, and then points him or her towards the specific objectives. Which of the ten sentencing objectives is relevant in a case of assault? Should the judge choose objective (a) ('to denounce unlawful conduct') and send the man to prison in order to convey a message that society will not tolerate criminal violence? Or should the offender be allowed to remain at liberty, provided that he attend some form of treatment program?

If rehabilitation is the more appropriate sentencing goal, then objective (d), 'to assist in rehabilitating offenders,' is the relevant aim to be pursued. This choice provides judges with a dilemma that they will probably resolve in their own individual ways, just as they have done in the past. If changing trial court sentencing practices is one of the goals of this statement, it is unlikely to be realised. The likely consequence is that judges will continue to sentence as before.

The Fundamental Principle of Sentencing

The next section of the statement contains a list of principles, in accordance with which the sentencing decision is to be taken. The list includes a fundamental principle (proportionality) and subordinate principles relating to the use of mitigating and aggravating factors, consistency in sentencing, totality, restraint, and the use of incarceration.

According to section 718.1: 'A sentence must[9] be proportionate to the gravity of the offence and the degree of responsibility of the offender.' This clear expression of proportionality in sentencing is important and represents a departure from the vacuum that existed in the Criminal Code. By endorsing a fundamental principle of this nature, the drafters of section 718.1 took a step toward making sentencing more consistent and philosophically coherent. In theory at least, this desert-based principle should limit the influence of the utilitarian sentencing objectives that precede it. Thus a judge wishing to impose a severe, exemplary sentence to 'send a message to others' will be restricted to the limits of a proportionate disposition. Disproportionately harsh sentences imposed in pursuit of some utilitarian goal (usually deterrence) will be discouraged by the existence of this fundamental principle.[10]

The weakness of this section of the statement is that the fundamental principle of proportionality is undermined from two directions: first, by the preceding ten objectives, and second, by the five subsequent principles. This in turn gives rise to two further problems: the influence of the principle of proportionality could be undercut by all these objectives, and there is no guidance provided for sentencing judges as to exactly how the objectives and principles affect the principle of proportionality, or how they relate to each other. Some legislated articulation of the interrelationships between all these components would have been appropriate, but none is provided.

Secondary Sentencing Principles

Judges are already very familiar with several of the principles outlined in the legislation. The first principle, for example, states that 'a sentence should be increased or reduced to account for any relevant aggravating or mitigating circumstances relating to the offence or the offender.' Since an important part of the process of determining the nature and quantum of punishment consists of evaluating relevant mitigating and aggravating factors, this principle merely codifies what is obvious. As such it will come as little surprise to judges in Canada and it will provide them with little additional guidance. This principle is the conceptual equivalent of saying to university professors that the grade assigned to a student's paper should reflect both the good and the bad points of the work.

After stating this principle, the statement then introduces four statutory aggravating factors. The first relates to hate-motivated crimes. Specifically, subsection 718.2(a)(i) states that 'evidence that the offence was motivated by bias, prejudice or hate based on the race, nationality, colour, religion, sex, age, mental or physical disability or sexual orientation of the victim' shall result in a more severe sentence. This provision attracted more commentary than any other section when Bill C-41 was being debated. Indeed, the bill itself became known in the news media as the 'hate crime' bill.

Should crimes motivated by hate be punished more severely? It is a complex question that cannot adequately be addressed in this chapter. However, it is clear that hate crimes are in several respects more serious than other forms of criminality.[11] Hate crimes carry the additional harm of a threat to other members of the community to which the individual victim belongs. As well, they convey an affront to the identity of the individual victim. In a multicultural society like Canada, they may well provoke social discord between cultures. For example, anti-Semitic vandalism carries an affront to the Jewish faith, as well as a message of hate which may provoke fear and promote social tension. Moreover, research has demonstrated that hate crimes directed against the person typically result in more severe and longer-lasting injuries than other assaults. In short, there are several justifications for harsher penalties for hate-motivated crimes. Hate-motivated crimes have in the past resulted in more severe sanctions, and it is also worth noting that aggravated penalties for hate crimes exist in other jurisdictions as well. Many American states have statutes that mandate harsher penalties for offenders convicted of bias-motivated crimes.

For these reasons, it seems reasonable, under a desert-based sentencing scheme, to treat hate motivation as an aggravating factor: the harm is greater, and the severity of the penalty should accordingly be enhanced. Whether this ground for aggravation should be placed in the statement of purpose is another matter, however. There are more important aggravating factors that affect far larger numbers of offenders. Criminal record, for instance, is central to the sentencing process, but it receives no mention in the statement of purpose.

Subsections 718.2(a)(ii) and (iii) state that 'evidence that the offender, in committing the offence, abused the offender's spouse or child,' or 'evidence that the offender, in committing the offence, abused a position of trust or authority in relation to the victim shall be deemed aggravating circumstances.' Both of these sections merely reflect current judicial practice to enhance penalties in such cases. But once again we ask whether they need to be one of only two aggravating factors contained in the Criminal Code. The same argument can be made for the fourth statutory aggravating factor, which relates to crimes committed on behalf of or in association with a criminal organization.[12]

According to principle (b), 'a sentence should be similar to sentences imposed on similar offenders for similar offences committed in similar circumstances.' Stating that there should be parity between the penalties assigned to offenders whose crimes are equally serious modestly strengthens the bill's statement on proportionality. Thus it has some degree of usefulness, in contrast to principle (a), which has little or no practical significance.

The third principle, (c), states that 'where consecutive sentences are imposed, the combined sentence should not be unduly long or harsh.' This is a statutory enunciation of the principle of totality, which the sentencing process has for some time articulated to prevent the imposition of excessively long sentences upon offenders convicted of multiple offences. Canadian courts of appeal have long provided guidance to trial court judges in this regard. Accordingly, few judges are unaware either of the problem or of the solution that has evolved in Canada, as well as in England and Wales (see Ashworth (1983); Thomas (1979)). It is not clear why the principle needs to be enshrined in the Criminal Code.[13]

Restricting the Use of Incarceration in Canada

The remaining two principles ((d) and (e)) are more interesting. They both relate to the overuse of incarceration. An overemphasis on incarceration as a penal sanction in Canada has been noted by many groups and individuals. Accordingly, reducing Canada's reliance on incarceration as a sentencing option has been a fundamental policy goal, supported by a wide constituency of experts. Any sentencing bill should attempt to reduce, to the extent possible, the number and duration of sentences of imprisonment, particularly for non-violent offenders, and this has in fact been a stated aim of federal government policy for some time.[14] The statement of purpose attempts to restrict the use of imprisonment by means of principles (d) and (e).

The Principle of Restraint

Principle (d) declares that 'an offender should not be deprived of liberty, if less restrictive alternatives may be appropriate in the circumstances.' This is the principle of restraint, which has been endorsed by several important commissions of inquiry in this country. As the Canadian Sentencing Commission noted in its report, restraint in the application of the criminal law is consistent with the position taken by every commission of inquiry in Canada, from the Brown Commission in the mid-nineteenth century to the Nielsen Task Force that reported in 1986. The notion of restraint is most closely associated with the work of the Law Reform Commission of Canada. However, earlier versions were far more general than the wording that eventually entered the Criminal Code as subsection 718.2(d).

As formulated by the Law Reform Commission of Canada, the principle of restraint encompasses many aspects of the criminal law and is not restricted to the issue of sentencing. In relation to sentencing in particular, both the Law Reform Commission[15] and the Sentencing Commission argued that restraint should encompass *all* kinds of dispositions. Thus in the latter's proposed statement of sentencing purpose, the principle of restraint followed the paramount principle (that the sentence be proportionate to the gravity of the offence and the degree of responsibility of the offender) and was expressed in the following way: 'a sentence should be the least onerous sanction appropriate in the circumstances' (Canadian Sentencing Commission 1987, 154). Subsection 718.2(d), however, restricts the application of restraint to sentences of imprisonment. While it is important to affirm this principle in statutory form, the application used here is, in our view, too narrow. Judges constantly need to question whether a less intrusive sanction would be appropriate if the law is to be truly faithful to the spirit of parsimony in sentencing. This means that if a discharge is appropriate, a fine should not be imposed, and so forth. The more restrictive wording contained in Bill C-41 is also a change from the Department of Justice policy document of 1990, which followed the exact wording of the Sentencing Commission's statement.[16]

Alternatives to Incarceration: Imprisonment and Offenders from Visible Minorities

Continuing the spirit of the preceding principle, the final principle, (e), argues that 'all available alternatives to imprisonment that are reasonable in the circumstances should be considered for all offenders, with particular attention to the circumstances of aboriginal offenders.' It has long been known that Canada's penal institutions contain a disproportionate number of aboriginal offenders. The most recent statistics from provincial correctional systems across the country show that almost one inmate in four is aboriginal. Over half of all admissions in some provinces (such as Saskatchewan and Manitoba) are aboriginals (Reed and Roberts 1998). However, aboriginal Canadians are not the only visible minority that is overrepresented in penal institutions.

Data from the Province of Ontario show that the racial disproportion of blacks in the province's jails is far greater than that associated with aboriginals. Thus custodial admissions data for 1993–4 reveal that 16 per cent of inmates admitted were black, compared to 6 per cent for aboriginals (Commission on Systemic Racism in the Ontario Criminal Justice System 1995). Discriminatory sentencing decisions account for a small but significant amount of this overrepresentation (see Roberts and Doob (1997)). Imprisonment also poses special problems for female offenders. The Daubney Committee reported a survey that found that over 80 per cent of female inmates were mothers, and over half of these were single parents. While incarceration clearly creates conditions of exceptional hardship for these categories of offenders, subsection 718.2(e) focuses primarily on aboriginal offenders. A more general formulation might have been more appropriate.

Will subsection 718.2(d) accomplish its stated goal of curbing the use of incarceration as a sanction in Canada, in general or for aboriginal offenders? Simply suggesting that judges consider other sentencing options is unlikely to have much impact upon sentencing practices across the country. In all probability, judges already consider alternatives to incarceration before they imprison offenders. (See La Prairie (1990) as well as her chapter in this volume, for discussion of this issue.) An effective statement would restrict judges from imposing imprisonment *unless specific conditions are met.* This would be the first step toward effective guidance. The second would consist of guidelines specifying the kinds of cases and conditions that should give rise to different dispositions. (For further discussion of this issue, see Doob (1990)).

The final wording of the statement's principle regarding the use of incarceration represents a significant dilution of the original formulation. The discussion document published by the Department of Justice in 1990 followed a much stronger tack. It laid down specific conditions that had to be fulfilled before a sentence of imprisonment could be imposed. The exclusionary nature of this document was modelled upon the Sentencing Commission's statement but is to be found in formulations in other jurisdictions as well. For example, subsection 1(2) of the English Criminal Justice Act of 1991 states:

> the court shall not pass a custodial sentence on the offender unless it is of the opinion –
> (a) that the offence, or the combination of the offence and one other offence associated with it, was so serious that only such a sentence can be justified for the offence; or
> (b) where the offence is a violent or sexual offence, that only such a sentence would be adequate to protect the public from serious harm from him.

In contrast to both these formulations, section 718 permits judges considerably greater latitude in terms of imposing sentences of incarceration. In short, the dilution of the principle of restraint is a clear weakness of the statement of purpose and principles now contained in the Criminal Code. The use of imprisonment as a sanction needs to be constrained to a substantially greater degree if any consequential impact upon incarceration rates is to be achieved. This is particularly true since sentencing guidelines are not a part of the government's reform package. In the absence of guidelines, all hope of changing sentencing practices resides with the statement of purpose, which accordingly must be expressed in language that is both unequivocal and forceful.

Conclusions

At the time that Bill C-41 was introduced, the press release from the minister of justice stated that the statement of purpose would provide 'clear direction from Parliament on the purpose and principles of sentencing.'[17] Do sections 718–718.2 provide such direction? In our view, the answer is that, with one exception, the statement merely codifies principles that have evolved already about the sentencing process. It will not provide much direction in the sense of giving judges a tool to promote consistency. The practical advice for judges contained in the statement is to be found in the fundamental principle, which, it will be recalled, states that a sentence 'must be proportionate to the gravity of the offence and the degree of responsibility of the offender.' This should constrain judicial behaviour. It will, in theory at least, discourage judges from imposing disproportionately harsh sentences in pursuit of deterrence.

The major hope of success for the statement contained in sections 718–718.2 lies with this fundamental principle. The weakness of the bill as a whole is that a rather confusing statement of purpose is all that is offered to change sentencing practices. This statement is the only means of giving life to the important policy goals of limiting unwarranted disparity and reducing the use of imprisonment as a sanction. It is unlikely to prove sufficient. If the statutory statement is the sole means of effecting change, then it should clearly specify the conditions under which certain sentencing options, such as custody, should be imposed. Sections 718–718.2 close off few options for the sentencing judge and, accordingly, offers little practical guidance.

The value of a statutory statement of sentencing purpose and principles cannot be overstated. As noted earlier, many people, judges, criminal justice professionals, and indeed all those with an interest in sentencing will look to such a document as a statement from Parliament about sentencing policy. The importance of the statement is enhanced in the Canadian context, because unlike other jurisdictions (such as the United States) sentencing reform in this country does not involve a formal guideline system. Thus the goals of reducing the use of incarceration, promoting proportionality in sentencing, and reducing the amount of sentencing disparity must all be accomplished, in large degree, by the statement of sentencing purpose. We can be hopeful, but not optimistic about the impact of sections 718–718.2 of the Criminal Code on Canadian sentencing practices.

ENDNOTES

1 This chapter draws on material originally published in the *Criminal Law Quarterly* (Roberts and von Hirsch 1995).

2 Andrew von Hirsch is the author of numerous books about the sentencing process, including *Doing Justice* (1976), *Past or Future Crimes* (1985b), and *Censure and Sanctions* (1993). He is currently Honorary Professor of Penal Theory and Penal Law at Cambridge University.

3 Criminal Justice Act (U.K.), 1991, c. 53. For commentary on the Act, see Ashworth (1992).

4 The federal government's response to the proposals advanced by the Canadian Sentencing Commission and the Daubney Committee was a hybrid statement of purpose and principle containing elements of these earlier proposals. Although shorter, it draws heavily upon the Canadian Sentencing Commission proposal. First proposed in Bill C-90, it was amended somewhat in Bill C-41, which eventually became sections 718–718.2 of the Criminal Code.

5 There are only six actual subsections in the bill but some contain more than one objective. For example, subsection 718(b) includes both general and special deterrence. For the purposes of clarity, we discuss the objectives independently here.
6 The commission attributed this purpose to the criminal law rather than sentencing per se. For further information on this issue, see Roberts and von Hirsch (1992).
7 The commission proposed two purposes, one for the criminal law and a related one for the sentencing process. See Canadian Sentencing Commission (1987), 125–56.
8 It is estimated that approximately 3 per cent of all offenders are sentenced (Statistics Canada 1996b; Ashworth 1995).
9 It is worth noting that section 718.1 uses the word 'must,' suggesting an even stronger endorsement of proportionality than the formulation of the Sentencing Commission, which was that the severity of sentences 'should' be proportionate to the seriousness of crimes.
10 For a discussion of the implications of the proportionality principle see Manson (1998) and Roberts and von Hirsch (1998).
11 For Canadian research on this issue see Roberts (1996b).
12 This factor was added after the others, and as such raises the possibility that Parliament will continue to add aggravating factors on a piecemeal basis.
13 A statement of purpose and principles need not, and in fact cannot, include all relevant sentencing principles. For example, a great deal has been written about the principle that has evolved whereby defendants who plead guilty are accorded a more lenient sentence than accuseds who are found guilty. Should this 'discount' be enshrined in the guiding statute as well?
14 See, for example, the report on sentencing published by the Government of Canada in 1982: *Sentencing* (Ottawa: Department of Justice Canada 1982) at 34, and also the discussion documents released by the federal government in 1990.
15 See *Brief Submitted to the Canadian Sentencing Commission by the Law Reform Commission of Canada* (Ottawa: Law Reform Commission of Canada March 1985).
16 See Government of Canada, *Directions for Reform: A Framework for Sentencing, Corrections and Conditional Release* (Ottawa: Ministry of Supply and Services Canada 1990).
17 News Release: Minister of Justice Introduces Sentencing Reform Bill. Department of Justice, Canada, 13 June 1994.

ADDITIONAL READING

Canadian Sentencing Commission. 1987. *Sentencing Reform: A Canadian Approach.* Chapter 6. Ottawa: Supply and Services Canada.

House of Commons Standing Committee on Justice and Solicitor General (Daubney Committee). 1988. *Taking Responsibility. The Report of the House of Commons Standing Committee on Justice and Solicitor General on its Review of Sentencing, Conditional Release and Related Aspects of Corrections*. Ottawa: Queen's Printer.

Roberts, J.V., and A. von Hirsch. 1992. Sentencing Reform in Canada: Recent Developments. *Revue Générale de Droit* 23:319–55.

4

Conditional Sentences

JACK GEMMELL[1]

Although it received little publicity at the time, one of the most important provisions of Bill C-41 created a new sanction called the conditional sentence. Since then, conditional sentencing has become the most visible and controversial element of the reform bill. It has generated a great deal of news media coverage and provoked questions in the House of Commons. Much of the debate focuses on what many people see as a paradox: offenders are first sentenced to prison, but they serve their sentence under supervision in the community. In this chapter, Jack Gemmell explores the nature and origin of the conditional sentence and evaluates its utility in accomplishing the goal of reducing the use of incarceration as a sanction.

Introduction

The new sentencing provisions contained in Bill C-41 ushered in an important addition to Canadian sentencing law and practice: the conditional sentence. Designed as an alternative to imprisonment and subject to surprisingly few limitations as to its availability, the conditional sentencing provisions allow a judge to permit an offender to serve a sentence of up to two years less a day in the community, subject to a conditional sentence order.

Conditional sentences do not fit comfortably either with prior Canadian sentencing practices or the purpose and principles of sentencing now (somewhat incompletely) codified by sections 718 to 718.2 of the Criminal Code. At first glance, they are paradoxical: on the one hand the trial judge must decide that only a sentence of imprisonment will suffice for a particular offender and a particular offence; but that judge subsequently authorizes the offender's release into the community. Such a disposition is inconsistent with Canadian sentencing practices for a wide range of offences, such as drug trafficking and theft from an employer, for which the courts of appeal have mandated jail terms except in exceptional circumstances, even where the offender is rehabilitated or poses no discernible risk to the community. And conditional sentences do not appear to convey the necessary public messages of general deterrence, denunciation, and retribution. In fact, the imposition of a conditional sentence could be said to subvert the message that the original sentence of imprisonment was meant to communicate.

However, conditional sentences represent a means of reducing Canada's high incarceration rate for non-violent offenders. Canada continues to have one of the highest rates of imprisonment among the Western, developed countries and an explicit alternative to imprisonment, like conditional sentencing, at least has the potential to reduce that rate, by diverting offenders away from the jail system into a form of community supervision. Indeed, as we will see below, one of the policy reasons for enacting this legislation was to provide an alternative to imprisonment. Whether the advent of conditional sentencing will actually reduce the rate of incarceration is an issue that will be explored later in this chapter.

This chapter will examine the nature of conditional sentences and two important related issues: when a conditional sentence is appropriate, and whether conditional sentences will actually reduce the rate of incarceration in Canada.

The Nature of a Conditional Sentence

Sections 742 to 742.7 of the Criminal Code govern the imposition, conditions, variation, and termination of conditional sentences. Section 742.1, which outlines the conditions according to which a court may impose a conditional sentence, and section 742.2, which prescribes the conditions that the court must and may attach to a conditional sentence order, are reproduced below.

Section 742.1

Imposing a conditional sentence

Where a person is convicted of an offence, except an offence that is punishable by a minimum term of imprisonment, and the court

(a) imposes a sentence of imprisonment of less than two years, and

(b) is satisfied that serving the sentence in the community would not endanger the safety of the community and would be consistent with the fundamental purpose and principles of sentencing set out in sections 718 to 718.2, the court may, for the purpose of supervising the offender's behaviour in the community, order that the offender serve the sentence in the community, subject to the offender's complying with the conditions of a conditional sentence order made under section 742.3.

Section 742.3

Compulsory conditions of conditional sentence order

(1) The court shall prescribe, as conditions of a conditional sentence order, that the offender do all of the following:

(a) keep the peace and be of good behaviour;

(b) appear before the court when required to do so by the court;

(c) report to a supervisor

(i) within two working days, or such longer period as the court directs, after the making of the conditional sentence order, and

(ii) thereafter, when required by the supervisor and in the manner directed by the supervisor;

(d) remain within the jurisdiction of the court unless written permission to go outside that jurisdiction is obtained from the court or the supervisor; and

(e) notify the court or the supervisor in advance of any change of name or address, and promptly notify the court or supervisor of any change of employment or occupation.

Optional conditions of conditional sentence order

(2) The court may prescribe, as additional conditions of a conditional sentence order, that the offender do one or more of the following:

(a) abstain from

(i) the consumption of alcohol or other intoxicating substances, or

(ii) the consumption of drugs except in accordance with a medical prescription;

(b) abstain from owning, possessing or carrying a weapon;

(c) provide for the support or care of dependants;

(d) perform up to 240 hours of community service over a period not exceeding eighteen months;

(e) attend a treatment program approved by the province; and

(f) comply with such other reasonable conditions as the court considers desirable, subject to any regulations made under subsection 738(2), for securing the good conduct of the offender and for preventing a repetition by the offender of the same offence or the commission of other offences.

While it is easy to say what a conditional sentence is, it is much more difficult to characterize it as a form of punishment. Simply put, a conditional sentence is a sentence of imprisonment of less than two years that the court has permitted the offender to serve in the community, subject to a conditional sentence order. As a punishment, it defies easy categorization. It is not equivalent to actual imprisonment, since the offender is not confined to jail; it is not the same as a probation order, because its method of enforcement is quite different, and it is not directly analogous to parole, since the offender is not confined initially and the releasing authority is the court and not correctional officials.

The problem of characterization goes to the central issue of the legitimacy and efficacy of this sanction in the eyes both of the public and the courts. In a sense, it may be a matter of perception. If the public (and ultimately the courts) regard conditional sentences as allowing offenders who by rights should be sent to jail to escape punishment, then they will be used less and less as an alternative to imprisonment and increasingly as a substitute for the less onerous sanction of probation. On the other hand, if the courts (and ultimately the public) come to see that the relatively widespread use of conditional sentences instead of jail sentences leads not to a rise in the crime rate, but rather to a reduction in correctional budgets and the promotion of the rehabilitation of offenders, then they will succeed in becoming a true alternative to incarceration.

Parliamentary Intent

The provisions creating conditional sentences envisage them as an alternative to imprisonment: only after the court imposes a sentence of imprisonment may it permit the offender to serve that sentence in the community, subject to a conditional sentence order. And judging from the statements from the minister of justice introducing Bill C-41 to the House of Commons, Parliament intended conditional sentences to be a true alternative to imprisonment. According to the minister, the conditional sentence sanction is 'obviously aimed at offenders who would otherwise be in jail but who could be in the community under tight controls.' He went on to add: 'It seems to me that such an approach would promote the protection of the public by seeking to separate the most serious offenders from the community while providing that less serious offenders can remain among other members of society with effective community based alternatives while still adhering to appropriate conditions.'[2]

The government's stated policy reasons for creating such an alternative to imprisonment ranged from the idealistic to the pragmatic. First, there was the hope that Canada could begin to reduce its rate of incarceration, which is high, relative to those of other industrialized countries. Second, there was the stated belief that jail may not be necessary for many non-violent offenders. Third, it was noted that jail can be harmful to inmates, tending rather to breed crime than to deter it. And finally, there was the pragmatic consideration: jail is much more expensive than community supervision and the scarce funds available could be better spent on incarcerating and treating offenders convicted of more serious crimes.

The Discretion of the Courts

In translating these policy goals into legislation, Parliament chose to give the courts a wide discretion about when to grant the offender release into the community on a conditional sentence. This is consistent with the prevailing practice in Canada to leave sentencing by and large up to the trial judge.

Section 742.1 prescribes four prerequisites for the imposition of a conditional sentence:

1. The court must impose a sentence of imprisonment of less than two years.
2. The offence for which the court is sentencing the offender cannot be punishable by a minimum term of imprisonment.
3. Serving the sentence in the community would not endanger the safety of the community.
4. Serving the sentence in the community would be consistent with the fundamental purpose and principles of sentencing set out in sections 718 to 718.2.

These four preconditions do not exclude many cases. The first two – that the sentence of imprisonment be less that two years and not a minimum term – are not stringent criteria. To begin with, most criminal sentences are less than two years in length – indeed, the maximum term of imprisonment for most criminal offences is now effectively less than two years. Very few offences are punishable by a minimum term of imprisonment, the most common of which are second or subsequent impaired driving offences, and they make up only a small percentage of the total criminal caseload.

What is also noteworthy is that the first two preconditions relate to the length of the sentence rather than the type of offence or the criminal record of the offender. Parliament did not see fit to exclude some obviously problematic offences from the ambit of conditional sentences, and instead contented itself to exclude only offences punished by minimum terms of imprisonment. Thus conditional sentences are theoretically available for child sexual offences, such as sexual interference and sexual exploitation, or more violent offences, such as assault with a weapon or assault causing bodily harm. Repeat offenders not facing a minimum term of imprisonment can also apply for a conditional sentence.

Similarly, the third precondition – that the court be 'satisfied that serving the sentence in the community would not endanger the safety of the community' – does not create a high threshold. Generally speaking, offenders serving less than two years will not pose a danger to the community: if they did, the prosecution and the judge would likely have taken a much harsher position on sentence. As well, many will have committed non-violent offences – thefts, breaches of court orders, drug offences, and the like – while those convicted of violent offences will frequently have committed relatively minor assaults, be first offenders for this type of offence, or be able to point to mitigating circumstances, such as previously good character, remorse, or reconciliation with the victim. Given these broad criteria, the conditional sentence is potentially available as a sentencing option in a high percentage of cases.

The practical limits on the wholesale imposition of conditional sentences stem from the fourth precondition – that serving the sentence in the community would be consistent with the fundamental purpose and principles of sentencing set out in sections 718 to 718.2 – and the court's possible residual discretion not to impose a conditional sentence even if the offender and the offence meet the preconditions.[3] Neither provide much real guidance to the courts and the result has been a confusing body of contradictory case law. The requirement that serving the sentence in the community must be consistent with the purpose and principles of sentencing is particularly unilluminating, especially when it is recalled that the sentencing court must have applied the same purpose and principles in deciding to impose a sentence of imprisonment in the first place, and found that only jail and no other less restrictive sanction was appropriate in the circumstances. If serving the sentence in the community was consistent with the purpose and principles of sentencing, why was the offender sentenced to jail in the first place?

Assuming that the sentencing court has a residual discretion to refuse to impose a conditional sentence even when the offender satisfies the four preconditions,[4] there are no statutory guidelines at all for its exercise. At most one could say that the court presumably must base it on considerations, whatever they may be, other than the statutory fundamental purpose and principles of sentencing identified in the Code. In the final analysis, the conditional sentencing provisions leave a great deal of discretion to the courts to develop, on a case-by-case basis, their own doctrines and principles about when a conditional sentence is appropriate, much like they had had to do in the past when deciding when jail was necessary and when a fine would do. How successful this process will be remains to be seen: after all, it was these same courts acting on the same case-by-case basis that created the high rate of incarceration that Parliament hoped partially to rectify through the mechanism of the conditional sentence.

Enforcement of Conditional Sentence Orders

Serving a conditional sentence order in the community is a little like complying with a strict probation order, except that the unexpired portion of the sentence hangs over the offender like the proverbial Sword of Damocles, waiting to drop should the offender violate the terms of release. The conditions of a conditional sentence order can be stricter than those in a probation order and in practice likely will be, given that the conditional sentence order is meant to be an alternative to imprisonment. Much more restrictive conditions, such as house arrest and electronic monitoring (theoretically available in a probation order) are easier to justify for a conditional sentence order. The main difference between the two types of order lies in their enforcement. Conditional sentence orders are easier to enforce than either probation orders or suspended sentences. For probation orders, the principal mechanism of enforcement is to lay a charge of breach of probation. But, strange as it may seem, this charge is often hard to prove because of the rule against hearsay evidence, the presumption of innocence, and the criminal standard of proof beyond a reasonable doubt.

For a suspended sentence, enforcement is more difficult. A court can revoke a suspended sentence and resentence the offender, but only after the offender has been convicted of a new criminal offence, after he or she has been brought before the sentencing court, and after a revocation hearing has been held. Because of these requirements, in practice hearings to revoke a suspended sentence are rarely even held. Finally, even if the prosecutor succeeds in proving the breach of probation charge or in convincing the court to revoke the suspended sentence, the ultimate question of sentence still rests in the hands of the sentencing judge, who may not be inclined to imprison the offender. As a result, some probation officers, police officers, prosecutors, and judges have tended to regard probation orders and suspended sentences as essentially toothless remedies.

By contrast, conditional sentence orders are designed for easy enforcement. An offender arrested on reasonable grounds for a violation of a conditional sentence order must justify his or her release on bail. The hearing into the violation is before the original sentencing court and should be quickly held –

generally within thirty days of the sentence. The prosecutor can prove its case using hearsay evidence, by way of a report from the conditional sentence supervisor and attached witness statements, and need only meet the civil standard of proof on a balance of probabilities rather than the criminal standard of proof beyond a reasonable doubt. And while the court has a number of noncustodial options should it find the offender in violation of the conditional sentence order, the expectation will be that the court will usually commit the offender to jail to serve the unexpired balance of the conditional sentence. After all, notionally at least, the offender is simply serving his or her sentence of imprisonment in the community. Accordingly, the offender serving a conditional sentence order might reasonably believe that the court will enforce any violation of the conditional sentence order quickly and effectively, with the penalty being the unserved balance of the conditional sentence.

When Should a Court Impose a Conditional Sentence?

There is no science of sentencing and sentencing decisions are notoriously hard to justify, both on their own terms and in comparison with other cases. This is particularly true for conditional sentencing. Exhibit 4.1 gives six examples of cases where the sentencing court has considered whether to grant the offender a conditional sentence; Exhibit 4.2 briefly sets out what the court decided. It should be noted that not only is it difficult to reconcile why a court ruled out a conditional sentence for one type of offence while a second court granted one for another, for each type of offence represented in Exhibit 4.1, decisions in similar cases can be found in which the court has come to the opposite conclusion.

EXHIBIT 4.1

Would you grant the offenders described below a conditional sentence? All were of previous good character and none had a prior criminal record. (See Exhibit 4.2 for the court's decision.)

1. A police officer who shot and killed a native demonstrator without legal justification?
2. A bookkeeper who defrauded her employer of $270,000?
3. A teacher who had sexual relations with a young female student from age eleven to thirteen?
4. A mule caught importing about 1.1 kilos of hashish into Canada?
5. A politician who forged election forms for a bogus candidate in order to get elected?
6. A drunk driver who lost control of his car, striking three pedestrians and injuring them, fortunately not permanently?

EXHIBIT 4.2

How the court decided the cases described in Exhibit 4.1.

1. Yes: *R. v. Deane* (unreported), Ont. Prov. Div., Fraser J., 3 July 1997
2. No: *R. v. Pierce* (1997), 114 C.C.C. (3d) 23 (Ont. C.A.)
3. Yes: *R. v. Scidmore* (1996), 112 C.C.C. (3d) 28 (Ont. C.A.)
4. No: *R. v. Dugas* (1997), 34 W.C.B. (2d) 248 (Que. S.C.)
5. Yes: *R. v. Taylor*, [1996] O.J. No. 4695 (Ont. Gen. Div.)
6. Yes: *R. v. Szawlawski*, [1997] O.J. No. 1016 (Ont. Gen. Div.)

Generally speaking, there are two schools of judicial thought about conditional sentencing. One is a conservative, business-as-usual approach that seeks to accommodate conditional sentences into the existing sentencing structure. A more liberal, reform-minded approach that has taken Parliament more at its word by seeking to use conditional sentences as a principled alternative to jail. This latter view has resulted in a critique of the inadequacies of current sentencing practice, with its reliance on imprisonment as a sanction.

Before the introduction of conditional sentences, jail was the centrepiece of Canadian sentencing practice. To bring some order to the jurisprudence of sentencing, the courts of appeal had promulgated sentencing tariffs for various categories of offences that were said to mandate jail except in exceptional circumstances. Thus, for example, an offender convicted of trafficking in any drug, even a soft drug like marijuana, had to be sentenced to jail in the absence of exceptional circumstances, a term which was narrowly defined and hence rarely found to arise. The Alberta Court of Appeal had gone even further by establishing specific jail terms as a starting point for the sentencing of certain offences. As one commentator noted, this presumption of jail came to encompass almost every criminal offence, including crimes of violence, welfare frauds, thefts from employers, most sexual offences, and drug trafficking (see Young (1988)).

The courts of appeal justified the presumption of incarceration largely by the need for a general deterrent: the jailing of the offender was believed to act as a deterrent for like-minded individuals (although considerations of denunciation, retribution, and the perceived gravity of the offence also played a role). The advent of conditional sentences posed the question of whether a conditional sentence could serve as a suitable alternative to the term of imprisonment dictated by the presumption of incarceration for certain types of offences.

The conservative approach to conditional sentencing has, by and large, been to deny the availability of conditional sentences for at least some of these types of offences, where the offender could be said to have taken a calculated, profit-seeking risk. Thus, as noted in Exhibits 4.1 and 4.2, some courts have refused to grant conditional sentences for crimes motivated by greed, such as major thefts from employers and trafficking in drugs, even though by no stretch of the imagination could the offender be considered a danger to the community.

But the existence of the conditional sentence option also challenges the underlying rationales for imprisonment and has, for the liberal school of conditional sentencing, inspired a rethinking of some of the principles and purposes of sentencing. Accordingly, one of the justifications for imposing conditional sentences for liberal-minded judges is that jail is not as effective a remedy for deterring criminal conduct as was formerly believed: fear of apprehension and the certainty of trial and conviction may be more important. Jail is expensive to maintain and often personally destructive to the offender, tending to further alienate him or her from society. In these circumstances, the conditional sentence can be said to be a rational alternative to jail, one which does not unduly undermine the benefits of general deterrence.

In the leading case from the liberal school, *R. v. Wismayer*,[5] Mr Justice Rosenberg of the Ontario Court of Appeal presented a kind of alternative to the usual presumption of incarceration: once the offender had met the first three criteria for the imposition of a conditional sentence – the sentence of imprisonment was for less than two years, it was not a minimum sentence, and the offender was not a risk to the community – the principal factor in deciding whether to grant a community sentence was 'whether permitting the offender to serve the sentence in the community under a conditional sentence order would endanger the safety of the community because of the risk that the offender will re-offend.'[6] While the sentencing court was also to take into account all of the other principles and purposes of sentencing when arriving at this decision, the practical effect of emphasizing this principal factor would be that many offenders would be released on conditional sentences.

By contrast, conservative jurists have declined to enter into the debate over the utility of jail sentences and generally content themselves with bald assertions that in this case or for this type of offence the principles of general deterrence, denunciation, and retribution require jail instead of a conditional sentence. In particular, they have often seen conditional sentences as inadequate to convey the sense of denunciation of and retribution for serious criminal misconduct. The principles of denunciation and retribution are a public means by which the state, via the courts and the justice system, can assert the primacy and authority of its laws and condemn affronts against the fundamental moral standards of society. Sentencing is their ultimate mode of expression and it would seem that only the most serious sanction – imprisonment – would be commensurate with serious breaches of the legal and moral standards at stake. A lesser penalty like a conditional sentence would not be proportionate to the gravity of the offence and it would not send the necessary message to a public that wants a public display of law enforcement.

To justify the imposition of a conditional sentence in the face of this argument, judges have stressed the punitive aspects of conditional sentences: the strict terms of supervision, the threat of jail for any violation, and the absence of parole. Through the investigation, apprehension, and prosecution of offenders the criminal process itself helps to satisfy this need for a public maintenance of legal and moral standards. But despite these arguments, the fact still remains that the court could have imposed a harsher penalty and chose not to do so.

The notion of a generous granting of a conditional sentence as an alternative to imprisonment has not met with widespread approval by either the judiciary, many of whom have tended to remain wedded to their old reliance on imprisonment, or some elements of the public, who have seen conditional sentences as the remittance of punishment rather than a viable alternative to jail. These two phenomena are related, as the courts prefer to reflect existing social norms rather than to initiate changes. Convincing the public at large of the justice of a conditional sentence will take some doing: in general, the public often only hears of the end result, the conditional sentence, and is not aware of the facts of the case or the history of the proceedings. In today's political climate, punishing criminals is popular; releasing them back into the community is not. Consequently the failures of such releases, even if rare, will be far more newsworthy than all the successes. Only time will tell whether the public and the judiciary can come to terms with what amounts to an easing of the penal regime in Canada in a time of increasing political popularity for more severe criminal laws and harsher penalties.

Will Conditional Sentences Reduce Canada's Rate of Incarceration?

One concern about alternatives to imprisonment like conditional sentences is that they will merely serve to widen the net of penal controls – a phenomenon well described in the literature – rather than to reduce the imprisonment rate to any significant degree. Indeed, conditional sentences could conceivably end up increasing the rate. The Canadian Sentencing Commission described this effect as follows: 'A widening of the net of penal controls is liable to occur when a new sanction is introduced with the intention that it should be used in lieu of another sanction, which is *more severe*' (1987, 367). The problem occurs when the new sanction is not used as a substitute for the more severe sanction, but rather replaces or supplements existing, less severe sanctions. Conditional sentences have the potential for widening the net. They are intended to provide an alternative to the more severe sanction of jail; the danger is that they may be used instead as a stricter form of probation, with more restrictive conditions, such as house arrest or electronic monitoring. The result would be a tightening of the penal regime in Canada, with offenders facing more restrictions on their liberties and more severe sanctions in the event that they breach the terms of their sentence.

Studies in England of a similar sentencing option, the English suspended sentence,[7] have found that it tended to widen the net. Some English judges must not only have been imposing suspended sentences on cases where imprisonment was not really at stake, but also making the suspended sentence of imprisonment longer than what might ordinarily have been imposed for a sentence of imprisonment. In fact, when first introduced, the decline in the rate of imprisonment caused by the substitution of suspended sentences for immediate jail terms was more than offset by the number of suspended sentences being imposed. The only reasonable conclusion was that a significant number of offenders who were never facing jail in the first place were being saddled with suspended sentences. Worse still, later studies showed that the lengths of the suspended terms of imprisonment were longer than equivalent cases of immediate imprisonment: presumably, judges were compensating for the perceived leniency of the suspended sentence by making it longer than a normal term of imprisonment. While it was impossible to determine definitively, some researchers argued that the English suspended sentence could well have had the effect of actually increasing the rate of imprisonment. If true, it pointed to a truly calamitous failure of a policy designed to reduce the jail population.

It is too early to assess the effect of conditional sentencing on the Canadian penal regime. However, some of the initial responses to the legislation by some of the courts of appeal have not been encouraging. A key issue is how long a conditional sentence should be. If the courts were to treat a conditional sentence as a pure alternative to imprisonment, then they should determine the length of the term of imprisonment first, applying ordinary sentencing principles, before deciding whether to release the offender into the community on a conditional sentence order. This was the approach adopted in England by the English Court of Appeal in an attempt to control the sentencing practices for their suspended sentences.

Some of the courts of appeal have rejected this approach, however, preferring that the trial judge first decide whether a reformatory sentence – one of less than two years – rather that a penitentiary sentence – one of two years or more – would be appropriate. If the lesser sanction is chosen, the judge is then to consider the whole range of sentencing options, from discharges, fines, and probation to conditional sentences and immediate imprisonment. The length of a sentence served in the community would not necessarily be the same as one served in custody. This approach has two pitfalls. It implicitly treats the conditional sentence not as an alternative to jail, but rather as a sentencing disposition in its own right, creating the prospect that it will displace other, less severe sanctions like probation order. And it explicitly permits the conditional sentence to be longer than the sentence of immediate imprisonment for which it is meant to serve as a substitute.

The result could well be a widening of the net of penal controls. Worse still, a combination of a miserly application of conditional sentences to cases of actual imprisonment, coupled with the relatively widespread imposition of conditional sentences on offenders who would never have faced jail in the first place, could potentially increase the rate of incarceration since, inevitably, some of the people on release on conditional sentences will be jailed for violating their orders. Regardless of how the appeal courts rule about the proper way to impose conditional sentences, a deeper question arises: whether appellate decisions have any real control over sentencing practices in the trial courts. This brings us back to the debate over actual sentencing guidelines and whether they would be a more effective means of implementing Parliament's intention to reduce imprisonment through conditional sentences.

ENDNOTES

1 Jack Gemmell has been a member of the Ontario Bar since 1979 and has practised criminal law at all levels of the court system. He published the first analysis of the conditional sentence regime.
2 House of Commons, *Debates*, 20 September 1994, 5873
3 When first enacted, paragraph 742.1(b) did not contain this fourth precondition and some early appellate decisions suggested that once the offender satisfied the first three conditions he or she was *ipso facto* entitled to a conditional sentence: see, for example, *R. v. Scidmore* (1996), 112 C.C.C. (3d) 28 (Ont. C.A.) and *R. v. Arsiuta* (1997), 114 C.C.C. (3d) 286 (Man. C.A.). There were two responses to this trend: first, other appellate decisions re-examined s. 742.1(b) and read in a residual discretion in the court to refuse to impose a conditional sentence if inconsistent with the fundamental purpose and principles of sentence: see, for example, *R. v. Pierce* (1997), 114 C.C.C. (3d) 23 (Ont. C.A.). Second, Parliament amended s. 721(b), purporting to clarify its interpretation by adding the fourth precondition. Now that

Parliament has amended s. 742.1(b) to give the courts more latitude in refusing to impose conditional sentences, the question becomes whether there is any more need for this residual discretion.

4 The existence of such a discretion arises from the general principle that sentence is in the discretion of the court (see ss. 718.3(1) and (2), *R. v. M. (C.A.)* (1996), 105 C.C.C. (3d) 327 at 374–5 (S.C.C.), and *R. v. Wismayer* (1997), 115 C.C.C. (3d) 18 at para. 34 (Ont. C.A.)), and an interpretation of the language of s. 742.1 – which says that the court may impose a conditional sentence if the conditions are met – indicating that Parliament intended the court to have such a discretion.

5 *R. v. Wismayer* (1997), *supra*, note 4.

6 Ibid., at para. 68.

7 The English suspended sentence bears some resemblance to our conditional sentence. Like the conditional sentence, it is an explicit alternative to imprisonment: the judge is first to sentence the offender to a term of imprisonment before considering whether to release him or her by suspending the sentence for a period of up to two years. Unlike the conditional sentence, the offender does not begin serving the sentence in the community; instead, the sentence merely remains suspended over the operational period, potentially to be reactivated in its entirety should the offender violate the terms of his or her release. By contrast, in Canada, the offender who violates a conditional sentence release will at least have served some portion of the sentence before being committed to jail, thereby reducing the balance of the unexpired portion which he or she is potentially liable to serve.

ADDITIONAL READING

Gemmell, J. 1997. The New Conditional Sentencing Regime. *Criminal Law Quarterly* 39:334–62.

Manson, A. 1997. Finding a Place for Conditional Sentences. 3 *Criminal Reports* (5th): 283–300.

5

Conditional Sentencing: Issues and Problems[1]

JULIAN V. ROBERTS

This chapter draws attention to some problems created by the conditional term of imprisonment. These issues will have to be addressed if conditional sentencing is to make an effective and principled contribution to sentencing, reducing the use of incarceration as a sanction.

Introduction

Conditional sentencing is a powerful new weapon in the struggle to contain the use of incarceration as a sanction. However, like any weapon, in the wrong hands it can produce as much harm as good. The courts have grappled with the conditional sentence since it was introduced, and it is clear that no consensus has yet emerged as to the most appropriate manner in which to use the disposition (see the subsequent chapter by David Cole for an update on appellate reaction to the conditional sentencing regime). Moreover, conditional sentencing has generated controversy beyond the judiciary; there have already been calls for amendment or repeal of the provision. The importance of such pressures should not be underestimated: they were directly responsible for provoking the significant amendments to the judicial review provision (see Chapter 17 of this volume). If the conditional sentencing regime it is to survive to make a contribution to reducing the number of admissions to custody, the problems associated with this new sanction must be identified and dealt with. In this chapter I draw attention to some of the issues surrounding the conditional sentence provisions. First, however, I note some trends in the use of the disposition since its creation in September 1996.

Recent Trends in the Use of Conditional Sentences

The data reported in Table 5.1 show that the judiciary across the country have embraced the conditional term of imprisonment with some enthusiasm. In the first year, 13,037 conditional terms of imprisonment were imposed across the country. Of these, 4,083, or almost one-third, were imposed in Quebec. Unfortunately, at the time of writing (February 1998), national data on the nature of optional conditions imposed, the breach rate, and the judicial response to breaches are still unavailable. More important, it is at present still unclear whether the introduction of the conditional sentence provision has actually reduced the number of admissions to custody. National conditional sentence data broken down by offence category are not yet available; Table 5.2, however, presents a breakdown of conditional sentence orders for the first year for the Province of Ontario. It shows that judges in this province, at least, have been using the conditional sentence order for a wide range of offences, including very serious crimes. Finally, Table 5.3 provides some preliminary data on the kinds of optional conditions imposed in the four jurisdictions for which this information was available. As can be seen, treatment orders and community service orders are frequently imposed, while house arrest, which is the most restrictive possible condition of a conditional sentence order, is seldom im-

TABLE 5.1
Number and Average Length of Conditional Sentence Orders, September 1996–August 1997

Province/territory	Number of orders	Median sentence length (in months)	% Female	% Aboriginal
Nova Scotia	380	6	16	n/a
Prince Edward Island	20	5	15	15
New Brunswick	386	4	19	n/a
Quebec	4,083	8	14	n/a
Ontario	3,775	5	24	7
Manitoba	228	6	22	38
Saskatchewan	684	8	15	76
Alberta	1,413	6	28	21
British Columbia	1,831	4	16	13
Northwest Territories	59	5	20	n/a
Yukon	48	3	25	n/a
Canada	13,037	5	20	n/a

Source: Department of Justice Canada

TABLE 5.2
Conditional Sentences by Offence Category, Ontario, 1 September 1996–31 August 1997

Offence category	Number of offenders	Percentage of Total
Homicide and related	11	< 1
Serious violent	82	2
Violent sexual	163	4
Break and enter and related	275	7
Non-violent sexual	92	2
Traffic/import drugs	181	5
Weapons offences	78	2
Fraud and related	845	22
Miscellaneous against the person	118	3
Theft/possession	634	17
Assault and related	611	16
Arson/property damage	55	1.5
Morals offences	19	< 1
Obstruct justice	39	1
Possession drugs	116	3
Traffic – Criminal Code	101	3
Breach court order	167	4
Impaired driving	66	2
Other	122	3
Total	3,775	100

Source: Statistical Services, Correctional Services Division

TABLE 5.3
Optional Conditions Imposed as Part of Conditional Sentence Order, Selected Jurisdictions

	Alcohol/ drug treatment	Other treatment	Restitution	Perform community service	Curfew	House arrest	Other
PEI	4	15	7	5	5	7	15
New Brunswick	267	58	90	120	42	–	129
Manitoba	126	111	47	145	229	7	761
NWT	28	30	15	42	6	5	87

posed. Since these data derive from a very limited number of jurisdictions, it is unwise to make generalizations about the country as a whole.

The trends discernible from the available data underline the breadth of the conditional sentence regime. The same point can be made by examining the ambit of the new disposition. Section 742.1 of the Criminal Code permits the use of conditional sentencing for a very wide range of crimes, including some of the most serious. In the *Wismayer* decision, the court noted, 'It must be borne in mind that for the most serious offenders the conditional sentence is simply not an available option because the offender will have been sentenced to the penitentiary.'[2] However, Parliament has set such a high threshold (up to two years less a day) that the vast majority of the most serious crimes are included within the ambit of the conditional sentencing regime. Table 5.4 provides a list of offences and the percentage of cases that resulted in a sentence of imprisonment of under two years over the most recent period for which statistics are currently available. As can be seen from this table, almost all convictions for these offences result in sentences of less than two years. According to section 742.1, these offenders are within the statutory limit of a sentence of less than two years imprisonment.

Distinguishing the Conditional Sentence Order from a Term of Probation

One problem is that a conditional sentence order is not necessarily more onerous, or may not be perceived by offenders or members of the public to be more onerous than a term of probation. As a judgment of the Ontario Court (General Division) noted: 'A conditional sentence order must be, and must be seen to be, more onerous than suspended sentence by way of probation.'[3] Without reliable statistics on the number and nature of conditions imposed in conditional sentence orders, it is hard to know how much more onerous they are than terms of probation. Still, it is worth comparing the statutory conditions and the consequences of conditional sentence orders and probation orders.

The conditions of a conditional sentence order do not differ substantively from the conditions of a probation order. Modelled closely on section 732.1 of the Criminal Code, there are only two principal differences. First, according to paragraph 742.3(1)(d), the condition to remain within the jurisdiction of the court unless written permission is obtained is a compulsory, rather than an optional condition, as it is with a probation order. Second, according to paragraph 742.3(2)(e), the court may order the offender to attend a treatment program approved by the province. Under the terms of a probation order, paragraph 732.1(3)(g) states that the court may order the offender to actively participate in a treatment program, but only 'if the offender agrees.' These distinctions are unlikely to be perceived by the offender as substantively different, and this may well undermine the credibility and hence the utility of conditional

TABLE 5.4
Use of Incarceration, Nine Jurisdictions, 1993 and 1994

Offence	Percentage of admissions to custody under two years	Maximum penalty
Sexual assault (s. 271)*	89	10 years
Aggravated assault (s. 268)	82	14 years
Assault with a weapon, etc. (ss. 267, 269)*	98	10 years
Assault (ss. 265, 266)*	100	5 years
Forcible confinement (s. 279)	86	10 years
Sexual touching child < 14 (ss. 151, 152, 153)*	94	10 years
Robbery (ss. 343, 344, 345)	66	Life imprisonment
Break and enter (ss. 348, 349)	95	Life imprisonment
Sexual assault with a weapon/ aggravated sexual assault (ss. 272, 273)**	51	Life imprisonment/ 14 years
Trafficking (NCA 4)	95	Life imprisonment
Procuring (s. 212)	71	14 years
Obstruct justice (s. 139)*	100	10 years
Forgery (ss. 366–71, 372(1), 374–8	100	14 years
Impaired operation causing bodily harm (s. 255)	99	10 years

Source: A. Birkenmayer and S. Besserer, *Sentencing in Adult Provincial Courts: A Study of Nine Canadian Jurisdictions: 1993 and 1994*. Ottawa: Statistics Canada 1997, Table A-7.
* Denotes hybrid offence
** These offences were combined in the analysis on account of small numbers.

sentencing. The Alberta Court of Appeal recognized this reality in a recent decision when it noted that 'many conditional sentences are either virtually identical in terms and effect to a suspended sentence or are only marginally more restrictive. Hence to contend that a conditional sentence is much more onerous than a suspended sentence is a highly debatable proposition.'[4] If the conditions of a conditional sentence order are usually little different from the conditions imposed as part of a probation order, what about the consequences of breach? How are the two distinguished?

The metaphor of the Sword of Damocles has been used to describe the suspended sentence of imprisonment in England and Wales (see Ashworth (1995)) and the conditional sentence in Canada.[5] Damocles, it will be recalled, was immobilized with fear by awareness of a sword suspended over his head. The sword was hanging by a single horsehair, with the consequence that the slightest false move by Damocles would lead to his instant death. In order to serve as an effective specific deterrent, the punishment that follows a breach must be certain, swift, and severe. The threatened consequences of a conditional sentence order are none of these.[6] In fact, a conditional sentence order is no more certain or severe than a probation order. While it has been argued that the threat of execution of the sentence of imprisonment makes the conditional sentence order more onerous than a suspended sentence accompanied by a probation order (see Walker (1985)), incarceration in the event of a breach is not mandatory.

Violation of a conventional probation order may also lead to the incarceration of the offender, since breach of a probation order, but not a conditional sentence order, constitutes a fresh offence. Since a conditional sentence is supposed to be more severe than a probation order, this seems paradoxical. The conditions associated with most conditional sentence orders are generally no more onerous than those associated with a conventional probation order. In practice, judges may distinguish between the two orders by adding more onerous optional conditions, or by incarcerating immediately for most breaches. We shall have to await the results of empirical research to know whether this is in fact happening. At the time this volume goes to press (February 1998) breach data are only available from the Province of Ontario. These data suggest that, for Ontario at least, judges have not been eager to imprison offenders who breach the conditions of a conditional sentence order. Of all the breaches proven in this province to date, one-quarter of the offenders were incarcerated for the balance of the sentence. A further 17 per cent were incarcerated for a briefer period, and the court elected simply to amend the conditions in another 26 per cent of cases. The most frequent judicial response (in one-third of cases) was to take no further action.[7]

If the conditional sentence order is not clearly distinguishable from a probation order, problems will arise in terms of the perceptions of offenders and members of the public, as will a conflict with the principle of proportionality (see below).

Conflicts with the Purpose and Principles of Sentencing

If the conditional sentence is significantly less onerous than a term of imprisonment, then a potential conflict between the conditional sentence and the purpose and principles of sentencing may arise. At the heart of the issue is the dichotomy that has always permeated the sentencing process. When imposing sentence, should the court focus on the past – that is, the seriousness of the criminal conduct – or the future, namely, the likelihood that the offender will reoffend? Two schools of sentencing philosophy exist, both of which are explicitly acknowledged by sections 718 to 718.2 of the Code, which specify the purpose and principles of sentencing. On the one side are desert theorists, for whom the seriousness of the offence and, to lesser extent, the offender's criminal record, are primordial considerations. Mitigating and aggravating factors must relate to the gravity of the offence or the extent of the offender's responsibility for the act. Sentencing theorists from the alternative perspective argue that the purpose of sentencing is to effect reductions in the crime rate, through mechanisms such as general and specific deterrence or incapacitation. The conflict between these two theoretical orientations is most apparent when one follows the logic suggested by the Code to be followed by a court before imposing a conditional sentence order.

The original wording of section 742.1 created significant potential for conflict. It suggested that the imposition of a conditional sentence order follows a two-step procedure, with different criteria relevant to each stage. First, the court must apply the statement of purpose and principles to determine the nature and severity of the sanction. Since subsection 718.2(e) specifically enjoins judges to consider 'all non-custodial sanctions other than imprisonment that are reasonable in the circumstances,' if a judge imposes a sentence of imprisonment it is presumably because no community-based disposition is appropriate. Central to this decision will be the fundamental principle of sentencing. According to section 718.1, 'A sentence must be proportionate to the gravity of the offence and the degree of responsibility of the offender.' The principle of proportionality is associated with sentencing according to a 'just deserts' orientation. According to the desert model, legal punishment expresses censure, and this takes precedence over utilitarian sentencing goals that aim to prevent crime (von Hirsch 1990). Once the decision to incarcerate had been taken, the court should proceed to the second stage, namely to determine whether the offender's presence in the community would endanger the safety of the community. At this point, different criteria (relating to risk of reoffending rather than just deserts) will apply.

The justification for the two-stage approach was clear. It ensured that the imposition of a conditional sentence order does in fact replace a sentence of incarceration rather than a non-custodial sanction (which would lead to 'net-widening,' or an increase in admissions to custody). This logic is followed in the British context involving the suspended term of imprisonment. However, it has its problems, not the least of which is the difficulty for a sentencing judge to separate in his or her mind the question of whether the sentence of incarceration is appropriate and, if so, whether it need be executed immediately. After all, during the sentencing hearing, judges are likely to be sensitized to the possibility of a conditional sentence by submissions from defence counsel. A two-stage model assumes that the court can lay aside such appeals unless and until the necessity for a custodial term has been established.

Undermining the Fundamental Principle of Sentencing

Perhaps the most obvious conflict that can arise when a two-stage approach is used involves the principle of proportionality, identified by section 718.1 as the fundamental principle in sentencing. Let us assume that a judge follows the purpose and principles articulated in sections 718 to 718.2 and sentences an offender to six months in prison, guided primarily by the principle of proportionality, which is central to desert-based sentencing. In other words, the severity of the sentence is determined primarily by the seriousness of the crime. However, if the court believes that serving the sentence in the community would not endanger public safety, the six-month term may be converted into a conditional sentence order. Thus some of the offenders for whom imprisonment is inevitable will now receive a noncustodial option. The logic is that desert considerations have determined that imprisonment is a necessity, while an evaluation of the offender's dangerousness may then remove the necessity for incarceration.

After having been guided by considerations relating to the seriousness of the crime, the judge has shifted to evaluating the issue of risk to the community. This evaluation will reflect different criteria, such as the offender's age or criminal history, to determine if the eighteen-month term should be made into a conditional sentence. The two-step process, then, with each stage using different criteria, can generate different results. A proportionate sentence may involve custody, while the absence of evidence that the offender is a risk may argue for a conditional sentence.

Given these arrangements, the conditional sentence will inevitably undermine the principle of proportionality in sentencing.[8] This will be effected in two ways. First, two equally culpable offenders, convicted of the same crime and sentenced to comparable periods of custody, may receive very different treatment if one of them is made the subject of a conditional sentence order. The principle may also be violated in another manner. Consider two offenders convicted of assaults that differ markedly in their seriousness. Offender A has committed the more serious assault and is accordingly sentenced to six months in prison. Offender B receives a six-month term of probation for a less serious assault. However, what if the court in case A makes the term of imprisonment conditional? Many people, including and especially offender B, are going to regard the two dispositions as being comparable in severity. This, too, is a violation of the principles of proportionality and equity, since offenders convicted of dissimilar crimes are receiving penalties of comparable severity.

The principle of proportionality could be violated across offences. Most crimes of violence are perceived to be more serious than property crimes (although the two categories can overlap). Accordingly, crimes of violence are generally punished more severely. This is consistent with the principle of proportionality. If risk assessment is allowed to determine whether a term of imprisonment will be made conditional, proportionality will be affected. The reason for this is that violent offenders tend to have shorter criminal histories and are less likely to reoffend than property offenders (Campbell 1993). This may encourage judges to use conditional sentences more often for offenders convicted of crimes of violence.

Conflict with Secondary Principles of Sentencing

After the fundamental principle of sentencing, section 718.2 specifies several other, secondary principles to be taken into account. For example, subsection 718.2(a)(iii) states that 'evidence that the offender, in committing the offence, abused a position of trust or authority in relation to the victim shall be deemed to be aggravating circumstances.' What effect is such a principle to have on the decision as to whether a term of custody should be made conditional? The *Scidmore*[9] decision by the Ontario Court of Appeal illustrates the difficulties that arise.

In *Scidmore*, the appellant was a teacher convicted of sexual misconduct involving an eleven-year-old pupil. There was a clear breach of trust over a two-year period. The majority of the court of appeal concluded that the imposition of a conditional sentence would not endanger the community and was therefore appropriate. The minority view was that the statutory aggravating factor (breach of trust) should be considered *before* a term of imprisonment is made conditional. Thus the statement of principle argues for a harsher than average penalty, while the invocation of the conditional sentence provision resulted in a less serious disposition. Should the conditional sentence be allowed to 'trump' the statutory statement of the principles of sentencing in this way?

Conflict with the Objectives of Sentencing

Another potential conflict arises with respect to the purposes of sentencing identified by section 718, of which denunciation is a good example. Denunciation is the first sentencing objective identified by section 718. Advocates of conditional sentencing argue that the sentencing purpose of denunciation is served by the imposition of the sentence of custody. This objective having been accomplished, another goal – namely, reducing the use of incarceration – can be achieved by making the term of custody conditional. Is this naive? How much denunciation can be conveyed by what is essentially an enhanced probation order, backed up the threat of incarceration?

Consider applying the logic of a conditional sentence to another disposition. (In fact, the first proposal for a conditional sentence, contained in Bill C-19, which died on the order paper in 1984, envisaged a provision which would apply to any disposition, not just a term of imprisonment.[10] This is consistent with the nature of conditional sentences in other countries.)[11] Imagine that a court imposes a fine of ten thousand dollars, the amount reflecting the purpose and principles of sentencing as well as the offender's ability to pay. The offender duly pays the fine. Now the court converts this fine to a 'conditional' fine. This means that certain conditions will be imposed on the offender for a period of six months. If, at the end of the six months the offender has abided by these conditions, that offender will receive his or her money back. Denunciation is served, we are told, by the imposition of a significant fine. But how much denunciation would be achieved with such a system?[12]

Resolving Conflicts between Sections 718–718.2 and 742: The 1997 Amendment

Conflicts arise between sections 718–718.2 and section 742 if the decision as to whether the sentence should be made conditional is not guided by the other purposes and principles of sentencing. More recent Ontario Court of Appeal decisions in *Pierce*[13] and *Wismayer*,[14] as well as the 1997 legislative amendment to section 742, take a different approach and close somewhat the door that was opened wide by *Scidmore*. In *Pierce*, the court rejected a rigid two-step process and suggested that the principles of sentencing should determine not just the length of the term of imprisonment but also whether it should be conditional in nature. The judgment in that appeal notes that 'the new guidelines for sentencing, while largely a codification of existing principles, are nowhere in the Code stated to be restricted to being used in what the appellant submits is the first stage.'[15] In *Wismayer*, the court also rejected a strict separation between the decision to incarcerate and the decision regarding whether the term could be made conditional, noting that: 'The principles and objectives of sentencing as they have been developed by the courts and as expressed in the *Criminal Code* are not wholly exhausted once the decision has been made to impose a term of imprisonment of less than two years. *These principles and objectives must also be brought to bear on the decision whether or not to impose a conditional sentence* (emphasis added).[16] However, the judgment continues to suggest that 'the primary consideration in determining whether the conditional sentence should be imposed must be the expressed statutory factor of danger to the community.'[17] The reasoning behind this is that 'it stands to reason that the fact that Parliament has specifically referred to only one factor, that serving the sentence in the community would not endanger the safety of the community, must mean that this factor is entitled to more weight than certain other factors of more general application.'[18]

In *Macdonald*,[19] the majority decision of the Saskatchewan Court of Appeal took a similar direction. A conditional sentence had been imposed in a case of criminal negligence causing death. The court concluded that a conditional sentence order violated the principle of parity in sentencing and was not proportionate to the gravity of the offence. In short, the decision to make the sentence of imprisonment had to be consistent with the principles of sentencing, even if the presence of the offender in the community would not endanger the community.

Prior to the legislative amendment, assuming the first two statutory prerequisites had been met (no minimum punishment; sentence of imprisonment of less than two years) the court needed to be satisfied of only a third requirement, namely that the presence of the offender in the community would not endanger the safety of the community. Now a fourth condition is present. The court must also be satisfied that serving the sentence in the community 'would be consistent with the fundamental purpose and principles of sentencing set out in sections 718 to 718.2.'[20]

This additional requirement will inevitably mean that fewer conditional sentence orders will be handed down than if the *Scidmore* reasoning had been followed. Before a court may impose a conditional sentence, it now has to be satisfied that the offender's presence in the community poses little risk to that community, and also that the conditional sentence order is not inconsistent with sentencing purposes, such as denunciation, or sentencing principles, such as proportionality or the statutory aggravating factors. Although fewer conditional sentences are now being imposed, they are less likely to generate conflicts with the purpose and principles of sentencing contained in sections 718–718.2.

Finally, the language used in section 742.1 suggests that the more circumscribed reasoning found in *Pierce*, *Wismayer*, and the revised wording of subsection 742.1(b) is closer to Parliament's intention. The original wording of subsection 742.1(b) stated that if 'the court is satisfied that serving the sentence in the community would not endanger the safety of the community, the court *may* ... order that the offender serve the sentence in the community' (emphasis added). If risk is the only consideration, and if the court is satisfied that community safety is not endangered, what other considerations can there be, apart from sentencing purposes such as those found in section 718?

If Parliament had wished the court to impose a conditional sentence in every case in which the three conditions obtained (no minimum punishment; sentence of less than two years; no threat to community safety), surely the language of the provision would have been 'the court shall order that the offender serve the sentence in the community.' The use of the more permissive 'may' suggests that Parliament envisaged cases in which these conditions would be met, but which still should not result in a conditional sentence. The seriousness of the offence would appear to be the most likely candidate for consideration which would exclude the imposition of a conditional sentence even when the three conditions stipulated in section 742.1 had been met.

In light of these decisions and the legislative amendment, the courts would be well advised to adopt a more integrated approach to the decision as to whether a term of imprisonment can be made conditional.

Public Reaction to Conditional Sentencing

A Nonsentence?

Polls have for many years shown that most Canadians are dissatisfied with sentencing patterns.[21] There is a danger that the conditional sentence of imprisonment will make matters worse, as it may be seen as yet another manifestation of leniency in sentencing. There will be a perception that a conditional sentence is a nonsentence. This has been the experience with the suspended sentence of imprisonment in the United Kingdom. The British public perceived the suspended term of imprisonment as letting the offender go unpunished. The Canadian public will have difficulty accepting what is a paradox for all but criminal justice professionals: a sentence of imprisonment which the offender spends at liberty. Consider the following analogy. Imagine being told that you have won a February vacation in the Caribbean. The only problem is that you will spend the week in frigid Ottawa. If you are not in the South, it is not a Caribbean holiday. Members of the public are likely to reason that if the offender is not in custody, then the sentence cannot reasonably be described as a term of imprisonment.

It may be naive to expect that the public will willingly embrace the paradox of a sentence of imprisonment in which the offender may never enter custody.

Counsel for the appellant in *Pierce* was of the view that the public would appreciate that the offender serving a conditional sentence is 'still serving a substantial sentence but just not in a conventional custodial setting'[22] But a sentence in the community is likely to be seen as more lenient than an 'unconventional custodial setting.' The only way in which the public is likely to accept a conditional sentence as a legitimate variation on, rather than a lenient replacement for, imprisonment is if the conditions imposed are sufficiently onerous as to be distinguishable from a probation order, and the sentence therefore constitutes a genuine penalty.

Public anger will focus on the judiciary under one of two conditions. First, the public will react strongly if a conditional sentence order is revoked when the offender is charged with a fresh offence. And with the judiciary imposing many conditional sentence orders, this will one day occur. The resulting headlines will be reminiscent of the treatment accorded parole boards when a parolee commits a crime prior to the end of his or her period of supervision. The other circumstance likely to generate public opposition is when an offender convicted of a serious personal injury offence receives a conditional sentence order because the court believes that he or she is not a threat to the community. The first issue relates to risk; the second to proportionality. This problem is likely to be particularly acute for the more serious cases involving violence.

Truth in Sentencing

The public may also regard a conditional sentence as undermining the concept of truth in sentencing. This notion lies at the heart of lay conceptions of sentencing (see Roberts and Gebotys (1989)). The public favour a sentencing process in which the sentence of imprisonment bears a close (or at least closer) resemblance to the sentence that was imposed in court. For this reason, public hostility is frequently directed at the parole authorities for undermining the sentence of the court.[23] Some of this resentment will now be directed at judges, for a conditional sentence will be viewed by the public as a form of 'judicial parole.'

The importance of public reaction should not be overstated. Misperceptions of the sentencing process abound, and there is research evidence that members of the public are less critical of sentencing decisions when they have more information than is usually contained in a newspaper account of a sentence (see Doob and Roberts (1988)). However, it is worth noting that according to section 718, the fundamental purpose of sentencing is 'to contribute, along with crime prevention initiatives, to *respect for the law* and maintenance of a just, peaceful and safe society' (emphasis added). The importance of this goal has also been acknowledged by some recent appellate decisions.[24] Conditional sentences clearly have the power to undermine public respect for the law in general and, in particular, for the institution of the judiciary.

What can be done to assuage public apprehension about conditional sentencing? A public legal education initiative is clearly needed. Such a campaign should attempt to convey a sense of the potential onerousness of a conditional sentence order in comparison to a probation order. As well, the low rate of default to date will reassure many people who are concerned about recidivism rates. Finally, judges will have to make an extra effort to explain the reasons[25] why a term of imprisonment is being made into a conditional sentence. This is particularly true when a conditional sentence is imposed for the more serious personal injury offences. Even then there is no guarantee that the news media will convey this judicial reasoning to the public. If news reports continue to stress the leniency of conditional sentences, it will be hard indeed for the new disposition to achieve the goal of reducing the use of incarceration.[26] The task of educating the public on this issue is not impossible, but it will not be easy.

Addressing the Problems with the Conditional Sentence

The twin issues of a loss of public confidence and a weakening of the principle of proportionality can be addressed simultaneously. There are several possible solutions.

Lower the Ceiling of Custodial Terms Which May Be Made Conditional

First, the ambit of sentences that may be converted to a conditional sentence could be reduced. The high ceiling of two years less a day – which encompasses such a large percentage of custodial terms – could be lowered. The most apparent violations of proportionality, and the cases likely to provoke the greatest degree of public disapprobation are to be found at the 'deep end' of crime seriousness. A sentence of eighteen months that becomes conditional is likely to prove far more controversial than a sentence of two months. Reducing the ceiling to one year would avoid the most egregious conflicts with the principle of proportionality or the sentencing purposes.[27] If conditional terms of imprisonment were restricted to offenders sentenced to prison for relatively brief periods of time – say up to ninety days – the provision would be far less controversial. The general public as well specific victims are likely to be more accepting of a conditional sentence that replaces a relatively brief period of custody.

It may be argued that reducing the 'ceiling' in this way would defeat the whole purpose of the conditional sentence of imprisonment, namely, reducing the number of admissions to custody. This argument overlooks the fact that the vast majority of provincial admissions to custody are for very brief periods. The median term of imprisonment at the provincial level is one month. Over one-third of all admissions are for periods of less than one month (Reed and Roberts 1998). There is accordingly great scope for reducing the number of admissions, even if the ceiling of the conditional sentence were reduced from two years less a day to something like six months.

Restrict the Use of Conditional Sentences to Certain Offenders

A second possibility would be to restrict the use of conditional sentences to certain categories of offenders, perhaps non-violent offenders or first offenders. Public opposition is likely to be far more muted if the only offenders whose terms of imprisonment becomes conditional are those convicted of crimes involving property, or first offenders. Advocates of the current conditional sentence provisions might argue that these changes would defeat the whole purpose of conditional sentencing (to reduce the use of incarceration). However, it should be recalled that significant percentages of property offenders are currently imprisoned, and they could benefit from the conditional sentence. Crimes of violence account for only a small proportion (17 per cent) of the provincial court caseload (see Birkenmayer and Roberts (1997)). Eliminating these offenders from consideration for a conditional sentence order would still leave much room for reducing the use of incarceration.

Alternatively, restricting the use of conditional sentence orders to first offenders would be consistent with the spirit underlying the use of a suspended sentence, namely, that of a judicial warning. This restriction is used in other countries, such as Italy.[28] It is also the route taken in several American states. In the State of Washington, for example, non-violent offenders without prior felony convictions who are being sentenced for an offence other than a sex offence or certain drug crimes receive what is termed a 'first-time offender waiver' (FTOW).[29] This is effectively a stayed sentence, which involves up to two years of community supervision and several conditions, such as a requirement to receive treatment. It is, in other words, a conditional sentence. The Washington criteria may seem too narrow, but the underlying principle may have some merit.

Increase the 'Penal Bite' of a Conditional Sentence Order

A third possibility may at first seem anathema to advocates of conditional sentencing. It consists of following the English model and permitting the court to activate the sentence in full, not just the remaining portion prior to warrant expiry. In fact, in 70 per cent of breaches of suspended terms of imprisonment in England and Wales the full prison term is implemented.[30] Jack Gemmell describes this as 'substantially more mischievous than the conditional sentence regime' (Gemmell 1997). But is it? An offender sentenced to one year in prison, made conditional, is relieved of the pains of imprisonment unless and until he or she violates the conditions of the conditional sentence order. If those conditions are not particularly onerous – and according to subsections 742.3(1) and (2) they need not be – the offender can avoid incarceration.

There is one other justification for following the route taken in England and Wales and activating the entire custodial term. Central to the notion of a conditional sentence is the threat implied by the sentence. Offenders are effectively told that in the event of breach, the consequences are more onerous than with a suspended sentence. Martin Wasik notes: 'Deterrence theory assumes that the conditional sentence will be the more effective where the sanction to be visited upon breach is known by the offender to be severe and where the chances of the court imposing these consequences are perceived by him to be high' (Wasik 1994).

This raises the notion of deterrence: the offender is deterred from breaching the conditions of the conditional sentence order by fear of imprisonment. Specific deterrence is clearly a principal goal of the conditional sentence. This is apparent from the language of paragraph 742.3(2)(f), which states that the offender 'must comply with such other reasonable conditions as the court considers desirable ... for securing the good conduct of the offender and for *preventing a repetition by the offender of the same offence or the commission of other offences*' (emphasis added). As noted earlier, under the present conditional sentence provisions, the offender does not know how long he or she will be incarcerated in the event of a breach, or even if he or she will be imprisoned at all. Making the consequences of breach more certain and severe will enhance the deterrent effect of the conditional sentence.

Develop Penal Equivalences

Perhaps the most fruitful approach to reforming the conditional sentence involves developing penal equivalences. The idea would be to create a conditional sentence order that is as punitive as the term of imprisonment that it replaces. As noted earlier, under the current legislation, the conditions associated with a conditional sentence order need not be more onerous than those associated with a standard probation order. The only difference may be the threat of imprisonment in the event of a default, but it is only a threat, and not a particularly certain one at that.

Little attention has been paid by scholars to the question of penal equivalences.[31] The advantages of having such equivalences are clear. They would permit the court to devise a conditional sentence order that would have the penal equivalent of a period of imprisonment, with the exception that the offender would remain in the community. The offender would avoid incarceration, but not punishment. This would permit the sentencing process to reduce the use of incarceration without disturbing the proportionality principle, which requires that the severity of sanctions be commensurate with the seriousness of the crimes for which they are imposed. Equivalence of impact is difficult but not impossible to achieve.[32] In fact, this route has been adopted in England and Wales, where the imposition of a suspended term of imprisonment is accompanied by a number of immediate noncustodial penalties, which would not have been imposed had the term of imprisonment been immediate. As Martin Wasik notes, this strategy has been endorsed by the 1991 Criminal Justice Act (Wasik 1994). Parity could be maintained in the following way.

Consider two co-accused being sentenced for serious robbery. Let us assume that on grounds of the seriousness of the offence, both individuals merit a term of imprisonment. Differential risk factors associated with the two offenders may suggest that one can serve his sentence in the community under a conditional sentence order without endangering the safety of the community. However, in order to preserve parity, the conditional sentence should carry the same penal bite as the period of imprisonment. This would include the addition of other sanctions, and/or the extension of the period of community supervision beyond the duration of the term of imprisonment of the incarcerated offender. Another means by which a conditional sentence order could be made more onerous would be to combine it with a probation order. As the Honourable Judge Cole notes,[33] paragraph 731(1)(b) permits the court to impose a term of probation to follow the expiry of the conditional sentence order. Thus a six-month term of imprisonment might be made conditional and followed by a six-month term of probation.

Split Sentences

Finally, another possibility that is unlikely to prove popular with advocates of the current conditional sentence provisions involves the creation of split or bifurcated sentences. Under the terms of a split sentence, a term of custody would be divided between a period of immediate imprisonment to be followed by a period served in the community. The custodial term would give the offender a clear idea of the consequences of breaching the subsequent conditional sentence order and prevent the total sentence from seeming like a variation on a term of probation. At the same time, the fact that the offender might serve as much as three-quarters of the sentence in the community would mean that the principle of restraint in the use of imprisonment was followed. Split sentences of this kind are also used in a number of other jurisdictions. Assuming that no net-widening took place, split sentences would also have a significant effect on the custodial population. Of course, the split sentence will make the notions of conditional sentencing and parole even harder to disentangle.

Alternatively, it has been suggested that a conditional sentence order could have two components. First, there would be a fixed period in which the offender would be required to serve under nightly house arrest, with release allowed for the purposes of work or to perform community service. This would comprise the denunciatory period of the sanction. Second, this period would be followed by a period in which the conditions would be less onerous, conforming, perhaps, closely to the current conditions of a conditional sentence order.[34] The advantage, it is argued, is that a denunciatory period is maintained.

Conclusions

Canada's high rate of incarceration has been noted by several commissions of inquiry (e.g., Canadian Sentencing Commission (1987)) and acknowledged by the federal Department of Justice. The recent sentencing statistics alluded to earlier in this chapter show that many minor property crimes result in terms of custody.[35] Reducing the number of custodial terms imposed is an explicit policy goal of the sentencing reform initiative that gave rise to Bill C-41. Accordingly, the question is no longer whether we should imprison fewer offenders, but how. What is needed, however, is a principled approach to decarceration. If imposing fewer terms of custody were the only goal, we could simply flip a coin each time an offender was sentenced to prison, with the outcome of the toss determining whether that offender received a conditional rather than a custodial sentence. This too would generate a reduction in the use of custody, but in an unprincipled way.

The goal of the conditional sentence is to reduce the use of incarceration in a way that preserves the integrity of the sentencing process. This means imposing conditional sentences without violating the purpose and principles of sentencing mandated by Parliament and now contained in sections 718 to 718.2 of the Criminal Code. The most important, indeed the fundamental sentencing principle identified by section 718.1 is proportionality, and conditional sentences need to be utilised without doing harm to this principle.

Conditional sentencing needs to be seen as part of a wider attempt to constrain the use of imprisonment as a sanction. The broader initiative should include the increased use of sentencing alternatives, diversion programs, and the decriminalisation of certain offences. These require a rational implementation policy and coordination by a permanent sentencing commission. In this respect, it is important to add that the ability of the courts to reduce the use of incarceration is limited to the resources provided by governments, particularly provincial governments. If the resources saved by a reduction in the use of incarceration are not used to enhance and expand the alternatives to incarceration and to ensure that conditional sentence supervision is effective, then little real progress will be made.

The new conditional sentence may prove to be of considerable use to judges in terms of reducing the use of incarceration. However, in order for this to be accomplished in a principled way and in a manner that does not arouse public antagonism, additional guidance from courts of appeal across the country, and from the Supreme Court itself, will be required.

ENDNOTES

1 This chapter draws on material previously published in the *Canadian Criminal Law Review* (Roberts 1997d).
2 *R. v. Wismayer* (1997), 115 C.C.C. (3d) 18 (Ont. C.A.).
3 *R. v. K.R.G.* [1996] O.J. No. 3867 at para. 30.
4 *R. v. Brady* (unreported), Alta. C.A., February 1998.
5 See Renaud (1996).
6 Once again, the judgment in *R. v. Brady* is telling: 'This metaphor exaggerates the severity of a conditional sentence.'
7 Data supplied by the Department of Justice Canada to the author, 22 February 1998.
8 The same undermining of proportionality is achieved by the influence of parole on terms of imprisonment. The problem is exacerbated by conditional sentences, however, since the entire sentence can be served in the community, not just a fraction of it, as with parole.
9 *R. v. Scidmore* (1997), 112 C.C.C. (3d) 28.
10 S. 661, Bill C-19, first reading 7 February 1984.
11 See *Alternatives to Imprisonment and Measures for the Resettlement of Prisoners.* Seventh United Nations Congress on the Prevention of Crime and the Treatment of Offenders. Milan, 1985.
12 If a conditional sentence carries a degree of denunciation under these conditions, how does it differ from a bail decision, in which certain restrictions are imposed on the accused, who also pays a surety, which is later returned to him?
13 *R. v. Pierce* (1997), 114 C.C.C. (3d) (Ont. C.A.).

14 *R. v. Wismayer, supra*, note 2.
15 *R. v. Pierce, supra*, note 13.
16 *R. v. Wismayer, supra*, note 2.
17 Ibid.
18 Unreported decision of the Ontario Court of Appeal, February 1997 at 18.
19 Unreported judgment of the Saskatchewan Court of Appeal, 5 March 1997.
20 S. 742.1(b).
21 For example, a nationwide poll conducted in 1994 found that 82 per cent of Canadians feel that sentences are too lenient. This is consistent with the results of surveys posing the same question over a decade earlier (see Roberts (1994a); Doob and Roberts (1983)).
22 Cited in *R. v. Pierce, supra*, note 13.
23 For example, a recent headline in the *Toronto Star* stated 'Swindler gets 6 months, but in jail for just 12 days.'
24 In *R. v. Brady, supra*, note 4, the Alberta Court of Appeal noted that '[t]he law must educate as well as condemn.'
25 According to s. 726.2, when imposing sentence, the court must provide reasons. This requirement was also part of Bill C-41. It is not clear at this early stage whether it has changed judicial practices regarding the provision of reasons for sentence.
26 See discussion of this point in Jull (1997).
27 Another way of restraining the use of conditional sentences would be to employ the maximum penalty structure. Conditional sentences could be restricted to offences whose maxima do not exceed some threshold, say five years. The problem with this approach is that the current maximum penalty structure is the result of ad hoc historical amendments and lacks a rational, proportional structure. This is why the Canadian Sentencing Commission called for a thorough revision of the current statutory maxima (Canadian Sentencing Commission 1987).
28 See *Alternatives to Imprisonment and Measures for the Social Resettlement of Prisoners, supra*, note 11.
29 See Sentencing Guidelines Commission, State of Washington, 1992, *Implementation Manual*, Olympia, Washington, I-17.
30 See Wasik (1994).
31 See, for example, Morris and Tonry (1990) and Tonry (1996). In one analysis it has been suggested that sanctions be ordered in terms of the extent to which they intrude on a person's living standard (von Hirsch, Wasik, and Greene (1989).
32 For Canadian research on this subject, see Tremblay (1989).
33 See D. Cole, memorandum dated 10 September 1996.
34 This suggestion was made by Judge David Cole of the Ontario Provincial Court.

35 For example, fully 7,353 offenders were incarcerated for theft under $1,000 (the monetary limit at the time these data were collected); for further information see Roberts and Birkenmayer (1998).

ADDITIONAL READING

Manson, A. 1997. The Appeal of Conditional Sentences of Imprisonment. 10 *Criminal Reports* (5th), 279–90.

– 1998. A Brief Reply to Professors Roberts and von Hirsch. 10 *Criminal Reports* (5th), 232–5.

Roberts, J.V. and A. von Hirsch. 1998. Conditional Sentences of Imprisonment and the Fundamental Principle of Proportionality in Sentencing. 10 *Criminal Reports* (5th), 222–31.

6

Conditional Sentencing: Recent Developments

DAVID P. COLE

Since the conditional sentencing regime was introduced in September 1996, a considerable volume of jurisprudence has evolved. In this chapter David Cole explores some of the important appellate decisions that have been decided over the first year of the new conditional sentence. As will be seen, the appellate courts have adopted rather different interpretations of the conditional sentence provisions.

This metaphor [Sword of Damocles] exaggerates the severity of a conditional sentence. Even if a conditional sentence could be equated to a sword, it does not hang by a thread, but by a rope. And the only way that this rope can break is if the offender himself cuts it. And with each passing day of the sentence, the 'sword' shrinks until it finally becomes a butter knife.[1]

During its short life span, the concept of conditional sentencing has been both vilified as being 'soft on criminals' and praised as one of the most enlightened sentencing revisions ever enacted. Whatever the truth may be, the changes seem to have been misunderstood by the general public and probably still are.[2]

Introduction

In the first twelve months since the proclamation of the legislation, over 13,000 conditional sentences were imposed. As this book goes to press (February 1998) the editors considered that it would be appropriate to summarize some of the significant case law that has been decided to date. The reader is cautioned that it is difficult to make any definitive statements about trends in conditional sentencing on the basis of such limited case law interpretation. Further, the Supreme Court of Canada has not yet considered conditional sentences,[3] and trial courts lack the benefit of that Court's guidance on these issues.

Balancing the Statutory Factors

It will be recalled from the description of the various criteria that must be considered by a judge in deciding whether to impose a conditional sentence (Chapter 4) that the third of these is whether the court 'is satisfied that serving the sentence in the community would not endanger the safety of the community.' Because this statement of parliamentary intent introduces a considerable measure of discretion into the sentencing process, this section was one of the first to undergo appellate scrutiny. What happened in Ontario is reasonably representative of the way in which appellate courts wrestled with this issue during 1997. In *Scidmore*[4] the trial judge had sentenced the accused, a teacher, to a reformatory-length custodial term for a series of 'historical' sexual assaults committed against one of his female students, aged eleven to thirteen at the time when the offences were committed. The accused appealed against that sentence. A majority of the panel of the court of appeal that heard the case considered that once the first two statutory prohibitions – a minimum term of incarceration and a sentence of two years or more – had been found not to apply or to be appropriate, 'it is the intent of the legislature that the term be served in the community unless that would put the community at risk.' Because the accused's antecedents, both prior and subsequent to the offences, raised no obvious concern that he would reoffend, the justices in the majority were prepared to substitute a conditional sentence for the custodial term that had been imposed by the trial judge. In dissent, Abella J.A. wrote 'that to permit the age of the offences and the community reputation of the appellant to trump an otherwise appropriate jail sentence would render s.718.2(a)(iii) [the subsection which expressly provides that a breach of a position of trust or authority in relation to a victim in the commission of an offence is an aggravating factor] almost meaningless ... In this case no exceptional circumstances exist to justify the suspension of the sentence imposed.'

A few weeks later a somewhat differently constituted panel of judges, examining a case of large-scale fraud, came to a different conclusion as to the manner in which the 'safety of the community' criterion should be approached. Writing for the court in *Pierce*[5] Finlayson J.A. expressly rejected the majority view in *Scidmore* that as part of the process involved in deciding whether to impose a conditional sentence a court is bound only to satisfy itself that serving the sentence in the community would not endanger community safety. He rejected the idea that the various sentencing 'guidelines' enunciated in section 718 are deemed to be exhausted once the length of the sentence has been determined and the court is considering whether to impose a conditional sentence. Finlayson wrote: 'It is difficult to accept that the elaborate sentencing guidelines which Parliament chose to introduce at the same time as s. 742.1 were only intended to be used within the framework of that section to determine the length of the sentence. Surely these sentencing guidelines also address whether a conditional sentence should be imposed.'

This view of the way in which section 742.1 is to be applied was soon further approved by another bench of the court in *Wismayer*.[6] Speaking for the court, Rosenberg J.A. wrote: 'The fact that the conditional sentence is available in a particular case because the conditions prescribed by s.742.1 are met does not absolutely entitle the offender to a conditional sentence. As with all other available dispositions, it is for the trial judge to determine whether such a disposition is appropriate in the particular circumstances of the case.'

Any remaining doubt that the views expressed by the panels in *Pierce* and *Wismayer* are to be preferred to those of the majority in *Scidmore* with respect to the proper approach to the application of section 742.1 was removed by the enactment (in April 1997) of an amendment to section 742.1 of the Code, by which the words 'and would be consistent with the fundamental purpose and principles of sentencing set out in sections 718 to 718.2' were added to paragraph 1(b).[7]

Although the reasoning in *Scidmore* has thus been overturned by Parliament, the question of whether to impose conditional sentences on non-violent offenders who apparently pose no risk to the community has been a notable feature of judicial consideration of the new sentencing legislation.

'Historical' Sexual Assault

The differing majority and minority judgments of the Newfoundland Court of Appeal in *W. (L.F.)*[8] present a representative summary of how the courts have dealt with this difficult issue to date. The facts were that the offences had occurred some twenty-five to thirty years previously, when the accused was between twenty-three and twenty-nine years of age. The victim, the accused's cousin, was between nine and fifteen years of age at the time. The victim lived next door to the accused in an isolated rural community. The accused would take her to a locked shed to commit the ten to twelve instances of sexual abuse that included masturbation and fellatio. In addition to warning the victim that she should not tell anyone, she was also led to believe that the accused had brought a gun home from his time spent in the military.

Not surprisingly, the abuse had had an enduring, traumatic effect upon the victim 'that had materially impaired her happiness and contentment.' Her childhood and adolescent years 'were marred by feelings of shame, isolation and low self-esteem ... These feelings ... continued into her adult years, posing particular problems in her marriage ... [T]he normal and happy lifestyle which Mr. W. has enjoyed for the most part ... has eluded the victim and may continue to do so over the residue of her life.'

In favour of the accused the court noted that the offences were the only blemish on an otherwise 'exemplary life.' While not admitting his guilt to the court, the accused had disclosed to his brother that the offences had occurred at a time in his life when he was abusing alcohol, a problem that he had subsequently addressed by abstaining from alcohol for over twenty years. He had thus 'transformed his life entirely'; he was reported to be a devoted family man and a positive contributor to society. Crown counsel agreed that the accused 'was fully rehabilitated and posed no danger to the community's safety through reoffending.'

The trial judge and the majority judges in the court of appeal rejected an argument advanced by the Crown that 'the sheer gravity of offences involving sexual abuse of children' mandated a carceral response. While it was true that the court's previous sentencing jurisprudence had held that, absent exceptional circumstances, application of the principles of general and special deterrence and denunciation 'resulted in jail terms for perpetrators of child sexual abuse,' Parliament had now changed the rules by authorizing the imposition of conditional sentences. These judges noted that Parliament had not excluded offences of this nature from consideration for a conditional sentence (except to the extent that an accused would not be eligible if a penitentiary sentence were to be imposed and/or the accused represented a threat to community safety). The majority judges of the court of appeal dismissed the Crown's arguments that nothing had changed with the proclamation of the new sentencing legislation as follows:

> In the first place, that argument assumes deterrence and denunciation cannot be achieved through a conditional sentence and reflects the traditional mind set that these objectives can be achieved only through incarceration in a jail. This is not tenable. As the trial judge aptly observed, the denunciatory and general deterrent effect of a conditional sentence ought not be underestimated. Not only may the offender's freedom be severely limited, but his or her continuing presence in the community, detained at home and

bearing the stigma of conviction, is calculated to serve as a daily deterrent to any like minded person and have real denunciatory consequences. These effects may perhaps be considered all the more pronounced in a rural setting such as Bay de Verde. The second weakness, which was pointed out by Mr. W.'s counsel, is that the Crown's argument pre-supposes nothing has really changed in the sentencing process. It is true, as the foregoing discussions acknowledge, that the overall purpose and principles set out in the legislation generally represent a codification of the common law. However, it is a mistake to depict the new provisions as making no changes. In particular, Part XXIII now contains the new option of conditional sentencing that was not before part of the process. While this court's stance that deterrence and denunciation are prime considerations in child sexual abuse cases is still operative, the option of serving sentence in the community under strict conditions is now available in certain circumstances to give effect to these ends. Finally, the Crown's position is flawed insofar as it attempts to set up certain categories of offences whose gravity is such that they will never, or rarely, be punishable by a conditional sentence notwithstanding the length of imprisonment imposed. As the trial judge underscored however, this is a restriction which Parliament did not elect to impose. The legislation does address the gravity of the offence through its confining eligibility for service in the community to sentences not serious enough to warrant a term of more than two years. It also brings a consideration of the gravity of the crime to bear in the conditional sentencing process through the amendment's explicitly engaging the principles of sentencing. However, it does not go beyond that point by restricting or qualifying the eligibility of certain classifications of offenders for conditional sentencing and this court must resist the Crown's urging to do so.[9]

The Crown also argued on appeal that, despite the accused's complete rehabilitation, he 'must nonetheless be sent to jail out of some sense of retribution.' As discussed elsewhere in this volume, the Supreme Court of Canada has recently discussed the proper definition of this term in considering whether sentences totalling twenty-five years were appropriate for a father who physically and sexually abused his children over many years. The court wrote that in its modern form, retribution must not be confused with vengeance (a sentencing philosophy which the court considered to be inherently unconstitutional): 'Retribution in a criminal context [as contrasted with vengeance], represents an objective, reasoned and measured determination of an appropriate punishment which properly reflects the *moral culpability* of the offender, having regard to the intentional risk-taking of the offender, the consequential harm caused by the offender, and the normative character of the offender's conduct. Furthermore, unlike vengeance, retribution incorporates a principle of restraint; retribution requires the imposition of a just and appropriate punishment, and *nothing more*.'[10]

Understood in this way, the Supreme Court concluded that retribution 'is an accepted, and indeed important, principle of sentencing in our criminal law.'[11] As such, in looking 'to provide a coherent justification for criminal punishment,' retribution must 'must be considered in conjunction with the other legitimate objectives of sentencing, which include (but are not limited to) deterrence, denunciation, rehabilitation and the protection of society.' Because the Crown wished to downplay the accused's rehabilitation entirely, the majority judges of the Newfoundland Court of Appeal held that these arguments were 'flawed as a result of their overstressing the objectives of deterrence and denunciation.'

A very different view was taken by Cameron J.A., the dissenting judge, who asked: '... if the factors under s.718 to 718.2 led the judge to conclude that imprisonment, as opposed to suspended sentence and probation, was the appropriate disposition, how can those same factors now lead to a different conclusion ...?'[12]

Although conditional sentences might be appropriate for some kinds of sexual assaults, she wrote: '... I do start from the premise that sexual assault of a child is a crime that is abhorrent to Canadian society and society's condemnation of those who commit such offences must be communicated in the clearest of terms. As to moral blameworthiness, the use of a vulnerable child for the sexual gratification of an adult cannot be viewed as anything but a crime demonstrating the worst of intentions.'[13] While agreeing with the trial judge and the majority judges that the enactment of the new legislation had changed the approach to sentencing which should be employed, Cameron J.A. considered that the trial judge had erred, in that 'he did not give sufficient weight to ... the principles of denunciation and general deterrence ... or to the moral blameworthiness of the offender.'

The Ontario Court of Appeal has now had several opportunities to pronounce sentences in cases involving forms of violence against vulnerable persons. One of the first of these was *Wismayer*, where the court expressly dismissed 'the misapprehension that societal denunciation can only be expressed by requiring the offender to serve a sentence of imprisonment in custody.' In that case the court declined to impose a custodial sentence for historic sexual assault short of intercourse, even though the offence had been committed against a vulnerable victim (seven to eight years old) in circumstances which 'to some extent involved a breach of trust,' thereby demonstrating that the offender had demonstrated a high measure of 'moral blameworthiness.' The panel of appellate judges hearing the case was obviously impressed by the proposal that the offender would be subject to a form of closely monitored house arrest by his parents, as well as concerned that the gains reported by the appellant's psychiatrist would likely be lost if the particularly psychologically frail appellant were now to be incarcerated after four years on bail.

In several subsequent cases, however, the court has adopted a different view. For example, in *L.S.*,[14] despite the fresh evidence admitted on appeal indicating that the seventy-one-year-old accused's medical advisor 'is of the view that incarceration would exacerbate [some of his health problems] and make him much more symptomatic,' the court was only prepared to reduce the custodial term, and declined to convert it into a conditional sentence. Although it seems clear that the court's thinking has not yet entirely crystallized, these cases may be read as saying that the emphasis on denunciation – generally in the sentencing 'guidelines' specified by Parliament in sections 718–718.2 of the Criminal Code, and most particularly in subsection 718(a) – mandate that a custodial sentence be imposed in cases of historic sexual assault, unless there are highly exceptional circumstances present.[15]

Dangerous Driving Causing Death or Bodily Harm

Prior to the enactment of the conditional sentence provisions, appellate courts across the country, mindful of the carnage caused by overly aggressive driving, routinely approved of or imposed penitentiary or upper reformatory length sentences even for first offenders, particularly when alcohol was found to be a contributing factor. Since the change in the legislation, some courts have modified their views, acknowledging that it makes little sense to incarcerate a person who has made a single mistake, albeit one with dreadful consequences for the offender and his victims.

In *McDonald*,[16] the accused, a thirty-three-year-old physically handicapped aboriginal woman, was the principal financial and care provider of her six children and an elderly parent. She had a previous conviction for impaired driving. The accused was extremely intoxicated (she had two and a half times the legal limit of alcohol in her system) when she drove her truck into a brawling crowd at a high rate of speed, killing one person. Since the offence she had completely rehabilitated herself, ceased to drink, and had become a very productive member of her band and community. Unfortunately, the offence had divided that community. The victim's husband had been forced to leave due to the tension resulting from the offence. This caused the secondary victimization of his children: because the father could not afford to take the children with him, they remained in the community with their grandparents.

After hearing extensive evidence the trial judge imposed a sentence of nine months' electronically monitored house arrest, followed by probation. The Crown appealed the sentence, arguing that a custodial sentence must be imposed. By the time the case reached the Saskatchewan Court of Appeal (the case took over three years before it was finally decided on appeal) the revisions to Part XXIII of the Criminal Code had been proclaimed in force.

The three judges who heard the appeal expressed radically different views as to whether a conditional sentence was appropriate in a case of dangerous driving causing death. Vancise J.A. issued a lengthy dissent, arguing that the new legislative provisions indicated Parliament's intention that imprisonment should only be used as a last resort. Given the special personal and family circumstances of the accused, the fact that a custodial sentence would result in meaningless punishment, and that such a sentence (necessarily served out of the community) might jeopardize rather than facilitate the accused's rehabilitation, a conditional sentence should now be imposed. In order to address punishment and denunciation for this most serious offence the conditional sentence should contain an order for electronically monitored house arrest for a further twelve months.

Sherstobitoff J.A. disagreed with Vancise J.A.'s proposed result 'or much of the foundation for it.' He pointed out that the trial judge had erred by imposing electronic monitoring; according to the court of appeal's pre-Bill C-41 jurisprudence, sentences short of imprisonment for criminal negligence causing death should not be imposed. Sherstobitoff J.A. was further of the opinion that very little had changed since the advent of the new legislative scheme. In his view, a conditional sentence would not be 'proportionate to the gravity of the offence or the moral blameworthiness of the offender.' It would also violate the principle of parity expressed in subsection 718.2(b) of the legislation, in that it would not be a similar sentence imposed on a similar offender for a similar offence committed in similar circumstances: '[in] disparity lies injustice.' After reviewing the 'purpose,' 'fundamental sentencing principle,' and 'other sentencing principles' expressed in sections 718–718.2, he concluded that 'there is nothing in these provisions to warrant a departure from' the court's previous sentencing jurisprudence.' As to the precise question of whether a conditional sentence would adequately address all of the various aspects of sentencing, he wrote that the 'offence is too serious, and the damage done too great, to permit anything other than a period of imprisonment' to be imposed. Given the accused's personal circumstances and the fact that she had, by the time the appeal was disposed of, served almost all of the term of electronic monitoring, he felt that a sentence of six months' incarceration would now be sufficient.

The other majority judge agreed in result with Sherstobitoff J.A., given the facts of the case and the various aggravating and mitigating factors. However, Lane J.A. was prepared to recognize that the changes introduced by the new legislation were 'a clear intention on the part of Parliament to reduce institutional incarceration and to adopt the principle of restraint.' He also generally agreed with Vancise J.A. 'concerning the use and imposition of a conditional sentence.' Nevertheless, on the particular facts, he could not agree that 'less restrictive sanctions are appropriate.'

Just two months later a different view of this difficult issue was taken by the Nova Scotia Court of Appeal in *Parker*.[17] In this case, the accused, speeding and weaving in a high-performance vehicle in a busy area, ran over four young teenagers sitting on a church lawn waiting for a bus near a designated bus shelter; two were killed instantly, while the survivors suffered serious bodily injury. They and the parents of all four of the victims suffered permanent emotional scarring. The twenty-year-old accused had come through a 'chaotic and dysfunctional' childhood relatively unscathed. He had no previous criminal or driving record. At the time of sentencing he was the primary caregiver for an older brother, who had been rendered a quadriplegic in a diving accident. It was agreed by all that the accused accepted full responsibility for the offences and was appropriately remorseful. Although the accused had consumed some alcohol, it could not be determined what effect, if any, such consumption contributed to the tragedy; following normal sentencing principles, the trial judge decided that he should sentence the accused as if his consumption of alcohol had not been a contributing factor.

The trial judge imposed concurrent conditional sentences of two years less one day. He placed the accused under a form of house arrest for the entire period, prohibiting him from leaving his residence except for work, school, attending for psychological counselling, and performing 240 hours of community service (the maximum permitted amount). The terms of house arrest also included conditions that the accused not receive friends into his residence; if any person other than an immediate family member came to his residence, he was required immediately to isolate himself. Part of his community service obligations required him to speak to designated groups about the consequences of dangerous driving. Once the conditional sentence was over, the accused was placed on probation for the next two years.

On appeal, the Crown argued that a conditional sentence was inadequate to reflect the need for general deterrence and denunciation. The Nova Scotia Court of Appeal disagreed, holding that '[a] properly informed public' would not perceive that a sentence as onerous as this, particularly given the 'substantial deprivation of liberty' implied in the form of house arrest ordered by the trial court, to be a lenient disposition. The court held that while the accused 'is morally culpable and criminally liable for his actions ... his crime is to be distinguished from an intentional criminal undertaking such as drug trafficking or fraud.' The court recognized that '[n]o sentence available in our criminal justice system could lessen or redress the devastating impact of th[e victims'] loss.'

In *Biancofiore*,[18] the twenty-three-year-old accused had been drinking for some hours when he decided to take two friends for a ride in his brother's sports car, which he did not have permission to do. At 2:35 a.m. he drove at a very high rate of speed, weaving in and out of traffic along major streets. While travelling at least 117 kilometres per hour (in a posted 60 km/h zone) the accused made an abrupt movement to avoid slower moving traffic. He lost control, mounted the curb, and struck a concrete pole and a guard rail. The sports car was completely destroyed by the impact of the crash. The accused was not seriously injured in the accident; however, both passengers were. The consequences of these offences for one of the passengers were described by the court of appeal as resulting in 'permanent serious injuries that had a devastating impact on her personal life and on the life of her family.' The accused had a prior conviction for public mischief, for which he was on probation at the time of the commission of these most serious offences.

In allowing a Crown appeal against concurrent conditional sentences imposed following guilty pleas to charges of dangerous driving causing bodily harm, 'over .80,' and taking an automobile without consent, the court considered how the sentencing principles of general deterrence and denunciation should have been more properly applied by the sentencing judge. On the subject of general deterrence, the court noted the considerable body of academic literature that challenges the assumption frequently made by courts (and others) that custodial sentences have or are likely to have the effect of causing or inducing others not to commit crimes. However, it also noted that there was some empirical support for the concept that harsh sentences had some general deterrent effect. But the court was not prepared to find that only custodial sentences could address such concerns. The court stated that it 'did not wish to foreclose ... the availability of a conditional sentence of imprisonment in a proper case' of dangerous driving causing bodily harm or death. However, in this instance, because of the presence of the aggravating features described above, combined with the fact that an alcohol-related offence had been committed, the court declined to uphold the conditional sentence imposed at trial.

Although 'the need for denunciation alone may not have made a conditional sentence inappropriate,' speaking for the court Rosenberg J.A. was clear that it was the need to denounce elements of the particular accused's course of conduct that mandated the imposition of an immediate custodial sentence in *Biancofiore*. Those aggravating factors included the accused breaching the 'keep the peace and be of good behaviour' clause of the order of probation he was subject to at the time of the commission of the offence, the unlawful taking of the vehicle, and 'a pattern of driving dangerously while his blood-alcohol level exceed the maximum permitted by law.' The presence of these factors indicated that the offender had demonstrated a high measure of 'moral blameworthiness.' This phrase comes from a number of decisions from the Supreme Court of Canada dealing with the constitutionality of several provisions of the Criminal Code. In *M. (C.A.).* Chief Justice Lamer explained that 'denunciation embraces two different but related concepts. A sentence with a denunciatory concept satisfies the community's desire and need to condemn "that particular offender's conduct." A denunciatory sentence can also play a more positive role in a rational and humane sentencing regime by communicating and reinforcing a shared set of values.'[19]

Although the case law will no doubt continue to evolve, it seems clear from these first decisions that the fact of maiming another individual or taking someone's life will no longer be considered sufficient in itself to justify a custodial sentence. Factors demonstrating that the accused exhibits evidence of an ongoing risk to the community or a high degree of 'moral blameworthiness' for the offence committed must be present before a custodial sentence is likely to be imposed.

Drug Trafficking

In *Stevens*[20] the Manitoba Court of Appeal held that a twelve-month conditional sentence was sufficient punishment for an unemployed forty-year-old woman (essentially a first offender; her only previous offence was for refusing to provide a breathalyser test) who made two deliveries of cocaine or a substance held out to be cocaine, as a favour to the major conspirator. She obtained no financial benefit from the transactions, nor was she an addict trafficker who obtained drugs in exchange for her services. Conversely, in *Ly*[21] the Ontario Court of Appeal held that conditional sentences should be imposed only in exceptional circumstances for drug trafficking. The court refused to interfere with maximum reformatory sentences imposed on two non-addict heroin traffickers.

A more stark contrast in approach is demonstrated by decisions of the Alberta and British Columbia Courts of Appeal released within days of one another. In *Phun*[22] the Alberta Court of Appeal made it clear that the 'starting point' for any case of commercial trafficking in cocaine in that province would be three years' imprisonment. However, in *Bui*[23] the British Columbia Court of Appeal refused to interfere with a conditional sentence imposed at trial on a man caught with twenty-five ounces of cocaine. Despite what the Ontario Court of Appeal had said in *Ly*, the British Columbia court felt that courts in that province were not bound to find 'exceptional circumstances' before imposing conditional sentences, so long as the three statutory criteria laid out in section 742.1 (as amended) are addressed.

Although the structure of the Canadian criminal justice system is in part designed to reflect regional differences and to allow local judges (and appellate courts) to deal with sentencing according to provincial priorities, such stark differences in approach show the need for steps to be taken to reduce disparity. Unfortunately, in its consideration of the Report of the Canadian Sentencing Commission, Parliament rejected the idea of a permanent sentencing commission whose mandate would include reducing unjustified sentencing disparities. In the absence of such a body, the Supreme Court of Canada must undertake this role. It is hoped that these remarkable and probably unjustified disparities will soon be brought to that court's attention.

The Sufficiency of Supervision of Conditional Sentences

Even prior to the advent of the new legislation provinces had different 'intermediate sanctions.' Saskatchewan and British Columbia, for example, had developed fairly extensive electronic monitoring programs, while other provinces continued 'to study' their feasibility. Also, the caseloads of probation officers (and conditional sentence supervisors) vary considerably across the country. Probation officers in New Brunswick and Quebec, provinces which have decided as a matter of policy to reduce emphasis on incarceration and replace it with much increased spending on community supervision, have somewhat lower caseloads than elsewhere in the country.

To date there has been relatively little judicial comment on these issues. However, it seems to be becoming known that in some parts of the country few or no new resources have been allocated to conditional sentence supervision. At least one Ontario judge has indicated that he will not impose conditional sentences of less than six months because he feels that no effective supervision will be conducted for lesser sentences. The Alberta Court of Appeal has written that breaches are not likely to be caught and that, in the absence of provincially funded halfway houses, 'house arrest' is not much of a penalty, since 'a man's home is his castle.'[24]

Again, the question of whether alleged breaches can be expeditiously dealt with is just beginning to come before the courts. At least one court[25] has interpreted that a breach hearing must be substantively commenced within thirty days of the laying of the allegation. In most parts of the country an offender cannot process an application for legal aid within such a short time-frame.

While these issues remain to be fleshed out, it seems clear that unless and until Parliament and the provincial legislatures are prepared to provide or reallocate funding, judges (and the general public) may rapidly lose faith in the experiment with conditional sentencing. Given that it took some twenty-five years to agree on this most modest of sentencing reforms, this would be a great pity.

ENDNOTES

1 *R. v. Brady*, [1998] A.J. No. 39 (Alta. C.A.).
2 *R. v. R. (R.A.)*, [1997] M.J. No. 539 (Man. C.A.).
3 The Supreme Court is scheduled to hear appeals in five conditional sentence cases in the spring of 1999.
4 *R. v. Scidmore* (1997), 112 C.C.C. (3d) 28 (leave to appeal to the Supreme Court of Canada discontinued, 7 March 1997).
5 *R. v. Pierce*, *supra*, note 3.
6 *R. v. Wismayer* (1997), 115 C.C.C. (3d) 18.
7 S.C. 1997, c. 18, s. 107.1, proclaimed in force 2 May 1997. In *R. v. Doughty* (unreported), 15 May 1997, the Ontario Court of Appeal interpreted this amended version of s. 742.1 as 'a clarification of the prior version of the same section.'
8 *R. v. W. (L.F.)* (1998), 119 C.C.C. (3d) 97. This is one of the cases which will be heard by the Supreme Court of Canada.
9 Ibid., 119–20, paras. 46–9.
10 *R. v. M. (C.A.)*, [1996] 1 S.C.R. 500 at 557–8.
11 Ibid., 554.
12 *R. v. W. (L.F.)*, 137, para. 97.
13 Ibid., 145, para. 117. It is perhaps no accident that among the various Newfoundland judges who considered this case, Cameron J.A. is the only female judge. In *Scidmore*, the first 'historical' sexual assault case considered by the Ontario Court of Appeal under the new legislation, Abella J.A., in contrast with her male colleagues, would have imposed a period of incarceration.
14 *R. v. L.S.* (unreported), 6 June 1997. See also *R. v. Oliver*, [1997] O.J. No. 1911; *R. v. Creighton and Travassos*, [1997] O.J. No. 2220; *R. v. Doughty* (unreported), 17 May 1997.
15 A similar conclusion seems to have been reached by the British Columbia Court of Appeal. In a series of decisions released simultaneously, *R. v. Ursel etc.* (1998), 117 C.C.C. (33d) 289, some of which involved sexual assault, in only one case was

the court prepared to impose a conditional sentence, due to the 'precarious physical state' of the eighty-two-year-old accused.

16 *R. v. McDonald* (1997), 113 C.C.C. (3d) 418.

17 *R. v. Parker* (1997), 116 C.C.C. (3d) 236.

18 *R. v. Biancofiore* (1998), 119 C.C.C. (3d) 344.

19 *R. v. M. (C.A.)*, 558–9.

20 *R. v. Stevens* (1997), 115 C.C.C. (3d) 372.

21 *R. v. Ly* (1997), 114 C.C.C. (3d) 279.

22 *R. v. Phun*, [1997] A.J. No. 1142. Strictly speaking the court was only dealing with the facts of the case at bar, which involved appellate consideration of a two-and-a-half-year sentence for trafficking in heroin imposed on an addict trafficker who had taken steps to cure himself of his addiction and was drug free at the time of sentencing. Despite this, the court of appeal increased the sentence to four years, while holding that a normal sentence for such trafficking henceforth would be five years.

23 *R. v. Bui*, [1997] B.C.J. No. 2761.

24 *R. v. Brady, supra*, note 1.

25 *R. v. Orlias*, [1996] N.W.T.J. No. 87.

ADDITIONAL READING

Manson, A. 1997. The Appeal of Conditional Sentences of Imprisonment. 10 *Criminal Reports* (5th), 279–90.

7

Sentencing Options in Canada

ALLEN EDGAR[1]

When most members of the public think about sentencing, they think of imprisonment. But imprisonment is just one of many dispositions at the disposal of judges in Canada. The list of different sentencing options grew even longer with the passage of Bill C-41, which created the new disposition known as a conditional sentence. In this chapter, Allen Edgar describes the various sentencing options in Canada. At the end of the chapter he outlines the kinds of sentences that are imposed for some high-frequency offences.

Introduction

A person facing the unpleasant situation of being sentenced is often quite aware of what the judge can do and is almost always intensely interested in what the judge will do. So is the victim and the victim's family. Much less interesting to those immediately involved is what goes into the judge's decision-making process. Once the stage has been set by the nature of the offence, the nature of the offender, and the advocacy skills of the lawyers involved, three key components are integral to the process: (a) direction given in the statutes (generally the Criminal Code) in relation to the particular offence; (b) rules and principles which give guidance to the judge as to which dispositions should be used; and (c) personal characteristics of the judge. The first two components determine the sentencing options, while the third shapes the ultimate choice made from the options in arriving at the actual sentence. This chapter will deal primarily with the first two components. The chapter begins by describing the various sentencing options created by the Criminal Code. Then the ways in which rules and principles limit the judge's choice in sentencing for a particular offence and provide guidelines both for the choice among available options and the extent to which these options should be used are examined. The chapter concludes by examining sentencing practices for three common offences.

Sentencing Options

The Criminal Code sets out the sentencing options available to the judiciary. Sometimes provincial statutes provide for the imposition of further consequences to the offender, as will be demonstrated in the discussion of impaired driving. The options available change over time, as some are abolished and new ones are created. The trend has been to abolish the harsher punishments (considered by many to be the more barbaric) while creating more enlightened ones. For example, the Criminal Code provided for whipping until 1972 and hanging as recently as 1974. These options are no longer available. Further back in our common law tradition, a judge could order mutilation or a period in the stocks. More recently, new forms of punishment, such as the discharge and the conditional sentence, have been added by new legislation.

Not all options are available everywhere in Canada: even though the Criminal Code is a federal statute, Parliament can declare a sentencing option to be available in a particular province or territory only if it sets up a program to implement it. If no program is set up, the sentencing option in question may be in the Criminal Code, but the judge cannot use it. The fine option program in section 736 is designed this way. Alternatively, the government can declare a particular option to be in effect only in named provinces or territories, which are named only if they want to be. The curative discharge provision for impaired driving offences in subsection 255(5) follows this route.

The sentencing options currently available to the judiciary are imprisonment, which is subdivided into actual incarceration (from now on referred to simply as incarceration), intermittent sentence, conditional sentence, and indeterminate sentence; fine; probation; discharge; restitution; and prohibition.

Imprisonment

Incarceration

The offender sentenced to be incarcerated goes to prison and stays there until the end of the sentence or release on parole, as discussed in later chapters of this book. Generally, parole will be granted after between one- and two-thirds of the sentence has been served. The maximum term of imprisonment that can be imposed varies with the seriousness of the offence. A few offences carry a minimum term of imprisonment. The maximum sentence for an offence will also depend on whether it was prosecuted by indictment or summarily. The general maximum on summary conviction is six months, although for a few offences it is eighteen months.[2] Maximum terms on indictment are two years, five years, ten years, fourteen years, and life.[3] These maximums are almost never imposed, however, as a result of rules and principles discussed below. Newspapers frequently report that someone has been charged with an offence and, if convicted, will be liable to be sentenced to prison for some astonishing period of time. Take for example, a basic sexual assault that involves no bodily harm or weapons. The accused is technically liable to ten years, but sentences actually imposed are nowhere near this long. The striking difference between the possible sentences and those imposed confuses the public and can create the impression that the sentencing judge in particular, and the courts in general, are soft on criminals. This impression in turn has a negative effect on the public's respect for and confidence in the courts. It looks to some as though judges are wilfully refraining from using incarceration to the extent intended by Parliament, thereby flouting the wishes of society.

The problem created by maximums far exceeding actual sentencing practice was identified by the Canadian Sentencing Commission (1987). The commission noted that, except for murder,[4] even the worst cases usually receive sentences far below the maximum, and life sentences occasionally imposed for other offences meant parole eligibility in seven years. Further compounding the problem was the fact that, with the broad jumps in maximum sentences noted above (e.g., two then five years, etc.), offences of different seriousness shared the same maximum, while offences of similar seriousness had different maximums. The commission recommended that, for all offences other than murder and high treason, the maximum penalty structure be revised downward to six months, one year, three years, six years, nine years, and twelve years. The proposed complement to this more finely tuned and realistic structure was a procedure for going above the maximum for the exceptional case. Sentences, instead of being heavily grouped near the bottom of the possible range and approaching the statutory maximums only for the worst examples of the offence, would be more evenly spread across the entire statutory range.

Ten years and many amendments of the Criminal Code later, the only apparent effect of this recommendation has been the inclusion of the eighteen-month summary maximum noted above. There has been more response in the area of drug offences, particularly in relation to marijuana. Under the Narcotic Control Act, which has been supplanted by the Controlled Drugs and Substances Act, marijuana was considered a narcotic and grouped with far more harmful drugs, like heroin. The statutory maximum sentence for trafficking in even tiny amounts of marijuana was life imprisonment; the maximum for possession on indictment was seven years' imprisonment and, on summary conviction, six months for a first offender and twelve months for subsequent offenders. Now, for small amounts of marijuana, trafficking carries a maximum of five years' imprisonment and possession six months. These limits are still far above the severity of actual sentences handed down, but much more realistic than the previously possible sentences.

Prison terms are divided into two categories: reformatory and penitentiary. All terms of two years or more are served in a penitentiary, while those of under two years are served in a reformatory. Many believe that there is a qualitative difference between the two prison systems, for various reasons. Penitentiary time might be considered as harder time, or programs available in one system might be considered more conducive to the rehabilitation of the particular offender than those in the other. A consideration of factors such as these can influence the judge in choosing between two years and two years less a day.

If the accused is being sentenced to prison for more than one offence, or is already serving a prison term, the sentencing judge may opt to have the sentences served concurrently or consecutively (subsection 718.3(4)). Sentences served concurrently are served at the same time, so the effective sentence is really the longest of the various concurrent terms. The existence of the other prison terms might affect a decision regarding parole, but it does not affect either the legal eligibility to apply for parole or the date of the expiration of the sentence. Sentences served consecutively are served one after the other. Thus two one-year prison terms served concurrently expire after one year, while the same two prison terms expire after two years if the judge orders them to be served consecutively.

An interesting variation on incarceration now available to judges in relation to some offences is the ability to increase the percentage of the sentence that must be served before the accused is eligible to apply for parole. Normally, a prisoner may apply for parole after having served one-third of the term of imprisonment, or after seven years in the case of a life sentence. Many receive parole at this point and most prisoners serve no more than two-thirds of their sentences before being granted parole. Only a few serve the entire sentence. This variability leaves the sentencing judge in the dark as to how long the offender will actually be in prison. A sentence of three years could result in incarceration for anywhere from one to three years. Now, for a great number of the more serious offences, section 743.6 of the Criminal Code gives a judge imposing a sentence of two years or more the power to increase the minimum that must be served from one-third up to the lesser of one-half or ten years.[5] This decreases the uncertainty factor. A judge using this option to its fullest extent would know that the same three-year sentence would result in at least one and a half years of incarceration.

Intermittent Sentence

A judge imposing a sentence of ninety days or less may order that the sentence be served intermittently, according to the times specified by the judge (section 732). Usually the sentence is ordered to be served on weekends. This permits the offender to continue with employment, education, or treatment programs not available in a custodial setting. The sentence must be accompanied by a probation order, which sets out terms for the accused while not in prison. This tool has fallen out of favour with some judges because the correctional facilities in their jurisdiction are often so crowded that there is no room for the part-time inmate. When the offender arrives Friday night to start serving time for the weekend, he or she may be told to sign in and then go home.

Conditional Sentence (section 742.1)

This new option, which came into effect September 1996, is discussed in detail in other chapters of this book. A judge intending to impose a prison term first determines whether a sentence of less than two years is appropriate. If so, the judge next considers whether the safety of the community would be endangered by the offender's serving the sentence there under certain conditions. Since fuller details are given in Chapter 16, it will be sufficient to note here that the mandatory and optional conditions are similar to the terms for probation described below.

Indeterminate Sentence

The use of this sentencing option can result in sentences above the maximum. On the sentencing for an offence involving violence, danger to life or safety, or which threatened to cause severe psychological damage, the Crown may apply to have the accused declared a dangerous offender, if the maximum sentence is ten years or more (section 752). The requirements for dangerous offender status are set out in section 753. If the sentencing judge finds the accused to be a dangerous offender, an indeterminate sentence must be imposed. (Prior to 1 August 1997 its use was optional.) While mainly imposed in relation to quite serious offences, the dangerous offender designation is also available for less serious offences meeting the requirements, since it is the dangerousness of the offender and not the seriousness of the current offence which is to be determined on a dangerous offender application (*Currie* (1997)).

Suspended Sentence

Pursuant to paragraph 731(1)(a), the judge who convicts the offender can suspend the passing of sentence and instead impose only a period of probation. If, before the period of probation expires, the offender is convicted of another offence, including the offence of breaching any of the terms of the probation order, the suspension can be revoked and replaced with any sentence that could have been awarded in the first place.

Probation

Probation, like parole, is a form of controlled release into the community. The customary form of probation is prescribed in section 731, while a new sort of 'super probation' for long-term offenders became available on 1 August 1997.

Probation (section 731)

The offender is bound by a probation order, which must have three compulsory terms and may contain any number of optional terms. The compulsory terms are to keep the peace and be of good behaviour; to appear in court when required; and to make notification of changes in address, name, or employment. The optional terms include specific items such as abstention from alcohol or drugs, abstention from owning a weapon, community service, etc. In addition there is a basket clause of other reasonable conditions for protecting society or rehabilitating the offender. Working within these requirements of reasonableness, protection, and rehabilitation, some judges have come up with quite creative conditions.[6]

Long-term Supervision (section 753.1)

Although it is coupled in the Criminal Code with the dangerous offender provisions discussed above, long-term supervision is actually more akin to probation than incarceration. A judge may find an accused to be a long-term offender if a sentence of at least two years is appropriate, there is a substantial risk that the offender will reoffend, and the there is a reasonable possibility of eventual control of that risk in the community. A judge who finds that an accused is a long-term offender must order the offender to be supervised in the community for a period of up to ten years following the end of the prison sentence. This option provides the possibility of supervision for a far longer period than probation or, in the vast majority of cases, parole. It would begin when any period of parole had ended.

Fine

A judge may almost always fine an accused through one of two avenues. The penalty sections applicable to many offences specifically provide for fines. For instance, the general penalty for summary conviction offences (section 787) provides for a fine of up to $2,000 as well as prison for up to six months. However, many offences are not specifically assigned fines as a possible penalty. Most offences prosecuted by way of indictment contain references only to the period of imprisonment, with no mention of fines. For these offences, section 734 provides a second avenue by granting a general power to fine; it permits the judge to impose a fine 'in addition to or in lieu of' any other punishment.

There are two limitations on the power created by section 734. The offence must not be subject to a minimum period of imprisonment and the judge must be satisfied that the offender can pay the fine or work it off under a fine option work program. A fine option program allows the offender to earn credits toward the payment of the fine by work performed according to the program. Not every province has established such a program. Ontario, for example, has no fine option program. Thus judges in Ontario can only impose fines under section 734 if satisfied that the offender can pay.

Time in Default

A judge who fines an accused through the first avenue has discretion to impose a period of imprisonment if the fine is in default: i.e., not paid. Subsection 718.3(3) applies to indictable offences and subsection 787(2) to summary conviction offences. The limitation imposed on this option is that the time in default may not exceed the maximum imprisonment available for the offence. When a fine is imposed under section 734, there is an automatic time-in-default mechanism imposed by subsection 734(2), which the judge may not either increase or decrease.

Victim Fine Surcharge (section 737)

In addition to any other punishment, the sentencing judge is required to impose a victim fine surcharge, unless the offender satisfies the judge that a surcharge would cause 'undue hardship' to the offender and his or her dependants. Money raised from the surcharge in a province is to be used to help fund victim assistance programs. When a fine is imposed, the surcharge may be any amount up to 15 per cent of the fine. If no fine is imposed the maximum surcharge is $10,000. A judge not imposing the surcharge is supposed to give reasons for this decision.

Discharge

The discharge provisions of section 730 permit a judge not to convict an accused who has just been found guilty of the offence. This option is available only for offences without a minimum punishment and with maximum prison terms of less than fourteen years. The decision whether to convict or grant a discharge is actually part of sentencing, even though it comes before conviction. This apparent contradiction in terms was created to avoid the necessity of imposing the stigma and disadvantages of a criminal conviction for minor offences on offenders who appeared ready and able to lead law-abiding lives. The impetus for the creation of the discharge, which came into effect in 1972, may well have been the large number of young people convicted for possession of marijuana in the 1960s. As they were starting their adult lives, the possible repercussions of a conviction on employment, travel opportunities, and immigration status would have been out of proportion to the gravity of the offence.

A discharge can be absolute or conditional. An absolute discharge becomes permanent immediately; a conditional discharge is coupled with a period of probation, which the offender must successfully complete. If the accused abides by all of the terms of probation (or is not caught violating them), the discharge becomes permanent when the probation expires. An accused who violates the probation order faces not only a possible charge of breach of probation, but also the prospect of having the discharge revoked and replaced with a conviction and a new sentence. In practice, very few probationers are brought up for breaches.

Restitution

Section 738 permits the court to order the accused to make restitution to the victim if the amount involved is 'readily ascertainable.' Where property has been damaged, or stolen and not returned, the amount of the order can be up to replacement cost. For offences involving bodily harm, the maximum is the actual monetary loss, including loss of income.

Section 739 permits restitution to be ordered to a person 'acting in good faith,' who might be called a secondary victim. For example, the primary victim of a car thief is the car's owner. The stolen car might pass through several people's hands before being purchased by someone in complete ignorance of its stolen nature. If the car is discovered, this purchaser in good faith must relinquish it to the original owner and is suddenly out the purchase price, with no car. The judge can order the convicted car thief to make restitution to this person. If the accused does not make the ordered restitution, the person to whom restitution was ordered to be paid can take the order, register it with a civil court, and pursue civil remedies to collect the amount.

Prohibitions

For certain types of offences, a prohibition order can be imposed ordering the accused not to possess something or do something for a certain period of time.

Although the court could impose the same restriction on the offender as a term of probation, this order is distinct from probation terms. A prohibition order can often operate over a longer period than probation and a violation of a prohibition order is a separate offence from violation of probation.

Firearms

An already tough firearms prohibition scheme was made even stronger on 1 December 1998 by new sections 109 and 110. Section 109 is a mandatory section, listing four categories of offences for which the judge is required to make an order prohibiting the possession of an extremely wide variety of weapons, including firearms, ammunition, and crossbows. The categories are (1) serious offences (maximum ten years or more) involving violence; (2) several listed weapons offences and criminal harassment; (3) drug offences of importing, exporting, or manufacturing; and (4) offences involving weapons while under a previous prohibition order. For the first timer, the order must be for at least ten years after release from prison or after the trial if prison is not ordered. Any subsequent order against the same person must be for life.

Section 110 creates a discretion to impose a prohibition order for two other categories of offences: (1) crimes involving violence with a maximum of less than ten years, and (2) offences involving weapons while not under a prohibition order. Again the order must be for at least ten years. Although the order is discretionary, the judge must give reasons for not imposing it.

The possibility for the judge to grant exceptions for people who hunt for sustenance or need firearms for their employment was added to the prior prohibition regime after several courts granted constitutional exemptions under the Charter of Rights as relief against cruel or unusual punishment. These exceptions were continued in section 113. This process Parliamentary response to court decisions is discussed below in Rules and Principals.

Association with Children

For various offences listed in section 161 committed against children under the age of fourteen, the judge must consider, and may make, an order prohibiting the accused from going to specified public places where children are likely to be, such as parks, public pools, day care centres, and schools; and/or being employed in or volunteering for any position that involves supervising children. The order can be for any period up to life.

Driving

For alcohol-related driving offences, subsection 259(1) requires the judge to make an order prohibiting driving. This applies anywhere in Canada and should not be confused with a driver's licence suspension imposed by a province. Many provinces impose automatic licence suspensions upon conviction for these offences, which may be for far longer periods than the prohibition imposed by the judge,[7] and which may come as a surprise to the accused. The maximum length of the order is three years plus the length of any term of imprisonment. The minimum varies: first offence, three months; second offence, six months; and subsequent offences, one year. For other designated offences committed by means of a motorized vehicle, subsection 259(2) grants discretion to use this option. There is no minimum period. The maximum period varies with the maximum prison term for the offence: life, no maximum prohibition; over five years and less than life, ten-year maximum prohibition; five years or less, three-year maximum prohibition.

Rules and Principles

Various rules and principles shape the choice of sentencing options and the degree to which the chosen options are used. Such rules and principles limit and influence the judge's discretion. What appears to be an unfettered discretion may in fact be quite circumscribed. A clear distinction between a rule and a principle is not always obvious, and there is a spectrum sliding from rigid rules to rules to principles. (These are not legal terms, but are used here in an attempt to impose some structure on the area.) If a rigid rule is not followed, the sentence is illegal or incomplete. The record will clearly show if it has been broken and an appeal will invariably succeed. A rule must be followed or the trial judge will have erred,[8] but the sentence will not be illegal. The record will not always show whether or not the rule was followed. A finding on appeal that the sentencing judge broke a rule does not necessarily mean the appeal will succeed. The sentence imposed can be upheld if, despite the error, that sentence was appropriate. A principle is something that the sentencing judge must keep in mind when devising the sentence. It is even harder to detect when a principle has been missed, or noted but not followed. A degree of judgment is generally required in determining whether a principle has been violated.

Rigid Rules

Anecdotal evidence indicates that rigid rules are not infrequently broken by sentencing judges, causing headaches for administrators of both the provincial and federal prison systems. Even though the resulting sentence is illegal, only an appellate or supervisory court has jurisdiction to declare it to be illegal and impose a legal sentence.

Probation

Probation can be imposed on its own, with a fine, or with imprisonment for two years or less. It cannot be imposed together with both a fine and imprisonment: *Blacquiere* (1975). This rule is easy to break because it does not make sense: there are numerous situations in which a short prison term and a fine, followed by probation, would be entirely appropriate. But if all three of these sentences are imposed an appeal will succeed, with the appellate court eliminating one and perhaps altering the length or size of the other two.

Probation can only be coupled with prison terms totalling two years or less. The two-year limitation on the prison term applies to the total period to which the accused is then subject, and it applies even if no single term is over two years. This limitation even applies retroactively: a probation order that was valid when imposed becomes invalid if the accused is subsequently given a new prison term that pushes the total left to serve over two years: *Miller* (1987). A probation order may be for up to three years. If coupled with imprisonment, it comes into effect on the expiry of the prison sentence. Probation cannot be used as a stand-alone tool; it must be accompanied by a conditional discharge, suspended sentence, fine, or imprisonment (section 731).

Deferred Parole

The offence must be listed on Schedule I (Criminal Code offences) or Schedule II (drug offences) of the Corrections and Conditional Release Act. When sentencing an accused for any other offence, a judge may not use this option.

Minimum Sentence

Where the statute calls for a minimum period of imprisonment, it means incarceration. The court must impose at least the minimum and cannot use the conditional sentence option. This rigid rule must be followed even if the defendant has already spent considerable time in custody prior to sentencing. Likewise, minimum fines required by statute must be imposed, even if the judge knows that the defendant cannot pay even the minimum. Minimum fines under financially driven statues, like the Income Tax Act and the Excise Tax Act, can be enormous.

Prohibition Orders

If the judge neglects to make a mandatory prohibition order, the sentence imposed is not illegal, but is simply incomplete. On a sentence appeal by either the offender or the Crown, the appeal court will add the missing prohibition order.

Exceptions: Charter of Rights

Since 1982, judges have been able to create exceptions to even rigid rules through the application of the Charter of Rights. The nature of these exceptions, and how their creation is mandated by the Constitution of Canada, is discussed below under 'Effect of the Charter.'

Rules and Principles

Many of the rules and principles that were common law creations of the courts have now been codified in the Criminal Code. The purpose of this section is to show how they interact with the available sentencing options to create the sentence awarded. The most obvious principles are the purposes and principles recently codified by Bill C-41 in sections 718, 718.1, and 718.2. We will neither address all of them here, as Chapters 2 and 3 are devoted to Bill C-41, nor confine ourselves to them. As we will see, in some cases a common law rule or principle can give added strength to its codified version.

Several of these principles can be illustrated by the case of *Priest* (1996). The offence was break and enter of a business. The nineteen-year-old accused pleaded guilty. He had cooperated fully when apprehended and returned everything he took. He had no criminal record. The Crown asked for a sentence of thirty to sixty days with probation. The trial judge, without finding out anything more about the accused, noted the prevalence of break and enter charges on the docket and imposed a one-year sentence for general deterrence. Although this sentence was perfectly legal, and well within the maximum allowed for the offence, the court of appeal appeared to be appalled by it and listed some of the principles broken by the judge:

- *Prevalence of crime in an area* is not to be the primary consideration in sentencing. It can only be one factor to be considered among many.
- A *custodial sentence on a first offender* should not be imposed without either a presentence report or some other very clear information about the accused's background and circumstances.
- With a *youthful first offender* the primary considerations are specific deterrence and rehabilitation. Noncustodial dispositions must be explored and rationally rejected before a custodial sentence is imposed.
- *Proportionality* requires the sentence to reflect the seriousness of the offence, the degree of culpability of the offender, and the harm occasioned by the offence. The offender must not be unjustly dealt with for the sake of the common good by way of general deterrence.

- The *role of the courts* requires the imposition of appropriate sentences, not unduly harsh ones. A just society is not promoted by sentences that are far beyond those imposed for similar offences in other parts of the province.

As we look at some other rules and principles, consider whether the sentencing judge violated any of them as well.

Joint Submissions

When the prosecution and the defence agree between themselves to suggest a particular sentence, they make a joint submission. This is usually the end result of a plea bargain, where the defence agrees to plead guilty, usually to a less serious charge or to only some of several offences charged, in return for the prosecution agreeing to a lower sentence than it would ask for after a trial. Without plea bargains and the tremendous savings in court time they provide, the administration of justice would quickly sink under its own weight. The sentencing judge is not required to accept their suggestion. However, as noted in the Report of the Attorney General's Advisory Committee on Charge Screening, Disclosure and Resolution Discussions (*Martin Report* 1993), a joint submission ought to be followed unless it would either bring the administration of justice into disrepute or it is not in the public interest. This statement has subsequently been endorsed by the courts, with the reputation of the administration of justice and the public interest being seen as two separate categories: *Kirisit* (1993), *Sriskantharanjah* (1994). This principle and its two exceptions apply to sentences both above and below the joint submission.[9] Trial judges can and do differ widely in their interpretation of these two exceptions. First, they will differ on what the appropriate range of sentence ought to be. They also differ on how far out of this range the joint submission has to be before it ought to be rejected and a different sentence imposed. A corollary to this principle is that the sentencing judge should not give a greater sentence than asked for by the Crown without good reason: *Bahari* (1994), *Farizah* (1994).

Credit for Pretrial Custody

Offenders can spend considerable time in custody between arrest and sentencing. Subsection 719(3) of the Criminal Code provides that the sentencing judge may take this time into account to give a shorter prison term than would otherwise be appropriate, or even no prison term at all. This is elevated into a rule by the common law so that a trial judge should give credit for pretrial custody unless there is a good reason not to: *Rezaie* (1996). Pretrial custody is considered worse than serving a sentence because it is 'dead time.' There is no earning of credit towards parole eligibility: six months' pretrial custody is six entire months in jail, not the two to four months that may be served of a six-month sentence. Also, no educational or rehabilitative programs are available to the offender. For this reason, trial judges often give credit on a two-for-one basis, reducing the sentence by two days for each day of pretrial custody. However, there is no set formula and each case should be decided on its own merits. Sometimes much less credit is given. *Rezai* illustrates the difference between a rigid rule and a rule or principle. Although the trial judge erred by breaking the rule, the sentence was still legal and upheld because it was a fit sentence despite the error.

Problems in following this rule have arisen when minimum sentences are involved, as we will see below under 'Offences.' If the sentencing judge did not think a sentence above the minimum was called for, there is no room for any credit for pretrial custody, unless the Charter of Rights was called into play. However, in *McDonald* (1998), a Court of Appeal for the first time held that a minimum sentence could be reduced for this purpose without directly resorting to the Charter. This issue is discussed further below under 'Effect of the Charter' and 'Offences.' Low maximums can also interfere with the application of this rule. This occurs most often under the Young Offenders Act, where most offences have a three-year maximum. Judges who feel that even three years is not sufficient are loath to reduce the time further by the application of the rule.

Credit for Guilty Pleas

A guilty plea should result in some reduction of the sentence. The earlier in the process that the plea is made, the greater the reduction. Two grounds support this proposition. First, a guilty plea can indicate remorse and acceptance of the offender's wrongful conduct. Second, the plea saves the expense, in both money and time, of a trial and the trauma that testifying can often cause witnesses, especially victims. Reducing the sentence involves some practical problems. The reduction of the sentence has to be sufficient to make pleading guilty appeal to the accused, yet it should not appear that other offenders who choose to go to trial are being penalized for exercising that right or that innocent people are pleading guilty rather than risking a much higher sentence if convicted at trial, or that the courts are awarding grossly inadequate sentences.

Deferred Parole

Along with the rigid rule limiting the offences for which deferred parole is available, the Criminal Code contains principles for its use in subsection 743.6(2). Having regard to the circumstances of the offence and the nature of the offender, the court is to use this option if denunciation and general and specific deterrence so require. These considerations are paramount; rehabilitation of the offender should be subordinate.

But the common law may have altered this principle somewhat: *Dankyi* (1993), *Goulet* (1995). The courts noted that the paramount considerations concerning the use of deferred parole were quite similar to the general principles of sentencing applied when the judge arrived at the length of the term of incarceration in the first place, and that the available range of sentence was large enough to accommodate the best and the worst offences. Therefore, the circumstances of the offence can rarely justify delaying parole eligibility. Generally the characteristics of the offender would be the basis for using this option. The court did concede that an offence of unusual violence, brutality, or degradation could provide the basis for choosing this option under the head of denunciation.

Probation

Probation should not be used to impose additional punishment on the accused, but only to assist in rehabilitation and to prevent further offences: *Ziatas* (1973).

Worst Offence, Worst Offender

The general principle is often stated to be that maximum sentences are reserved for the worst offence and the worst offender. However, the correct statement should be 'worst offence or worst offender': *Stairs* (1994), *Boucher* (1991). For summary conviction proceedings on offences with which the Crown could have proceeded by indictment, the statement becomes 'the worst cases that could be expected to come before a Provincial Court judge on a summary conviction proceeding': *Sanatkar* (1981), *Soucie* (1988).

Consecutive Sentences and the Totality Principle

Although the Criminal Code appears to grant complete discretion as to when to order sentences to be served consecutively, there are guidelines for its use. First, sentences should generally not be consecutive if the offences were committed together. Second, even if the offences were totally unrelated, sentences should not be ordered to be served consecutively if the total time in prison would be too long. This is the totality principle. Individual sentences that are fit and proper in themselves can add up to a total sentence that is so long that it crushes any hope in an offender who still has prospects of being rehabilitated.

The application of this principle can cause some victims to feel unvalued. The judge may feel that the rapist before the court requires three years in prison. Yet convictions for seven sexual assaults have just been made. Each offence on its own might attract a three-year sentence, but a twenty-one-year sentence would be far too long. A three-year sentence is imposed for each offence, but they are ordered to be served concurrently. The victims might well feel that the offender is only being made to 'pay' for the first offence and the others are 'free.'

Effect of the Charter

The Canadian Charter of Rights and Freedoms can be seen as a sort of trump card in relation to the rigid rules of sentencing. Because Parliament is supreme, judges are compelled to follow these mandatory statutory rules when sentencing. However, Parliament in its supremacy has declared all laws to be subject to the Charter. The Charter is part of the Constitution. Subsection 52(1) of the Constitution Act, 1982 states: 'The Constitution of Canada is the supreme law of Canada, and any law that is inconsistent with the provisions of the Constitution is, to the extent of the inconsistency, of no force and effect.' Rights protected by the Charter are not guaranteed absolutely. Section 1 provides that a law can impose a reasonable limitation on a right, if that limitation is necessary to achieve some important societal objective. When a judge uses the Charter to avoid imposing a mandatory punishment, he or she is not flouting the will of Parliament but actually obeying it. As shown below, a sort of dialogue between the courts and Parliament goes on with respect to minimum punishments and the Charter.

One of the rights guaranteed by the Charter is the right not to be subjected to cruel and unusual punishment (section 12). Thus this provision permits, or rather compels, the courts to create exceptions to rigid rules of sentencing if following them would result in cruel and unusual punishment. 'Cruel and unusual' means 'so excessive as to outrage standards of decency' or 'grossly disproportionate to what would have been appropriate': *Smith* (1987). The rigid rules of sentencing found to violate section 12 invariably involve minimum punishments or mandatory prohibition orders.

There are two avenues for the creation of Charter exemptions to rigid rules. The first is under section 52 where the judge determines that the provision itself offends section 12. The judge can either strike down the provision or add something to it to make it conform to the Charter. This is quite a broad approach, as it effectively changes the actual statute.

A much narrower approach is afforded by subsection 24(1) of the Charter, which allows a judge to prevent a violation of section 12 by granting an exemption on a case-by-case basis. If the exemption is granted, the statute remains the same and any other accused who wants an exemption must convince the judge by whom he or she is being sentenced that applying the provision would violate section 12 in his or her particular case.

Section 52

The Supreme Court of Canada used the broad approach afforded by section 52 in *Smith* when it struck down the minimum sentence of seven years for importing narcotics under the Narcotic Control Act, even though it felt that this minimum did not violate section 12 in that particular case. The court outlined the basic criteria for determining whether an exemption is required. The test for a violation of section 12 involves an examination of the gravity of the offence in general, the characteristics of the offender, and circumstances of the particular offence to determine what sentence would be appropriate. If the minimum required by the statute is grossly disproportionate to this, it violates section 12. The issue of 'grossly disproportionate' involves the effect of the sentence, not merely its quantum or duration. The judge must then determine whether the minimum is nonetheless necessary to achieve some important societal objective, or whether that objective can be achieved through less harsh means.

The court held that the seven-year minimum had to be struck down because the offence of importing 'cast too wide a net.' It applied both to extremely serious crimes such as the importation of huge quantities of heroin by a long-term criminal, and relatively innocuous offences, such as a first offender bringing in a couple of joints for personal consumption. Both would be guilty of importing a narcotic and both would be subject to at least seven years' imprisonment if convicted. While the first example might call for a sentence far longer than seven years, seven years would be grossly disproportionate for the second example. And cases at the low end of the spectrum were not only conceivable but certain to occur. This certainty created the violation of section 12 by the provision itself, and not merely its use in certain cases.

For approximately ten years after it was struck down the provision for a seven-year minimum sentence remained in the Narcotic Control Act, but no judge in Canada was obliged to impose it. When Parliament replaced this Act in 1997 with the Controlled Drugs and Substances Act, it finally took the hint from *Smith* and did not include a minimum sentence for importing.

The broad approach of section 52 was also used by the Ontario Court of Appeal in *Hamilton* (1986) to give judges in Ontario the sentencing option of the curative discharge for impaired drivers when it had not made available in Ontario by Parliament, thus creating an exemption to the rigid rule that a judge can only use the tools that Parliament has provided. As noted above in 'Sentencing Options,' curative discharge was made applicable in much of Canada, but not Ontario. The court held that this discrepancy violated the guarantee of equality in section 15 of the Charter. Instead of creating equality by striking down the provision creating the tool, the court did so by 'reading in' that the tool was applicable in Ontario. About three years later, the same court held in *Alton* (1989) that the discrepancy did *not* violate section 15 and read it right out again.

Subsection 24(1)

Probably the most well-known application of subsection 24(1) of the Charter to create an exception was *Latimer* (1997). Robert Latimer had killed his severely disabled daughter to free her from a life of unremitting pain. On a conviction for second degree murder, the sentencing judge did not apply the mandatory life sentence without eligibility for parole for ten years. Instead, he sentenced Mr Latimer to two years less a day. Whereas the motive for murder is generally 'somehow related to self interest, malevolence, hate or violence,' this case involved a 'rare act of homicide that was committed for caring and altruistic reasons.'

Striking down the minimum under section 52, as many courts had previously refused to do, was not appropriate. The cases in which its imposition would violate the Charter would not be common and inevitable, as in *Smith*, but extremely rare. However, in this particular case, the minimum sentence would be grossly disproportionate to what Mr Latimer deserved, so a one-time exception under subsection 24(1) was granted.

The mandatory firearms prohibition in section 100 of the Criminal Code was the subject of numerous one-time exceptions. Originally, section 100 allowed no exceptions. Judges granted subsection 24(1) exceptions to people who did not pose a serious threat to society despite their crime and who needed to use a firearm to earn their livelihoods: people like subsistence hunters or police officers. While not being able to possess a firearm is not much of a hardship for most people, for those who depend on firearms to earn their living, the effect of the prohibition might well ruin their lives. Shortly after two provincial courts of appeal upheld such exceptions in *Chief* (1989) and *McGillivary* (1991), Parliament added its own provisions for exceptions to section 100,[10] which mirrored the grounds cited by the courts.

Minimum fines have also been found to violate section 12 with fines below the minimum then being imposed: *MacFarlane* (1997), *Piscione* (1997).

In conclusion, although virtually every minimum punishment has been challenged under the Charter of Rights, these challenges have had no effect on the vast majority of sentencing matters. Case-by-case exemptions under subsection 24(1) are rare; broad section 52 exemptions are *extremely* rare. However, Parliament does take note of these rare cases and, when multiple provincial courts of appeal or the Supreme Court of Canada have found a violation of section 12, keeps the results in mind when passing new legislation.

Charter as a Tool of Statutory Interpretation

The Charter can also have an indirect effect on rigid rules of sentencing where the court uses it as a guide in interpreting a sentencing provision. Before striking down legislation under section 52, the court should see if there is another rational interpretation that will not violate the Charter. Until *McDonald*, the courts consistently interpreted the sentencing provisions of the Criminal Code to mean that a sentencing judge may not go below a minimum sentence in order to give credit for pretrial custody. In that case, on a Charter challenge to the minimum four-year sentence for robbery using a firearm, the court held that credit for pretrial custody could be given to reduce the sentence below four years and that to hold otherwise would mean that the four-year minimum would violate the charter guarantee against cruel and unusual punishment. Rather than strike the minimum down under section 52 as was done in *Smith*, the court gave a new interpretation to the interaction between minimum sentences and the provision permitting credit to be given for pretrial custody so that the legislation would conform to the Charter.

Offences

In this section, the options, and their range, available for particular offences (robbery, assault, and break and enter) will be described, with the exception that those options, such as probation and restitution, which are always available and whose range is either not variable or dictated by the particular facts of each case will generally not be included. We will explore the sentencing practice for the offences in question: first through case law, to illustrate the range of sentences, and then through statistics, to see the patterns. The statistics are taken from Statistics Canada (1996b).

Robbery (section 343)

Robbery is essentially theft involving violence, the threat of violence, or a weapon. It can range from a purse snatching where the victim is knocked over to the most horrific situations involving extended terror and serious injuries. Robbery is considered by Parliament to be such a serious offence that it punishable only by indictment. The sentencing options available depend on whether or not a firearm was used in the robbery. Rather than categorized as indictable and summary, this offence is subdivided into robbery and robbery with a firearm.

Sentencing Options

The maximum sentence for robbery is life imprisonment. There is no minimum. Conditional sentence, intermittent sentence, suspended sentence, and indeterminate sentence are all available. The maximum sentence for robbery with a firearm is life imprisonment; the minimum sentence is four years in prison. Conditional sentence, intermittent sentence, and suspended sentence are not available; indeterminate sentence is available for both forms of robbery. A fine of any amount may be imposed as long as the judge is satisfied that the accused can pay it, or work it off where fine option programs are available. Discharge is not available for either form of robbery, because the maximum is not less than fourteen years.

Sentencing Practice

Robbery. The full range of available sentences has been used, from suspended sentence (*Scott* (1996) and *Cain* (1993)), through conditional sentence (*McMillan* (1996)), to life (*Stairs* (1994) and *Boucher* (1991)). A maximum can be imposed to protect society if the offender is incorrigible, with a terrible record, or where the offence is so heinous as to override all other considerations. *Stairs* resulted in a life sentence even though no violence was actually used. Mr Stairs had been committing robberies since 1968 and had been constantly in the penitentiary system, except when he was unlawfully at large committing more robberies. He showed no sign of changing his ways. Yet the accused in *Elliot* (1995), who had a similar record, had concurrent life sentences for three robberies reduced to a total of nine years because no violence was used. In *Boucher*, the life sentence was justified by the 'stark horror' of the offence rather than by the record of the offender.

A suspended sentence was given on appeal in *Scott*, despite the violence used in the robbery. Ms Scott was an unwilling participant under the domination of her abusive husband. After the robbery, she had left him and turned her life around. Ms Scott had dependant children and no record. The court of appeal noted that the sentencing judge had put too much weight on deterrence and underestimated the deterrent value of a suspended sentence. It imposed a three-year term of probation and a firearms prohibition.

At least eight sentencing decisions have given serious consideration to whether a conditional sentence should be imposed for the robbery charge before the court. Ironically, the only conditional sentence given was in *McMillan*, in which a BB gun was used. If the offence had been committed after the new four-year minimum came into effect, the conditional sentence would not have been available. The court imposed the conditional sentence because the accused had no record, the offence was out of character, in the two years between the offence and the trial the accused had done very well and was rehabilitated. In the other seven cases, the courts all concluded that either proportionality, deterrence, the safety of the community, or a bad record precluded the use of a discharge. It appears that conditional sentences for robbery will be extremely rare.

In 1994 and 1995, 91 per cent of robbery sentences included prison. About one-quarter of those also included probation. Suspended sentences were given in 7 per cent of the cases. Fines were imposed in only 3 per cent and restitution in less than 2 per cent of the cases. The average sentence was around twenty-one months; only 6 per cent of the sentences were over five years. A third of the offenders were sentenced to the penitentiary: two years or more. Almost half of the sentences were for one year or less.

Robbery with a Firearm. Few reported cases of sentences imposed for offences in this category exist and no statistics have been published. Prior to the creation of this special category, the courts had already recognized that the use of a firearm was an aggravating factor and had drawn a deep division between loaded and unloaded: *Aylward* (1978), *Doyon* (1979). *McDonald* (1997) involved a robbery using a BB gun. The twenty-one-year-old accused showed the butt of the gun to a store clerk while demanding money; he cooperated when arrested and returned all the money. The accused had a prior conviction for assault. He served six and a half months' pretrial custody. Prior to this amendment, it is doubtful that this offender would have received a penitentiary term, yet he was given four years on top of his pretrial custody. Principles regarding rehabilitation and credit for pretrial custody had to be ignored because of this limitation. It is easy to imagine far worse scenarios for robberies involving knives, which would not be the subject of any minimum. Yet the judge refused to grant an exemption to the minimum under either section 52 or subsection 24(1) of the Charter. However, the Ontario Court of Appeal held that Mr McDonald should be given credit for his pretrial custody without resort to the Charter as discussed above under 'Effect of the Charter': *McDonald* (1998). The British Columbia Court of Appeal had already considered this four-year minimum in *Wust* (1998) and had given the traditional response that pretrial custody could not reduce the sentence below four years. After reading *McDonald*, the court decided to revisit the issue in *Mills* (1998) before a five-judge panel instead of the traditional three judges.

Assault (section 266)

Assault is defined as the application of force to another without that person's consent. Simple assault involves no weapon or bodily harm. The vast majority of assaults are simple, or level one, assaults.

Sentencing Options

Assault as an indictable offence carries a maximum sentence of five years' imprisonment. There is no minimum sentence. If treated summarily, the maximum sentence is six months' imprisonment and again there is no minimum. Conditional sentence, intermittent sentence, and suspended sentence are all available. There is no maximum or minimum fine for an indictable assault. When tried summarily the maximum fine is $2,000; there is no minimum. Both probation and discharge are available.

Sentencing Practice

Minor cases are often dealt with by way of a discharge. In *Black* (1991), a school teacher struck a young student on the head, causing a lump. Her appeal from a conditional discharge with one year of probation was granted and replaced with an absolute discharge. Offenders with records for assault can often expect a short jail term.

Where the victim is the offender's spouse, and especially if the judge finds that the offence was part of a pattern of abuse, these circumstances will be considered aggravating factors. Hence, domestic assaults can attract somewhat longer terms. *Brown, Highway, and Umpherville* (1992) provides a good description of the problem of domestic violence. In this case sentences of eighteen months were given for simple assault to accused who had substantial records for domestic violence.

Prison was imposed in 20 per cent of the cases involving only one charge, with an average term of fifty-one days. The majority of these prison terms, 59 per cent, were for one month or less. Ninety-nine per cent were for six months or less. Where more than one charge was involved, the rate of imprisonment rose to 45 per cent with the average term rising to eighty-five days. Probation was given in 69 per cent of the cases of one charge, fines in 31 per cent.

Break and Enter (section 348)

Breaking into and entering a place and either committing or intending to commit an indictable offence – usually theft – is often referred to simply as B & E. The options available depend on whether the 'place' was a residence or not. Offences involving a dwelling are considered to be more serious and are only indictable; those involving any other place have recently been made punishable by summary conviction as well. The maximum for this newly hybrid offence has been reduced from fourteen years' imprisonment to ten.

Sentencing Options

A maximum sentence of life imprisonment is available where the offender broke and entered into a dwelling. For breaking and entering into any other premises the maximum sentence is ten years' imprisonment. Breaking and entering into non-dwelling premises may also be tried summarily, in which case the maximum sentence of incarceration is six months. Whether tried by indictment or summarily, there is no minimum sentence of imprisonment. Conditional sentence, intermittent sentence, and suspended sentence are all available.

For indictable forms of B & E, any amount may be fined as long as the court is satisfied that the accused can pay it, or work it off where fine option programs are available. When punishable by summary conviction the maximum fine is $2,000. There is no minimum fine. Probation is available for both indictable and summary conviction offences. Discharge is not available for offences involving a dwelling. It is newly available for non-dwelling offences on both indictment and summary conviction, since the maximum was reduced.

Sentencing Practice

B & E of a Dwelling The higher maximum for dwellings reflects the sanctity of the home and the possibility for violence if the occupants are at home. The highest sentences have been reached when the offence was associated with another of serious violence: thus the twelve years in *Keefe* (1978) was concurrent to a twelve-year sentence for wounding committed in the house, and the eleven years in *Spurway* (1996) was coupled with attempted murder. At the low end, suspended sentences and intermittent sentences are common. A recent example is *Jenks* (1997). The accused pleaded guilty, had no record, was remorseful, and cooperated with police. In *Blue* (1989), with no recovery of the $6,000 worth of goods stolen, an eighteen-year-old with no record was unable to get his sentence of ninety days intermittent imprisonment plus one year probation reduced on appeal.

B & E of Other Places The usual target of non-dwelling B & Es is a commercial establishment. Despite the lower maximum for this offence, this type of B & E generally attracts higher sentences than those involving homes,[11] although suspended sentences and short custodial terms can be granted to first offenders. A couple of reasons can be suggested for the higher sentences. Homes are more often broken into by younger offenders on the spur of the moment, whereas commercial premises are more likely to be targeted by serious criminals after advance planning. A typical example of a case deserving of a short sentence is *Priest* (1996), described above under 'Rules and Principles.' The youthful first offender made full restitution, cooperated with the authorities and pleaded guilty. The sentence was reduced on appeal as far as possible to the time already served, which was thirty-five days. Had the offender managed to be released on bail sooner, the sentence might well have been reduced further.

At the high end, an older accused with an extensive record of B & Es of commercial establishments received four years for breaking and entering business premises and stealing a camcorder which was not recovered: *Kendall* (1996). Because of the bad record, general and specific deterrence, together with the protection of society, required the long sentence, although it had been reduced on appeal from five years to give some hope to rehabilitation.

Available court statistics do not differentiate between B & E of dwellings and other places. Only the cases involving a single charge of B & E will be examined. Prison was imposed in the majority of cases: 61 per cent of the time. The average term was seven months; the median term was between three and six months. Over a quarter (27 per cent) of offenders received sentences of less than three months, which made them eligible for intermittent sentences. About 5 per cent received penitentiary terms, hardly any of which were over five years. Suspended sentences were quite common, being granted 29 per cent of the time. Probation was also imposed in the majority of cases (59 per cent), with the average length being fifteen months. Fines (16 per cent) and restitution (13.9 per cent) were used much less often. The average fine was a little over $400, with only 3 per cent of cases involving fines of more than $1,000.

ENDNOTES

1 Allen Edgar is Research Director for Criminal Law at the Judicial Research Centre in Toronto. His research interests include criminal and constitutional law. He is the author of the annual publication *Conduct of a Trial*.
2 Uttering threats, s. 264.1; assault with a weapon or causing bodily harm, s. 267; unlawfully causing bodily harm, s. 269; Sexual assault, s. 271; forcible confinement, s. 279(2); and, failure to comply with probation order, s. 733.1.
3 The Controlled Drugs and Substances Act has more variety. Summary maximums are six months, twelve months, and eighteen months. Indictable maximums are eighteen months, two years, three years, five years, seven years, and ten years.
4 Both first and second degree murder have mandatory life sentences. First degree murder has a minimum period before parole eligibility of twenty-five years; second degree murder a minimum period of ten years.
5 The offence must either be set out in Schedule I (Criminal Code offences) or II (drug offences) of the Corrections and Conditional Release Act, or be a criminal organization offence.

6 Two examples illustrate the creativity of some judges. A young man who had been drinking was convicted of dangerous driving for an accident that killed his two best friends. The judge gave him a suspended sentence when incarceration was almost always imposed for such an offence. One term of his probation was that he perform several hundred hours of community service, going to high schools and describing the event and the effect it had on him and the families of the victims: *Hollinsky* (1995). A less dignified term of probation was imposed in the 1980s by a Toronto judge (none of these sentencing decision were reported) on men convicted of propositioning prostitutes in public. They were required to clean up used condoms from home owners' property near to where to offences occurred.

7 For example, the Ontario Highway Traffic Act, s. 41, provides for an automatic licence suspension for anyone convicted of a Criminal Code alcohol-related driving offence: one year for first offenders, three years for second offenders, life for third offenders (with the right to apply for reinstatement after ten years), life with no hope of reinstatement for fourth and up.

8 This is a polite term used by appellate court to mean the trial judge was wrong.

9 In *Sriskantharanjah*, the accused was charged with the first degree murder of her two children. A joint submission of six years on a guilty plea to manslaughter was made and accepted by the trial judge. The Ontario Court of Appeal held that, in the circumstances of this case, six years was not in the public interest. The accused had been suffering from major depression, isolation, and spousal abuse, presented a low risk of reoffending, and a suitable treatment program was available. The sentence was reduced to two years less a day with three years' probation.

10 S.C. 1991, c. 40, s. 12(1).

11 Ruby (1994), 597.

ADDITIONAL READING

Birkenmayer, A., and S. Besserer. 1997. *Sentencing in Adult Provincial Courts: A Study of Nine Jurisdictions: 1993 and 1994*. Ottawa: Statistics Canada.

Ruby, C. 1994. *Sentencing*. 4th ed. Toronto: Butterworths.

8

Sentencing Trends and Sentencing Disparity[1]

JULIAN V. ROBERTS

This chapter reviews sentencing statistics released by Statistics Canada. Canada has lagged behind other countries with respect to sentencing data. Although we have reliable, annual information on crimes reported to and recorded by the police across the country, sentencing trends are not released on an annual basis. In fact, the data summarized in this chapter derive from the most comprehensive sentencing database for decades. These data should be of interest to many groups working in the area of sentencing. The trends revealed allow us to explore issues such as the utility of the maximum penalty structure, the existence of proportionality in sentencing, and the extent of sentencing disparity.

Introduction

Ask the average Canadian what he or she thinks about sentencing, and the response will be negative. Nationwide surveys over the past twenty years have repeatedly shown that most Canadians believe that sentences should be more severe, particularly for violent offenders (Doob and Roberts 1983; Roberts 1994a). As well, almost half the population believes that excessive leniency is the main reason for a perceived increase in violent crime rates (*Maclean's* 1995). However, few individuals have an accurate idea of sentencing patterns. One reason for this is that systematic sentencing statistics have not been available until fairly recently. Accordingly, the public's impressions of sentencing are based upon the sentences reported by the media – and content analyses of the news media have demonstrated that the dispositions reported are unrepresentative of sentencing trends. As well, the accounts of the sentencing hearings published in newspapers are frequently incomplete, failing to convey the judicial reasoning underlying the sentence (Canadian Sentencing Commission

1987). This explains, in part at least, public dissatisfaction with the sentencing process.

The lack of information about sentencing practice has implications for the judiciary as well. At present, judges in Canada have little concrete idea of statistical patterns within their own province or across the country. Judges appear aware of this impediment to the sentencing process: four out of five judges surveyed by the Canadian Sentencing Commission believed that it would be helpful to have better sentencing statistics (Canadian Sentencing Commission 1987). Judicial knowledge of sentencing patterns, like that of the public, is haphazard, and not founded upon a sound body of data. This may well have important consequences for variability in sentencing patterns, an issue to which we shall return later in this chapter.

But sentencing statistics have recently been made available. The sentencing survey created by the Canadian Centre for Justice Statistics (in Statistics Canada) is producing data that will be of considerable interest to criminal justice professionals, including and especially judges, as well as the news media and the general public. The data reported here come from the Adult Criminal Court Survey located in the Canadian Centre for Justice Statistics. These sentences are drawn exclusively from provincial or lower courts. Cases transferred to superior courts are not yet included in the database; consequently, a small number of the more serious cases of any particular crime (ones which would result in more severe sanctions) are not included. However, since only approximately 3 per cent of cases are transferred to superior courts, this has little impact on the sentencing trends. Unfortunately, the database lacks detailed information on important case characteristics, such as the extent of the offenders' criminal records or the presence of other important aggravating and mitigating factors. Without this critical level of detail, it is impossible to explain variation in sentencing patterns between jurisdictions. Nevertheless, the sentencing database provides good aggregate data on a large (over a million) number of sentencing decisions (see Birkenmayer and Besserer (1997) for further information about the database and additional findings).

Data are drawn from nine jurisdictions[2] across Canada, representing approximately 85 per cent of the cases reported to the police (Canadian Centre for Justice Statistics 1996). The statistics derive from the calendar years 1993 and 1994, the most recent period for which data are available at the time of writing.[3]

Findings

Table 8.1 provides a breakdown of the number of cases, charges, and sanctions for eight principal offence categories. As can be seen, the vast majority (79 per cent) of cases involved only a single charge. For cases in which an offender was sentenced for multiple charges, it is impossible to know which component of the sentence is associated with which charge. For example, an offender convicted of two crimes, such as break and enter and possession of burglary instruments, is sentenced to a one-year term of imprisonment. It is not clear, however, what portion of the sentence was imposed for the break and enter and what portion for the possession of burglary instruments. This makes it impossible to determine the average sentence for a specific offence such as break and enter. For this reason, the sentencing patterns presented in this chapter involve only the cases in which an offender was sentenced for a single criminal charge.

Although crimes of violence are more likely to be reported by the news media, they accounted for a minority (17 per cent) of all sentenced cases. Property crimes (28 per cent of all the cases) constituted the single largest offence category, followed by motor vehicle offences (23 per cent), and offences against the administration of justice[4] (15 per cent). The other offence categories accounted for the remaining 33 per cent of cases. A small number of less serious offences made up a large percentage of convictions. Five specific offences (impaired driving (section 253 of the Criminal Code); failing to appear in court (section 145); simple assault (section 266); failing to comply with a judicial order (section 740); and theft under $1,000 (this monetary limit has

TABLE 8.1
Sentencing Survey Overview
Number of Cases, Charges, Sanctions
(All Jurisdictions)

Offence category	No. of cases	No. of charges	No. of sanctions	Percentage charge	Percentage multiple charge
Person	91,939	117,234	203,935	73	27
Property	151,771	247,159	418,909	72	28
Motor vehicle	126,908	149,233	290,753	83	17
Morals	10,506	11,762	16,402	89	11
Administration of justice	82,997	165,755	233,264	83	17
Other Criminal Code	10,106	17,255	27,677	84	16
Drugs	33,888	44,470	63,623	85	15
Other federal statutes	43,567	67,812	76,694	90	10
Total	551,682	820,606	1,331,183	79	21

subsequently been raised to $5,000)) accounted for almost half (42 per cent) of all charges. Impaired driving was the single most frequently occurring offence, accounting for fully 13 per cent of all charges. This finding is important because it identifies the high-volume offences that are clogging the courts. Some of these offenders could have been candidates for diversion programs.

The numbers of sentences imposed also contain a lesson. Over the one-year period covered by the database, there were 3,114 convictions for sexual assault. This represents a very small percentage of all incidents of sexual assault recorded by the police. In the year preceding these statistics, the police recorded almost 40,000 reports of sexual assault, a figure which itself represents a small percentage of all crimes of sexual assault actually committed. The Violence Against Women Survey conducted by Statistics Canada found that only approximately one incident in ten was ever reported to the police (Statistics Canada 1993). In short, a sentence is imposed on a very small number of offenders for this particular crime. This finding supports the view that the sentencing process can play only a very limited role in preventing crime. If such a small percentage of offenders is actually sentenced, whether the sentence imposed is six months' or six years' imprisonment will have little impact on the crime rate. Although the point is illustrated here by using data for sexual assault, it holds true for other crimes and other jurisdictions. The leading British sentencing authority noted that judges in that country deal with no more than 3 per cent of all crimes. Andrew Ashworth concluded that 'if criminal justice policy expects sentencing to perform a major preventive function, it is looking in the wrong direction' (1995, 23). The same can be said for Canada.[5]

Distribution of Sanctions

Table 8.2 provides a breakdown of all sanctions imposed for the eight offence categories. As can be seen, overall, 1.6 sanctions were imposed per charge. When the public learn of sentences of imprisonment, they are seldom aware that whatever the term of custody imposed, it is frequently accompanied by some other sanction. In almost half the cases of imprisonment judges imposed a second sentence as well, and in four cases out of five this additional sanction consisted of a period of probation to follow the period of imprisonment. The warrant of the court does not necessarily end with the expiry of the term of custody.

As the data in Table 8.2 indicate, a fine is the most frequently imposed sanction, handed down in just over half of the cases. This finding reflects the fact that only a small minority of offenders sentenced have been convicted of serious crimes (see above). A term of probation was imposed in one-third of all

TABLE 8.2
All Sanctions Imposed
(All Jurisdictions)

Offence category	Prison (%)	Probation (%)	Fine (%)	Restitution (%)	Other (%)	Average no. sanctions per case
Against the person	28	68	29	2	51	1.8
Property	27	49	39	13	42	1.7
Motor vehicle	20	17	80	—	81.8	2.0
Morals	13	28	47	—	47.6	1.4
Administration of justice	47	23	38	2	27.8	1.4
Other Criminal Code	18	37	53	—	39.3	1.5
Drugs	26	23	58	—	29.5	1.4
Other federal statutes	4	3	91	—	10.1	1.1
Total	26	34	54	4	47.2	1.6

charges, while approximately one-quarter (26 per cent) of the charges resulted in a term of imprisonment. Table 8.2 also reveals that offences against the administration of justice attracted the highest incarceration rate: 47 per cent of offenders in this category were imprisoned, although for relatively brief periods of time, in comparison to sentence lengths imposed for crimes of violence. Property crimes and crimes of violence were equally likely to result in the imposition of a term of imprisonment.

Use of Imprisonment as a Sanction

Figure 8.1 shows the offences that generated an incarceration rate of 50 per cent or higher. There were eighteen such crimes. The presence of some offences in Figure 8.1 may provoke surprise among some readers. Why, for example, does a crime such as possession of burglary instruments (subsection 351(1)) generate a higher incarceration rate than sexual assault (section 271)? This may appear to constitute a violation of the principle of proportionality, according to which the severity of punishments should be directly proportional to the seriousness of the crimes for which they are imposed. Thus offenders convicted of sexual assault should be more likely to be incarcerated than offenders convicted of possessing instruments for the purposes of burglary, since the former offence is generally perceived to be more serious than the latter. The principle of proportionality has long been a part of the sentencing process in Canada and elsewhere (see Ashworth (1995); von Hirsch (1976), and, as a result of the recent sentencing reform bill, it is now part of the statement of the purpose and principles of sentencing (see Chapter 3 by Roberts and von Hirsch).

The answer to this paradox with respect to the use of incarceration may reside in the criminal records of the offenders. Research has shown that property offenders have significantly more extensive criminal histories than violent offenders (Campbell 1993). Offenders convicted of possessing burglary instruments are more likely to have previous, related convictions than offenders convicted of sexual assault. As well, burglars are more likely to be perceived by judges as 'career criminals' or professional offenders. Both of these grounds are likely to trigger a punitive response, and this may explain the high incarceration rate for burglary, relative to other offences, such as sexual assault.

FIGURE 8.1
Cases with One Charge: Prison as the Most Severe Sanction
(Offences with at Least 50% Incarceration Rate; Nine Jurisdictions; 1993 and 1994)

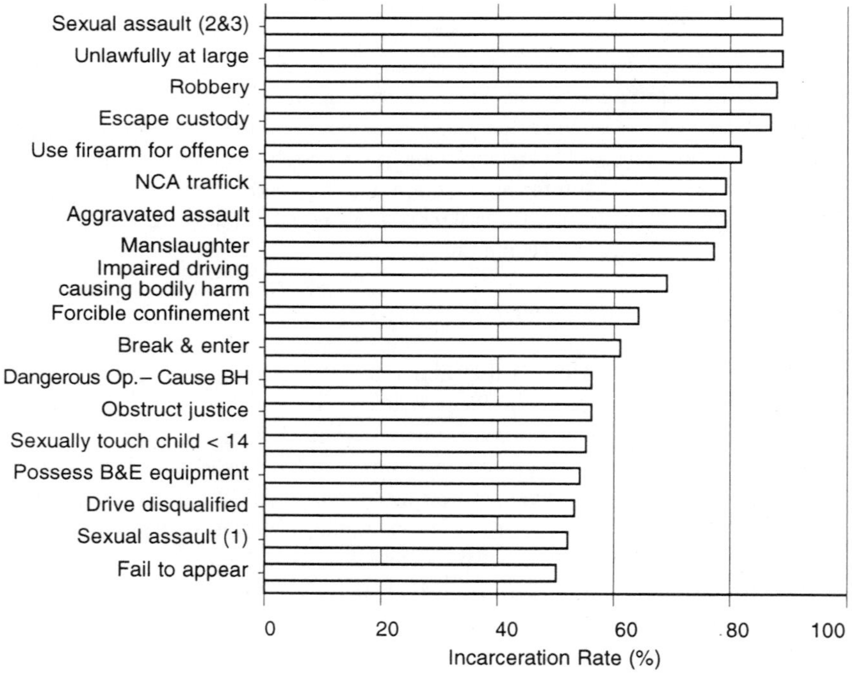

However, other evidence in the sentencing database demonstrates the existence of the principle of proportionality. Offences with a tiered penalty structure provide a good test of this principle. For example, the Criminal Code defines three levels of assault, based upon the seriousness of the harm inflicted. The least serious level (section 266) generated an incarceration rate of 20 per cent. The intermediate level of seriousness (assault with a weapon or causing bodily harm; section 267) had an incarceration rate of 48 per cent, while the most serious level (aggravated assault; section 268) had an incarceration rate of 79 per cent. Thus the seriousness of the offence was clearly a factor in determining the incarceration rate, a finding which is consistent with the principle of proportionality. The same phenomenon was observed for another tiered offence: the first level of sexual assault generated an incarceration rate of 52 per cent while the higher levels of sexual assault combined had an incarceration rate of 89 per cent. The seriousness of the offence also had an impact on the average length of prison sentence imposed. Thus the average prison term imposed for aggravated assault was 440 days, more than three times the average term for simple assault.

The next table (Table 8.3) provides a list of common offences, together with the number of cases per offence, the incarceration rate, the number of offenders who were imprisoned, the median[6] sentence of imprisonment, and the longest term that was imposed during the time period included in the database.

A report of the National Crime Prevention Council of Canada in 1997 noted that Canada has always had a high incarceration rate compared to other Western nations. Comparing international incarceration rates is complicated and analyses must taken into account many factors, including the crime rate and charging practices. Nevertheless, the sentencing database provides indirect support for the hypothesis that Canada imprisons a number of offenders who could be dealt with in the community. The data presented in Table 8.3 show that significant numbers of offenders were sentenced to prison for crimes that are not particularly serious. For example, 528 individuals were incarcerated for possession of a firearm, 1,363 for possession of stolen goods under $1,000, fully 7,353 for theft under $1,000, 1,665 for mischief under $1,000, and 3,455 persons were incarcerated for simple possession of a narcotic.

These crimes may not be trivial, but do they really require the incarceration of the offender, even if there are previous convictions? Is there no community-based sanction that will suffice to accomplish the goals of sentencing as specified by the statement of the purpose of sentencing contained in section 718 of the Criminal Code? While these offenders were detained for short periods of time, they still cost on average $127 a day while in detention. Several provi-

TABLE 8.3
Selected Offences: Prison as the Most Severe Sanction in Case

				Prison sentences (days)		
Offence category	Number of cases	Prison sentences	Incar-ceration rate (%)	Median	Longest sentence	Maximum penalty
Robbery	1,483	1,304	88	480	3,650	Life
Sexual assault (2&3)	57	51	89	720	4,745	14 yrs
Sexual assault (1)	2,163	1,134	52	120	3,285	10 yrs
Assault (aggravated)	408	323	79	300	2,920	14 yrs
Assault (with weapon)	5,725	2,777	49	90	2,190	10 yrs
Assault (simple)	41,799	8,435	20	30	1,095	5 yrs
Assault police	2,034	813	40	30	730	5 yrs
Sexual touching of child under 14	748	413	55	120	1,825	10 yrs
Careless use of firearm	2,827	573	20	60	1,460	10 yrs
Possession of firearm	2,292	528	23	30	1,095	5 yrs
Break & enter	9,363	5,693	61	120	2,190	Life
Possess b&e equipment	309	167	54	60	913	10 yrs
Possess stolen goods > $ 1,000	3,210	1,482	46	90	2,190	10 yrs
Possess stolen goods < $ 1,000	4,443	1,363	31	30	730	2 yrs
Theft > $ 1,000	3,702	1,697	46	90	1,740	10 yrs
Theft < $ 1,000	37,056	7,353	20	30	730	2 yrs
Credit card theft/ forgery	1,562	445	28	45	913	10 yrs
Forgery	1,890	647	34	60	1,095	14 yrs
Personation	1,134	274	24	30	1,095	10 yrs
Fraud > $ 1,000	3,203	1,211	38	90	2,555	10 yrs
Fraud < $ 1,000	3,404	886	26	30	730	2 yrs
False pretenses	2,591	707	27	30	900	10 yrs
Mischief > $ 1,000	2,292	426	19	30	390	10 yrs
Mischief < $ 1,000	12,495	1,665	13	30	730	2 yrs
Impaired driving causing bodily harm	354	243	69	90	913	10 yrs
Impaired driving – over .08	87,337	14,118	16	21	1,825	5 yrs
Impaired driving – refuse sample	4,336	739	17	21	1,095	5 yrs

TABLE 8.3 *(continued)*
Selected Offences: Prison as the Most Severe Sanction in Case

				Prison sentences (days)		
Offence category	Number of cases	Prison sentences	Incar-ceration rate (%)	Median	Longest sentence	Maximum penalty
Dangerous operation	2,655	600	23	60	1,640	5 yrs
Drive disqualified	9,271	4,957	53	30	730	2 yrs
Obstruct justice	675	377	56	30	730	10 yrs
Give false information	2,225	368	17	30	365	5 yrs
Obstruct police	6,088	1,282	21	30	365	5 yrs
Escape custody	1,111	971	87	60	730	2 yrs
Unlawfully at large	4,361	3,882	89	30	730	2 yrs
Fail to appear	31,676	15,946	50	30	730	2 yrs
Fail to comply	20,278	9,097	45	30	180	6 mos.
NCA traffick	4,013	3,187	79	120	4,380	Life
NCA possession	23,160	3,455	15	30	2,190	7 yrs
Total	343,730	99,589	29			

Source: Julian V. Roberts and Andy Birkenmayer. 1997. 'Sentencing in Canada: Recent Statistical Trends,' *Canadian Journal of Criminology*, 39:459–82.

sions of the Sentencing Reform Act are aimed at reducing the use of incarceration for such offenders. These data show that this is an important policy goal for the courts in this country.

Relationship between Maximum Penalty Structure and Sentencing Trends

Although each offence in the Criminal Code carries a maximum penalty, these are almost never imposed. There are two principal reasons for the discrepancies between potential and actual sentences. First, the maxima are generally very high, and second, they fail to reflect current perceptions of the relative seriousness of the crimes for which they can be imposed. Offences of differing seriousness carry the same maximum penalty, and most maxima derive from the last century, and public perceptions of the seriousness of various offences have evolved considerably since that time. Accordingly, the maximum penalty structure does not serve as a guide for judges as to the relative seriousness of different crimes. As well, the maxima are inconsistent. For example, selling defective stores to Her Majesty carries the same maximum penalty as sexual assault with a weapon. Since the maxima are unrealistically high, they may well encourage false expectations among members of the public.

Both problems can be illustrated by the current sentencing database, as can be seen in Table 8.3. The crime of break and enter (private dwelling; paragraph 348(1)(d)) illustrates the first problem. Although the maximum penalty for this crime is life imprisonment, the theoretical maximum bears no relation to current practice. Almost a quarter of offenders convicted of break and enter received a noncustodial sanction, and of those who were imprisoned, the median term of custody was only four months. No sentence for break and enter exceeded three years; fully 95 per cent of prison terms for this offence were under two years. Other offences show the same pattern: trafficking in contravention of the Narcotics Control Act is also punishable by life imprisonment, yet the median custodial term was four months.[7]

The second problem can be illustrated by comparing sentencing patterns for different offences. Sexual assault (section 271) carries a maximum penalty of ten years,[8] yet it is actually punished more severely than break and enter, a life imprisonment offence.[9] Thus when sentencing offenders, judges are following contemporary perceptions of the seriousness of various crimes, rather than the hierarchy of seriousness established by the maximum penalty structure. Clearly, if the maximum penalty structure is to guide judges (and the public) with respect to the relative seriousness of different crimes, a complete revision is necessary.[10] It is to be hoped that such a revision will be part of the next stage of sentencing reform, now that Bill C-41 has become law.

Use of Probation

A period of probation was the most severe sentence imposed in one-quarter of the cases in the database. In fact, over half of the single charge cases involving offences against the person received a term of probation as the most severe sanction. Probation was less likely to be used for crimes involving property: only 40 per cent of property offenders received a probation term. There are two explanations for this rather surprising outcome. First, over two-thirds of the crimes against the person category were accounted for by the first level of assault, some incidents of which are relatively minor. Second, criminal record may well once again be exercising a strong influence on sentencing patterns. Since property offenders are more likely to have previous convictions than violent offenders, the former are more likely to have been given a period of probation in the past. This may discourage judges from imposing probation on this second (or third) occasion, hence the lower rate of probation as the most severe sanction for property offenders.

Harassment charges and making indecent phone calls generated the highest percentage of cases in which probation was imposed as the most severe sanction. Approximately two-thirds of the cases of uttering threats resulted in a term of probation as the most severe sanction. The average duration of probation orders was fourteen months. As with the use of incarceration, the severity of probation sentences increased with the seriousness of the offence of conviction. Thus the average length of probation terms for the first, least serious level of assault was fourteen months, while the average length of probation terms for aggravated assault was twenty months.

Use of Fines

As noted above, a fine was imposed in just over half (54 per cent) of cases. In fact, a fine was the most severe sanction in almost half (45 per cent) of the single charge cases. Table 8.4 presents a breakdown of the use of fines across different offence categories. As would be expected, the offence category, 'Other Federal Statutes,' which includes a diverse collection of regulatory crimes, had the highest percentage of cases in which a monetary fine was the most severe sanction (91 per cent of cases). For regulatory offences such as these, a fine is the usual sanction. The category with the next highest use of fines was motor vehicle offences: 70 per cent of these cases resulted in the imposition of a fine as the most serious sanction. Taken together, these two offence categories (regulatory crimes and motor vehicle offences) accounted for over half of the fines imposed. The category of offences against the person resulted in the least frequent use of a fine as the most severe sanction (see Table 8.4). The average fine imposed over the period covered by this survey was $430.

Sentencing Disparity

Everybody has his own point of view, and everybody has a different one at different times ... Thus we see the fate of a citizen change several times in going from one court to another, and we see that the lives of the poor wretches are at the mercy of false reasonings of the momentary churning of a judge's humors.

Caesare Beccaria, *On Crimes and Punishments*

One of the principal justifications for sentencing guidelines is to remedy the problem of unwarranted disparity in sentencing. If sentencing disparity exists,

TABLE 8.4
The Use of Fines

	Number of cases	All fines imposed N	All fines imposed %	Most serious sanction N	Most serious sanction %
Against person	67,242	19,230	29	10,684	16
Property	109,916	43,345	39	30,856	28
Motor vehicle	105,855	85,134	80	74,500	70
Morals	9,381	4,445	47	3,842	41
Administration of justice	68,897	26,071	38	22,873	33
Other Criminal Code	8,529	4,547	53	3,745	44
Drug	28,915	16,631	58	14,612	51
Other federal statutes	39,114	35,580	91	35,062	90
Total	437,849	234,983	54	196,174	45

then guidelines are necessary to promote greater uniformity in sentencing. If sentencing disparity is not a problem, reformers should concentrate their attention on other issues, such as the excessive use of imprisonment as a sanction. As the quotation by Beccaria, the famous eighteenth-century philosopher, shows, speculation about sentencing disparity has been around for some time. In this chapter we review the research on sentencing patterns in Canada. First, however, it is necessary to touch upon the definitional problems surrounding the concept of unwarranted disparity.

Defining Unwarranted Sentencing Disparity

Intuitively, we all have an idea of what is meant by 'unwarranted disparity,' but after a little reflection it will become apparent that disparity of sentence can have several meanings. Consider an example that many people would regard as evidence of disparity. Two offenders, co-accuseds convicted of break and enter, are sentenced to one year and five years' imprisonment, respectively. But if this is evidence of unwarranted disparity, which sentence is disparate? Is it the shorter term or the longer term? Perhaps we need more information; perhaps knowing the average custodial sentence for this offence will tell us something.

Supposing the average is one year in prison. Is the five-year term the disparate sentence? Perhaps. But what if the offender who received this sentence was ten years older than the other individual, largely responsible for the planning of the crime, had a long criminal record, showed no remorse, and had pleaded not guilty (but was subsequently convicted)? Now the sentences, while still arithmetically disparate, no longer seem unreasonable and most people – although not all – would regard the difference as appropriate and principled. So one obvious point to bear in mind is that we frequently need more information than simply the difference between two sentences imposed upon offenders convicted of the same Criminal Code offence. Before examining the evidence for the existence of sentencing disparity, it is worth noting the results from systematic surveys of criminal justice professionals.

Perceptions of Sentencing Disparity

Judges are the most important participants in the sentencing process. We might expect most judges to deny the existence of unwarranted disparity; to respond otherwise is to make a statement that some may interpret to question their professional competence. In the only comprehensive survey of the views of the judiciary conducted in this country, over four hundred judges were asked: 'Do you think that there is unwarranted variation in sentences being handed down in Canada?' Over 60 per cent of respondents conceded that there is a fair amount of variation from judge to judge. Only 26 per cent endorsed the position that 'the variation that does exist is not significant' (Research Staff of the Canadian Sentencing Commission 1988). From this it seems reasonable to infer that most judges are willing to concede that sentencing disparity exists. Crown and defence counsel across the country were asked a slightly different question by the Sentencing Commission: 'Do you think that there is unwarranted variation in sentences?' Usually these professional groups have strikingly divergent views on matters relating to sentencing. On this occasion, however, both groups responded similarly: 40 per cent endorsed the view that 'there is a great deal of unwarranted variation.' Fifty-seven per cent indicated that there is some unwarranted variation. Only 3 per cent perceived no unwarranted disparity. Lawyers actively engaged in the sentencing process on a daily basis also appear to be aware of the problem.

One of the goals of any sentencing system should be to foster the perception among offenders upon whom sentences are imposed that these dispositions are just. It would be naive to expect all sentenced offenders to accept their particular sentences, yet if there is widespread cynicism toward the criminal justice system we can never hope to accomplish one of its primary goals: rehabilitation. It is important, therefore, to know something of the perceptions of offenders. What little we do know comes from two surveys, one of general inmates and the other of Native offenders. The results of both suggest that the perception of disparate treatment is widespread. Seventy per cent of Native inmates surveyed shared the opinion that different sentences would be imposed by different judges. A second, independent survey of inmates incarcerated in British Columbia generated similar results. Fully 98 per cent believed that some judges send offenders to prison more frequently than others. The authors of the report succinctly note: 'Judges did not emerge with the offenders' confidence.' And further: 'it appears offenders do not operate under the assumption that the judge is a neutral, objective arbiter, but instead they ascribe to him or her idiosyncratic decision-making and sentence formation.' The target population most affected by sentencing thus believes that unwarranted sentencing disparity is a reality and not just a perception.

Finally, in this context it is important to note the conclusion of the most important review of sentencing in Canada conducted to date. The Canadian Sentencing Commission (1987), reviewing the evidence upon disparity, concluded: 'These findings, and others like them, taken in the context in which sentencing occurs in this country, strongly suggest that there is considerable unwarranted variation in sentencing' (77).

Research on Sentencing Disparity

Empirical research on sentencing disparity has been accumulating in this country and in other jurisdictions for some time now. In fact, the first empirical study of sentencing disparity appeared in 1919. Everson studied over 100,000 sentencing decisions in New York City and found considerable variation in the severity of penalties imposed. He concluded that sentences reflected 'to an astonishing extent' the personality of the individual judge (Everson 1919, 20). In another early study, researchers concluded that 'a prisoner who was found guilty ... will have about three chances out of ten of going to jail or penitentiary if sentenced by Judges 1 or 2, but will have six chances out of ten of being given some form of imprisonment if sentenced for the same crime and under the same circumstances by Judge 3' (see Gaudet (1938)). These studies used relatively unsophisticated statistical analyses. Since then, however, a great deal of research on sentencing disparity has accumulated, much of it in America. The general finding is supportive of the earlier research. Michael Tonry, one of the world's leading sentencing experts, has written that: 'Research in many countries documents the existence of disparities in sentencing that cannot be accounted for by reference to the characteristics of offenders, or the circumstances of offences' (Tonry 1996, 177).

The empirical literature on sentencing patterns has addressed the issue of disparity using a number of different methods. As will be seen, none of these alone provides incontrovertible evidence of unprincipled disparity in sentencing. In order to know whether (and to what extent) sentencing disparity exists, it is necessary to examine all types of research, to see if a consistent pattern emerges. Let us begin with the most frequently employed way of studying disparity: by examining sentencing patterns across different regions of the country.

Regional Variation in Sentencing Patterns

A significant degree of variation emerged between provinces. The extent of variation depended on the offence. Thus the range in custody rates for theft under $1,000 did not vary greatly, ranging from 4 per cent in Newfoundland to 26 per cent in the Yukon. This may well be explained by variation in legally relevant but unmeasured case characteristics. Another explanation of the fairly uniform custody rates for this offence is that the presence of a monetary limit on the value of stolen property places a constraint on the variability in offence seriousness. Other offences generated far more variation from jurisdiction to jurisdiction. Incarceration rates for break and enter ranged from 37 per cent in the Northwest Territories to 78 per cent in Prince Edward Island. Table 8.5 provides incarceration rates and average terms of imprisonment for eleven high-frequency offences.

In the absence of case-specific information – such as the extent of injuries inflicted, the value of the property stolen, or the offender's criminal history – it is not possible to state whether this variation reflects legally relevant variables or unprincipled variation in sentencing. In fact, it would be imprudent to infer that variation in incarceration rates for a crime such as burglary reflects differential punitiveness across the country. The higher incarceration rate in Ontario might reflect the fact that more cases of break and enter in that province occurred in an urban setting and resulted in greater loss to the victim than burglaries in less affluent rural settings. This would explain a more severe sentencing pattern in Ontario in a principled way; such an explanation cannot be verified at present, however, as the database does not include information on the value of the property stolen.

This approach to research has been criticized. If differences emerge between two jurisdictions, if the average sentence for assault is eighteen months in Toronto and six months in Orillia, is this really evidence of disparity of treatment? Does it conclusively establish that the same offence results in a much more severe sentence in one part of the province? Critics will argue that the pattern of offending may be different, that offenders with more extensive criminal histories may gravitate to certain areas, or that there are obscure but perfectly legal explanations for the discrepancy. Consider crimes involving loss of property. Perhaps the average break and enter in Toronto results in greater property loss (or damage) than the average break and enter in a small town. This would result in a discrepancy in the severity of sentences for this crime imposed in

TABLE 8.5
Incarceration Rates and Average Prison Sentences by Jurisdiction

Offence category	Nfld.	P.E.I.	N.S.	Que.	Ont.	Sask.	Alta.	Yukon	N.W.T.	Total
				Percentage of cases with a prison sentence						
Assault (2)	50	43	32	19	59	32	45	61	77	49
Assault (1)	10	39	8	5	25	22	16	23	26	20
Break & enter	55	78	46	33	72	47	56	33	37	61
Possess stolen goods (UK)	18	16	16	12	43	29	25	43	18	39
Theft < $1,000	4	9	7	20	26	9	11	27	24	20
Mischief < $1,000	14	16	4	9	19	7	6	8	11	13
Impaired driving – over .08	20	75	4	8	23	12	12	29	20	16
Drive disqualified	42	14	16	36	78	20	41	65	30	53
Fail to appear	51	38	22	24	62	22	16	47	37	50
Fail to comply	50	63	31	28	62	25	28	57	21	45
NCA possession	5	3	3	9	20	6	5	6	2	15
Total for all offences	19	42	10	15	34	17	19	31	25	26
				Average prison sentence (days)						
Assault (2)	61	167	147	164	115	195	161	119	200	132
Assault (1)	56	20	59	83	46	97	66	66	78	51
Break & enter	92	270	337	275	190	245	236	70	171	210
Possess stolen goods (UK)	44	11	73	114	83	123	111	53	45	85
Theft < $1,000	14	36	41	63	46	78	66	27	52	47
Mischief < $1,000	38	17	33	67	38	66	55	38	54	44
Impaired driving – over .08	47	10	44	55	45	34	54	61	45	46

TABLE 8.5 *(continued)*
Incarceration Rates and Average Prison Sentences by Jurisdiction

Offence category	Nfld.	P.E.I.	N.S.	Que.	Ont.	Sask.	Alta.	Yukon	N.W.T.	Total
					Average prison sentence (days)					
Drive disqualified	53	85	29	51	47	79	67	30	30	53
Fail to appear	22	17	39	32	32	37	33	23	26	32
Fail to comply	27	32	37	53	39	49	40	29	36	42
NCA possession	29	9	37	48	39	42	55	25	14	41
Total for all offences	48	33	101	71	54	85	80	54	84	60

Note: Only includes offences in which each jurisdiction had at least ten cases

the two communities. But the variation would be perfectly justifiable, since the extent of harm inflicted is greater in Toronto and the sentence imposed should accordingly be more severe.

It is certainly true that some of the research that involves making comparisons between jurisdictions or courts or judges can overestimate the extent of unwarranted disparity. Researchers may fail to measure some legally relevant variable and simply attribute variation in sentencing to extralegal factors, such as the personality of the judge. Some more careful research, which has measured a larger number of variables, finds greater consistency in sentencing. Don Andrews and his colleagues, for example, conducted research in which they attempted to account for variation in sentencing severity. By the use of careful statistical controls, they found that far more variation in sentencing could be attributable to legal, rather than extralegal factors. Other researchers (e.g., Brantingham (1985)) have found similar outcomes. This line of research underscores the importance of measuring as many variables as possible before attributing variation to extralegal factors. However, it does not undermine the general conclusion that sentences do vary as a function either of the personality of the judge or his or her sentencing objective.

If sentencing disparity exists, is it unwarranted? The attribution of variation uncovered in this fashion remains problematic for the reasons noted above. However, it is unlikely that case characteristics alone could account for these differences. In order to explain this pattern of results without resorting to the concept of unwarranted disparity requires an explanation that lacks parsimony and plausibility. Why, for example, would the most serious cases of any particular offence gravitate to one province? These data remain highly suggestive that unwarranted disparity exists across Canada. They also underscore the necessity of developing a national database that would permit unequivocal attributions about the source of such variations.

Experimental Studies of Sentencing Disparity

The difficulty with cross-jurisdictional comparisons is that while we observe significant variation, we are not sure what is responsible. The only way we can be certain that variation is due to differences between judges rather than legally relevant differences between cases is to conduct an experiment. Of course we cannot, in real life, randomly assign cases to judges, but some researchers have done the next best thing: they have given the same case to judges in what is known as a sentencing simulation. Perhaps the best-known study in this tradition is a classic experiment carried out by Ted Palys and Stan Divorski (1986). The study employed over two hundred provincial court judges attending judicial conferences. Each judge read descriptions of a series of cases which contained information relating to the offence and the offender (e.g., presentence reports, victim impact statements, and so on). After reading the case descriptions, the judges were asked to assign a sentence. Since the cases were exactly the same for all judges, any differences in sentencing patterns must be attributable to the judges and not to other factors.

Palys and Divorski found substantial variation. For example, in one case of armed robbery, sentences ranged from a suspended sentence to thirteen years in prison. Another armed robbery case generated a range of sentence from eight months to thirteen years. For a case of assault causing bodily harm, the range was a $500 fine to five years' imprisonment. These differences – unlike those generated by cross-jurisdictional comparisons – have to be due to the 'judge' factor and not to characteristics of the case (such as the extent of the offender's criminal record), for all judges read exactly the same set of facts.

There are, however, some interpretational difficulties (although of a different kind) with this research method as well. Several aspects of a sentencing simulation set it apart from sentencing in the courtroom. In a simulation there are no consequences for an offender (or for the judge, for that matter, in terms of a possible appeal). The amount of information at the disposal of the judge in a simulation is a fraction of that which is encountered in a sentencing hearing. With the exception of routine cases in a high-volume court, decisions made by judges in court usually take much longer than the decisions in a sentencing experiment. Finally, the judges who participated in these simulations were aware that they were in an experimental study, and this awareness may have changed their reactions. In short, 'sentencing' in a simulation is a bird of a very different plumage than sentencing in court. According to this criticism, the disparity that arises in a simulation is in no way representative of the actual amount of disparity in 'real life.' Critics of the sentencing simulation would thus argue that this approach overestimates the amount of disparity that actually exists. The question then arises: Can we extrapolate the conclusion that sentencing disparity exists in courts on the basis of the results of simulation experiments? Probably not. But these experiments complement the research taking other approaches.

Qualitative Research

The qualitative research category encompasses virtues of both the first two. Here the attempt is to assign the variation in actual sentencing patterns to factors relevant to the case and factors relating to the judge. The most important Canadian study in this area was conducted by John Hogarth in 1971. Although not directly addressing the topic of disparity per se, Hogarth's research sheds much light upon the problem. Having gathered a great deal of information about both judges and actual cases, Hogarth set about testing two competing models of sentencing. One, called the 'Black Box' model, suggests that what is important in explaining sentence variation is critical information relevant to the case. This information would include aspects of the offence (seriousness, number of victims, number of counts, plea) as well as the offender (age, sex, marital status, criminal history). The competing model of sentencing attempts to explain sentences by reference to the judge and his or her perceptions of the case.

When Hogarth compared the relative ability of the two models to explain sentencing variation, he found the so-called Black Box model to be vastly inferior. Or, put more simply, knowledge about the judge and the judge's attitudes was more relevant than knowledge of the facts of the case. To quantify the effect, we can add the following. On average, the facts of the cases accounted for less than 10 per cent of the variation in sentencing practices. However, the judges' perceptions and sentencing philosophies explained about 50 per cent of the variance in sentence length. Hogarth concluded: 'It appears from the analysis that one can explain more about sentencing by knowing a few things about the judge than by knowing a great deal about the facts of the case' (350).

As with the other categories of research, there is a consistent pattern here, too. Other studies adopting this perspective have found it hard to account for much variation in sentencing without considering the personality of the judge. Several studies from the U.S. (e.g., Sutton 1978) have generated similar results. Of course this approach also has its critics. It has been argued that this kind of analysis fails to take into account important variables that may be legally relevant in terms of explaining variation in sentencing. A great deal of consistency in sentencing could remain obscured in variables that were not measured by the researchers. This is a recurrent problem in research using this methodological approach: it is generally impossible to gather information on all potentially relevant factors (legal as well as extralegal) and yet without doing so, much of the variation in sentencing that remains unexplained is also enigmatic. Does it represent unwarranted variation or is it legally justifiable but caused by factors unnoticed by the researchers? While this criticism is a cogent one, it cannot explain away all the results.

Summary of Sentencing Disparity Research

The sentencing trends emerging from the latest Statistics Canada survey are consistent with previous research, and there seems little doubt that a degree of unwarranted disparity exists in the Canadian criminal justice system. The problem of sentencing disparity in Canada has been approached by researchers from a number of different directions. Each approach has its own particular drawbacks, but taken together the results have been consistent, not only across methodologies but also over time. The most recent Canadian data show substantial cross-jurisdictional variation, in keeping with the results of a study on sentencing disparity from the U.S. that appeared in the Archives of Psychology over half a century ago.

Is it really surprising that the bulk of research evidence suggests that sentencing disparity is a problem in Canada? After all, over 1,300 individuals are asked to make complex decisions without a great deal of guidance. This is not a criticism of judges. Take an example closer to (my) home: consider grading practices at university. Several sections of a course have different instructors. The major component of the course grade is a final paper, twenty pages in length. If one professor assigns a grade of 70 per cent to a particular assignment, what are the chances that the paper would receive the same mark if it had been evaluated by other instructors?

Although he was writing of another time and another place, it seems that Beccaria was on the mark when he described the problem of sentencing disparity. We end this chapter with a quotation from David Daubney, the member of Parliament who headed the 1988 House of Commons Committee on Sentencing and Parole, which reported in 1988. Daubney noted, 'Clearly, the kind of disparity we're seeing is unacceptable and doesn't do anything for the public image of the criminal justice system' (*Ottawa Citizen,* 31 October 1987). With regard to sentencing disparity, little would appear to have changed since Beccaria's time.

Conclusions

Although they are the most systematic data ever available in Canada, the sentencing statistics contained in the Canadian Centre for Justice Statistics database are in many respects only a beginning. Several steps need to be taken to generate a more comprehensive sentencing database. There are clear limits to the utility of an aggregate database. With regard to the issues of disparity and proportionality, it is imperative that additional information relating to the characteristics of the case and important mitigating and aggravating factors be incorporated into the database. It is particularly important that criminal history information be incorporated, in light of the fact that, after the seriousness of the crime, it is the most important determinant of the nature and quantum of punishment.

If comprehensive sentencing statistics, complete with important aggravating and mitigating factors, were available, they could form the basis of an advisory sentencing guidelines system. Judges across the country would be able to access sentencing patterns for their courthouse, their province/territory, and for the country as a whole. The benefits in terms of reducing disparity would be considerable, and if the database was purely advisory, there would be no opposition from those members of the judiciary for whom the concept of 'sentencing guidelines' is anathema. The suggestion of a computerized information system is not new; it was first mooted in the late 1970s and two computerized information systems were implemented on a trial basis in the 1980s (Doob 1986).

The news media, too, have an important stake in access to systematic sentencing statistics. At the present, when newspapers report a particular sentence, there is no framework within which to place the disposition, in order to determine whether it was too harsh, too severe, or about right. The only available context is the maximum penalty which, as has been demonstrated here, is no guide to current practice. In fact, two factors work to convey a misleading impression of sentencing practices. First, the sentences reported by the news media tend to be those that are unusual or newsworthy in some respect. This usually means that the sentence was lenient in light of the seriousness of the crime. The Canadian Sentencing Commission found that the manslaughter cases reported by the media were the most serious instances of this crime, particularly those that did not result in a severe sentence (see Roberts (1995c)). Public reaction to sentences reported in the media is founded in the context of a maximum penalty which is far above the average sentence. If sentences reported in the media were placed in the context of the average sentence for the crime in question, public reaction to the sentencing process might be rather different.

Finally, we should not lose sight of a clear link between sentencing statistics and sentencing reform. Bill C-41 introduced a number of significant reforms to the sentencing process in Canada, not the least of which was the creation of a new disposition, the conditional sentence (see other chapters in this volume). An important objective of these reforms was to reduce Canada's excessive reliance on imprisonment as a sanction. The only way that we can know whether this goal has been achieved in a principled way, or whether there has been any improvement at all, is through a careful examination of sentencing statistics. The sentencing database should play a critical role in any evaluation of Bill C-41 undertaken.

A number of important questions will need to be answered in the years to come. First, has there been a decrease in the use of sentences of imprisonment? With regard to the conditional sentence, has it generated a reduction in the use of incarceration, or has it resulted in a 'widening of the net,' drawing more, not fewer, offenders into custody? For what kinds of cases is this new disposition being used? Have important decisions of the provincial courts of appeal been followed by trial court judges? The statement of purpose and principles contained in the bill and now found in sections 718 through 718.2 of the Criminal Code was designed to promote greater uniformity of approach in the sentencing process. Has it in fact reduced the amount of variability in sentencing? We can only hope that within a few years we shall have a sentencing database in place that will be adequate to answer these and other important questions.

ENDNOTES

1 This chapter draws upon findings reported in Roberts and Birkenmayer (1997). I would like to thank Andy Birkenmayer from the Canadian Centre for Justice Statistics for his assistance in generating these statistics.

2 Newfoundland and Labrador, Prince Edward Island, Nova Scotia, Quebec, Ontario, Alberta, Saskatchewan, the Yukon, and the Northwest Territories.

3 Since these data were collected before Bill C-41 was proclaimed (September 1996), we do not have information on the new sanction, the conditional sentence, which is described and discussed in other chapters in this volume.

4 This category includes crimes such as obstructing justice (section 139), obstructing police (section 129), and failing to comply (section 740).

5 Of course, it might be argued that the mechanism of general deterrence would be effective even if such a small percentage of offenders are actually sentenced. If general deterrence were effective, then the imposition of very severe sentences on even a small number of offenders might prevent crime, if the other potential offenders were deterred. Research on this point is quite clear, however, that general deterrence is very ineffective (see, for a review, the report of the Canadian Sentencing Commission (1987)).

6 The median sentence is the value that divides the distribution of sentence lengths; 50 per cent of sentences are longer than the median, 50 per cent shorter.

7 It might be argued that a high maximum penalty is still needed to take into account the exceptional case, which just happened not to have occurred over the period covered by this analysis. However, there is such a gap between the sentencing patterns in the provincial courts that it is clear that the maxima could be revised downward while still providing 'room' for the exceptional case.

8 The maximum penalty if the Crown proceeds by way of indictment.

9 These incongruities are apparent even without reference to current sentencing practices. For example, forgery and certain forms of fraud carry the same maximum penalty as sexual assault with a weapon.

10 A revision of the maximum penalty structure was one of the reforms proposed by the Canadian Sentencing Commission and endorsed the majority of witnesses who testified before the House of Commons Standing Committee in 1988 (see Daubney Committee (1988), 72).

ADDITIONAL READING

Birkenmayer, A., and S. Besserer. 1997. *Sentencing in Adult Provincial Courts: A Study of Nine Canadian Jurisdictions: 1993 and 1994*. Ottawa: Statistics Canada.

Birkenmayer, A., and J.V. Roberts. 1997. Sentencing in Adult Provincial Courts. *Juristat*, 17 (1).

Canadian Sentencing Commission. 1987. *Sentencing Reform: A Canadian Approach*. Chapter 6. Ottawa: Supply and Services Canada.

Palys, T., and S. Divorski. 1986. Explaining Sentence Disparity. *Canadian Journal of Criminology* 28:347–62.

9

Sentencing Mentally Ill Offenders

RICHARD D. SCHNEIDER[1]

If an accused is found, according to the legal criteria, to have been mentally disordered at the time of the commission of the offence, the law will not hold him or her legally responsible for the act. The issue of mental disorder also arises at the sentencing stage, however. In this chapter, Richard Schneider examines the way in which the sentencing process is affected when the offender being sentenced suffers from a mental disorder. Although only a small minority of sentenced offenders suffer from a mental disorder, they nevertheless pose a particular challenge for the sentencing judge.

Introduction

As we have seen in earlier chapters, the variety of sentencing options, alternatives, objectives, and principles allow a court considerable flexibility in sentencing an individual accused to ensure that the sentence is the best possible 'fit,' not only for the offence but for the accused. Prior to considering the ways in which sentencing principles are modified when applied to the mentally disordered accused, it is important to examine briefly the legal notion of criminal responsibility, generally, as it is applied to the determination of guilt or innocence – the verdict.

A mentally disordered accused is one who, according to the Criminal Code of Canada (the 'Code'), suffers from a 'disease of the mind.' A disease of the mind was defined by the Supreme Court of Canada in the leading case of *Cooper v. The Queen*[2] as follows: 'In summary, one might say that in a legal sense "disease of the mind" embraces any illness, disorder, or abnormal condition which impairs the human mind and its functioning, excluding however, self-induced states caused by alcohol or drugs, as well as transitory mental states such as hysteria or concussion. In order to support a defence of insanity the disease must, of course, be of such intensity as to render the accused incapable of appreciating the nature and quality of the violent act or of knowing that it is wrong.'

Where an accused suffers from a mental disorder at the time of the commission of a criminal act, the law recognizes that he or she should not be held responsible or punished if the mental disorder is of a particular intensity and quality. This principle, incorporated in the Criminal Code since it was first enacted in Canada in 1892, has been recognized, in essentially the same language, since the famous British trial of Daniel M'Naghten in 1843. M'Naghten was eventually found not guilty by reason of insanity in the murder of Sir Robert Peel's secretary. Not knowing how to deal with the facts of the case, the House of Lords put a number of questions to the court and, after much debate, rules were formulated which have come to be known as the M'Naghten rules. Section 16 of the Code is a version of the rules which reads as follows:

16.(1) No person is criminally responsible for an act committed or an omission made while suffering from a mental disorder that rendered the person incapable of appreciating the nature and quality of the act or omission or of knowing that it was wrong.

(2) Every person is presumed not to suffer from a mental disorder so as to be exempt from criminal responsibility by virtue of subsection (1), until the contrary is proved on the balance of probabilities.

(3) The burden of proof that an accused was suffering from a mental disorder so as to be exempt from criminal liability is on the party that raises the issue.

While there is a very large body of law defining in great detail the parameters of the 'not criminally responsible' defence,[3] a discussion of that case law is beyond the scope of the present chapter. What should be recognized, however, is that mental disorder, if it causes the requisite degree of impairment in the accused at the relevant time, results in an absolute acquittal. Upon the verdict the state discharges the accused absolutely, ending any further obligation to the criminal justice system, unless the accused remains a significant threat to the safety of the public.

Where the accused suffers from a mental disorder that has not caused the requisite degree of impairment to afford the accused an absolute acquittal pursuant to section 16 of the Code, the court must nevertheless consider the mental disorder in deciding whether the accused had the requisite intent (*mens rea*) to be convicted of the offence charged. Lesser degrees of mental disorder may result in the accused being convicted of a less serious crime. For example, an accused who was charged with first degree murder may, because of his or her mental disorder, be convicted of the much less serious offence of manslaughter. In order to obtain a conviction for first degree murder, the Crown must prove that the accused not only intended to kill his or her victim but also planned and deliberated upon the killing. However, if a mental disorder was operative it may only be possible to prove a general intention to assault the victim but no specific intention to kill. The difference in punishment may be tremendous. Whereas there is no minimum penalty for manslaughter, a conviction for first degree murder results in a life sentence, with no possibility for parole until twenty-five years have elapsed.

Mental disorder is therefore considered by the courts in deciding not only whether the accused should be convicted of the charge laid but also whether he or she should be convicted but of a much less serious offence. In addition, as we shall see, even where the verdict is not affected, mental disorder is a factor to be considered by the court in sentencing an accused.

When the mentally disordered accused has not qualified for, or has elected not to participate in, the 'Diversion of Mentally Disordered Accused' program[4] and has been unsuccessful with or chosen not to avail himself or herself of the 'not criminally responsible' defence and is subsequently convicted, the accused's mental disorder should nevertheless be considered by the court in the final disposition of the criminal charge.

Mental disorder may have been operative in the commission of the offence but not to an extent sufficient to have an impact upon the verdict; or, the accused may have quite rationally elected not to raise the issue during the course of the trial, notwithstanding the likely success of the defence. An accused has the right to decide whether or not he or she will put forth the defence of not criminally responsible.[5] The court must nevertheless take into consideration evidence of mental disorder during the sentencing process in that a just sentence must fit the offender as well as the offence.

In general, the mental disorder, in order to be afforded any weight in sentencing, must have caused or contributed to the commission of the criminal act or have a bearing upon the extent to which the principles of sentencing will be relevant to the accused or like-minded individuals. For example, depression occurring subsequent to arrest as a result of the legal predicament would generally not be taken into account in sentencing.

Although mental disorder, operative in the commission of a crime, is generally seen as a factor in mitigation it may, in extreme situations, have the reverse effect where protection of the public overshadows all other concerns. An accused who suffers from an untreatable personality disorder resulting in repetitive and/or violent crimes may attract a more severe sentence than usual, or even a dangerous offender designation. This was the case in *R. v. Pontello*,[6] where the accused had committed offences of violence and the psychiatric evidence suggested that this particular pattern of violence was likely to continue. The present discussion does not consider these extreme examples.

Justifications for the Mitigating Effect of Mental Disorder

There are a number of reasons why a mental disorder that operates during the commission of a crime generally has the effect of mitigating an otherwise fit sentence.

The Accused Is Viewed as Less Culpable

It is a fact that, generally speaking, relative to so-called 'normal' accused, accused who suffer from mental disorders are seen as somehow less blameworthy and inspire more sympathy from both the Crown attorneys prosecuting their cases as well as the courts hearing them. While there is often no purely logical basis for this sentiment, it is nevertheless prevalent. It may be that the courts do not wish to further oppress the disadvantaged. In *R. v. Pegg*,[7] the Ontario Court of Appeal considered the sentence appeal of an accused who pleaded guilty to a number of charges arising from breaking and entering two residences and committing acts of vandalism to each, resulting in approximately $34,000 damage. The accused was sentenced to twenty-three months of incarceration by the trial judge. The court of appeal allowed the appeal against sentence and reduced the sentence to seventeen months. It was observed that in addition to a number of mitigating factors, the accused was emotionally disturbed and had at the time of the incident been in counselling designed to stabilize his condition. He had made good progress: 'he has gone to the root of his problems and obtained counselling from which he has benefitted. In all the circumstances, the sentence was unduly long.'

The Accused Copes Poorly in Prison

Courts often recognize that while an accused suffering from a mental disorder copes poorly in society, his or her problems are exacerbated in prison. Accused with mental disorders are often physically abused by other inmates and kept in segregation for their own protection. In *R. v. Brown*,[8] the court reviewed the accused's appeal against sentence in respect of one count of kidnapping for which he received fifteen years in prison. The accused had approached a ten-year-old girl, indicating to her that her father had asked him to pick her up and take her to school. After driving to a remote area the accused choked the girl to 'insensibility' and left her for dead, covered with garbage, in a dump. At the same time the accused was charged with one count of attempted murder, for which he received an acquittal as a result of a finding of not guilty by reason of insanity. On appeal the accused put before the court psychiatric evidence falling short of insanity consisting of a psychosis that caused the accused not to 'appreciate what he was doing and what would happen to the girl and to himself as a result of it.' While the court upheld the conviction, it stated that 'having regard to the mental condition of the appellant ... the sentence is too severe in the circumstances and we would allow the appeal and vary the sentence by reducing it to a term of seven years imprisonment.'

A Reduced Sentence May Allow for Psychiatric Treatment

The business of sentencing is one of balancing competing interests, objectives, and principles. Different institutions have different programs and treatment facilities. As well, there are optimum time frames within which certain programs must be implemented and completed if they are to achieve their intended objectives. It is generally recognized that the prognosis for most types of mental disorder worsens the longer the disorder is left untreated. It is also the case that 'treatment' is often left until the end of a period of incarceration, because of the view that it is not necessary until sometime close to the release of the accused into society. Accordingly, it may be appropriate to attenuate an otherwise appropriate sentence in order to facilitate treatment or improve the prognosis.

In the case of *R. v. Wallace*,[9] the accused appealed against his sentence of eight years and two years consecutive for convictions for robbery and assault, respectively. The facts giving rise to the convictions were as follows. The appellant robbed a storekeeper while holding her at gunpoint with a double-barrelled shotgun. The accused then threatened the storekeeper and a customer with death and required them to lie on the floor. The conviction for assault arose in the following way. Some three hours after an argument with his landlord, the accused struck him over the head with the shotgun. The accused was sentenced to a lengthy period of incarceration as a result of his substantial record. However, the issue of insanity was never raised at trial and the trial judge was not aware of the accused's psychiatric difficulties, which were apparently never raised in mitigation by his defence counsel. A variety of psychiatric reports were admitted at the appeal, which indicated that the accused was a paranoid schizophrenic. The reports further indicated that prolonged incarceration would be detrimental to the accused's rehabilitation. The court went on to observe as follows: 'If the primary object of the criminal law is the protection of society, how apt is this sentence? Perhaps such a sentence as this one offers immediate protection to society but clearly it does little to protect it for the future. The best future protection for society lies in imposing a sentence which will make the appellant's rehabilitation probable through the provision of medical treatment that can be made available to him. It seems then that if a moderate term of imprisonment had been imposed, the medical treatment which he needed would have been available during such term and the sentence must be altered so that we can accomplish his cure and protect the community.' The sentence was reduced to four years and two years concurrent.

In the case of *R. v. Lockhart*,[10] the accused, originally charged with attempted murder, received a sentence of two years less a day plus three years probation as a result of pleading guilty to the lesser, included offence of aggravated assault. The Crown appealed against the sentence. The facts before the court were that the accused committed a vicious, unprovoked assault upon a prostitute whom he had invited to his apartment for the purpose of engaging in sex. The victim had suffered life-threatening head injuries which required immediate surgery, and from which she would never fully recover. At the time of the offence the accused was twenty-four years of age and worked as a caretaker. He had a very minor unrelated record. Although psychiatric assessments revealed that the accused did not suffer from a major mental illness, he did suffer from a number of personality difficulties, which included paranoid features, feelings of inadequacy and hostility, and unreliable controls. In particular, psychosexual testing revealed that the accused was afflicted with sadistic tendencies which could not conclusively be linked to the assault. Despite the accused's serious problems, the psychiatric evidence indicated that the accused was a reasonable prospect for treatment and recommended that he be sent to a correctional facility. At the time of the sentencing the court recognized that the accused had come to accept that he had difficulties and that the behaviour constituting the offence was out of character. The court of appeal found that the trial court had not erred in placing too much emphasis on the rehabilitation of the accused and indeed that society would be better protected with a sentence that would allow for the treatment of the accused that could be followed up with a period of probation, which would not have been possible if he had received a penitentiary sentence.

The Principle of General Deterrence is Not Relevant

General deterrence is a factor to be made part of the sentencing formula in order to deter like-minded individuals – individuals who, were it not for the deterrent effect of the present sentence, might be inclined to commit the same sort of offence. Logic would dictate that where the accused is mentally disordered, 'like-minded' accused are not likely to be deterred by considering the fate that befell the present accused.

In *R. v. Robinson*,[11] the court considered the case of a man who pleaded guilty to four charges of rape, attempted rape, and indecent assault committed within an eleven-day period. Although the defence of insanity was not raised at trial, expert psychiatric evidence raised by both the defence and the Crown at sentencing concluded that the accused suffered from a mental illness falling short of insanity and as a result represented a danger to women. The accused was sentenced to reformatory sentences, which were the subject of the Crown's appeal. The relatively 'light' sentences were imposed because the judge believed that there was a considerable chance for successful treatment and that the public would be adequately protected by the offender's treatment at the Ontario Correctional Institute, a provincial institution. The court of appeal, in deciding that the length of the sentence was inadequate and that treatment concerns must not outweigh the need to protect the public, emphasized the provisions of the federal and provincial legislation that allow for the transfer of federal inmates to psychiatric facilities for the purpose of treatment. It was nevertheless recognized that '... it is not really accurate to say that the sentence should be a deterrent because others like him lose touch with reality and as such the deterrence of this sentence is of course meaningless to them. Furthermore, the sentence should not proceed on the basis of punishment because the Court should not punish people who commit crimes because of mental illness ... the sentence must be of sufficient length to ensure full treatment but of course conversely, if that is not successful, that the public must be protected as best as can be accomplished ... Of course, the sentence must not exceed that which would otherwise be fit for the offence.'

The Principle of Specific Deterrence Is Not Relevant

The same logic applied above with respect to the applicability of general deterrence is also recognized with respect to specific deterrence. Mentally disordered accused will generally not be capable of the sort of reflection necessary for specific deterrence to achieve its intended objective. The case of *R. v. Valiquette*[12] involved an appeal against sentence on a conviction for manslaughter. While the accused was originally charged with first degree murder, she eventually entered a plea of guilty to a charge of manslaughter and, upon a joint submission, the trial court imposed a sentence of ten years' incarceration. The reduced plea was accepted, in part as a result of a 'psychologist's' report filed with the court. It was subsequently discovered that the author of the report was not a qualified psychologist. A psychiatrist was later retained who offered the opinion, which was received by the court of appeal, that the accused had had a very difficult childhood marked by incest and family violence. The accused was married to a man who was extremely violent with her. She had a baby in 1984 but by 1987 she felt that her personal situation was deteriorating and sought the assistance of social service agencies, which placed her child in foster home. The accused, however, was permitted to visit the child. The psychiatric report indicated that despite being allowed to visit the child, the accused began to suffer episodes of severe depression coupled with psychotic elements. She began to believe that the child was being abused in the foster home. The accused herself wished to commit suicide, but was unwilling to leave the child alone in what she perceived as a threatening world. She did not want the child to experience the same suffering that she had been through and thus killed the child to save him from suffering.

In part because the trial court had received a report which had not been prepared by a qualified psychologist, the court of appeal set aside the sentence, even though it had been the product of a joint submission. The court, in reviewing the particular facts of the case, indicated the following:

> In the present appeal, it is our duty to consider the 'fitness' of the sentence imposed in the court below. Fitness must, of course, be measured not only against the objective gravity of the offence but also in the light of appellant's mental state when she committed it and all the circumstances in which she found herself ...
>
> Quite clearly, [the] appellant was suffering from extremely serious mental and emotional problems when she committed the offence. While they may not have been such as to justify a defence of insanity requiring an acquittal on grounds of insanity, these problems are nonetheless very relevant to her sentence.
>
> Persons suffering from severe mental illness of this kind do not, in my respectful opinion, require exemplary sentences to deter them from repeating the offence. Nor is a severe sentence imposed on a mentally ill person of much value for purposes of general deterrence. Mothers, generally, do not need exemplary sentences to deter them from killing their young children. And most people understand that the mentally ill require treatment and supervision, not punishment.

The sentence was subsequently reduced to a suspended sentence and probation.

Sentences Must Not Be Made Longer in Order to Facilitate Treatment

We observed above that a sentence may be reduced from that of an otherwise fit sentence in order to accommodate treatment concerns. It may appear somewhat inconsistent that the courts have generally held that a sentence may not be increased in order to accomplish the same objective. While it is generally the case that the mentally disordered accused attracts greater sympathy than a 'normal' offender committing the same offence, paternalism does not permit a court to sentence a mentally disordered accused to a longer period of imprisonment in order to facilitate the obtaining of treatment. This principle was alluded to by the court in the above-mentioned case of *R. v. Robinson* and dealt with specifically in *R. v. Luther.*[13] It is an error in principle to impose a sentence disproportionate to the nature of the offence in order to obtain treatment at a facility that has a 'minimum stay' requirement in order to participate in its rehabilitative program.

In *Luther*, the accused was convicted on a charge of assault occasioning actual bodily harm and was sentenced to one year's imprisonment. The trial judge indicated that he was sentencing the accused to a lengthy period of incarceration so that she would get treatment for her drug addiction. On appeal the court stated that it is not the function of the criminal court to order confinement solely for the purpose of treatment of a physical or mental disorder.

Sentences for Mentally Disordered Accused Must Not Exceed the Tariff That Would Otherwise Fit the Offence

Just as the length of a sentence cannot be increased in order to facilitate treatment, a sentence may not be increased merely because the accused suffers from a mental disorder which may or may not render the accused more likely to commit future offences. In *R. v. Keefe*[14] the accused was charged with breaking and entering a dwelling house and therein committing the offence of wounding. The accused was found to have broken into a woman's home after she had refused his request that she give him a ride. He obtained a kitchen knife and said he would 'fix' her for keeping him out in the rain. The accused then lashed out at the victim, cutting her on the neck and hands, pulled the telephone out of the wall, and struck the victim with the cord. The victim escaped and when the police arrived the accused was found with the victim's children, holding a saw and attempting to cut his wrists. The accused then dropped the saw and was arrested. The children were not hurt. Although an insanity defence was raised at trial, it was not successful: the accused was convicted and a life sentence imposed. The accused was twenty-two years old, single, and unemployed at the time of the sentencing. The psychiatric evidence adduced at the trial indicated that he was mildly retarded and had a tendency to react impulsively; the accused was diagnosed as having a personality disorder with immature and anti-social features. The prison psychologist indicated that the accused was less hostile than the perpetrators of most violent crimes. The court of appeal emphasized that it was not justifiable to impose a lengthy sentence disproportionate to the offence merely because the accused suffered from some form of mental retardation, especially where the presence of the mental disorder has not elevated the offence into the category of offences characterized by 'stark horror,' as observed above in *Pontello.* In *Keefe* the court of appeal reduced the accused's sentence to twelve years.

A Court Has No Jurisdiction to Order That an Accused Serve His or Her Sentence at a Psychiatric Hospital

In *R. v. Deans,*[15] the accused was convicted of manslaughter. The evidence adduced indicated that the accused suffered from severe mental illness, but that he had considerable treatment potential. As a result, the accused was sentenced to five years' imprisonment, to be served at the Oak Ridge Division of the Mental Health Centre at Penetanguishene (a hospital). The Crown appealed the sentence on the ground that the judge had no power to direct that the sentence be served at a hospital. The trial judge's objective to have the sentence, or a part of it, served at a hospital could be the subject of a recommendation, but this was entirely within the discretion of the penitentiary and hospital officials on the basis of a transfer. Normally, such a recommendation should not be made by a court unless there is evidence that the hospital is willing to accept the accused and that the accused is willing to accept treatment.

Psychiatric Assessments

Although there is, unfortunately, no direct means of obtaining a court-ordered psychiatric assessment for the purposes of sentencing through section 672.11 of the Code, the court may employ subsections 21 and 22 of the Mental Health Act of Ontario to obtain out-of-custody or in-custody assessments, respectively (*R. v. Snow*).[16] Where feasible, defence counsel generally find that it is prudent to obtain a psychiatric assessment privately so that counsel and accused are aware of the results of the assessment before deciding whether or not to rely upon any such information. An assessment obtained early in the proceedings may also assist in the fundamental tactic of whether or not to raise the defence of 'not criminally responsible.' It may be that proceeding through the normal route of trial or guilty plea, with psychiatric factors raised in mitigation of sentence, will result in a faster track to liberty than a successful defence of 'not criminally responsible.' If a psychiatric assessment is obtained early in the proceedings for the purpose of getting an opinion as to criminal responsibility, it would be quite useful to obtain at the same time an 'off-the-record' view as to sentencing in the hypothetical event that the accused is ultimately convicted. In short, it should not be forgotten that a client's mental disorder is relevant not only to the issue of criminal responsibility, but also to the alternative issue of sentence.[17]

Terms of a Sentence That May Be of Particular Assistance to a Mentally Disordered Accused

With the proclamation of Bill C-41, the prospect of court-ordered treatment has been formally recognized in the context of both probation orders and conditional sentences. While it is recognized that the 'revolving door' phenomenon of mentally disordered accused in the criminal courts is very often attributable to the accused discontinuing medications, it is doubtful that the courts will have a better grip on the problem as a result of the recent amendments. Treatment has, unfortunately, not been defined.

Within the context of a probation order, the court may order the accused '... [i]f the offender agrees and subject to the program director's acceptance of the offender, [to] participate in a treatment program approved by the Province.' The term is contingent upon the accused's consent and, although not yet formally decided by the courts, quite likely does not extend to the ordered ingestion or injection of drugs. On the other hand, within the context of a conditional sentence, the court may order that the accused '... [a]ttend a treatment program approved by the Province.' This term is also, arguably, the accused's 'option,' in that declining the conditional sentence containing the offensive term is the accused's prerogative. The option is to serve the sentence in jail. The real value, it is submitted, in having the accused report to or participate in a particular 'treatment' program lies not so much in the fact that treatment can be ordered but in the fact that the accused can be monitored so that if he or she fails to follow the treatment, appropriate action can be taken, pursuant to the relevant civil legislation.

Conclusions

Although the principles of sentencing are the same for the mentally disordered accused as for the 'normal' accused, we have seen that the courts have considerable flexibility in emphasizing or de-emphasizing the importance of the various objectives of the sentencing 'mix' so as to ensure that the sentence 'fits' not only the offence but also the offender. Considering the flexibility the court has in sentencing, one is drawn to the tremendous importance of knowing the accused and the specifics of the mental disorder with which he or she has been afflicted. It is only with such knowledge that informed submissions may be made regarding the optimal sentencing fit, the treatment/program options, where the accused might best be placed, the utility of the various supports or lack of supports the accused has in the community, and therefore his or her ability to live autonomously. Arguments may be made that the otherwise appropriate sentence should be attenuated because the 'deterrent' considerations are not terribly relevant to the mentally disordered accused. As well, counsel should be vigilant that the accused is not detained longer as a result of well-meaning treatment considerations. In general, the assumptions we make and take for granted when dealing with the general population cannot be automatically made for the mentally disordered accused. It is critical that counsel take the time to know the peculiarities of their clients and the options that the law allows for in dealing with them.

ENDNOTES

1 Dr Richard Schneider is a clinical psychologist and assistant professor in the Department of Psychiatry and a lecturer at the Faculty of Law, University of Toronto. He is also a barrister and solicitor who serves as counsel to the Ontario Review Board. He has published extensively in the area of mental disorder and the criminal justice system.

2 (1980), 51 C.C.C. (2d) 129 (S.C.C.).

3 This new terminology replaced the old terminology of 'not guilty by reason of insanity' in 1992; while the wording was modernized the substance of the test has not changed.

4 This is a program available in Ontario for mentally disordered accused who have committed less serious non-violent offences where the accused is 'diverted' into the mental health system and the criminal charges are withdrawn.

5 For tactical reasons, it may be in an accused's best interest to proceed through the trial process and end up convicted rather than to obtain a verdict of not criminally responsible. As mentioned above, the 'not criminally responsible' accused is discharged absolutely only if he or she is not a significant threat to the safety of the public. However, if the accused is, as a result of his or her mental condition, a significant threat to the safety of the public, the accused's liberty may be curtailed for an indeterminate period of time, even where the index offence is minor.

6 (1977), 38 C.C.C. (2d) 262 (Ont. C.A.).

7 (1987), 24 O.A.C. 74.

8 (1972), 8 C.C.C. (2d) 13 (Ont. C.A.).

9 (1973), 11 C.C.C. (2d) 95 (Ont. C.A.).

10 (1987), 19 O.A.C. 158.
11 (1974), 19 C.C.C. (2d) 193 (Ont. C.A.).
12 (1990), 60 C.C.C. (3d) 325 (Que. C.A.).
13 (1971), 5 C.C.C. (2d) 354 (Ont. C.A.).
14 (1979), 44 C.C.C. (2d) 193 (Ont. C.A.).
15 (1977), 37 C.C.C. (2d) 221 (Ont. C.A.).
16 (1992), 76 C.C.C. (3d) 43 (Ont. Gen. Div.).
17 The business of psychiatric assessment and the 'medicalization' of determinations of criminal responsibility in general has generated tremendous debate and produced an enormous literature. The following provocative quotation provides a good example: 'Skepticism and mystery surround forensic psychiatry hearings. Experts from both camps testify with equal fervor concerning the sanity of the defendant. Abstruse conceptions of insanity and mental illness are bandied about the courtroom as religious incantations are bandied about a temple. Like religious ceremonies, these hearings appear more concerned with ritual than with truth' (Lipkin 1990, 331).

ADDITIONAL READING

American Psychiatric Association. 1994. *Diagnostic and Statistical Manual of Mental Disorders*. 4th ed. Washington, D.C.: American Psychiatric Association.

Kaplan, H.I., B.J. Sadock, and J.A. Grebb. 1994. *Kaplan and Sadock's Synopsis of Psychiatry*. Baltimore: Williams and Wilkins.

Schneider, R.D. 1996. *Ontario Mental Health Statutes* ('The 1996 Annotated'). Scarborough, Ont.: Carswell.

10

Sentencing Aboriginal Offenders: Some Critical Issues

CAROL LA PRAIRIE[1]

In this chapter, Carol La Prairie explores what is clearly one of the most pressing problems in the area of sentencing: the high imprisonment rates of aboriginal offenders. It has long been known that, in some provinces, aboriginal Canadians are highly overrepresented – relative to their incidence in the general population – in prison statistics. This finding is representative of a broader, international phenomenon. Most Western nations imprison their ethnic minorities at a higher rate than majority group members. How can we explain this phenomenon in Canada? La Prairie reviews the substantial body of Canadian literature which has addressed the role that sentencing plays in generating a high rate of Native incarceration.

Introduction

Why are aboriginal and racial minorities overrepresented in prison statistics? The criminology literature in the United States, Britain, Australia, New Zealand, and Canada contains many references to the role that race plays in the overrepresentation of certain minority groups in the courts and correctional systems. In the United States and Great Britain, most references are to African Americans, but aboriginal peoples are the focus of attention in Canada and Australia. In some provinces in Canada, however, attention is shifting to include the black population as well (Roberts and Doob 1997; Wortley and Brownfield 1996). As Smith (1994) argues, it is not clear whether the same explanations for overrepresentation can be applied to African-American and aboriginal groups; different explanations, depending on other factors – including the geographic location of minority populations or even different geographic locations of the same group – may be required.[2]

In Canada, there is a pervasive belief that discrimination by agents of the criminal justice system explains the over-involvement of aboriginal people in the criminal justice and correctional systems. This belief has been reinforced in reports of public inquiries and by a variety of commentators (e.g., Rudin 1995; Jackson 1988). Clarifying the question of discrimination is difficult, however, given that research knowledge is limited. And scant attention is paid to the literature if it does not fit within the prevailing ideology and conventional wisdom about the relationship between the criminal justice system and aboriginal people.

Recent international findings (Tonry 1994) suggest that explanations involving class and socio-economic disparity, grounded in historical processes, may be more powerful than ones based exclusively on discrimination. Tonry (1994, 158) notes that despite two decades of initiatives and programs based a belief that the overrepresentation of minority groups (i.e., blacks in the United States; Afro-Caribbean in Britain; and aboriginal people in Canada, Australia, and New Zealand) in prisons is a result of racism in criminal justice processing, 'a consensus is emerging among researchers in most countries that the disparities result primarily from racial differences in offending patterns.' Tonry further suggests that group differences in offending patterns are the consequence of historical experiences and contemporary social and economic circumstances. He writes: 'The criminal justice system, however, is incapable of serving as the engine that can drive fundamental changes in a state's systems for distributing goods or opportunities' (1994, 160).

It is important to understand the role that sentencing plays in the overrepresentation of aboriginal inmates in order to define what is and what is not within the power of the criminal justice system to change. Unfortunately, however, one of the serious gaps in Canadian criminology is the contribution of the various processes and practices of criminal justice, including judicial decision making, to the overrepresentation of aboriginal people in community corrections and correctional institutions.[3] Moreover, unlike the United States, England, and Australia, where criminal justice data relating to the race of the accused are maintained and considerable research into disparity in sentencing has occurred, little research in Canada has addressed this issue, primarily because of the cost and time involved in participant observation research. Even when resources have been available to explore the relationship between aboriginal people and the criminal justice system (such as the Canadian Sentencing Commission (1987), the Standing Committee on Justice and the Solicitor General (Daubney Committee 1988), the Royal Commission on Aboriginal Peoples (1996), and the Law Reform Commission (1991), the results are long on recommendations but short on data.[4] It is interesting that the best data on these issues emerged from research conducted in the 1970s and 1980s (e.g., Canfield and Drinnan 1981; Hagan 1975; Moyer 1987; Moyer et al. 1987; Muirhead 1982), despite the fact that in those decades researchers lacked the resources that have subsequently been devoted to the issue of aboriginal people and criminal justice in the late 1980s and 1990s.

If one compares the state of research knowledge about possible disparity in the sentencing of minority groups and especially aboriginal people in Canada to other countries with similar populations, it is obvious that, despite a number of very expensive and prolonged public inquiries into aboriginal justice, we still lag far behind. Central sentencing questions remain. Is there unwarranted disparity in the disposition and length of sentences given aboriginal and non-aboriginal offenders? If disparity exists, how can it be explained? What social and demographic differences in aboriginal populations across the country may affect involvement in the commission of offences and sentencing?

Sentencing and Sentencing Disparity

Dispositions

Participant observation research in sentencing disparity is virtually non-existent and the Canadian Centre for Justice Statistics (CCJS) adult criminal court data do not distinguish between aboriginal and non-aboriginal accused. As a result, few research studies explore the sentencing of aboriginal and non-aboriginal offenders. York's (1995) research on federal offenders revealed that disproportionately higher numbers of this group were incarcerated, even when controlling for offence type. One problem with understanding the finding, however, is the lack of information about the number and nature of previous offences. That is, higher incarceration rates for aboriginal offenders may be justified by their longer or more serious criminal histories.

A provincial court study in Manitoba conducted during the course of the Manitoba Inquiry (Report of the Aboriginal Justice Inquiry 1991, 108–9) found that aboriginal offenders were more likely to receive incarceration as a sentence. However, the aboriginal group also had more counts and charges and had committed more offences against the person. The authors make the argument that overt discrimination is the reason for the greater use of incarceration for the aboriginal group, as both groups had an equal number of previous offences. However, no information about possible differences in type of previous offences is provided and it is well known that both the number and the nature of previous offences affect sentencing. While additional research of this kind is required, more complete information about the factors that influence sentencing is also necessary.

By contrast, in analysing aboriginal and non-aboriginal adult homicide data from 1962 to 1984, Moyer et al. (1987) found that the outcome of preliminary hearings showed no difference by race or gender. In terms of conviction rates, aboriginal offenders were more likely to be convicted of manslaughter, and non-aboriginal offenders of first or second degree murder. Almost half of the non-aboriginal group received life imprisonment, compared to one-fifth of the aboriginal group; half of the aboriginal group received sentences of less than five years, compared to less than a quarter (23 per cent) of non-aboriginals (Clark and Associates 1989, 22). The Cawsey Inquiry (1991, 199), found that only 18 per cent of the new aboriginal cases in community corrections programs in 1989 were on probation, as compared to 34 per cent of the new non-aboriginal cases. However, nearly twice as many aboriginal offenders were involved in fine option programs compared to non-aboriginal offenders.

Sentence Lengths

As early as 1982, Correctional Services Canada (CSC) data 'showed that native admissions tended to be very similar or marginally shorter, than their non-Native counterparts with the same admitting offence' (Moyer et al. 1987). Since that time, similar findings have been generated in other studies, particularly research involving federal offenders. For example, Hann and Harman (1993) found that non-aboriginal offenders generally receive longer sentence lengths than aboriginal offenders. More recently, York (1995) found that non-aboriginal offenders have a longer mean sentence length (5.2 years) than aboriginal offenders (4.2 years). At the same time, York also found that more aboriginal than non-aboriginal offenders had served a previous sentence and that approximately 75 per cent of the aboriginal offenders had been convicted of the more serious offences. This compares to 59 per cent of non-aboriginal offenders. For federally sentenced females, the shorter sentence length finding also holds true. The mean sentence length for aboriginal females was shorter in all offence categories, including total offences (York 1995). In Ontario provincial institutions, Shaw (1994, 80) found aboriginal women to be serving slightly shorter sentences, despite the fact that they had more prior incarcerations.

Disparity in sentence lengths among aboriginal and non-aboriginal provincial offenders is less apparent. Provincial correctional data for the years 1988–95 show that sentences for aboriginal offenders are only marginally shorter than those for non-aboriginals. Alberta had the largest difference between the groups, with only 9 per cent of the aboriginal population receiving a sentence of 367 or more days, as compared to 15 per cent of the non-aboriginal group. Information on sentence length by type of offence was available only for Alberta and Saskatchewan. In both provinces, non-aboriginal offenders received longer sentence lengths for prison, property, administration/public order, and weapon offences. In Alberta, aboriginal offenders receive longer sentences for driving offences, but in Saskatchewan aboriginal offenders did not receive longer sentences in any of the offence categories (La Prairie 1996, 42–3). Interestingly, the Manitoba Inquiry report stated that in its provincial court study, sentences for aboriginal males for 'common offences' (mischief, wilful damage, common assault, and theft under) were more severe than those for the non-aboriginal group (109). However, provincial data from Manitoba for the years 1988–95 show that, on average, aboriginal offenders received slightly shorter sentences overall than did the non-aboriginal group (La Prairie 1996, 172).

Data from the Cawsey Inquiry (1991) revealed that in 1989 the average aggregate sentence to Alberta Correctional Centres for non-aboriginal offenders was 149 days, compared to 122 days for aboriginal offenders. One reason for the shorter sentence lengths for aboriginal offenders, as Clark's (1989, 28) qualitative analysis of judicial decision making in Nova Scotia suggested, may be that the majority of provincial court judges are aware of the difficult conditions facing aboriginal accused. Earlier, Hagan (1975) had reached a similar conclusion. He found a difference in sentencing between 'law and order' judges and those with less concern about these issues, but that advocacy of law and order did not lead to the abuse of discretion or differential treatment of minorities. On the other hand, he noted that 'Judges who are less concerned about the maintenance of law and order appear to use part of their discretion to provide lenient treatment to Indian and Metis offenders. It can be hypothesized that this favourable treatment is intended to compensate for the differential life chances and cultural experiences of persons of native background' (1997, 38).

Factors Affecting Sentencing

Criminal record and the seriousness of the offence are the two principal factors determining the severity of sentence imposed. It is important, therefore, to determine if there are any differences between aboriginal and non-aboriginal offenders in relation to each of these variables. Differences between the two groups with regard to either variable could explain, in a legally acceptable way, the disproportionately high levels of aboriginal incarceration.

Prior Record

Although comparative data on prior records of aboriginal and non-aboriginal accused are limited, recent research findings shed some light on this issue. For example, an evaluation of the Saskatoon Community Mediation Services revealed that aboriginal accused referred by prosecutors were more likely to have a prior record than were non-aboriginal accused (49 per cent of the aboriginal group had a prior record, compared to 30 per cent of the non-aboriginals). In addition, 32 per cent of the aboriginal accused had a prior conviction in the five years prior to the date for which data were collected. This finding explains the lower referral rates of the aboriginal group to the mediation program, compared to the non-aboriginal group. It also suggests the need for diversion guidelines that are broad enough to include the aboriginal group.

Nature of Offences

Community-based and correctional research into aboriginal offending patterns has consistently documented the higher proportion of personal injury offences among aboriginal offenders. In 1989, Statistics Canada reported that aboriginal people make up 3 per cent of Canada's population but constituted 22 per cent of Canada's homicide suspects and 18 per cent of its victims. But aboriginal people are also overrepresented in the statistics relating to less serious offences – fine default, crimes against the administration of justice (failure to appear, breaches of probation), and public disorder offences – which often result in periods of detention.

Aboriginal offenders in federal institutions are more likely than non-aboriginal offenders to be incarcerated for offences against the person. In a parole decision-making and release study, Hann and Harman (1993) found the most likely admitting offence for non-aboriginals was property, whereas the most likely admitting offences for the aboriginal group were against the person and break and enter. More recent data reveal that aboriginal males and females are still disproportionately incarcerated for offences against the person, as non-aboriginals are for drug and property offences. Aboriginal offenders had also served more previous federal sentences (York 1995, 10). York's examination of federal offenders in 1995 revealed that the five most frequent offences for federal aboriginal offenders were assault causing bodily harm, robbery, second degree murder, manslaughter, and sexual assault. For non-aboriginal offenders they were robbery, assault causing injury, trafficking, second degree murder, and firearm offences.

Provincial sentence admission data for the years 1988–95 demonstrated that the most common Criminal Code offences for aboriginal offenders varied by jurisdiction. For example, in British Columbia they were driving related; in Alberta and Ontario, property; in Saskatchewan, administration of justice; and in Manitoba, crimes against the person. Generally, non-aboriginal offenders were incarcerated for more property, drug, and driving offences, and aboriginal offenders for more against the person and administrative offences, except in Ontario, where aboriginal and non-aboriginal offences were similar. Remand data were similar (La Prairie 1996, 40–1).[5]

Regional Variation in Levels of Aboriginal Incarceration

The incidence of crime, the socio-economic and other characteristics of aboriginal offenders, type of offences, migratory patterns, birth rates, age distributions, and standards of measurement for calculating overrepresentation should be included in any viable explanation of overrepresentation and may reveal more about the phenomenon than the normally accepted explanations. Variation in these conditions among aboriginal people in Canada may account for variation in levels of overrepresentation and these factors may be more influential than sentencing practices in determining levels of incarceration.

Such an approach is consistent with recent work in the United States on the effects of socio-economic status (SES) on black versus white violence. Paschalli et al. (1996) found that racial differences in violent behaviour exist only among young adults of low SES, and exposure to violence, a correlate of SES, accounted for black–white differences in this sub-group. Blacks in the low SES groups were twice as likely as whites in the same SES category to report at least one violent incident. Involvement in the illicit economy, lack of a supportive environment, psychological distress, and substance abuse were also strongly associated with violent behaviour. There was a lack of association between race and violent behaviour among young adults of high socio-economic status. While considerable attention has been given to the issue of the overrepresentation of aboriginal people in the Canadian criminal justice system, racial, SES, and geographic explanations of overrepresentation have attracted little notice.

Variation in Incarceration Levels

The extent to which aboriginals are overrepresented in the prison population varies across the country. It is highest in Saskatchewan, Alberta, and Manitoba, where it ranges from three to six times higher than the comparable aboriginal population in each province, and lowest in Quebec, the Northwest Territories, and Nova Scotia, where it is approximately 2 per cent higher than the comparable aboriginal population (La Prairie 1996). There is also variation in the extent to which different aboriginal groups are overrepresented in prison statistics. Status Indians are the group most overrepresented in correctional systems. For example, in a daily count in Saskatchewan institutions in 1994, 78 per cent of the aboriginal inmates were Status Indians, as compared to 12 per cent Métis and 10 per cent non-Status Indians, even though the combined Métis and non-Status group comprises 46 per cent of the aboriginal population in Saskatchewan and Status Indians comprise only 54 per cent. In recent risk and recidivism research using a Manitoba probation sample, the Status Indian group, particularly those living off-reserve, had higher risk/need levels than the Métis or non-aboriginal groups. However, both the on- and off-reserve Status groups had the highest levels of reoffending (Bonta et al. 1997).

While comparative regional data are sorely lacking, research (see Task Force Report, Indian Policing Policy Review 1990; Canadian Centre for Justice Statistics 1991, 1993; La Prairie 1995) shows a greater volume of crime committed by aboriginal people, particularly in western provinces, and differences in the socio-economic and other demographic characteristics of aboriginal populations across the country. Where aboriginal populations are more marginalized, particularly in relation to the non-aboriginal population, criminological theory suggests they would be a higher risk for the commission of crime, particularly for those crimes which are likely to result in the incarceration of the offender.

Since involvement in crime is influenced by socio-economic factors, decisions made at various stages of criminal justice processing may reflect this. For example, the decision to sentence an offender to probation rather than incarceration may depend upon the kind of employment, family, and other institutional supports at his or her disposal. Therefore, better knowledge about these kinds of differences between groups is critical if changes in sentencing are to occur.

Migration

Previous research suggests that living in urban areas, particularly in inner cores of western cities, greatly increases the vulnerability of aboriginal people to involvement in the criminal justice system (La Prairie 1995; McCaskill 1988). The provinces with the highest levels of off-reserve migration also have the highest aboriginal incarceration levels. For example, the off-reserve registered Indian population in Canada increased from 50,300 to 226,872 between 1967 and 1993. The largest increase was in Saskatchewan, where the proportion of people living on-reserve declined and the off-reserve population increased by 32 per cent. The proportions are now almost equally divided. Quebec and the Atlantic region had the lowest increases (Indian and Northern Affairs Canada (INAC) 1995b). The Prairie provinces have the highest, while Quebec and the Maritimes have the lowest levels of aboriginal incarceration.

Population Characteristics

The overrepresentation of Status Indians in correctional institutions is also consistent with the proportion of Status Indians living in the Prairie provinces. The majority of the Canadian aboriginal population who identified themselves as North American or Status Indian in the 1991 *Aboriginal People's Survey* lived in the three Prairie provinces. The registered or Status Indian population more than doubled in all regions of the country between 1967 and 1993, and the provinces with the highest gains were Saskatchewan, Alberta, and Manitoba – the provinces with the highest levels of aboriginal incarceration.

Age Distributions

The aboriginal population in Canada also has a much larger proportion of the age group most likely to be involved in the criminal justice system. For example, in Canada, 35 per cent of the general population is under twenty-four years of age, compared to 56 per cent of the aboriginal population. At 62 per cent, the aboriginal group under twenty-four years of age in Saskatchewan is the largest in the country. Saskatchewan also has the highest involvement of adults and youth in the criminal justice system.

Education

Education levels in the Prairie provinces are also consistent with the incarceration situation. For example, Saskatchewan and Manitoba have the largest groups of on-reserve registered Indians with less than Grade Nine education in the entire country. However, the off-reserve registered Indian group with less than Grade Nine education is half as large, and the Saskatchewan off-reserve registered Indian group with university education is among the highest in the country. The other interesting national finding is that there are more on- and off-reserve Status Indians in Nova Scotia and more off-reserve Status Indians in P.E.I. and New Brunswick with university educations than the non-aboriginal population.

Labour Force Participation and Income

Labour force patterns from the Prairie provinces may play a major role in contributing to levels of incarceration. For example, in 1991, 47 per cent of registered Indians living on reserve in Canada were in the labour force. British Columbia and Ontario had the highest participation rates (55 per cent and 50 per cent, respectively), while Saskatchewan had the lowest (37 per cent) of all provinces and territories. Labour force participation for on-reserve Status Indians in Saskatchewan at 38 per cent, is lower than for off-reserve Status Indians at 43 per cent, and for Métis/non-Status Indians at 55 per cent. However, these data are in contrast to those from the Maritimes, Ontario, and Quebec, where the total aboriginal participation rate is the same or higher than the non-aboriginal rate, and where the differences between registered Indian and non-aboriginal are much less extreme. In Newfoundland and P.E.I., the registered Indian labour force participation level is higher than the non-aboriginal level.

Census data from 1990 show that Saskatchewan Status Indians on- and off-reserve had lower incomes than the comparable groups in all other provinces and territories. However, other aboriginal groups in Saskatchewan (Métis, non-Status) had somewhat higher incomes than the Status groups and, while on the low end in provincial and territorial comparisons, are not the lowest. The differential between Status Indian and non-aboriginal incomes is greatest in the territories and least in the Maritimes and Quebec.

Discussion

The findings summarized in this chapter suggest that the incidence of crime, the socio-economic and other characteristics of aboriginal offenders, type of offences, migratory patterns, birth rates, and age distributions must be included in any viable explanation of overrepresentation of aboriginals in the Canadian criminal justice system and may explain more about overrepresentation than the normally accepted explanations of discrimination in criminal justice system processing. Variation in these conditions among aboriginal people in Canada may account for the variation in levels of overrepresentation. Tonry (1994, 160) supports this broader interpretation when he argues that 'group differences in offending patterns are the consequence of historical experiences and contemporary social and economic circumstance ... Poverty, disadvantaged childhoods, welfare, educational deficiencies, and lack of marketable skills are powerfully associated with a number of social pathologies, including criminality.'

These issues, coupled with higher aboriginal birth rates and a disproportionate number of aboriginal people in the age group most vulnerable to involvement in the criminal justice system, would suggest that aboriginal overrepresentation in the criminal justice system must surely follow. The variation in socio-economic and migration and incarceration data for aboriginal populations across Canada would indicate that is the case.

But an understanding of the impact of these issues on aboriginal involvement with the criminal justice system does not eliminate the need for better information about sentencing practices and about offence and prior record characteristics of aboriginal and non-aboriginal offenders. Boutellier (1996, 4) notes that: 'The criminal justice system is by definition narrow in its scope. It cannot cope with socio-economic problems and it should not be judged in these terms. Criminal justice operates given the material conditions of a society and not in order to change them.' However, there are ways in which the criminal justice system can respond more effectively to socio-economic and other disparity. Alternatives to reduce the use of imprisonment are now commonplace but research shows, guidelines for the application of these measures may not result in the inclusion of many aboriginal offenders because they are too narrow to include the criminal justice circumstances of this group. It is essential to conduct research into type of offence and prior records of aboriginal and non-aboriginal offenders to assist policy makers in developing appropriate alternative measures and sentencing guidelines. While aboriginal offenders may have more extensive prior records, many of the offences that contribute to these records may be related to the administration of justice, such as breaches of the peace and failures to appear in court. Given the propensity of aboriginal offenders to commit these kinds of offences, it will be important to monitor the use of the new conditional sentence to ensure that breaches of these sentences do not increase the use of incarceration of aboriginal offenders.

Conclusions

The absence of reliable and comprehensive information about judicial decision making when dealing with aboriginal and non-aboriginal offenders results in continued misunderstanding and misinformation about the sentencing of aboriginal offenders which, in turn, creates even deeper divisions and suspicions among aboriginal people about the 'justice' of the criminal justice system. A recent case in Regina illustrates the problem. Two young white men found guilty of manslaughter in the death of a young aboriginal prostitute were sentenced to six and a half years of incarceration. This sentence provoked considerable public criticism and also generated accusations of racism by aboriginal groups (*Globe and Mail* 1997).[6] However, an examination of research on sentence lengths for aboriginal and non-aboriginal offenders in Canada, particularly for those who are incarcerated for the most serious offences, suggests that aboriginal offenders consistently receive shorter sentences than non-aboriginal offenders. Moreover, recent field work in a remote aboriginal community in Saskatchewan revealed that aboriginal concern about the apparent leniency of sentences is not restricted to non-aboriginal accused. Several people complained about a homicide that resulted in what they considered a lenient sentence for the aboriginal offender, who was also a member of the community (La Prairie 1997).

The need to conduct more research into the sentencing of aboriginal and non-aboriginal offenders and to examine the impact of the sentencing reform law, especially the provisions related to conditional sentencing, cannot be overemphasized. The former would allow for the kinds of modifications to bail and probation requisites advocated by Smith (1994); the latter would permit a better understanding of the value and utility of the conditional sentencing approach for aboriginal offenders, particularly those in inner cities and isolated communities, who typically have higher breaches of probation orders than other aboriginal and non-aboriginal groups. Reforms such as expanding the use of conditional sentences to more adequately reflect the realities of aboriginal people may be required. If better information about these issues is not forthcoming, we will continue to be guided by limited information and, worse still, misinformation.

ENDNOTES

1 Carol La Prairie is a principal researcher in the Department of Justice Canada with responsibility for sentencing research. She has worked and published in the area of aboriginal justice for the past twenty years.

2 In relation to different geographic locations of aboriginal people, Hagan (1975) observed, for example, that in rural areas with less bureaucratized courts, Indian and Métis offenders tended to receive more severe sentences than the same group of offenders in urban courts (Clark 1989, 28). Since that time, however, there has been no further research on the impact of geography or region on the criminal justice processing of aboriginal people.

3 The lack of comparative data is mainly a result of the absence of offender designations of aboriginal or non-aboriginal status at all stages of criminal justice processing. The exceptions are sentenced admissions and daily population counts of inmates in correctional institutions, where race is and has been designated for some time. These are the only systematic and comparative sources of sentencing data presently available.

4 See also the Report of the Aboriginal Justice Inquiry in Manitoba (1991); *Report of the Saskatchewan Indian Justice Committee* (1992); and the Cawsey Inquiry (1991). None of these inquiries, except, to a limited extent, the Manitoba Inquiry, conducted the kind of systematic participant observation and/or file data research that would have allowed for a better understanding of the contribution of decision making at

various stages of criminal justice processing to the overrepresentation of aboriginal people in correctional institutions.

5 Some data suggest that aboriginal offenders face more counts and are convicted of more charges than the non-aboriginal group (Report of the Aboriginal Justice Inquiry in Manitoba 1991; Nuffield 1996). While this may affect sentencing decisions, it may also suggest overcharging of the aboriginal group. Participant observation research into police decision making in their contacts with aboriginal and non-aboriginal suspects is required in order to better understand the overcharging issue.

6 In fact, taking time served in custody into account, these two offenders actually received ten-year terms of imprisonment. Moreover, the individuals were subject to judicial determination, which means that they would not be able to apply for parole until half the sentence had been served in prison (most offenders are eligible to apply for parole after one-third of the sentence has been served).

ADDITIONAL READING

La Prairie, C. 1996. *Examining Aboriginal Corrections in Canada.* Ottawa: Ministry of the Solicitor General, Corrections Policy Branch.

Roberts, J. V., and A.N. Doob. 1997. Race, Ethnicity and Criminal Justice in Canada. In M. Tonry and R. Hood, eds., *Ethnicity, Crime and Immigration: Comparative Cross-National Perspectives. Crime and Justice: An Annual Review of Research.* Volume 21. Chicago: University of Chicago Press.

11

Punishing Female Offenders and Perpetuating Gender Stereotypes

DIANNE L. MARTIN[1]

In this chapter, Dianne Martin explores the sentencing and confinement of female offenders. For too long, this special category of offender has been largely overlooked by the criminal justice system. One reason for this neglect is the fact that women have represented a small minority of persons charged or convicted. Although the system is attempting to respond more equitably to women, many issues remain to be addressed before female offenders receive just treatment at the hand of the sentencing and correctional processes.

Tracy's Story

Tracy Watson, aged twenty-two, has two children: Josh (fourteen months old), and Helena (four years old). Tracy has been receiving social assistance as a single parent since Josh was born. Their father, Kevin Anderson, gives her money when he is around and living with her (which he does off and on). He has been her boyfriend since she ran away from home when she was fifteen.

Kevin is also a runaway. He has trouble keeping a job and has been drinking heavily since Josh was born. He says that he loves Tracy and the kids and wants them to be a family. He hit Tracy the first time when she was pregnant with Helena. Since Josh was born, it happens all the time. When Tracy threatens to call the police or tells Kevin to leave, he becomes even more angry. He tells her that he will 'turn her in' to welfare, or kill them all, including himself. Last month, Kevin beat Tracy so badly that a neighbour called police. Tracy did not want to testify against Kevin, who eventually pleaded guilty. He was sentenced to thirty days in prison and one year's probation.

When Kevin got out of jail he gave Tracy's address to his probation officer and said she was his wife. Tracy allowed him to do so. She felt guilty that he had been sent to jail and remained afraid of him. Someone called the welfare office and told them that Tracy was working and living with a man. As result, Tracy was notified that she is responsible for an overpayment of $28,000 and charged with welfare fraud. Kevin told her that if she did not 'cover' him with his probation officer by confirming that he does in fact live with her, he would kill her and the kids and then himself. Tracy pleaded guilty to 'fraud over $5,000' – welfare fraud. What sentence will she receive? What should the sentence be?

Introduction

This chapter will provide some answers to the questions about the sentence Tracy would – or should – receive. To do that, it will look at the women who appear before the criminal courts and the sentences that are imposed on them. In this context, some of the current rationales and theories about the punishment of women will be considered. More detailed examination of the way in which women are punished for the offence popularly known as 'welfare fraud' will then be provided. We will be seeking to understand both how the courts are responding to the offence and how their response is affecting female offenders. Finally, the chapter will take a look inside Canada's notorious Prison for Women ('P4W'). After many critical reports and reform recommendations it is finally slated to be closed, but 'P4W' still has much to teach us about the punishment of female offenders.

Some Theoretical Questions

Crime is a masculine occupation. Women are the exception in criminal courts – whether as judges, lawyers, police officers, victims, witnesses, or accused. Consequently, the sentencing principles that guide courts were developed in response to male crime, with little or no regard to female offenders. Because so few women commit crimes and, until recently, women played no part in formulating the legal principles that define crimes and defences to them, female offenders are frequently lumped together as anomalies in the system, often with unfortunate consequences. Sometimes the experiences unique to women are ignored in the name of judicial neutrality, and matters such as pressures from family violence, which should be considered, are ignored. At other times the simple fact of gender is acknowledged as if it is relevant in itself, and that acknowledgment produces unintended harms by perpetuating stereotypes and reinforcing biases. The identification of difference can also produce overly harsh sentences.

For example, it is becoming clear that sentences that were intended to deter or reform the male offender too often simply crush or brutalize a woman. Penal institutions that were designed to confine and correct men have proven to be a poor model for the imprisonment of women. Imprisonment itself, now recognized as harmful and degrading to men, is often even more traumatic for women. There are many reasons for this, not least because prison separates women from their children, but also because the small number of female prisoners has been the justification for prison budgets that are too small to allow for adequate treatment or training.

Women are not only less likely to be prosecuted for a crime than men, they are also less likely to be imprisoned for their behaviour. For example, charges of impaired driving (or driving with more than 80 milligrams of alcohol in the bloodstream) constitute the single largest category of crimes dealt with at the provincial court level, against both men and women. Of a total of 97,281 impaired driving charges processed in provincial courts in 1993/4, the overwhelming majority (90 per cent) were brought against men. Of those, almost one-quarter received a prison sentence (Birkenmayer and Besserer 1997). The situation of women charged with impaired driving is markedly different. Women represented just over 10 per cent of those charged, and of those only slightly more than 10 per cent were sent to prison.

The differences run through the entire criminal justice process, perpetuating sometimes contradictory stereotypes of female offenders as 'simply sad,' 'mostly mad,' or 'basically bad,' and rarely recognizing them as diverse human beings, sometimes struggling with enormous social burdens, and always active participants in their own lives. Indeed, it is as important to appreciate the diversity of the women before the courts as it is to distinguish them universally from the dominant group of male accused. That is, it is as important to discuss particular women and particular crimes as it is to draw conclusions from the aggregate figures. Explanations for these differences have tended to consist of oversimplistic generalizations that fail to locate the women and their offences within more complex circumstances.

The 'Simply Sad'

Differences among dispositions that apparently favour women are attributed by some to a 'chivalry in sentencing.' Proponents of this explanation argue that proportionately fewer women are imprisoned than men (true), because judges treat women more leniently, out of sympathy or consideration for them (questionable), viewing female offenders as 'sad' rather than a genuine threat. This so-called chivalry has generated considerable critical attention. For one thing, if some sort of chivalry or sympathy is operating to benefit female offenders, it is at best patronizing to women and at worst unfair both to male offenders and to victims seeking 'just deserts' for the wrong done to them. However, a more careful look at the data about female offenders and the punishment they receive suggests that leniency may be more apparent than real in many cases, at least in view of the particular circumstances of the case. That is, in many cases, the more lenient sentences were quite justified, given the lesser involvement of the woman, or the fact that the crime was less serious than originally described. For example, more men than women are charged with a second or subsequent act of impaired driving. Subsequent charges of impaired driving carry a mandatory jail sentence, while first offences do not. This is a factor that will significantly inflate the incarceration rate for men or lower it for women.

However, it is also possible that certain women, in particular, those who are physically attractive, young, and middle class receive preferential treatment. When such a woman can point to a man either as the prime actor in the crime or the source of her rehabilitation, this claim is likely to be sympathetically received by the court. If this kind of favouritism is indeed occurring (the evidence is not definitive), it supports the view of some theorists that while there is little direct bias operating for (or against) women, the criminal sentencing process does act to preserve certain social relationships and thus indirectly to reinforce mainstream stereotypes.

Chivalry of a kind may also be responsible for a disproportionately high number of women being sent to psychiatric institutions. The idea that 'normal' women do not commit crimes unless compelled to by a man also reinforces the idea that the women who do commit crimes are 'abnormal.' It is a short step to conclude that they are also 'sick.'

The Mostly Mad

Studies in England have shown that women whose conduct and location bring them into conflict with the law are far more likely than men to be institutionalized in a psychiatric facility, and thereafter labelled as 'sick.'[2] There are good reasons to believe that this is true in Canada as well (see Adelberg and Currie 1987; Chunn and Menzies 1990). The tendency to try to understand criminality in women purely as a psychological anomaly is as firmly established here as elsewhere. In terms of data that would support or refute these labels, there is nothing definitive. We do know that three-quarters of the female inmates serving penitentiary terms report being, or having been, addicted to drugs or alcohol, and that this illness persists largely untreated in prison. We also know that most women in prison want better counselling and mental health services, which reveals more about the inadequacies of women's prisons than the illnesses of female offenders. However, leniency for the 'sad' and treatment for the 'mad' are not the only stereotypes perpetuated in the punishment of female offenders. There is also evidence that in regard to some behaviours and certain crimes, women are sentenced more harshly than men.

The Inherently Bad

The interest in explaining the anomaly of the female offender may justify very harsh dispositions in some circumstances. Thus when a court imposes a very severe sentence on a woman, the accused is somehow characterized as 'not a real (or at least not a good) woman.'[3] Harsh sentences are imposed on women convicted of violent crimes, because the violence is seen as contrary to their 'proper' role as gentle victims. These are the cases in which the accused is described as 'more deadly than the male,' or in similar terms. For example, Marlene Moore was found to be a 'dangerous offender,' a designation that could have resulted in indefinite imprisonment. (This classification was recently applied to the notorious Paul Bernardo.) Moore was the first woman ever designated a DO in Canada. The label was based on her lengthy record for assault and other violent offences, her unruly behaviour in prison, and her tendency to self-mutilation. However, if Moore's record is contrasted with the records of any number of male offenders, it seems outrageous to categorize her in that way (see Kershaw and Lascovich (1991)). Once again, the perception of the accused woman draws on stereotypes about how women are 'supposed to be'; it does not respond to who they really are.

What Kinds of Women Are Sentenced?

Female offenders in Canada are broadly typical of female prisoners throughout the Western world (although we are far more likely than European countries to use imprisonment as a sanction). They are generally poor, young, white, single mothers with few, if any, previous convictions. They are involved primarily in minor crimes such as shoplifting, prostitution, and drug-related offences, rather than corporate crime or serious crimes such as bank robbery. Although aboriginal women are significantly overrepresented in our criminal courts and prisons, as are all women of colour, the majority of offenders are white. The majority are also survivors of violence, a link that has only very recently been acknowledged. Surveys of women serving sentences of more than two years, and thus under federal jurisdiction, indicate that the majority of inmates are survivors of physical or sexual abuse (or both). The violence was in their families of origin or with their intimate partners.

In 1990, 82 per cent of 102 women surveyed at the Kingston Prison for Women and 72 per cent of 68 women surveyed inside provincial prisons reported being survivors of physical or sexual abuse. Abuse was found to be more widespread in the lives of aboriginal women, 90 per cent of whom reported having been physically abused, while 61 per cent said that they had been sexually abused. Most female prisoners wanted access to help in dealing with the effects of abuse on their lives. However, these women are also unusual in that they are in conflict with the law in the first place. Most women, whether poor, members of a minority, or single parents, are not in prison or facing criminal charges. In 1992 women were charged with just 16 per cent of the 704,859 criminal charges laid in Canada. The figures for offences resulting in more than two years are similar, although the raw numbers are much smaller. In 1995 there were 322 federally sentenced women in prison in Canada (a significant increase from 174 in 1975).

The Crimes That Women Commit

> Study after study shows that offences by those at the bottom of social and economic hierarchies are more likely to be policed, prosecuted and punished [more] severely than offences committed by wealthier people.[4]

After experience with abuse, poverty is probably the next single most unifying factor among women in conflict with the law, and it plays a major role in the crimes that women commit. A study in Nova Scotia identified poverty and family need as the cause of 42 per cent of crimes committed by women. The frequency of shoplifting, for example, was at its highest in August, the 'back to school' month, and December, with the demands of Christmas (see Chunn and Gavigan (1995)). It is also important to remember who is most likely to be arrested and charged in the first place: the poor, the visible, and the unruly.

Poverty is associated with other factors that put people at risk of arrest: poor education and few marketable skills; dependence on welfare, alcohol and drugs. Poor women are also most vulnerable in their dependence on men. A majority of female offenders are also single parents, solely responsible for child care. A 1990 survey of female prisoners found that two-thirds of federally sentenced women were mothers. Many had lost custody of one or more of their children, or were fearful that this might occur, and reported that contact with their children, regardless of their age, was essential to them. Unlike male prisoners who were parents (who report that their spouse or partner is caring for the children), most women prisoners were solely responsible for their children's care.

Poverty also explains a lot about the types of offences women commit: 'even if criminal activity is widespread, patterns of offending behaviour differ according to the opportunities available. Those with access to other people's money through their employment or profession, for example, are much more likely to embezzle funds than to sell drugs on a street corner. They are also less likely to be caught. Crimes committed in the privacy of corporate offices tend to be more difficult to detect and prosecute than street crimes because of their low visibility, and because the law generally shelters these private spaces from state officials' (Gordon 1991, 100).

The broad picture, then, of the offences that women commit is that they are situational, opportunistic, and motivated by poverty. With the exception of impaired driving (the criminal offence charged most frequently against both men and women), the offence that results in the highest number of charges against women is shoplifting – theft under $1,000. Next highest are other property offences, such as fraud, followed by prostitution-related offences, such as communicating for the purpose of prostitution. For men, the equivalent offence is level one assault, with theft a distant second (or third, if one counts impaired driving). In terms of percentages of the total charges laid, the only offence that is committed by a higher percentage of women than men is communicating for the purposes of prostitution (see Table 11.1).

A Woman's Crime: Welfare Fraud

Although women constitute a minority in the criminal justice system, and even more so within the prison system, this does not necessarily reflect chivalry in sentencing. Men face the lion's share of fraud charges overall and receive more time in jail for those charges, but this bias seems to reverse when we look at the type of fraud that women are most likely to commit: welfare fraud. It appears from the available data that women represent the majority of those charged with welfare fraud and are very likely to be sentenced to at least a short term in prison (a trend that may change with increased reliance on conditional sentences, described in later chapters of this volume). Why this might be so raises some interesting insights into the anomalies associated with the punishment of women generally. Understanding the ways in which the criminal law operates ideologically, that is, reinforcing some attitudes and beliefs over others, may be the most useful way to understand the sentences imposed for

TABLE 11.1
Persons Charged, by Gender: Selected Incidents, 1994

Offence	% Males	% Females
Violent Crime		
Homicide	88	12
Assaults	85	15
Sexual assaults	98	2
Robbery	90	10
Total	87	13
Property Crime		
Breaking and entering	94	6
Motor vehicle theft	92	8
Fraud	70	30
Theft over $1,000	82	18
Theft under $,1000	67	33
Total	78	22
Criminal Code		
Mischief to property	89	11
Arson	86	14
Prostitution	45	55
Total	82	18

Source: Commission of Inquiry into Certain Events at The Prison for Women in Kingston (Ottawa: Public Works and Government Services Canada 1996), 205.

welfare fraud. By stigmatizing those who need social assistance in the first place, and by punishing their wrongs harshly, the criminal justice system favours some women over others – and the poor, single mother defrauding the public purse in order to support her family is the loser.

There are many reasons for this situation. The increase in the need for social assistance caused by the recent recession has been accompanied by the usual increase in resentment expressed toward recipients. This resentment translates into support for harsh punishment for those who break the rules, even where the offence is motivated by 'need not greed,' and where poverty and privation have compelled a recipient to fail to disclose the contributions of a boyfriend or the extent of part-time employment earnings. In these difficult cases, pitiful and understandable circumstances seem to cry out for mercy, but the mercy received is often minimal and a jail sentence is a real risk. Tracy's story, which began this chapter, is a very common one.

The Sentencing Principles at Work

At least until very recently, the most likely sentence that a woman like Tracy would have received is imprisonment. For more than twenty years the paramount principle in sentencing welfare fraud offenders has been general deterrence, the principle that looks to the sentence imposed on a particular offender to serve as a deterrent to others who might be thinking about committing the same crime. Some judges have also said that in the case of a breach of a public trust, like welfare fraud, the sentence must 'denounce' the conduct. If these principles of deterrence and denunciation dominate, jail is the penalty most likely to be imposed, even in cases that would in other situations result in a lesser penalty, where, for instance, the accused had no prior record and the crime was compelled by circumstances of poverty and genuine need. When the woman has a prior record, and/or she does not present a very appealing picture to the court, a jail sentence has been almost inevitable. This harsh attitude was expressed more than twenty years ago by Chief Justice Gale in *R. v. Thurotte* (still a leading case): 'Although this case is pitiful in many respects, this Court is unanimously of the opinion that the paramount consideration in determining the sentence is the element of deterrence. Welfare authorities have enough difficulties without having to put up with persons who set out to defraud them.'[5]

It is sobering to recall that despite the court's recognition that this was a 'pitiful case,' Thurotte received a five-month jail sentence for defrauding welfare of $1,700. This was not an unusual case. Nikki McGillivray[6] pleaded guilty to defrauding Alberta Family and Social services of $23,263 between 1 April 1977 and 31 October 1991. She had failed to inform welfare about her common law relationship or the assistance she had received from her partner's student loan. She was sentenced to six months in prison and a year's probation. Ms McGillivray, a twenty-seven-year-old with two children under the age of six, committed the offence in order to support herself and her two children. She was described by the judge as 'an emotionally abused, battered wife who is very much manipulated by her boyfriend.' But the judge also noted that the abusive boyfriend 'was certainly not standing over her shoulder at the Welfare Office' when the false applications were made, and that she had two prior convictions for 'theft under.' In summarizing her view that jail was called for, Judge Daniel said: 'It is commonly the case that offenders of this type present themselves as quite sympathetic figures. They usually had a difficult life and their circumstances are often pitiful. But, they are not unlike the thousands of others who find themselves driven to depend on the largesse of the welfare System. Given the absolute necessity for honesty on the part of welfare applicants, it is evident the Courts have time and time again stressed deterrence both for the individual and the public at large must be the paramount consideration in these types of sentencing.'[7]

The case of *Leaming* makes a similar point. In *Leaming*, Judge Fradsham held that the poverty of the accused and her use of the money to support her family were not mitigating circumstances (although it would have aggravated the crime if she had spent the money on 'items of extravagance'). Despite the fact that Leaming had no prior record and had had 'a most difficult life,' this thirty-eight year-old woman was sentenced to eighteen months in prison because she had not disclosed that she was living with her common law husband.[8]

Just as pressure from an abusive spouse is not enough to avoid prison altogether, neither is the well-being of a woman's children, although sometimes this will shorten a prison sentence. The British Columbia Court of Appeal recently approved a nine-month prison sentence for welfare fraud and refused to allow the accused to serve her sentence at home under electronic monitoring, in spite of the fact that her absence was markedly affecting her young son's behaviour at school. Deterrence of others had to take priority over his (and her) well-being.[9]

However, there is some indication that this punitive attitude is being softened by the availability of the conditional sentence. Although she had to serve one week of a four-month sentence, the Ontario Court of Appeal recently substituted a conditional sentence for the original four-month prison term so that the accused could serve the balance of her sentence in the community. She was required to make restitution and do community service for failing to disclose a common law relationship for almost three years, however.[10] It is too soon to tell whether the wide use of conditional sentences will reduce the increasing numbers of women in prison, although it appears likely that it will. However, conditional sentences, particularly when accompanied by strict conditions, are not always the solution either. The next difficulty facing the courts will be to sentence the women who could not meet the conditions imposed. A wise judge, almost twenty years ago, commented on the downside of a community service sentence: 'you have got your hands full looking after your two children, certainly your one child, and earning yourself your own proper livelihood without finding some extra hours after five or six or seven o'clock at night to perform some kind of public service or community service. I would interpret a community service order in this case, especially having regard to your age and your own position, as a case of refined cruelty quite frankly.'[11]

That women are being imprisoned for their poverty is troubling, and it is not just as a result of committing the offence of welfare fraud. Many more women are in jail because they could not or did not pay a fine. Others will follow because they could not or did not fulfil a condition. What is obscured by the relatively small numbers of women serving prison sentences and, indeed, the relatively short sentences imposed, is that even gender-neutral dispositions have a harsher impact on women than on men. For example, women are proportionately more likely than men to be imprisoned for non-payment of fines. Because women have less access to jobs or money than men it is not unreasonable to conclude that their relative poverty is one cause of that disparity.

Women's relative poverty may also help to explain why more women than men are placed on probation, a disposition involving considerable constraints on liberty, rather than being fined. However, the most disparate effects are experienced by women serving prison sentences. Prison is hard on women not only because confinement separates them from their children and creates real hardships for many of those children, but also because the prisons themselves are harsher. Due to the small numbers of inmates, women's prisons have not been able to provide anything like the range of programs and facilities available to men. However, prison statistics do not really tell us very much about what prison does or does not do for the women sent there. For that one needs more detail.

The Prison for Women in Kingston

Female prisoners have long been recognized as representing a case very distinct from that of male prisoners and this is most obviously true for women serving penitentiary terms (more than two years). The history of Canada's only penitentiary for women has been marked by repeated calls for its closure from various commissions and inquiries, the first just a few years after the prison was built. That pressure finally came to a head in the late 1980s, when a coalition of feminists and feminist organizations, within and without the official corrections hierarchy, joined together to produce a report that finally led to the closing of 'P4W' (see Task Force on Federally Sentenced Women (1990)).

That decision was hailed as a victory for women, for feminist reform, and for prison reform generally, but institutions do not change so readily. The tensions associated with the imminent closing of the penitentiary and the related low level of staff expertise (many more senior officers had already transferred to other institutions) contributed to a climate in which tensions were high and relatively minor incidents were likely to escalate. And escalate they did, in April 1995, in what was at the time one of the most disturbing prison scandals ever.

A dispute over delayed medication led to an assault on a guard, which escalated into some quite serious assaults by other prisoners on guards. The assaults were soon coupled with threats of death and plans to escape and to take hostages until, finally, the prisoners were subdued with mace and isolated. The prisoners ultimately pleaded guilty to criminal charges based on these allegations and in the normal course of events that would have been the end of it. However, following this brief but violent incident the prisoners involved, who had been isolated in the segregation unit, did not settle down. Feelings still ran high on both sides. There were episodes of slashing and attempted suicide, urine throwing, and general uproar throughout the segregation cells as the prisoners protested when mace decontamination procedures were not followed and calls to their lawyers were denied. The guards were equally agitated and, in addition to the lockdown and denial of calls and privileges, demonstrated outside the prison to protest the failure to transfer the women involved in the 22 April incident to another (inevitably male) institution. The guards' version of events, that the episode was part of a planned escape conspiracy and the weapon used was an HIV-infected syringe, was never substantiated, but it clearly became as true for guards as the brutality experience became true for prisoners. This was the climate at the prison when, four days after the initial incident, the warden called in the (male) institutional emergency response team (IERT) to conduct a 'cell extraction and strip search.' The entire process was videotaped – ironically, as it turned out, to protect the IERT from allegations of inappropriate conduct.

It is difficult to underestimate the impact of that videotape. As powerful as the images of police officers beating the supine Rodney King in Los Angeles were, the Prison for Women images were in some ways even more disturbing. The sight of the masked, helmeted, booted members of the all-male IERT ordering thin, frightened, yelling women to strip, occasionally restraining them, using knives to cut open their clothing and inserting the tips of their billy clubs to pull it off, was deeply shocking. The entire procedure seemed sadistic and the humiliation and degradation of the women left casually with paper shifts – after long periods of full nudity – was poignant and obvious.

Despite many complaints, the prison administration initially resisted any suggestion that they had done anything wrong, but ultimately, almost a year after the incident, the solicitor general appointed Madame Justice Louise Arbour of the Ontario Court of Appeal to conduct an inquiry (see Arbour (1996)). Justice Arbour concluded that there had been a brief and violent incident of assaults by prisoners on guards, but she rejected the other allegations, including that the assaults represented attempted murder. However, she noted that the guards in question certainly believed that they had faced death and that the incident had enormous significance for everyone, including the guards. Many left prison work altogether and many left working with women. She also found that there were many and serious policy breaches and a subsequent cover-up. There is no doubt that if the male emergency response team had not videotaped their subsequent actions in further 'subduing' the women in segregation, and if that video had not become public, few outside the prison would ever have known what happened. Certainly the prisoners would never have been believed.

Perhaps the most troubling of many worrisome conclusions drawn by Justice Arbour is the extent to which the Prison for Women was dominated by lawlessness on the part of the law enforcers, from guards to the senior administrators. According to Justice Arbour, one of the worst aspects of the events at 'P4W' was that this brutality and the cover-up occurred at the women's prison, where many progressive influences were operating, which should have prevented these events from ever taking place. The violence and its cover-up were of equal concern to Justice Arbour, particularly as the abuse most of the women had suffered outside in the community had been repeated inside prison: 'The society in which many women offenders live is neither peaceful nor safe. By the time they go to prison, they should be entitled to expect that it will be just.'

Conclusions

Justice Arbour's conclusion should be the legitimate expectation of all Canadians; that justice will be equal and fair and that punishment will be merciful and just. The expectation is not always met, of course, and that is why, in considering the punishment of women offenders, it is important to be attentive to the effects of punishment on all of us: men and women of different ages and ethnic origins and different locations in life. Just as the poignant and vulnerable position of female offenders convicted of welfare fraud does not save them from prison sentences, the gender of prisoners is no guarantee of fair and humane treatment. At least part of the solution for reducing the harsh impact of the criminal justice system on female offenders is to reduce the impact of incarceration on all offenders.

ENDNOTES

1 Dianne Martin is a Professor of Law at Osgoode Hall Law School. She is co-director of the Innocence Project, a clinical program devoted to investigating cases of wrongful conviction. She is co-author of *Sentencing Digest*.

2 Allen (1987) found that women were twice as likely as men to be given psychiatric dispositions instead of incarceration.

3 This tendency is quite apparent in some of the decisions we will look at below, under 'Welfare Fraud.'

4 Turk (1969), *Criminality and the Legal Order*, 9.

5 *R. v. Thurotte* (1971), 5 C.C.C. (2d) 129 at 129 (Ont. C.A.).

6 *R. v. McGillivray* (unreported), Daniel, J., Docket # 21054671P1, Calgary, Alberta, 16 September 1992.

7 Ibid.

8 *R. v. Leaming* (1992), 17 *Weekly Criminal Bulletin* (2d) 558, (Alta. Prov. Ct.).

9 *R. v. Friesen* (1994), 22 *Weekly Criminal Bulletin* (2d) 593 (B.C.C.A.).

10 *R. v. Jantunen* (unreported), Ont. C.A., 4 April 1997.

11 (Unreported) CCJC, Oxford, Misener J.; Ont. D. Crim. Sent. 7260-02, 21 November 1980.

ADDITIONAL READING

Birkenmayer, A., and S. Besserer. 1997. *Sentencing in Adult Provincial Courts: A Study of Nine Jurisdictions: 1993 and 1994*. Ottawa: Statistics Canada.

12

Sentencing Black Offenders in the Ontario Criminal Justice System[1]

TONI WILLIAMS[2]

Incarceration rates of black offenders have increased dramatically in recent years in Ontario. As well, black offenders are disproportionately represented in prison populations relative to their numbers in the general population. This is true in Ontario and also in the United States and the United Kingdom. In this chapter, Toni Williams explores the role that sentencing plays in accounting for the high numbers of black inmates in the province.

Introduction

Over the last twenty-five years, several studies in the United States and United Kingdom have documented a disturbing problem: the dramatic and rapidly increasing overrepresentation of black people among persons who receive the harshest sentences. In the United States, which is the only Western industrialized nation to execute people, most persons on 'death row' are black men (Wolfgang and Riedel 1973). Black men and women are also overrepresented in American prisons (Tonry 1994, 1995a; Miller 1995), as they are in British prisons (Hood 1992; Cook and Hudson 1993). These studies raise important questions about racial discrimination in the criminal justice systems of these jurisdictions, and they also lend support to general concerns about disparity in the sentencing processes. The two problems are closely related in that disparate sentencing of otherwise similar white and black persons is one important sign of possible racial bias. Still, they are different. Not all discriminatory conduct has an observable impact on decisions, so discrimination may exist even if there is no racial disparity in sentencing outcomes. Conversely, judges may sentence convicted persons inconsistently, regardless of race, in which case sentencing may be disparate but not racially discriminatory. Canadian academics and policy makers have long identified disparity as characteristic of sentencing practices in this country (Hogarth 1971) and over the last ten years they have been highly critical of differential sentencing in cases that have similar facts (Canadian Sentencing Commission 1987). Whether the disparity lies in the case-to-case decisions of individual judges, or in differences from judge to judge or court to court, significant inconsistency in penalties is condemned as unfair. By the early 1990s, this view was so well established that it formed the basis for legislative reform of the sentencing system.

Discriminatory sentencing of black persons in Canada, by contrast, is contested. Many black Ontarians have long been convinced that the criminal courts in general and sentencing judges in particular do not treat them fairly (Equal Opportunity Consultants 1989; Commission on Systemic Racism in the Ontario Criminal Justice System 1995). Their concerns have been noted, but the responses have been muted. In part, it has been easy to deflect complaints about racial discrimination in sentencing because of the lack of systematic data on sentencing. Canadian criminal justice data do not normally identify non-aboriginal people, so little research exists into how black people fare in criminal proceedings (Roberts and Doob 1997). A few studies of the 1980s suggested that some Canadian courts might sentence black people more harshly than white people (Renner and Warner 1981; Clairmont 1989; Clairmont, Barnwell, and O'Malley 1989), but the small samples of these studies made their findings inconclusive. In the absence of a body of academic scholarship or policy analysis that endorses and reinforces the claims of discriminatory treatment, the experiences of black Ontarians have been discounted as 'perceptions' and 'anecdotes' that lack an objective basis.

In October 1992, the Government of Ontario appointed a commission of inquiry to investigate the treatment of racial minority persons throughout the criminal justice process. The creation of the commission was the outcome of a long political struggle that began as an organized response to police shootings of black men and developed into a critique that identified 'systemic racism' as a pervasive problem of Ontario society. The origins of the commission lie in the fifteen-month period between August 1978 and November 1979, during which officers of the Metropolitan Toronto Police shot and killed three black men: Andrew 'Buddy' Evans, Albert Johnson, and Michael Sargeant. No charges were laid in respect of the deaths of Buddy Evans or Michael Sargeant, and the officers who killed Albert Johnson were acquitted of manslaughter charges. These deaths, and the legal proceedings that followed (Glasbeek 1994) galvanized many black Ontarians, particularly in Metropolitan Toronto. They established organizations, which, together with progressive lawyers and social action groups, called for investigation of racism in policing and greater accountability from the criminal justice system.

More police shootings of black Ontarians occurred during the 1980s. Few officers were charged with criminal offences and none were convicted. Each death or injury provoked expressions of anger and outrage from black organizations and their loose coalition of supporters, and intensified the calls for recognition of 'racism' in existing practices and reforms to policing. In response to these demands, special inquiries into policing were struck (Metro Toronto Task Force on Human Relations (Chair Walter Pitman) 1977; Carter 1979; Gerstein (Chair) 1980; Lewis (Chair) 1989). The task forces consulted, reported, and recommended changes. Some reforms were implemented, but many were not, and the shootings continued.

Once the community groups were established they became a vehicle for expression of concerns about discrimination against black people throughout Ontario's criminal justice system. Stories emerged of black persons experiencing mistreatment in prisons and in the criminal courts. There were complaints about bail and sentencing decisions and about the conduct of trials and other hearings (Equal Opportunity Consultants 1989). As these stories circulated within black communities, thematic connections were made with the shootings. It was thought that a system that appeared not to care about black victims of police violence would make little effort to ensure fair treatment of black persons accused or convicted of a criminal offence. Thus the perceived failure adequately to address the concerns raised by the shootings came to be seen as part of a pattern of indifference toward, and unequal treatment of, black people in the criminal justice process.

On 2 May 1992, a Metropolitan Toronto police officer killed another black man, Raymond Lawrence. This shooting, which was the fourth in eight months in Metro Toronto, coincided with the acquittal of the American police officers who had beaten an African-American man, Rodney King. The beating of Mr King had been captured on videotape and beamed across the continent. The death of Mr Lawrence passed unobserved by anyone other than the police officers involved. In a bold political move, one of the most active groups in the black community, the Black Action Defence Committee (BADC) organized a rally that explicitly encouraged participants to see connections between the American officers' use of force against African Americans and the shootings of black people in Ontario.

At the end of the BADC rally, many of the large contingent of young people who had attended broke away to form a spontaneous protest. They challenged police authority over the streets and created considerable disorder. These disturbances rocked the political establishment, provoking a swift response. Then premier Bob Rae appointed a Special Advisor on Race Relations – Stephen Lewis – who was given a one-month time-frame to develop a comprehensive action plan for resolving whatever problems lay behind the disturbances.

Lewis's extensive consultations led him to identify a general problem of 'systemic discrimination' in social institutions, which was experienced with particular force by black persons in Southern Ontario (Lewis 1992, 3). More specifically, he identified a pressing need for a fresh approach to the criminal justice system to correct 'a curious distortion' caused by the exclusive focus on policing of previous inquiries. The goal of this approach was to generate official, systematic knowledge about the possibility of racial discrimination in 'those parts of the Justice System which cry out for assessment and evaluation but always seem to escape it' (Lewis 1992, 14).

Four months after Lewis reported, the Ontario government created the Commission on Systemic Racism in the Ontario Criminal Justice System. Put at its simplest, the commission's mandate was to investigate concerns that the courts and correctional systems in Ontario (as well as the police) inadvertently treat black and other racial minority people unjustly. Empirical research into 'key decision-making points' of the criminal justice system, such as sentencing, was identified as a specific focus of the inquiry. This focus placed the critical questions of disparity and discrimination at the forefront of the commission's work.

This brief summary of the commission's origins shows how a struggle that was born of police use of deadly force broadened to encompass the entire coercive matrix of the criminal justice system. Despite this shift, the main demand continued to be institutional accountability for the mistreatment of black people. It was to be achieved by research that would generate official knowledge about discriminatory practices. Such knowledge was seen as the foundation for structural reforms that would establish clear and visible responsibilities for securing – not simply assuming – fair treatment of black people within the criminal justice system.

The Commission's Findings on Imprisonment and Sentencing

Prison Admissions

One of the commission's most important pieces of research is a background study on admissions to Ontario prisons. Its original purpose was to serve as a tool that would assist in the identification of specific areas of discretionary decision making that warranted further investigation. The research findings were so dramatic in their own right, however, that they ultimately became a focal point of the report. The study examined adult admission trends over a six-year period, 1986/7 to 1992/3, and 1992/3 data on race, sex, age, and charges of prisoners, and the reason for custody (detention before trial or a prison sentence). Prisoners were first classified into different groups based on 'race,' as recorded by correctional officers in admission units. The representation of different 'racial groups' among prisoners was then compared to census estimates of their representation in the population of province.

The findings of the six-year study are startling. They show that from 1986/7 to 1992/3 the total number of black admissions to Ontario prisons rose by 204 per cent, as compared to a 23 per cent increase in white admissions and a 40 per cent increase in total admissions. In this period, Ontario's black population increased from 2.4 per cent to 3.1 per cent of the province's population, which is a growth of about 36 per cent. The net effect of these changes was that, although the number of white prisoners grew significantly over the study period (from 49,555 in 1986/7 to 60,929 in 1992/3), they are a declining proportion of all admissions (from 84 per cent in 1986/7 to 73 per cent in 1992/3). By contrast, the dramatic growth in the number of black prisoners (from 4,205 in 1986/7 to 12,765 in 1992/3) meant that black admissions increased from 7 per cent to 15 per cent of total admissions. This shift from white to black prisoners was particularly marked among men and women charged with drug trafficking and importing offences and admitted to prisons serving the Metro Toronto area. Across the prison system as a whole, there was a massive growth in the total number of prisoners admitted for these offences over the study period. Data from two prisons that hold sentenced prisoners illustrate the impact of this growth on the imprisonment of black men and women.

In 1986/7, Maplehurst Correctional Centre, a prison for sentenced men, admitted 49 white and 4 black men convicted of drug trafficking/importing offences. In 1992/3, the same prison admitted 61 white men, an increase of 25 per cent, and 136 black men, which amounted to a growth of 3,300 per cent in the number of black admissions for trafficking offences. The effect of this trend was that the proportion of black prisoners sentenced for drug trafficking rose from 8 per cent to 68 per cent of all trafficking admissions at Maplehurst.

Data from Vanier Centre for women, Ontario's only prison exclusively for sentenced women, are also dramatic, although the number of individuals is, predictably, smaller. In 1986/7, Vanier admitted six white women and one black woman convicted of drug trafficking/importing offences. In 1992/3, forty-six white women and fifty-three black women were admitted to serve sentences for these offences. The six-year period saw a 667 per cent increase in the number of white admissions, and a 5,200 per cent increase in the number of black admissions. As a result, the proportion of black women sentenced for drug trafficking rose from 14 per cent to 54 per cent of all trafficking admissions at Vanier.

Analysis of 1992/3 admissions data also produced some striking findings on disproportionate imprisonment. Census estimates for 1991 indicate that about 3 per cent of the province's total population is black. Among prison admissions, however, about 13 per cent of adult males and 17 per cent of adult females are black. This pattern of greater overrepresentation of females than males also holds true for prisoners of aboriginal heritage. None of the other identified racial groups is overrepresented among adult male or female prisoners.

The commission analysed the reason for custody to see if the overrepresentation of black and aboriginal people was due to sentencing or to pretrial decisions, such as denial of bail. These data show that disproportionate imprisonment occurred at both stages of criminal proceedings. For black admissions, however, the overrepresentation was more pronounced before trial than after conviction. This difference is apparent among adults and youth admissions, although it is more marked among adults. Thus, in 1992/3 black adults were 16 per cent of remand (pretrial) and 9 per cent of sentenced admissions and black youth were 13 per cent of remand and 10 per cent of sentenced admissions. Aboriginal adults and youth, by contrast, appear in about the same proportions among pretrial and sentenced admissions. In 1992–3 they were about 6 per cent of adult admissions and 7 per cent of youth admissions at both stages of the criminal justice process.

Findings from analysis of the charges for which prisoners were admitted in 1992/3 indicate that drug charges contributed significantly to the overrepresentation of black people among both remand and sentenced admissions. The commission found that admission rates on drug possession charges are eleven times higher for black than white persons. For drug trafficking/importing charges the ratio of black to white admissions is 22:1.

That black people are overrepresented among prisoners before trial and after conviction indicated a need to study the exercise of discretion at bail and sentencing proceedings. It also suggested that it would be useful to design the study with as much linkage as possible between the two stages of the system. These insights, together with the findings about the significance of drug charges to the overrepresentation of black people, influenced the direction and content of the commission's research program. Other important findings of the imprisonment study, however, did not receive any further attention. Perhaps the most significant omission is the failure to explore further the finding that black women are more overrepresented among female admissions than are black men among male admissions. Roger Hood's study in the United Kingdom found a similar pattern, which he explained in terms of a substantial number of foreign women of African heritage who had been convicted of drug-importing offences (Hood 1992). In the absence of more information, however, we do not know if this factor accounts for the Ontario findings.

The Sentencing Study

The commission conducted an integrated analysis of the exercise of discretion at bail and sentencing (see Morrison (1993); Roberts and Doob (1997) for further information). Data were collected on a sample of white and black men charged by the Metro Toronto police in 1989/0. The entire sample was used to compare imprisonment decisions before trial and data on the sub-sample of convicted men was analysed for the sentencing study. Metropolitan Toronto was selected because this jurisdiction has the highest concentration of black people in Ontario and the commission wanted to ensure that it could gather a large enough sample of black men to permit meaningful comparisons.

There are two reasons for the selection of 1989/90 as the study period. First, a person may not be convicted and sentenced until long after charges are laid. Since the commission was using the same database for its analysis of bail and sentencing decisions, it wanted to be sure that all of the relevant criminal proceedings had been completed. At the time of the data collection (1993), 1989/90 was the most recent year for finding completed files. The second reason for choosing 1989/90 was that it marked the middle of the dramatic rise in the disproportionate imprisonment of black people. It therefore seemed to be a good point at which to take stock of the exercise of sentencing discretion.

An important aspect of the design of the sentencing research was the decision to select a limited number of offence types for the comparisons of black and white convicted men. This approach differs from that of many other major studies of disparate sentencing, such as Hood's (1992), which adopt a comprehensive strategy of analysing sentences for all offences that resulted in convictions in the jurisdiction under review. The commission explains its choice in terms of ease of interpreting the findings. Comprehensive studies provide a fuller picture of sentencing practices, but they suffer from the disadvantage that it may be difficult to determine how far racial disparity in sentencing is independent of differences in the patterns of convictions for white and black persons. In the commission's study, by contrast, the limited number of offence types significantly reduces the possibility that differential sentencing of black and white men is due to differences in charges.

On the other hand, the restricted number of offence types is also a limitation of the commission's research design. There is no way of generalizing from its findings to all criminal offences. Nor is it possible to say whether sentencing outcomes for other offences would show more disparity, less disparity, or no difference in the treatment of black and white convicted persons. This limitation might not matter if the underlying theory is that sentencing judges always discriminate against black people in the same way, no matter what the offence (or, conversely, if the theory had been that judges never discriminate against black people). But the commission's working model – supported by its imprisonment research – was that discrimination, at least in its direct form, is most likely to be associated with specific offences. The problem was that it was difficult to know in advance which offence types would be most likely to yield patterns of differential sentencing.

The commission chose five categories of offences: drug offences, sexual assaults, bail violations, serious non-sexual assaults, and robberies. Drug offences were an obvious choice, given the findings about prison admissions. Selection of the other offence types was based on consultations that had revealed significant concerns about black people being unfairly charged with these offences. The question for the sentencing study was whether there was any evidence that judges treated black men convicted of these offences unfairly. In responding to this question, the commission adopted a traditional strategy for researching racial disparity at sentencing. The research attempted to take account of every difference that might be thought legitimately to affect sentencing decisions. Once these differences have been accounted for, any residual disparity that remains may then be attributed to direct discrimination in the sentencing process. Because the commission's focus was systemic racism, however, there was also a more complex layer to the analysis. Systemic racism, as defined in the commission's mandate, refers to policies, procedures, and practices that have an adverse impact on racial minorities, even if they are not intended to have such an impact.

This type of indirect discrimination could not be identified by taking account of 'legally relevant' factors and looking for residual disparity, because the adverse impact may be due to reliance on those factors. The analysis instead requires close scrutiny of the legally relevant factors to see what impact they have and what role they play in sentencing practices. Ideally, those factors that are found to have an indirectly discriminatory impact, and hence to contribute to systemic racism, should then be excluded from sentencing practices unless their continued use can be justified by reference to two criteria. Reliance on the indirectly discriminatory factor must advance a legitimate and nondiscriminatory goal that is judged to be more important than racial equality, and reliance on this factor must be the least discriminatory method of advancing the goal.

The Sample

At the beginning of the integrated analysis, the total sample of charged persons consisted of 1,653 adult males. Of this total, 821 were classified by the police as black and 832 were classified as white. For ease of analysis the original sample was drawn to produce roughly equal numbers of black and white men in each offence category. The convicted sample was inevitably smaller, due to the impact of attrition and acquittals. In total, 871 were convicted, 488 white offenders and 383 black offenders. Another consequence of attrition and acquittals was that the matching of black and white men by offence was much less precise than in the original sample, although the samples remained comparable.

The sentencing study compared incarceration rates for black and white convicted men. A considerable quantity of data on criminal histories and personal characteristics were collected and these were included in the analysis. The study also examined characteristics of the offences and considered the impact on incarceration rates of decisions taken earlier in the process, such as detention before trial, plea, and, for some offences, Crown attorneys' choices about whether to proceed by summary conviction or by indictment.

Incarceration Rates

The commission began by looking at incarceration rates to see if there was any evidence of racial disparity in outcomes. It analysed the entire sample of convicted men, a sub-sample of men convicted of bail violations, sexual assaults, and drug offences (the three-offence sample), and it also compared sentences imposed on men convicted of drug charges. These analyses show that more black than white men are sentenced to prison. The extent of the disparity varies with the specific sample. Interestingly, the variation is almost entirely due to differences in the imprisonment rates of white men in the different samples. For each comparison, the data show that about two-thirds of the black men received a prison sentence. By contrast, the proportions of white men sentenced to prison ranged from 57 per cent of the entire sample to 47 per cent of the three-offence sample to 36 per cent of the drug-offence sample.

After documenting this basic finding of racial disparity in outcomes, the commission considered whether it could be explained by differences in factors such as characteristics of the offences, criminal histories and personal characteristics of the convicted men, and choices made earlier in the proceedings. There are some observable differences between the black and white samples that would contribute to higher imprisonment rates for black men, although these were generally quite small. Other differences ought to have led to harsher punishment of white than black men in the sample. Beyond the effect of these differences, the findings raise questions about whether some of these factors ought to play a role in the exercise of discretion at sentencing.

Differences That Contribute to Disparate Sentencing

Perceived seriousness of the offence is generally accepted as a legitimate influence on the severity of punishment. For the most part, little measurable difference appears between white and black convicted men in the commission's samples, which is not surprising, given the research design. Within the drug-charge sample, however, more white (90 per cent) than black (67 per cent) men were convicted of a simple possession offence as opposed to a trafficking offence. This difference would contribute to the differential incarceration rate, but it tells only part of the story. Analysis of sentences imposed on white and black men convicted of simple possession showed that the pattern of disparate sentencing persisted among those who faced the same charge. A much higher proportion of black (49 per cent) than white (18 per cent) men convicted of possession of a narcotic received a prison sentence.

Criminal history is another conventional explanation of sentencing differentials, and studies in other jurisdictions suggest that this factor accounts for some racial disparity in prison sentences. The Ontario data do not support this explanation. Data on the criminal records of the sample show that white men (72 per cent) were more likely than black men (65 per cent) to have at least one criminal conviction. White men (36 per cent) in the sample were also more likely than black men (28 per cent) to have acquired a lengthy criminal record, consisting of more than five previous convictions. Other aspects of criminal history, such as whether the person was on bail when charged or serving a sentence in the community while on probation or parole, also failed to explain the differential incarceration rates. While these factors had a significant impact on sentencing, they were no more likely to be found among the black than the white samples.

The commission identified one aspect of criminal history that may have contributed to the higher incarceration rates of the black sample, but it could account for disparity only among convicted men who already had a criminal record. This factor is the length of time since the last conviction ('clean time'). In general, older convictions on a criminal record have a less severe impact on sentencing than more recent convictions and this principle was confirmed in the commission's data. Across the entire sample of convicted men with a criminal record, those with more recent convictions were more likely to be sentenced to prison. Comparison of white and black men in this group showed that black men (21 per cent) were much more likely than white men (12 per cent) to have been last convicted within three months prior to the charge for which they were being sentenced.

In addition to assessing criminal record and the seriousness of an offence, sentencing judges may take into account the 'age, mode of life, character and personality' (*Iwaniw* (1959)) of a convicted person. One of the most important elements of this package of traits is employment status. Consistently with other sentencing studies, the commission found that this factor had a significant impact on incarceration rates. Within the sentenced sample as a whole, unemployed men (76 per cent) were much more likely than employed men (50 per cent) to receive a prison sentence.

This sentencing practice is highly contentious because it directly discriminates against poor people. The commission found that it also indirectly contributes to racial disparity in sentencing outcomes. A much higher proportion of black (62 per cent) than white (44 per cent) men were described as unemployed, which meant that the harsh impact of the sentencing practice fell disproportionately on the black men in the sample.

Another controversial sentencing practice, at least in some jurisdictions, is the policy of 'rewarding' those who plead guilty with a more lenient sentence than if they had been convicted after a contested trial. This practice is sometimes justified on the basis that the guilty plea shows that the individual takes responsibility for the offending behaviour and demonstrates contrition, both of which are viewed as desirable character traits. A more practical concern is that the guilty plea, especially if it comes early in the process, saves court time and resources.

The main criticisms of this policy are that it conflicts with the presumption of innocence and unduly pressures people into giving up their right to a trial. Studies in other jurisdictions have also found that the policy of discounting guilty pleas may contribute to racial disparity in imprisonment because black accused are consistently less likely than white accused to take advantage of it (Hood 1992). The commission's research indicated that the same may be true in Ontario. Analysis of the sentenced sample showed that black men (20 per cent) were almost twice as likely as white men (11 per cent) to have pleaded not guilty to the charges of which they were ultimately convicted.

For many charges, sentence severity may be influenced not only by the seriousness of the offence but also by how it is prosecuted. A large number of offences now offer Crown attorneys a choice between proceeding summarily or by indictment. This decision may have an important impact on sentencing outcomes because the two methods of proceeding are associated with very different maximum penalties. Even though maximum penalties are rarely awarded in practice, judges are likely to perceive a charge proceeded with by indictment as denoting a more serious offence than a charge proceeded with summarily.

Evidence of differential decision making by Crown attorneys appeared within the commission's study. Only some of the men in the sample had been convicted of charges that offered Crown attorneys a choice about mode of prosecution. Analysis of this group showed that Crown attorneys were significantly more likely to have proceeded summarily against white (61 per cent) than black (55 per cent) men. In a brief comment on this finding, the commission notes the lack of any evidence on the files to indicate that the black men had committed more serious offences. This suggests that Crown discretion may have independently contributed to racial disparity in sentencing outcomes.

The final factor identified by the commission as influencing sentencing disparity is detention before trial. Once again there is considerable research support from other jurisdictions for the finding that people denied bail and imprisoned before trial are more likely to be imprisoned after conviction than those who awaited trial in freedom. Unlike some of the other research findings on factors that influence sentencing, however, the explanation for this finding is unclear, because pretrial detention is not an explicit sentencing consideration. One possibility is that the exercise of discretion before trial and after conviction is intended to secure the same goals or is based on the same criteria (Meyer and Jesilow 1997). The primary ground for detention before trial, which is to ensure that the accused attends court when required, is of no significance to the punishment of a convicted person. It could be argued, however, that the secondary ground for denial of bail – crime prevention during the period before trial – resembles sentencing objectives such as individual deterrence and incapacitation.

The commission found that detention before trial was strongly related to imprisonment after conviction and that it also accounted for some of the racial disparity in sentencing. Within the sentenced sample, convicted black men (39 per cent) were significantly more likely than convicted white men (29 per cent) to have been ordered detained before their trials.

Conclusions about Disparity and Discrimination

The commission supplemented its separate analyses of the individual factors that contributed to racial disparity with multivariate analyses of the entire sentenced sample and the three-offence sample (men convicted of drug offences, bail violations, and sexual assaults). The purpose of this part of the study was to see if racial disparity remained when all of the other influential factors were simultaneously taken into account.

These analyses show that within the three-offence sample, the racial disparity in incarceration rates could not be fully explained by the combined effects the other factors. Instead, the 'race' of the convicted men had a small but independent impact on sentencing. This finding indicates that the higher incarceration rates of black than white convicted men is partly due to judges treating them more harshly for no legitimate reason. The disparity, in other words, is partly attributable to direct discrimination in the sentencing process. A second important finding about the three-offence sample is that unemployment rates and plea (as well as prosecution by indictment and detention before trial) have a significant impact on incarceration. This finding indicates that reliance on these apparently neutral factors in the exercise of sentencing discretion contributes to racial disparity of outcomes. In short, sentencing practices concerning unemployment and plea have an indirectly discriminatory impact, which contributes to the disproportionate imprisonment of black men.

Across the entire sentenced sample 'race,' plea, and prosecution by indictment had no direct impact on incarceration rates. Thus none of these factors contributed to the racial disparity of outcomes in the total sample. Unemployment and detention before trial, however, did have a discernable effect in that both were associated with higher imprisonment rates. Again, the implication is that sentencers who rely on these factors are likely to discriminate against black men without ever intending to do so.

Explanations for Racial Disparity in Sentencing

There are three basic models for explaining findings of racial disparity in sentencing outcomes. One focuses on offenders and their actions (offence/offender model); the others are centred on the decisions and practices of those who make and administer the criminal law (decision-maker models). An offender/offence model presumes that the criminal justice system is working as designed, and that racial bias – whether direct or indirect, explicit or implicit – is not part of its overall scheme (Wilbanks 1987). The criminal law and the standards of behaviour it demands are assumed to be neutral and universal, the administration of criminal justice is assumed to be impartial. Racial disparity in sentencing outcomes is, therefore, taken to reflect some other type of legally relevant – and by definition nondiscriminatory – difference between black and white persons convicted of criminal offences, such as criminal record or the seriousness of the incident that resulted in the conviction. Whatever the specific reason for disparity, the answer lies in the characteristics of offenders and offences; neither the law nor its administration is to blame.

Proponents of this model might challenge the commission's findings on the basis that more and better information about the offences and offenders would demonstrate that there is no direct discrimination. The claim is that the entire pattern of disparity could be explained by a legally relevant characteristic, which is currently invisible. Such claims can always be made, secure in the knowledge that unless perfect information is available they are in some sense unanswerable. One response is to turn an apparent weakness of the study into a strength. Direct discrimination appeared for some but not all charges. If the explanation were simply the missing data, then the expectation might be that all offence categories would be affected in the same way. It would seem likely that direct discrimination would appear in the sentencing for all offences or for no offences. Since the data vary with the different charges, they suggest that something needs to be explained. If the answer is not discrimination, what is the reason for the pattern of racial disparity?

In contrast to the offender/offence model, decision-maker models interpret racial disparity in sentencing outcomes as indicating bias in the standards or the practices of the criminal justice system (Meeker, Jesilow and Aranda 1992; Mann 1993; Cook and Hudson 1993). Bias may be subtle or explicit, it may inhere in the definitions of offences or in the application of the law and it may affect decisions at any stage of the criminal justice system. These models may accept that racial disparity in sentencing outcomes is partly or even largely explained by factors such as criminal records or differences in the perceived seriousness of offences, but they maintain that such factors reflect earlier discriminatory treatment by decision makers or bias in how offences are defined or interpreted. For example, evidence that black offenders have shorter periods of 'clean time' on their criminal records may be taken to indicate that they are the target of discriminatory police practices.

All decision-maker models start from the position that there is no connection whatsoever between 'race' or 'culture' and the propensity to harm other people. Racial differences in the distribution of bad things, such as punishments, or good things, such as wealth, are therefore due to choices that a society makes about how it should be organized, rather than the characteristics of individuals from different groups. Beyond this starting point, there are different versions of the decision-maker model. Some analysts treat class as the key social relationship that shapes the operation of the criminal justice system (structural bias). They draw on evidence that accused and convicted persons are mostly poor to argue that the criminal law and its administration function to control social classes that may pose a threat to those with wealth and power in a society (Reiman 1990). Class bias exists in legal standards (the criminal law) when, for example, injuries and deaths caused by corporations are not defined as crimes or are defined as less serious crimes than the harmful conduct of individuals. Bias exists in the administration of criminal justice when crimes committed by members of the upper classes generally escape detection and prosecution.

This model explains disproportionate imprisonment of black people as a manifestation of class, not racial, bias within the criminal justice system. Overrepresentation of black people in prisons occurs not because they are black but because structural features of the society, including systemic racism, place them disproportionately within the classes that are perceived to be a threat to the social order. The class-bias version of the decision-maker models may account for much of the disproportionate imprisonment of black people, including that which is due to indirect discrimination based on factors such as employment status, but it does not explain direct discrimination at sentencing or any other stage of the process. If most convicted persons belong to the same class, why would those who are black receive harsher punishments than their white counterparts convicted of the same offences?

Another version of the decision-maker model treats this question as its key concern. This model does not necessarily deny the significance of class to criminal proceedings, but it maintains that independent racial bias also operates at various stages of the process (Mann 1993). Proponents treat the over-representation of black people as the product of cumulative racial bias throughout the criminal justice system. The source of racial bias is not individual but social. Sentencing, like other social practices, is shaped by the values and assumptions of the society in which it exists. If negative racial stereotypes exist in the society at large, then judges may be influenced by them when evaluating convicted persons and their characters.

It can be seen that this model does not assume that judges consciously discriminate against black people – although some might. The claim, rather, is that cultural beliefs and assumptions about black people may implicitly shape judges' assessments of the individuals before them and that this bias is particularly likely to occur when judges are asked to assess intangible factors such as the attitude or personality of a convicted person. Since Canadian sentencing practices expressly refer to such factors, the conditions for discriminatory treatment exist. Findings of disparate outcomes at sentencing lend concrete support to the thesis.

Conclusions

The commission's research into sentencing and imprisonment shows that the criminal justice system in Canada's largest province is imprisoning disproportionate numbers of black people, and that the extent of this problem increased dramatically during the late 1980s and early 1990s. Much of this differential imprisonment occurs after decisions taken at an early stage of the criminal justice system, but direct and indirect discrimination at sentencing appear to make their own contribution to differential prison admissions.

These studies raise further questions. One important issue is the extent to which sentencing outcomes for other offences would reveal patterns of racial disparity. This question is posed by any selective study of sentencing practices because considerable research shows that disparity is more likely to occur for some offences than for others (Hood 1992) It is particularly pressing in the case of the offences selected by the commission because it appears that Ontario judges view most of them as serious offences that generally merit prison sentences (Canadian Centre for Justice Statistics 1993). This fact suggests that most of the convicted men in the study would receive a prison sentence, regardless of race. If judges seldom exercise the discretion to impose a punishment other than incarceration for these offences, then there should be little racial or other disparity of sentencing outcomes. Selection of offences that in practice ,receive a greater range of punishments might have revealed more about the relationship between sentencing discretion and racial disparity in imprisonment (Hood 1992).

It is also important to be aware of the possibility of variation in the sentencing practices of different courts. Hood's British study found, for example, substantial differences among courts serving the same area. In some courts the judges were 'acting in an even-handed way' (Hood 1992, 107); in others, sentencers imposed significantly harsher punishments on black than white convicted men. One consequence was racial disparity of outcomes for black and white men sentenced at these courts; another was that black men sentenced by the different courts received quite different punishments. Some interpret findings such as these to mean that racial disparity in sentencing is due primarily to black people being more likely than white people to be sentenced in courts that impose harsh sentences (Langan 1994). But this interpretation in turn requires explanation. It is possible, for example, that a court's practice of imposing harsher sentences than others in the same district has arisen partly because it deals with a large proportion of black convicted persons in the area and the judges serving in that court discriminate directly or indirectly.

Other aspects of the commission's study deserve further exploration. Of particular interest is the relationship between sentencing and decisions taken earlier in the process. The commission addressed this issue to some extent by analysing the detention decisions of the police and bail courts (Commission on

Systemic Racism in the Ontario Criminal Justice System 1995, 113–46), but the impact of other important decisions, such as choices about which charges to lay and which ones to withdraw, also need to be studied.

Despite the unanswered questions, the findings of the Commission on Systemic Racism lay a foundation for institutional accountability for how the criminal justice system treats black people. As such, they should be sufficient to prompt action from those responsible for the administration of criminal justice in Ontario. Some important initiatives occurred during the first year after the release of the report. For example, both provincial division judges, who conduct the majority of criminal proceedings, and federal Crown attorneys, who prosecute drug offences, have carried out significant training programs. At the time of writing, however, eighteen months after the report was released, the provincial government has yet to respond publicly to its findings and recommendations. The struggle for accountability continues.

ENDNOTES

1 The author thanks Judy Fudge, Valerie Holder, and Iain Ramsay for insightful and constructive comments on an earlier draft.

2 Toni Williams is an associate professor at Osgoode Hall Law School. She was a commissioner with the Commission on Systemic Racism in the Ontario Criminal Justice System, and she was responsible for writing the commission's reports.

ADDITIONAL READING

Commission on Systemic Racism in the Ontario Criminal Justice System. 1995. *Report of the Commission on Systemic Racism in the Ontario Criminal Justice System.* Toronto: Queen's Printer for Ontario.

Roberts, J.V., and A.N. Doob. 1997. Race, Ethnicity and Criminal Justice in Canada. In M. Tonry and R. Hood, eds., *Ethnicity, Crime and Immigration: Comparative and Cross-National Perspectives. Crime and Justice: A Review of Research.* Volume 21. Chicago: University of Chicago Press.

13

The Role of Victims in the Sentencing Process[1]

SANDRA BACCHUS[2]

What role should the victim play in a sentencing hearing? The traditional view of criminal justice in Canada has been that the criminal trial is a dispute between the state and the accused. This view, which excludes the victim, has been strongly criticized by many. More recently, however, the sentencing process has attempted to give the victims of crime a greater voice in the sentencing and parole process. In this chapter, Sandra Bacchus explores the issues surrounding the role of the victim in sentencing.

Introduction

It has often been said that a victim of crime is doubly victimized by his or her experience with the criminal justice system. This chapter examines the role of the victim in the sentencing process and the ways in which recent legislative changes seek to alleviate revictimization. How has the role of the victim evolved as a result of recent legislative changes? What rights, if any, does the victim now have during the sentencing process? To what extent should the victim's need for restitution affect whether an accused is incarcerated?

Evolution of the Victim's Role

Historically, the victim has been viewed as somewhat of an interloper in the sentencing process. Although in the vast majority of cases victims are the criminal justice system's *raison d'être*, their voice has traditionally been restricted. The role of the victim in sentencing proceedings has perhaps been best stated by the British Columbia Court of Appeal in *Re Regina and Antler*:[3] 'The Criminal Code contemplates prosecution of the accused by the Crown. It does not accord to persons affected by an offence status as parties to the proceedings against the accused apart from the provisions relating to restitution ... Nor does it grant to them the right to make representations against the accused independent of those which the Crown chooses to put forward.'

The victim of a crime is usually the person most profoundly affected by the offence. However, in Canadian law, the victim is not a formal party to the criminal proceeding. Unlike a civil action, in which one person sues another to seek compensation (usually financial) for a wrong done, the only parties to a criminal case are the state and the accused. Because the criminal act is considered to be a wrong done to the community, the Crown prosecutes the case on behalf of the state. Victims who wish to be compensated often discover that their needs and their perceptions of justice do not always coincide with the practice of the criminal justice system. As a result, a tension sometimes exists between the interests of the state (as represented by the Crown) and the interests of the victim.[4] For example, a victim may wish the accused to be charged with the most serious offence, carrying the most severe penalty. After examining the facts, Crown counsel may conclude that there is no reasonable prospect of a conviction, and therefore be obliged to abandon the conviction against the wishes of the victim.

At the sentencing stage, the lack of formal party status for the victim (only partially addressed in the recent sentencing reform bill) has important implications. Crown counsel may be obligated to refrain from placing certain material before the sentencing judge because that material is irrelevant or otherwise inadmissible. Crown counsel may be obliged, on the basis of precedent and the range of penalty usually imposed, to recommend penalties other than those favoured by the victim. It remains for the reader to decide whether the victim should have a voice, independent of the state, in the sentencing process.

In recent years this view of the role of victims, as articulated by the court in *Re Antler*, has altered considerably. Although victims do not have the right to make independent representations to the court, the active participation of victims in the sentencing process is now encouraged. Recent legislation has enhanced victims' rights in three areas: the right to information, the right to participation in the sentencing process, and the right to restitution. The evolution of victims' rights can be traced to several legislative initiatives that have developed throughout the last decade. In 1985, the United Nations General Assembly adopted a Charter of Victims' Rights, thereby officially recognizing the victim's voice in the criminal justice process. This declaration pronounced the rights of victims to fair treatment, access to justice, restitution from the offender, compensation from the state, and provision of support services. In 1988, Parliament passed Bill C-89,[5] which contained a set of principles to act as a guide to promote access to justice, and fair treatment of victims, and to provide assistance to victims of crime. This Act legislated the introduction of the victim impact statement. In addition, it expanded the victim's right to restitution by establishing a scheme prioritizing the payment of restitution to the offender over the imposition of a fine in cases in which the offender is unable to accomplish both. The Act also established the victim fine surcharge.

In Ontario, specific measures have been implemented to assist victims throughout the criminal process, including the sentencing stage. During the late 1980s, victim/witness assistance programs began to operate a number of sites throughout the province.[6] The victim/witness assistance program provides information to victims of crime, emotional support during the trial and sentencing phase, referrals to community agencies for counselling and support, and information about what the system can and cannot do for the victim in relation to repairing the harm done. Program staff assist the victim in the completion of victim impact statements.[7] After the trial or sentencing hearing the victim is usually 'debriefed' by victim/witness staff. Part of this process involves explaining the reasons for sentence and the appeal process. A copy of the probation order is given to the victim and the victim is encouraged to report any further incidents should they occur.[8]

In June 1996, Bill 23[9] was proclaimed in force in Ontario. This legislation was seen as a significant step in acknowledging the needs of victims of crime in the criminal justice system. The Act outlined principles and standards for the treatment of victims through the justice process, focusing on increasing access to information for the victim, the entitlement to have property returned as promptly as possible, and the victim's right to input in sentencing proceedings. Known as the 'Victims' Bill of Rights,' the Act provides guidance to those who come into contact with victims in the criminal justice system. The preamble reads: 'The people of Ontario believe that victims of crime who have suffered harm and whose rights and security have been violated by crime, should be treated with compassion and fairness. The people of Ontario further believe that the justice system should operate in a manner that does not increase the suffering of victims of crime and that does not discourage victims of crime from participating in the justice process.'

The Crown policy manual, which directs the conduct of Crown counsel, adopts the philosophy of the Bill of Rights and states that 'victims should be given an opportunity to attend court at the time of plea and sentencing and should be informed of their right to do so ... Victims should be consulted regarding significant decisions made by the crown regarding sentence, plea, withdrawal of charges.' Crown attorneys are directed to ensure that the interests of victims of crime are brought forward at every stage of the prosecution to a degree consistent with the primary role of a prosecutor, although comments of the victim that are not relevant to issues on sentencing should not be placed before the court. As a result, Crown counsel is sometimes required to act as a screen or filter for the concerns of the victim and must balance the victims' right to dignity and some level of participation in the process with the Crown's function as an officer of the court.

These legislative and philosophical changes detail the status of the rights of victims prior to the enactment of the most recent federal legislation, known as Bill C-41.

Bill C-41

The provisions of Bill C-41 amended the Criminal Code of Canada to specifically codify the rights of victims of crime to participate and benefit in the sentencing process in several key ways. Section 722 of the Criminal Code addresses the admissibility of victim impact statements in sentencing hearings. Sections 738 to 741.2 further expand the parameters of the type of restitution to which the victim is entitled. Subsection 745.6(2) entrenches the role of victim participation in some types of parole eligibility hearings. Victims now have standing to participate in eligibility hearings and can provide information to the court about the effect of the crime on their lives.

Restitution

Sections 738 to 741.2 of the Code constitute the revised restitution provisions pursuant to the C-41 amendments. The new sections set out the instances in which restitution may be ordered and include compensation for pecuniary damages, loss of support, and loss of income incurred as a result of bodily harm. Bodily harm includes psychological harm that the victim may have suffered. These specific circumstances were not incorporated in past legislation.[10] In each instance that restitution is available, the amount of the loss must be readily ascertainable.

Aside from expanding the number of instances in which restitution is available, section 738 grants the victim an automatic right to restitution. The previous version of the legislation required the aggrieved party to apply for restitution.[11] Section 738 now makes it clear that the Crown may apply for restitution or the court may consider the imposition of a restitution order of its own motion. The victim is not required to request restitution or even to attend court for the order to be imposed. This amendment reflects the emphasis to be placed on restoring the victim back to his or her original position as a means to further the ends of justice.

An example of this new emphasis on restitution for victims in the sentencing process is found in a recent case in which the judge was sentencing multiple accused convicted of the robbery of a convenience store. The following formula was employed by the sentencing judge in considering the issue of restitution to the victim:

> Since one of the important aspects of the revisions to part XXIII of the Code is that sentencing judges are directed to consider the needs of victims in considering intermediate sanctions, I turn first to [the] victim impact statement. As it does not detail any financial losses resulting from the bodily harm which he sustained, the various provisions of s. 728 would not seem applicable. I next consider whether it would be appropriate to make an order for restitution (or reparation) equivalent to the salary [the victim] is now forced to pay in order to hire another staff person to assist him during the evenings on weekends, and to pay his mother for her participation as a 'watchdog' on the other evenings. After calculating and dividing the total sum (which will be from the date of the offence until the date of issuance of these reasons), and apportioning it equally between the accused, I shall make an order in favour of the victim by way of restitution on a payment schedule, initially to be enforced by way of a probation order. In the event payment is not made, the victim will be at liberty to file the order and the clerk's certificate as to non-payment and outstanding balance and to enter a judgment in the amount outstanding as of the date of default payment.[12]

Two other aspects of the amendments to the restitution provisions suggest the emphasis that Parliament has placed on the concept of restorative justice. Subsection 740(b) provides that where a court is contemplating a restitution order and the offender may not have the resources to satisfy both restitution and a fine, the judge is first required to consider ordering restitution. This provision requires that the sentencing judge direct his or her mind to the interest of the victim as a priority in crafting a sentence that is fit.

The second aspect of the legislation that furthers this concept of restorative justice is the change to the way in which restitution orders are enforced. Restitution orders are now freestanding orders. This means that it is not necessary to place an offender on probation to make an order for restitution.[13] As a result, section 741 provides that if restitution is not paid forthwith, the aggrieved party may file the order and enter it as a judgment in civil court. The order is then enforceable against the accused as if it were rendered in civil court proceedings. Section 741.2 seems to envelop the common law principle that the existence of a restitution order does not preclude obtaining a civil remedy[14] with the practical problems involved in trying to obtain the civil remedy.[15] It has expanded the common law by obviating the need for the victim to commence a civil action. In collapsing two processes into one, this provision seeks to minimize the further revictimization of victims by limiting the steps required to recover their money. As well, the victim and the system are no longer solely dependent on overburdened, understaffed probation services to police the recovery of moneys.

Some might argue that free-standing restitution orders do little to further assist the victim's actual recovery of his or her loss, given that enforcement of the court order is the most difficult aspect of obtaining restitution from the civil courts. Once the restitution order has been filed with the court, the victim must still embark on lengthy, complex, and often unsuccessful proceedings to determine if the debtor possesses any assets. The skilful defendant can turn these proceedings into an exhausting game of 'hide-and-seek,' as assets disappear or are deliberately never accumulated in order to avoid payment. Thus it might well be that overburdened, understaffed probation services have been far more effective in recovering at least some of the money owed to the victim in light of the realities of the civil process.

Victim Impact Statement

A victim impact statement is defined as a description of the physical, emotional, and financial harm inflicted on the victim as a result of the offence before the court. It provides the victim with the opportunity to inform the court about the impact of the offence. The statement is not a retelling of the crime or an opportunity to raise other issues or discuss other offences not before the court. Nor is the victim entitled to tell the court what, in his or her view, the sentence should be. The statement is typically (but not always) written. On 28 March 1994 Ontario implemented the use of a standardized victim impact statement form, which is currently used in courts throughout the province.

Alternative forms of victim impact statements include oral statements presented by the victim to the court or given behind a screen or via closed circuit television, and audio- or video-taped statements of the deceased.[16] The victim may be called as a witness on sentencing or to answer questions that might arise from comments made in the victim impact statement. The introduction of the victim impact statement has been viewed as one of the most dramatic developments in Canadian sentencing history.[17] This reform, designed to increase victim participation in the sentencing process, directly addressed the issue of public discontent and dissatisfaction with the sentencing process.[18]

The impetus for developing what was then called 'victim impact statement programs' followed a 1983 report of the Federal and Provincial Task Force on Justice for Victims of Crime, which recommended the introduction of victim impact statements to be considered at the time of sentencing. In 1986, as part of the policy development process, the federal Department of Justice conducted a series of test projects in six locations across Canada. The findings demonstrated that victims did not seem to use such statements as a retributive tool. Completing a statement did not necessarily lead to greater satisfaction with the system; however, an overwhelming majority of victims found the experience of completing a statement to be a positive one and would participate again if victimized. Completing a statement appeared to result in an increase in the belief that the criminal justice system was interested in the victims of crime.[19]

Section 722 addresses the admissibility of the victim impact statement in the sentencing hearing. It is important to understand that neither this provision nor subsection 2(b) of the Charter of Rights and Freedoms gives the victim the right to make submissions regarding the length of sentence to be imposed. In *Coehlo v. B.C.*,[20] the accused had been convicted of dangerous driving causing death. At the accused's sentencing hearing a victim impact statement from the deceased victim's mother was filed. This statement included a passage which stated: 'Mrs Coehlo wants the court to impose the severest penalty available in this case as she has suffered irreparably in her mind.' No statement was filed by the victim's father but, at the family's request, counsel sought to supplement the previously filed statement with oral submissions relating to the impact of the crime. The trial judge restricted counsel's submissions to discussing only the victim and nothing else. The father of the victim sought to review the sentence (by way of prerogative writ) on the ground that the trial judge erred in denying him the opportunity to make submissions on the appropriate sentence. In dismissing the petition, the British Columbia Supreme Court noted: 'I find that Mr. Coehlo's rights to fully express his strongly held views by all means does not give him the right to audience in a court of law. While he is a victim of this crime, neither the Criminal Code nor the Charter of Rights and Freedoms requires that he be permitted to speak in addition to Crown counsel on the severity of penalty to be imposed.'[21]

The previous version of the legislation dealing with victim impact statements (section 735) did not compel a sentencing judge to consider such a report, although they were admissible as evidence at the sentencing hearing.[22] Section 722 now requires the judge to consider any such statement, describing the harm done or loss suffered by the victim, in his or her determination of the sentence. Currently the law is somewhat unsettled on the issue of whether the victim impact statement must be authored by the actual victim of the offence unless he or she is dead, ill, or otherwise incapable of making a statement.[23] However, there is strong precedent in Ontario for the position that the definition of 'victim' for the purposes of a victim impact statement should be given a broad and liberal interpretation, and that the victim can be someone other than the person who directly suffered physical or emotional loss as a result of the commission of the offence. In *R. v. Phillips*[24] the court expressly rejected the strict interpretation of the definition of 'victim.' It was the view of the court in *Phillips* that to impose a strict interpretation upon the definition of 'victim' would be contrary to the intent of the legislature to ensure that members of the deceased family be permitted to provide victim impact statements. It was the court's view in *Phillips* that the societal concern for victims' rights and the retributive aim of sentencing requires that there be a broad interpretation of the definition of 'victim.'[25]

Victim Fine Surcharge

The victim fine surcharge is a sum of money that the offender is required to pay in addition to the sentence imposed under the Criminal Code and/or certain other Acts. The surcharge is one of several new measures designed to make the justice system more responsive to the needs of victims. The amount of the surcharge to be imposed depends on the sentence. If the sentence is a fine, the surcharge cannot exceed 15 per cent; if the sentence is some other form of penalty, the fine cannot exceed $10,000.[26] The surcharge has been instrumental in expanding and improving support to the victims of crime. In Ontario, revenue generated by the fine surcharge is held in the victim assistance fund, which is to be used solely to maintain and expand assistance to victims of crime. Services that receive monetary assistance from the fund include the criminal injuries compensation board, and the victim witness assistance program, the victim crisis and assistance referral service, as well as other community-based agencies.[27]

General Issues

Section 718 sets out the fundamental purpose of sentencing and the objectives that the sentence should attempt to achieve. It is significant that notions of restorative justice are included in the fundamental purposes of sentencing. Subsections (e) and (f) direct the sentencing court to take into account the loss and harm done to the victim in fashioning an appropriate sentence. Pursuant to section 718.2, Parliament has deemed offences against certain classes of vulnerable victims and certain forms of harm to be specifically aggravating factors in sentencing. Victims who are subjected to offences motivated by racial hatred, bias, physical disability, or sexual orientation, and offenders who abuse positions of trust in relation to the victim or who victimize their spouse or child will be subject to sentences that denounce the conduct and express the public's particular abhorrence for such conduct. In this context the impact of the offence as outlined by the victim is important in assessing its gravity.

This author has prosecuted many cases in which victim impact statements were extremely important in this respect. In one such case the offence had involved severe and prolonged violence to the victim at the hands of her husband. At the accused's sentencing hearing an expert on the impact of domestic abuse testified that the victim was suffering from one of the most severe cases of post-traumatic stress disorder in his experience. The victim impact statement filed with the court detailed the agony she had endured and still suffers: severe nightmares and panic attacks and periods when she is so severely immobilized that she can only bring herself out of an attack by repeatedly sticking herself with a pin or sharp object. The humanizing of the impact of the offence could have only been achieved by entering the impact statement of the victim as evidence. Her statement was effective in conveying to the court the horrendous nature of this offence and its subsequent prolonged impact.

The introduction of conditional sentences raises issues related to the victim's right to restitution. I have discussed earlier in this chapter the emphasis that the recent amendments place on the concept of restitution. Given the centrality of restitution to the concept of victims' rights, is it appropriate that a court not incarcerate the offender and prefer a conditional sentence in order to permit the offender the opportunity to compensate the victim? Consider these comments made by the sentencing judge in *R. v. Visanji et al.*: 'I make one further common sense inference from Parliament's new emphasis on the need to reimburse victims as expressed in the revisions to the Code, that being that, as a practical matter, victims are unlikely to be reimbursed until the offender has been released from close custody. While this cannot itself serve as a justification for reducing an otherwise fit custodial term, it seems to me that in this case, where dangerousness is not obviously in issue, properly informed members of the public would think it entirely fit and proper that offenders be released from close custody in part to commence repaying their victims once the minimum appropriate denunciatory period has been served in close custody ...' [28]

Is such an approach consistent with the retributive and other aims outlined in section 718?[29]

Notification

The Corrections and Conditional Release Act is federal legislation which came into effect in 1992.[30] It provides for the notification of victims regarding the length of sentence imposed as well as parole eligibility and review dates. The victim may, upon application, also receive further information regarding the location of the penitentiary and the date of release from custody and the destination of the offender upon release.

Conclusion

In 1997 the Honourable Anne McLellan, the federal minister of justice, outlined the government's position regarding victims in the criminal justice system. In her address, the Honourable Minister expressed concern that not enough has been done to accommodate the interests of victims within the criminal justice system. The legislative changes detailed in this paper, culminating in the recent amendments to the sentencing provisions, clearly constitute significant improvements in the manner in which victims are treated in the criminal justice system. Minister McLellan suggests, however, that further innovative strategies are required to support the unique role that victims play.[31] It will be interesting to observe the direction that victims' rights will take in Canada in the coming years.

ENDNOTES

1 The author wishes to acknowledge the assistance of Brian Manarin and Susan Physick in the preparation of this paper.
2 Sandra Bacchus is an assistant Crown attorney in Scarborough, Ontario. She is currently completing her Master of Laws at Osgoode Hall Law School.
3 (1982), 69 C.C.C. (2d) 480.
4 This tension may arise throughout the criminal process, not just at the sentencing stage. A victim may, for instance, decide not to report a crime and resent the interference of criminal justice professionals who insist on arresting and prosecuting an offender, sometimes against the express wishes of the victim. A common example of this is domestic assault prosecutions, where large numbers of victims either fail to report crimes or refuse to cooperate with the Crown in the prosecution of the offender, who is also the victim's partner.
5 Bill C-89, An Act to Amend the Criminal Code (Victims of Crime)
6 Approximately twenty-three sites currently exist in Ontario, but the program is rapidly expanding. The program operates on a priority basis dealing primarily with

victims of violence and its involvement begins after a charge is laid. Referrals are made by the police, Crown attorneys, community agencies, and women's shelters. In addition to its other functions, the program ensures that the victim is provided with information, updates regarding the case, and any special needs, such as interpreters, housing, or counselling, as well as court preparation and court support.

7 See 'Some Views on the Sentencing Process,' remarks by Susan Lee at the Canadian Institute for the Administration of Justice Conference, 24–26 April 1997.

8 See Prince (1996).

9 An Act Respecting Victims of Crime

10 Sections 738(1)(a), (b), and (c) sanction the availability of an order for restitution in circumstances that include damage to or loss or destruction of property and bodily harm.

11 In practice these formalities were usually dispensed with.

12 *R. v. Visanji, Lall, and Akbar* (unreported), Ont. Ct. Prov. Div., 2 July 1997, at p. 3.

13 A restitution order may still be made part of a probation order under s. 732.1(3)(h). It may also be ordered as part of a conditional sentence. Section 742.3(2)(f) allows the court a discretion to impose such 'other reasonable conditions' as the court desires, in fashioning the terms of conditional sentence.

14 See *London Life v. Zavitz* (1992), 12 C.R. (4th) 267 (B.C.C.A.).

15 Many of the victims in *R. v. Stuckless* (see note 16, below) have joined together to launch a civil action against Maple Leaf Gardens.

16 At the sentencing hearing in *R. v. Stuckless*, a case in which an accused pleaded guilty to twenty-four counts of sexual offences involving young boys at Maple Leaf Gardens, seventeen victim impact statements were filed with the court. Eight complainants gave *viva voce* testimony about the impact of the sex abuse on their lives, in addition to submitting impact statements. At the sentencing hearing in *R. v. Bernardo*, Debbie Mahaffy, the mother of Leslie Mahaffy, produced a video of her daughter's life in order to give the court a more complete sense of her daughter and to underscore the tremendous sense of loss felt by the family as a result of her murder.

17 A. Young, 'Two Scales of Justice: A Reply,' [1993] 35 C.L.Q. 357.

18 One research study found that people given complete information about sentencing decisions were far more content than other individuals who had been given only a brief newspaper summary of the same case (Doob and Roberts 1983). As well, systematic content analysis of news media accounts of sentencing decisions have found that the reasons for sentence are almost never reported (Canadian Sentencing Commission 1987).

19 Project evaluations were completed prior to the proclamation of any legislative authority permitting the introduction of victim impact statements. Although victim

impact statements could be filed with the court without this authority, the use of these statements was viewed by some as problematic.

20 (1995), 41 C.R. (4th) 324 (B.C.S.C.).

21 *Coehlo v. B.C.* (1995), 41 C.R. (4th) 324 at 328 (B.C.S.C.).

22 Section 735(1.1) states that for the purpose of determining the sentence to be imposed on an offender or whether the offender should be discharged pursuant to s. 736 in respect of any offence, the court *may* consider a statement, prepared in accordance with s. (1.2), of a victim of the offence describing the harm done to, or loss suffered by, the victim arising from the commission of the offence.

23 See *R. v. Curtis* (1992), 69 C.C.C. (3d) 385 (N.B.C.A.)

24 (1995), 26 O.R. (3d) 522.

25 In *R. v. Phillips* (1996), 26 O.R. (3d) 522, McIsaac Gen. Div. J. held at p. 528: 'The provision of the three contested [statements] herein will assist me in lifting the character of P.C. Nystedt [the victim] from the status of a "faceless human cipher." I see no potential for them to distort the sentencing hearing into an exclusive process to rectify the purely private interests of their authors. They will merely provide a balance to the anticipated evidence that will be advanced on behalf of the offender in mitigation of sentence. Accordingly, both sides will be afforded a hearing that reflects the principles of fundamental justice ... I am persuaded that the definition of victim in s. 735(1.4) should be given a broad and liberal interpretation. For these reasons, I am compelled to the conclusion that I should not follow the judgement of the New Brunswick Court of Appeal in *R. v. Curtis, supra.*'

26 Criminal Code, s. 37.

27 See *R. v. Crowell* (1992), 76 C.C.C. (3d) 413 at 418 (N.S.C.A.): 'The victim fine surcharge is like a tax for the purpose of raising a revenue, but unlike a tax in that it is also a further expression of public reprobation at the time of sentencing. In an important aspect it is penal in its application and its consequences. In its fund-raising aspect it represents an effort to rectify the harm done by criminal activity, a public purpose wholly related to the field of criminal law.'

28 *Supra*, note 12.

29 See *R. v. Horvath* (1997), 117 C.C.C. (3d) 110 (Sask. C.A.); see also *R. v. L.F.W.* (unreported), Nfld. C.A., 22 September 1997.

30 S.C. 1992, c. 36.

31 Department of Justice – Minister's Address on Justice Issues, 23 August 1997.

ADDITIONAL READING

Giliberti, C. 1990. Study Probes Effectiveness of Victim Impact Statements. *Justice Research Notes* 1:1–8.

Hall, D. 1997. Victims' Voices in Criminal Court: The Need for Restraint. In M. Wasik, ed., *The Sentencing Process*. Dartmouth: Aldershot.

Waller, I. 1988. *The Role of the Victim in the Sentencing Process.* Research Reports of the Canadian Sentencing Commission. Ottawa: Department of Justice.

14

Appellate Review of Sentencing Decisions

GARY T. TROTTER[1]

This chapter addresses a critical but little-researched issue in the area of sentencing: the role of the appellate courts. Once a judge has imposed a sentence, either the Crown or counsel for the offender may appeal to have the sentence reviewed by a higher court. This means that the appellate courts can play a critical role in regulating sentencing at the trial court level. As well, appellate courts can influence sentencing practices on a broader level, when they hand down guideline judgments. Gary Trotter reviews the role that appellate courts have played in the evolution of sentencing in Canada.

Introduction

After a sentencing judge sorts through the innumerable sentencing provisions in the Criminal Code (described in previous chapters) and imposes a sentence that he or she feels is appropriate, the offender or the prosecutor may seek to have this decision reviewed by a higher court. This chapter examines the manner in which sentencing decisions are reviewed by the provincial and territorial courts of appeal. It also explores the role of the Supreme Court of Canada in the sentencing process.

Traditionally, the appellate courts (particularly the provincial courts of appeal), have played a very important role in the Canadian sentencing process. Apart from providing a means by which disgruntled litigants may test the appropriateness of a sentencing judge's decision, trial courts often look to the courts of appeal for guidance on sentencing matters (both in terms of the type of sentence required in a particular case and the quantum (or amount) of punishment that is merited). Decisions by the courts of appeal on sentencing matters are meant to reduce disparity in the lower courts, although the extent to which they are successful in this enterprise is debatable (Young 1988). This traditional role of the appellate courts has been disrupted somewhat by three recent cases from the Supreme Court of Canada that restrict the power of the provincial courts of appeal to review sentencing decisions. Unfortunately, these decisions were released close in time to the enactment of Bill C-41, the sentencing reform bill. The consequences of this temporal intersection of legislative and judicial activity is considered below.

The Appellate Courts: Finding the Pathways

The Classification of Offences: Indictable, Summary, and Hybrid

The procedure regarding the appellate review of sentences is complicated by the distinction made in the Criminal Code between indictable and summary conviction offences. Space does not permit a comprehensive explanation of this classification (see Quigley (1997)). For the purposes of this chapter, it is sufficient to understand that the Criminal Code classifies its most serious offences (such as manslaughter, break and enter, and aggravated sexual assault) as indictable offences. Indictable offences are generally punishable by the following maximum terms of imprisonment: two years, five years, ten years, fourteen years, or life. At the other end of the spectrum are those offences considered to be among the least serious (e.g., causing a disturbance, soliciting for the purposes of prostitution). These are known as summary conviction offences and carry a maximum punishment of six months' imprisonment, a fine of $2,000, or both (see section 787).

The vast majority of offences in the Criminal Code are classified as hybrid offences (e.g., sexual assault, criminal harassment, dangerous driving). Hybrid offences may be prosecuted either by indictment or by summary procedure. The decision as to which way to proceed, which is called an 'election,' is taken by the prosecutor. If the prosecutor elects to proceed by indictment, the greater maximum penalties will be available to the sentencing judge. Similarly, if the prosecutor elects to proceed by summary procedure, the sentencing judge will be limited to the lower maximum penalties described above. However, Parliament has recently altered this scheme somewhat by providing for a maximum penalty of eighteen months' imprisonment, a $2,000 fine, or both when certain hybrid offences (e.g., assault with a weapon, assault causing bodily harm, sexual assault) are proceeded with summarily. Separate avenues of review are available for sentences that result from summary conviction proceedings and proceedings by way of indictment. While this chapter touches on the procedure for appealing sentences in summary conviction proceedings, the focus of the discussion is on appellate review in the context of proceedings by indictment.

Appellate Review of Summary Conviction Sentences

Appeals of sentences imposed for summary conviction offences are heard by a single judge of the province's (or territory's) superior court of criminal jurisdiction (section 829). Section 813 of the Code permits both the accused and the attorney general[2] (or informant) to appeal against a sentence imposed in summary conviction proceedings. In terms of the power of a summary conviction appeal court to review a sentence, section 822 makes the powers of the court of appeal on indictable appeals applicable to this process. Thus, the power to review the 'fitness' of a sentence (found in section 687, discussed below) is also applicable to summary conviction sentence appeals.

Once the summary conviction appeal court has dealt with an appeal against sentence, the Criminal Code provides limited circumstances in which the offender or the attorney general may take the case before the court of appeal of the province. Section 839 provides that the party wishing to appeal must obtain 'leave to appeal' (permission to bring the case before the court) from the court of appeal (or a single judge of that court) and that the proposed appeal must be based on a question of law alone. A number of courts have held that an appeal that merely questions the 'fitness' of a sentence is not a question of law alone, although the matter is not free from controversy (*Thomas* (1980); *Guida* (1989); *Loughery* (1992); *Culley* (1977)).

Appellate Review of Indictable Sentences

With respect to indictable offences, the Criminal Code provides avenues of appeal directly to the courts of appeal of the provinces (or territories) for both the offender (section 675) and the attorney general (section 676). There are two limits placed on these appeal rights. First, the party seeking to have the sentence reviewed must obtain 'leave to appeal' from a single judge of the court or a panel of three judges. Second, the sentence appealed from cannot be one that is fixed by law.[3] Sentence appeals are heard by a panel of court of appeal judges. Panels are usually composed of three judges, although sometimes a panel of five judges may consider a sentence appeal, especially if the case raises a question of public importance or an issue with broad implications.

Joint Review of Summary Conviction and Indictable Sentences

Sometimes, an offender is convicted and sentenced in a single proceeding for both indictable offences (or hybrid offences for which the prosecutor has elected to proceed by indictment) and summary conviction offences (or hybrid offences for which the prosecutor has elected to proceed summarily). For example, an individual who pleads guilty or is found guilty of break and enter (a purely indictable offence) and breach of probation (where the prosecutor has elected to proceed summarily) falls into this category. If the offender or the attorney general wishes to appeal, must separate appeals be launched as described above (i.e., one in the summary conviction appeal court and one in the court of appeal)? Until very recently, the answer to this question was 'yes.' Now, subsection 675(1.1) (right of appeal of the offender) and subsection 676(1.1) (right of appeal of the attorney general) of the Criminal Code allow an appeal of both sentences directly to the court of appeal. This avoids the wasteful duplication of proceedings and enables a single court to consider the offender's situation from a more global perspective.

Sentence Appeals to the Supreme Court of Canada

The Criminal Code does not provide a direct avenue of appeal to the Supreme Court of Canada from a sentencing decision of a provincial or territorial court of appeal. However, under section 40 of the Supreme Court of Canada Act, the Supreme Court may grant leave to appeal sentence in both summary conviction and indictable cases. There are serious constraints on the ability of a litigant to obtain leave to appeal on a sentencing issue. On its own terms, section 40 requires that the issue raise a question of law alone or a question of mixed fact and law. Moreover, the issue must be of sufficient importance to justify the court's attention (Sopinka and Gelowitz 1993). As a matter of self-imposed policy, the Supreme Court does not hear many sentencing cases. The court will not consider cases that only raise the fitness of a sentence (Price 1983). The sentencing cases the court decides to hear usually involve significant legal or constitutional issues. A prominent example is the important case of *Gardiner* (1982), in which the court decided that where contested facts are presented at the sentencing hearing, the standard of proof required before they may be relied upon by the sentencing judge is the same standard as contested facts at trial, namely, proof beyond a reasonable doubt.

In recent years, the court has heard a number of cases that have raised the issue of the proper role of the courts of appeal in reviewing the fitness of sentences (*Shropshire* (1996); *C.A.M.* (1996); *McDonnell* (1997)). This issue occupies a large part of the following discussion.

The Nature of Appellate Proceedings: What Do Appeal Courts Base Their Decisions On?

In terms of practice and procedure, appeals are very different from trials (Sopinka and Gelowitz 1993). Appellate proceedings tend to be less dramatic than trials and rarely catch the attention of the media. Consequently, the general public is probably less informed about what takes place in the appellate courts, even though the decisions of these courts often have broader implications than most trial court decisions. Although there is some variation between provinces,[4] the practice of most of the courts of appeal is very similar. Appellate proceedings in Canada rarely involve the presentation of testimonial evidence. Sentence appeals are based upon the transcript of proceedings before the judge who originally sentenced the offender. The transcript usually includes a reproduction of evidence called at the original hearing (i.e., victim impact evidence, character evidence, medical/psychiatric evidence) and the submissions of defence counsel and the prosecutor, as well as the decision and reasons of the sentencing judge. Exhibits filed at the sentencing hearing are forwarded to the court of appeal. In most provinces, this material is supplemented by briefs written by the prosecutor and the offender's lawyer. These briefs (referred to as 'factums') set out the circumstances of the case, review legal precedents, and make recommendations as to the appropriate outcome of the appeal.

There is some scope to present the court of appeal with new information that might have an impact on the decision it is called upon to make. Section 687 of the Criminal Code allows a court of appeal to receive further evidence to assist in deciding the case. In legal jargon, the presentation of new evidence on appeal is referred to as an application to present 'fresh evidence.' While the rules respecting the presentation of fresh evidence are quite strict on appeals from conviction (*Palmer* (1979); *Stolar* (1988)), the courts are much more accepting of fresh evidence on sentence appeals. Fresh evidence applications are usually made on behalf of the offender and often include updates on the offender's life/family circumstances and progress while incarcerated prior to the hearing of the appeal. This type of material is considered to be relevant to the decision the appeal court judges are called upon to make about the sentence that was imposed.

The Scope of Review: When Should an Appellate Court Intervene to Alter the Decision of a Sentencing Judge?

The scope of review is really at the heart of any discussion about appellate review. The scope of permissible review plots the outside limits of what an appellate court is entitled to do in a sentencing case. It describes the type of inquiry the judges are required to undertake. Moreover, the powers that are granted to courts of appeal define the institutional role of the appellate courts in the overall sentencing process, especially in terms of their relationship to the lower courts. There is no special substantive law of sentencing for the courts of appeal. The same principles and provisions discussed in the previous chapters apply at this juncture. The only difference is the position in which sentencing judges and appeal court judges stand in relation to this substantive law. In other words, the scope of review determines who has the last word: sentencing judges or the courts of appeal.

The nature of the scope of review also has implications that reverberate outside of the strictures of the court process. Decisions about sentencing (or the allocation of the punitive power of the state) raise important questions of social policy. The degree to which society, through its criminal sanctions, reflects its disapprobation of certain types of conduct engenders questions of value and social meaning (Garland 1990). For instance, the manner in which a society punishes child or elder abuse conveys the degree to which that society values the physical integrity of some of its most vulnerable members. Decisions on these issues also raise questions about the allocation of scarce government resources. These considerations in turn pose the question of whether these types of decisions ought to be decided by a democratic body or by the courts. These issues are subsumed in the question of how much power we are prepared to grant courts of appeal to review and alter sentences, especially since Parliament has not legislated with great specificity in this area. A broader scope of review furnishes the courts of appeal with more latitude to influence public policy issues (Trotter 1997).

The Two Paradigms: Laissez-Faire or Interventionist?

The statutory core of appellate review of sentences is found in section 687 of the Criminal Code, which provides:

687(1) Where an appeal is taken against sentence, the court of appeal shall, unless the sentence is one fixed by law, *consider the fitness of the sentence appealed against,* and may on such evidence, if any, as it thinks fit to require or to receive,

(a) vary the sentence within the limits prescribed by law for the offence of which the accused was convicted; or

(b) dismiss the appeal. (Emphasis added.)

The courts of appeal have differed in their interpretation of this section. Some courts have held that the italicized words of section 687 should be read liberally, such that a court of appeal may substitute its own view of the appropriate sentence (*Simmons* (1973); *Cotton Felts Ltd.* (1982)). This interventionist paradigm devalues the contribution made by trial judges and reposes almost complete power in the courts of appeal. This approach is thought to foster greater consistency in sentencing; it also affords appellate courts greater scope to effect changes in sentencing policy.

At the other end of the spectrum is the standard of review which demonstrates considerable deference to sentencing judges. This model allows the courts of appeal to intervene and alter the decision of a sentencing judge only if the judge erred in principle, proceeded on an erroneous basis, or imposed a sentence that was either manifestly excessive or clearly inadequate (*Pepin* (1990); *Muise* (1994)). This approach has greater regard for the discretion of sentencing judges, but is thought to result in greater disparity.

Until recently, both of these paradigms were evident in different provinces,[5] although the more robust approach to appellate review seemed to predominate (Manson 1997b). Shortly before effecting dramatic changes in the sentencing review process (discussed below), the Supreme Court of Canada in *Dunn* (1995) made some statements about sentence appeals. Writing for a majority of the court, Mr Justice Major made the curious statement that section 687 conferred a discretion on courts of appeal similar to that of the trial judge assessing the fitness of sentence at first instance. He further stated that the scope of review does not involve *de novo* sentencing, nor does it contemplate a highly deferential standard requiring 'patent unreasonableness.' Instead, he held that the standard of review 'lies somewhere in between': *Dunn* (1995, 256).

The Supreme Court's Recent Decisions

The ambiguous comments in *Dunn* likely had no impact on the differing approaches to appellate review, because the Supreme Court of Canada released its decision in *Shropshire* (1996) not long after. Unlike *Dunn*, *Shropshire* was clear and unequivocal in its approach to the appellate review of sentences. This view was soon reinforced by the court's decision in *C.A.M.* (1996), and more recently in *McDonnell* (1997). We now have the luxury of certainty. However, it is doubtful that the Supreme Court resolved this important issue in a satisfactory manner.

In *Shropshire*, the accused killed the victim in the course of a drug transaction. Shropshire entered a plea of guilty to second degree murder, an offence requiring life imprisonment with a period of parole ineligibility between ten to twenty-five years (to be determined by the sentencing judge). Both the prosecutor and counsel for Shropshire suggested that the appropriate period of parole ineligibility was ten years. The sentencing judge disagreed and imposed twelve years. Shropshire then appealed his sentence to the British Columbia Court of Appeal. The court of appeal allowed Shropshire's appeal and reduced the period of parole ineligibility to the minimum (ten years).

The Supreme Court of Canada held that the British Columbia Court of Appeal was wrong in allowing Shropshire's appeal against sentence and reducing the period of parole eligibility. In allowing the appeal, the Supreme Court passed comment on what it described as the 'interventionist' approach of the court of appeal in reviewing sentences imposed in murder cases. The Supreme Court described the sentencing function as 'profoundly subjective' and noted that sentencing judges enjoy advantages over appellate judges in the sentencing process. The court was alluding to the fact that sentencing judges have the benefit of first-hand observation of the parties and the proceedings, which somehow gives them an advantage in applying the principles of sentencing. Primarily for this reason, the court held that a court of appeal should not intervene in a sentencing case unless it considers the sentence to be 'clearly unreasonable,' 'manifestly unfit,' or based on erroneous principles (*Shropshire* (1996), 287).

Academic commentary on this aspect of the decision was highly critical (Quigley 1997; Norris 1996; Manson 1996; Trotter 1996). First, the onerous standard of review created by the Supreme Court is unfaithful to the plain language of section 687, which merely requires that courts of appeal calibrate sentencing decisions for 'fitness,' not some more exacting standard. More fundamentally, the court's reasons for deferring to sentencing judges are unconvincing. In many aspects of appellate review, most of which relate to the review of convictions or acquittals, deference is shown to trial judges in certain situations. These are situations where the trial judge has made a finding of fact or credibility based on his or her first-hand observation of the evidence presented at trial. Given the subjective nuances and mental processes that are involved in these assessments, courts of appeal often defer to the more advantageous position of the trial judge. However, situations that call for deference rarely arise in the sentencing process. Although they may arise when the sentencing hearing follows a contested trial, the vast majority of sentencing decisions are made following a guilty plea. It is the exception (and not the rule) when testimonial evidence is presented at a sentencing hearing. As discussed above, most sentence appeals are based upon a transcription of the reasons of the sentencing judge, the submissions of counsel, the sentencing exhibits, and the factums of counsel. Indeed, given that 'fresh evidence' may be presented at a sentence appeal, court of appeal judges may actually be better informed than the sentencing judge (Norris 1996).

The approach in *Shropshire* was soon reinforced by the Supreme Court's decision in *C.A.M.* In *C.A.M.*, the Supreme Court considered whether the British Columbia Court of Appeal erred in reducing a twenty-four-year sentence for multiple counts of sexual and nonsexual physical abuse of the offender's children.[6] In determining that the court of appeal was wrong (again) to have reduced the sentence, the Supreme Court reiterated the need to defer to the decisions made by sentencing judges. The court stated that, 'absent an error in principle, failure to consider a relevant factor, or an overemphasis of the appropriate factors, a court of appeal should only intervene ... if the sentence is demonstrably unfit' (*C.A.M.* (1996), 315). The court offered an alternative formulation in emphasizing that a court of appeal ought to intervene to reduce disparity of sentences only where the sentence appealed from is 'in substantial and marked departure from the sentences customarily imposed for similar offenders committing similar crimes' (ibid, 319).

Perhaps aware of the weaknesses of its assertion in *Shropshire* that the 'first-hand' experience of sentencing judges demands curial deference, the Supreme Court in *C.A.M.* held that the ability of sentencing judges to 'directly assess' the sentencing submissions of the prosecutor and the offender ought to attract a certain level of deference. The court also pointed to sentencing judges' 'unique qualifications' of experience and judgment from having served on the front lines of the criminal justice system (ibid, 315). While recognizing that courts of appeal serve an important function in minimizing disparities for sentences imposed throughout Canada, the needs of particular communities must be recognized and expressed through the individualized decisions of sentencing judges. The court suggested that sentences should be 'expected' to vary somewhat across certain communities and regions in Canada as a function of local needs (ibid, 315–16).

While *C.A.M.* is more valiant in its attempt to justify the reasons for a highly deferential standard of appellate review, it is still unconvincing. The ability to 'directly assess' the sentencing submissions of the prosecutor and defence counsel, as opposed to reading transcribed versions, is not a compelling argument in favour of deference. Indeed, the opposite might be true: appeal court judges may peruse transcribed submissions at their leisure, while sentencing judges, who usually impose sentence immediately or shortly after the submissions of counsel, must rely upon their notes and memories (Trotter 1997). Reliance upon the specialized experience of sentencing judges is also misplaced, since most appeal court judges were formerly trial judges (Norris 1996).

The concerns expressed by the court about local needs and permissible disparity are even more problematic. Occasionally, the idiosyncratic needs of a local community may require a unique response from a sentencing judge. Again, this will be the exception, not the rule. On their facts, neither *Shropshire* or *C.A.M.* fell into this category. *Shropshire* involved a drug-related killing in an urban centre; *C.A.M.* is an all-too-common example of familial sexual abuse against children and did not give rise to any special needs in the community where the offences occurred.

The court addressed the issue of appellate review once again in *McDonnell* (1997). McDonnell entered a plea of guilty to two counts of sexual assault against individuals to whom he stood in a relationship of trust (a foster child and a baby-sitter). The trial judge imposed a total sentence of one year's imprisonment. On appeal to the Alberta Court of Appeal by the Crown, the sentence was increased to a total of five years' imprisonment. The court of appeal held that the sentencing judge was wrong in not imposing a sentence in accordance with the starting point created by the court of appeal for 'major sexual assaults.'

On further appeal, by a slim (5:4) majority, the Supreme Court of Canada ruled that the Alberta Court of Appeal was wrong to have increased the sentence imposed by the sentencing judge. In allowing the appeal, the court dealt a serious blow to the 'starting point' approach, which makes the viability of this sentencing paradigm rather tenuous (Manson 1997b). The majority's disapproval of the 'starting point' approach was based on two concerns. First, the court held that the creation of 'starting points' unduly encroached into the realm of Parliament by the judicial sub-categorization of offences (for sentencing purposes) based on their seriousness (*McDonnell* (1997), 454). Second, and related to the major theme in this chapter, the court held that the 'starting point' approach is at odds with deference that should be shown to the sentencing decisions of trial judges.

The Supreme Court offered no further justifications in support of its stance on appellate review. Instead, it quoted at length from its two previous decisions, relying upon the articulation of the standard of review set out in *Shropshire* and on the bulk of the reasoning advanced in *C.A.M.* Like these two previous decisions, *McDonnell* involved a guilty plea and did not present circumstances that required an approach tailored to the specific needs of the community.

The Implications

There can be no doubt that, for the foreseeable future, the courts of appeal of this country will be greatly constrained in their review of sentencing decisions. This development is peculiar. Admittedly, the dynamic explored in these decisions (the 'reviewability' of discretionary decisions) is a familiar one. It may even be said that there is a degree of antagonism between sentencing judges and the courts of appeal.[7] Still, it was not necessary for the Supreme Court to take the law in this direction.

It is too early to determine the implications of this development, although some consequences seem predictable. From a practical perspective, these cases ought to result in fewer sentence appeals to the courts of appeal. However, this will depend in large measure on the faithfulness of the courts of appeal to this development.[8] Greater disparity in sentencing may well result from the diminution of power in the appellate courts. Strengthening the 'bottom-up' current in sentencing (in direct proportion to the weakening of the 'top-down' influence of the appellate courts) can only realistically result in more disparity in the lower courts. This runs counter to the momentum of Canadian sentencing reform over the last decade or so (Roberts and von Hirsch 1992; Canadian Sentencing Commission 1987) and recent legislative activity in this area.

The timing of the Supreme Court's most recent forays into the world of sentencing is truly unfortunate. They come at a time when Parliament, drawing on years of penal policy formulation, finally turned its attention to substantive sentencing issues with the enactment of Bill C-41. Key among the aspects of this legislation is a statement of the purpose and principles of sentencing. However, this statement of purpose and principles is not self-applying (Roberts and von Hirsch 1995). We require guidance from our courts of appeal on how to approach these new provisions and Parliament undoubtedly contemplated that the courts of appeal would continue to provide significant guidance to the lower courts on sentencing matters. Conspicuously, section 687 of the Criminal Code was not amended by Bill C-41. This recent narrowing of the appellate review of sentencing decisions may make the implementation of the new legislative program more difficult (Trotter 1997). Parliament might consider responding to the scope of review fashioned by the Supreme Court.[9]

ENDNOTES

1 Gary Trotter is a Crown counsel with the Ministry of the Attorney General (Ontario). He also teaches sentencing courses in the Faculty of Law at the University of Toronto.

2 As discussed below, the attorney general may also appeal a sentence in respect of an indictable offence. The right of an attorney general to appeal against a sentence is considered to be an extraordinary power. In England, the attorney general must invoke a cumbersome reference procedure in order to have the court of appeal determine whether a sentence imposed in the Crown court was unduly lenient.

3 This limitation relates to the few situations in the Criminal Code where the sentence for a particular offence is mandatory. An example of this is the sentence for first degree murder. Section 742(a) provides that an individual convicted of first degree murder shall be sentenced to life imprisonment without eligibility for parole until he or she has served twenty-five years. There can be no appeal from this sentence.

4 All courts of appeal have detailed rules of court, which regulate the procedure for ensuring that all relevant material is put before the court.

5 Sometimes, the same court of appeal may employ a different paradigm, depending upon the nature of the case. It is often difficult to determine the precise approach of a court in any particular case, because most reasons for judgment in sentence appeals tend to be rather cursory (Young 1988).

6 Stating that the case was the worst he had ever encountered, the sentencing judge imposed a sentence of twenty-four years' imprisonment. The court of appeal reduced the sentence to eighteen years and eight months.

7 For an interesting example of this tension, see *R. v. Jackson* (1994). The case involved an appeal from a judge who refused to follow the starting point or guidelines set out by the Saskatchewan Court of Appeal. When the sentencing judge was asked by the prosecutor to sentence the offender in accordance with the guideline, the judge asked: 'where do they get the authority to say that we ignore what Parliament has said and start at another level than what is set out in the Criminal Code?'

8 It may be that a counterintuitive result might obtain and that the number of sentence appeals would remain constant (or even increase). As McCormick (1993) demonstrated, even though the Alberta Court of Appeal is reputed to provide the greatest guidance to the lower courts on sentencing matters, *per capita*, it entertains the greatest number of sentence appeals and appellants tend to be quite successful before that court.

9 This type of response was witnessed recently in another area of criminal procedure. In 1992, the Supreme Court of Canada struck down an aspect of s. 515(10)(b) of the Criminal Code for offending the vagueness doctrine embedded in s. 7 of the Charter (*Morales* (1992)). In a recent amendment to the Code (Criminal Law Improvement Act, R.S.C., c. 27 (1st Supp.)), Parliament responded by re-enacting the invalidated provision in language that purports to be more precise.

ADDITIONAL READING

Manson, A. 1996. The Supreme Court Intervenes in Sentencing. 43 *Criminal Reports* (4th) 306–16.

Price, R.R. 1983. The Supreme Court of Canada and Sentence Appeals. 30 *Criminal Reports* (3d) 333.

Sopinka, J., and M. Gelowitz. 1993. *The Conduct of an Appeal*. Toronto: Butterworths.

Trotter, G.T. 1996. *R. v. Shropshire*: Sentencing, Murder and the Supreme Court of Canada. 43 *Criminal Reports* (4th) 288–316.

15

Sentencing and Conditional Release

MARY E. CAMPBELL[1]

The presence of parole complicates the task of a sentencing judge. While parole authorities do not change the duration of the term of imprisonment imposed, they do affect the location in which the sentence of the court is discharged. This raises the complex issue, explored in this chapter, of the relationship between sentencing and parole.

Introduction

Each year in Canada approximately 6,000 offenders are released from federal penitentiaries and more than twice that number are released from provincial correctional facilities. The vast majority are released prior to the expiration of their custodial sentence, subject to what is known as 'conditional release.' As the next chapter outlines, this is a generic term encompassing temporary absence, day parole, full parole, statutory release, and remission-based release. While the specific nature of each varies somewhat, what is common to almost all is that the offender serves a portion of the sentence in the community, subject to various conditions and restraints.

Proponents of conditional release point to its importance in offsetting the deleterious effects of institutionalization, the benefits of a controlled, graduated return to the community, maximizing the use of community-based programs and treatment, and its relative rate of success as measured by recidivism statistics. Conditional release is seen as an integral part of the sentence and an effective contribution to the overall protection of society. Critics emphasize the limits of predicting human behaviour, the lack of public tolerance for error, and the uncertainty which, they argue, conditional release adds to sentencing and sentence administration. Some also argue that conditional release undermines the intention of the sentencing court: imprisonment should mean being behind bars.

Is conditional release complementary to or at cross-purposes with the sentence? In order to evaluate these competing claims, this chapter will consider how conditional release interacts with sentencing. The approach is two-pronged. First, where did the idea of conditional release originate, what was its purpose, and how did its creators see the link between sentencing and conditional release? Second, to what extent is it appropriate for contemporary sentencing judges to take conditional release into account when sentencing? Can or should, for example, a judge lengthen what would otherwise be an appropriate sentence to offset the possibility of the offender's early release? What if the offender is not subsequently released on parole?

Purpose of Conditional Release

History of Forms of Release[2]

Life was harsh in pioneer Canada, and nowhere more so than in the custodial facilities housing those who ran afoul of the law. Imprisonment itself was intended to mitigate the severity of such earlier punishments as execution, banishment, public whipping, or the pillory. However, jail conditions were chaotic at best, brutal at worst, and the penitentiary, while intended to be, at least in part, an institution of penitence and reform, was merciless in the rigour of its conditions. Convicts were expected to earn their keep and were released only when the sentence had been completed, unless 'gaol fever' (typhoid), industrial accidents, madness, or suicide had claimed them first. Occasionally, the monarch would extend clemency and pardon an offender or group of offenders serving sentences, resulting in immediate release.

The desirability of a system of graduated return to the community was recognized as early as 1839, only four years after the Kingston penitentiary first opened. In their report for that year, the Board of Inspectors for the Upper Canada penitentiary stressed that a program of post-release supervision was essential if real reform of the offender was to be achieved.[3] However, it was well into the second half of the century before there were serious calls for the adoption of measures similar to those introduced by Sir Walter Crofton in the Irish prison system in 1854. These recommendations for better classification of inmates and gradual freedom reflected two important ideas. The first was the emphasis on promoting and rewarding good behaviour while in the institution, one consequence of which would be earning a 'remission' or reduction in the length of the sentence. The second was the recognition that at least some portion of the sentence should be devoted to preparing the offender for return to society (a move away from viewing the achievement of reformation solely or primarily through punishment). Inherent in this was the recognition that a graduated return to the community, and normalization of the offender in the community, were important parts of the sentence.

There were also calls for the adoption of a 'ticket of leave' system in Canada. Such a system originated primarily in the cases of offenders sentenced by English courts to transportation to America or Australia: upon satisfactory behaviour, the inmate could be granted licence to be at large. Unlike sentences terminated early due to remission, the sentence would notionally continue to run after the licence was granted to the inmate, but, since there was no supervision in place, generally only a subsequent criminal conviction elicited revocation of the licence.

The enactment of a new Penitentiary Act was one of the first items of business on post-Confederation Canada's agenda. The 1868 Act introduced a scheme of earned remission, of up to five days per month. The purpose of the scheme was to 'encourage convicts to good behaviour, diligence and industry, and to reward them for the same.' The criteria were that the offender, for each month, 'shall have been exemplary in industry, diligence and faithfulness in his work, and shall not have violated any of the Prison Rules.' The effect of the remission was explicitly stated to reduce the sentence: offenders were not supervised or otherwise controlled upon release, but rather were discharged as free citizens. Until the introduction of mandatory supervision on the remission portion of the sentence for penitentiary inmates, this model of remission-based release was essentially the status quo for the next hundred years.

The next milestone in the development of conditional release was the passage of the Ticket of Leave Act in 1899. This Act formed the basis of the current system of parole. The Act was short and contained neither criteria for granting leave nor criteria for revocation. An offender released on leave was required to notify the local police of his or her address, and normally to report to them once a month. In addition, four conditions were provided by statute: the offender was required to produce his or her licence on demand; to refrain from breaking the law; 'not [to] habitually associate with notoriously bad characters, such as reputed thieves and prostitutes'; and 'not [to] lead an idle and dissolute life without visible means of obtaining an honest livelihood.' The penalties for breaching the conditions of the leave were severe. A return to custody for the offender was particularly harsh, since the Act required that he or she serve the sentence remaining to be served at the time the licence was granted – i.e., the offender was given no credit for the time served in the community under conditions.

Unlike the remission provisions of the Penitentiary Act, the Ticket of Leave Act was debated at length in Parliament. The speeches at second reading in the Senate reveal that the legislators saw the new Act as being primarily directed at expediting the reform of young, first-time, nonserious offenders. The prevailing view was that offenders fell into one of two classes: older, hardened recidivists (the 'criminal classes') and young miscreants whose crimes were simply a temporary lapse in judgment or fortune in an otherwise law-abiding life. The classification system in the penitentiary (such as existed at the time) was designed to keep these two groups apart, if the physical layout of the institution permitted, so as to minimize the contaminating influence of the first group. The ticket of leave was essentially an extension of this approach: the grant of a leave would 'be advantageous in bringing about the reformation of the offender, advantageous in giving him an opportunity of continuing in the employment of those who are in the law-abiding class, and relieving him from all the disadvantages to which he would be subjected if he were kept in constant contact with the criminal classes.'[4]

Three conclusions can thus be drawn about the motivation for the enactment of this legislation. First, the perception of offenders as falling into one of two classes led to a desire to find effective means of preventing the one from contaminating the other: existing architecture and costs limited the ability to physically separate inmates within the institution, and thus actual removal of reformable offenders would better promote their reform. Second, there was no inclination to consider alternatives that would have been a further draw on the public purse. The ticket of leave was attractive because it involved no additional costs (offenders would simply report to the police), and would in fact result in a measurable cost saving if a substantial number of offenders were successfully removed from custody. Third, the scheme had been in existence for a number of years in both England and America: encouraged by its reported success (though the indicia of that success were never noted in the Debates), and already under long-standing encouragement from England to adopt the system, Parliament clearly felt there was little to lose in implementing the program, at least on a trial basis.

Among the concerns expressed about the Act was the potential that it would 'imperil the deterrent efficiency' of punishment,[5] introduce uncertainty into punishment,[6] and contaminate decision making with sentimentality.[7] It was also argued (without any supporting evidence) that the legislation had been used primarily for political offenders in England, and that, in any event, it had not been 'a gratifying success' there.[8] The government was urged to delay the bill until it could be given further study (particularly with respect to the experience in England) and until more members of the House were present (the debate taking place during early August). But the prime minister was adamant that the matter had been amply reviewed by officials and was well supported by the English experience, and the Act was passed.

The ticket of leave program, which from the start was also referred to as parole, continued to expand in the years thereafter. A Dominion parole officer was appointed in 1904, who provided a limited amount of support to offenders. Aftercare support was not extensive, and it is likely that most offenders, as long as their parole period remained free of detected crime, were unencumbered by substantial supervision.

The first major evaluation of both remission-based release and the ticket of leave system occurred in the Archambault Report (1938). A three-man commission was appointed in 1936 on the recommendation of the minister of justice to enquire broadly into the operation of the Canadian penal system; their report made eighty-eight recommendations, touching on all aspects of the system. The report is important for, amongst other things, its clear articulation of a commitment to a rehabilitative objective for corrections: 'The great majority of prisoners will be called upon at some time to live again the ordinary life of a free man. Therefore, entirely apart from humanitarian grounds, and from a purely economic point of view, for the eventual benefit of society, the task of the prison should be, not merely the temporary protection of society through the incarceration of captured offenders, but the transformation of reformable criminals into law-abiding citizens, and the prevention of those who are accidental or occasional criminals from becoming habitual criminals' (Archambault 1938, 9).

The report recommended substantial revamping of both the ticket of leave program and remission to better reflect the rehabilitative ideal. In particular, it was critical of the failure to provide either meaningful rehabilitative treatment while the offender was in custody or support once he or she released.

The report reveals certain underlying assumptions about judicial involvement in both programs. It seems clear that the commissioners assumed that judges could take the possibility of remission-based release into account when sentencing. The commissioners' rationale is also clear: 'This remission has the effect of arbitrarily shortening the sentence of the prisoner. When remission has been granted to a prisoner, his sentence has been executed and he is entitled to be discharged and set at liberty ...' (Archambault 1938, 231). The commission's own observations that the system of crediting and forfeiting remission was often highly arbitrary and uncertain does not seem to have modified its view that remission shortened the sentence and hence was something that could be validly taken into account by sentencing judges.

Many of the recommendations of the Archambault Report were reflected in a revised Penitentiary Act, but the new version was not proclaimed in force for another decade, and it was not for another five years that parole was the subject of substantial reform.

Creation of the National Parole Board

The Fauteux Committee was struck in 1953 at the request of the minister of justice, at a time when relief was being sought from massive post-war overcrowding in the penitentiary system. The principal legacy of this four-man committee was the creation in 1959 of the National Parole Board to administer a system of parole, replacing the ticket of leave system.

The committee's philosophical commitment to parole was unqualified: 'Parole is a well-recognized procedure which is designed to be a logical step in the reformation and rehabilitation of a person who has been convicted of an offence and, as a result, is undergoing imprisonment ... It is a transitional step between close confinement in an institution and absolute freedom in society' (Fauteux 1956, 51). The committee stressed that it was not a reduction in the sentence or an undermining of the sentence: 'Parole should be an integrated part of the whole correctional process. Indeed, the entire system of prison treatment should, from the beginning, be directed toward the probability that parole will constitute the last phase of the sentence of imprisonment. It should not, therefore, be interpreted to the prisoner or to the public as clemency, leniency, or mercy' (Fauteux 1956, 53). Among the recommendations directed at greater integration of all players in the criminal justice system, the committee emphasized the importance of judges visiting custodial facilities: 'It goes without saying that judicial officers should be familiar with the types of institutions to which they sentence offenders, and the facilities available in them for the treatment and training of inmates' (Fauteux 1956, 17).

While the committee adhered to the view that conditional release was not a reduction in sentence, it was paradoxically uncritical in its acceptance that judges could take the likelihood of parole into account when sentencing. The commissioners wrote that the informal rule that offenders should not be considered for parole until one-half of the sentence had been served 'is still followed to a substantial extent. The justification for the rule is really its usefulness, which is manifold. Existing for many years, it is generally known to the courts and presumably is considered by them when they determine the length of sentence to be ordered' (Fauteux 1956, 62).

At the same time, the government of the day endorsed the underlying principle that conditional release was not a reduction in the sentence: as the minister of justice stated in Parliament, 'It is necessary to bear in mind that an inmate out on parole has not received a remission of his sentence. He is on parole for the balance of his sentence; he is merely serving that balance outside the institution.'[9] Moreover, the minister of justice hoped that an improved parole system would also reduce custodial numbers by reducing recidivism. The minister's hopes for a marked effect were realized: the number of offenders granted parole more than doubled from 1958 to 1959, the first year of operation of the board, for an effective grant rate of 42 per cent.[10] The recidivism rate (i.e., those returned to custody for either a breach of conditions or a new offence) for this group was a very low 7 per cent.[11] Notwithstanding these impressive figures, which were sustained in the early 1960s, members of Parliament were critical that the Fauteux Report was not being implemented as vigorously as possible. The minister of justice himself emphasized the Fauteux recommendation that judges better educate themselves about the correctional system, so that they would be 'better informed as to the type of training and rehabilitation program which is available for inmates and can determine the sentence, the length of sentence and perhaps the type of sentence, accordingly, on the basis of what this accused and guilty person needs.'[12]

Interaction between Sentencing and Conditional Release

Perhaps not surprisingly in any matter of social policy, the history of conditional release in Canada has been a mix of ideology and pragmatism. Its avowed ideological foundation has been rehabilitation, while its development has often been motivated by practical considerations, such as a lack of institutional treatment programs (and a lack of willingness to make funds available for such programs), as well as overcrowding. All of these factors led legislators to look for rehabilitative solutions through a phased reintroduction of the offender into the community. While correctional authorities and legislators consistently emphasized that parole was not to be viewed as a reduction in the sentence, paradoxically, they generally expected that judges would take it into account when fixing sentence. They also saw two other points of intersection between judges and conditional release: first, judges would have input into parole decision making in individual cases, and second, judges would cultivate a knowledge of corrections and conditional release that would allow them to sentence more effectively. How have these links developed in more recent history?

Judges' Input in Conditional Release Decisions

Historically, judges had at least on occasion been asked by release authorities for their views as to a particular offender's suitability for release. Both Archambault and Fauteux had recommended against this practice: while the judge might have useful input at the time of sentencing, by the time of a parole application he or she would usually know little, if anything, about the offender's progress.

The role of judges has now been codified in both the Criminal Code and the Corrections and Conditional Release Act. Judges are required to provide reasons for sentence, and courts and corrections officials are required to include those reasons in the offender's file. Such information may include details about the offence and the offender, the expectations of the judge in imposing the particular sentence, and recommendations about treatment. Other information admitted into court is also to be forwarded to corrections officials, such as psychiatric or psychological reports, or victim impact statements. This process allows correctional decision makers to take that information into account in any subsequent decisions, such as security classification, provision of treatment programs, and conditional release. Recognizing that their role is concluded when sentencing is finished and that they will not have current knowledge about the offender at the time of the subsequent correctional or conditional release decision, judges are not given any role to make their views known at the time of the correctional or conditional release decision.

Conditional Release Considerations in Sentencing

The question of whether judges should take parole eligibility into account when sentencing has followed a much more complicated path. In its review of sentencing and conditional release in 1987, the Canadian Sentencing Commission concluded that more often than not, judges took parole eligibility into account when sentencing, regardless of what appellate case law instructed them to do. In so doing they deliberately imposed longer sentences than they otherwise thought appropriate, in order to ensure that the offender spent what they considered would be a suitable period of time in custody. The commission was of the view that this added a further layer of confusion to an already apparent lack of 'equity, clarity and predictability' in sentencing and sentence administration. Taken in conjunction with the commission's view that parole had not lived up to its rehabilitative ideals, they recommended that it be abolished and that sentencing move to a 'real time' basis, i.e., that offenders would serve most of a sentence of imprisonment behind bars. Campbell and Cole (1985) acknowledged that 'an analysis of the case law indicates that conditional release has been a troublesome and confusing consideration for trial and appellate judges.'[13]

Ontario appellate case law has been divided on the appropriateness of taking conditional release into account. In *Bezeau* (1958) and *Bailey* (1970), the Ontario Court of Appeal was firm that trial judges should not pay any attention to conditional release eligibility. However, in *Roberts* (1963), the court of appeal suggested that conditional release was an appropriate consideration in deciding to reduce a twenty-four-year aggregate sentence for arson to twelve years, out of concern that twenty-four years, even taking into account statutory remission, was so long that it would impede rehabilitation (see also *Wilmott* (1966)).

Conversely, the British Columbia Court of Appeal during this time period was consistent in holding that conditional release was an irrelevant consideration in the discharge of judicial duties.[14] This was clearly articulated in *Heck* (1963), where the trial judge had imposed an aggregate term of five years for false pretenses, having taken into account parole eligibility. The court of appeal reduced the sentence to two and a half years, and held: 'It is thereby evident that the learned magistrate, in imposing sentence, has considered the parole system, although it is not clear whether he considered that the sentence should be increased so as to offset any possible reduction by the parole board or that, as advocated by the learned chairman of the board, there should be a long sentence, leaving it to the parole board to release the prisoner when it thinks proper to do so. His considering of either was an error' (143; see also *Holden* (1963)).

More recent judgments have generally adhered to this principle. In *Meilleur* (1981), the Ontario Court of Appeal implicitly continued to distinguish between sentencing and parole functions. The Quebec Court of Appeal has been unequivocal in its view that parole eligibility or the impact of consecutive or concurrent sentences are inappropriate considerations in sentencing:

> In my humble opinion, a judge who has to determine the appropriate length of imprisonment must assume that the accused will in fact remain imprisoned throughout the entire period fixed by the judge. The latter may not ignore the fact that an accused may obtain remission of part of his sentence or parole but that does not concern the judge. Logically, and at the appropriate time, remission of his sentence or parole are the subject of a decision which is rendered by the competent authorities after the judge has rendered his decision, and on the basis of the judge's decision. If the judge fixes his sentence in accordance with what the other authorities might decide, he warps the system which then begins to go around in circles. I am of the same opinion with respect to the effect that a sentence made consecutive to another may have for the purposes of applying the laws which concerns sentence remission or parole. The *Criminal Code* does not require, and in fact, does not allow the judge to fix the period of imprisonment in light of other legislation which may more or less influence the period of time during which the accused will remain imprisoned. On the contrary, it is the period of imprisonment determined by the judge which forms the basis upon which the other relevant legislation will be applied.[15]

The courts have been willing to distinguish other situations where conditional release considerations may be taken into account by the sentencing judge. For example, judges have traditionally doubled the credit for time spent in custody prior to trial and sentencing, to reflect both the more onerous nature of that incarceration (remand prisoners have virtually no access to programs or activities) and the fact that remand prisoners cannot earn remission. Notwithstanding the 1992 abolition of remission in the penitentiary system, at least one court of appeal has held that the 'double credit' is still acceptable, if only because of the conditions of confinement.[16]

A separate line of cases raises another issue: whether appeal courts should take into account what has transpired with the offender since he or she began serving the sentence, as it pertains to either conditional release eligibility or demonstrated performance while on release. In such cases, appellate courts have generally regarded conditional release as a relevant consideration.

For example, in *Katsigiorgis* (1987), the Ontario Court of Appeal dismissed the Crown's appeal of a sentence of two years less a day for criminal negligence causing death, notwithstanding that it felt that a sentence of three years would have been more suitable. The offender's good performance in provincial custody since sentencing and his imminent parole eligibility were cited as factors leading the court to conclude that 'in the circumstances no societal interest would be served by an increase at this time of the sentence which would place the respondent in a penitentiary setting.'[17]

The dilemma that appellate judges perceive in these situations was amply reviewed by the Newfoundland Court of Appeal in *Oates* (1992). The offender had been sentenced to two years less a day for conspiracy to traffic in cocaine, and was released on day parole at first eligibility (i.e., one-sixth (four months) of the sentence). The appeal court was unanimous in its view that the original sentence was too lenient and failed to give adequate weight to deterrence. At the same time, the offender had been living in a halfway house for some months and was successfully employed and pursuing university courses. Could the court take this into account? Was it required to? In its analysis, the court of appeal noted the general rule that conditional release is not a relevant consideration at sentencing; however, '[w]hatever validity this position may hold in the sentencing court where parole and remission can only be future contingencies, it can have no applicability to an appeal court when these events are no longer eventualities but realities. It is generally well settled now that an appeal court may take into consideration post-sentence conduct ...' (367).

The reasons for, and the application of, this exception to the general rule are clear: 'If one accepts, therefore, that appellate courts are entitled to consider post-sentence conduct, this must include all events which have impacted upon the individual's life, since sentence was imposed upon him or her – including parole or remission of sentence and events ensuing therefrom. Otherwise, the appeal disposition risks being reached on outdated criteria relevant at the time the sentence was pronounced but out of tune with the reality of changing circumstances in the individual's life. The respondent's parole and the positive developments in his life since being granted it are therefore relevant considerations' (368).

Courts have also grappled with parole eligibility in disposing of appeals against conviction rather than sentence. In *G. (K.R.)* (1991), the Ontario Court of Appeal ordered a new trial on appeal by the accused, but suggested that the Crown exercise its discretion and not proceed with such a trial: 'The appellant has now served almost the period of time in penitentiary necessary to make him eligible for parole. Having regard to the fact that he has no previous record, it seems likely that he would be a good candidate for parole when, or shortly after, he becomes eligible for it. In those circumstances, in the exercise of their discretion, the law officers of the Crown might decline to proceed with a new trial' (272).

The same approach was taken by the Newfoundland Court of Appeal in *B. (A.J.)* (1994), which applied a similar holding by the Quebec Court of Appeal in *Zurlo* (1990). In the former case, the offender had been convicted of various sexual assaults and sentenced to five years. The court of appeal agreed that the convictions should be quashed, and ordinarily would have ordered a new trial. However, the court noted, 'the difficulty is that the appellant is still serving his sentence though I assume he is, or will be very shortly, eligible for parole. In any event, it is almost three years since his trial. In these circumstances it is clear that an order for another trial would be pointless and unjust.'[18] In fact, the court held that a new trial under these circumstances would amount to a miscarriage of justice, and while ordering a new trial also entered a stay of proceedings to prevent such a trial from taking place.

An unusual line of cases that appears to contradict the principle that conditional release eligibility is not a relevant consideration in sentencing centres on sentences in excess of twenty years. As detailed in the next chapter, an offender is normally eligible for full parole after serving the lesser of one-third or seven years of his or her sentence. Consequently, any sentence of twenty-one years or more will have parole eligibility 'capped' at seven years. Similarly, an offender subject to a life sentence imposed as a maximum sentence is eligible for full parole after seven years; however, in this case, as with all life sentences, the offender receives credit for any time served in custody between arrest and sentencing.

Some courts have taken these provisions into account in elevating an otherwise appropriate fixed sentence to a life sentence, ostensibly to the benefit of the offender. For example, in *Hayes* (1996), the offender was convicted of importing heroin and sentenced to twenty years. He appealed both conviction and sentence. His conviction appeal was dismissed, and the Manitoba Court of Appeal held that the length of his sentence was 'not unfit.' However, given that he had spent twenty months in pretrial custody, the court held that 'in terms of parole eligibility, the accused would be better off with a life sentence.'[19] Consequently, the court gave the offender thirty days to decide whether he wished to keep the twenty-year sentence or accept a life sentence.

This alleged anomaly between lengthy fixed sentences and life sentences has led to a line of decisions that have held that the next step up from a twenty-year sentence should normally be a life sentence (for a review of these cases, see Rice (1994)). These courts have concluded that because there is no difference in parole eligibility in any fixed-length sentence beyond twenty years, Parliament must have intended that such sentences are not warranted.

This issue was put squarely before the Supreme Court of Canada in *M. (C.A.)* (1996), which also provided the court with the opportunity to speak more broadly to the question of conditional release and sentencing. The offender had been sentenced to a total term of twenty-five years upon conviction for brutal assaults on his children over a period of years. On appeal, his sentence was reduced to eighteen years and eight months, the British Columbia Court of Appeal holding that where a life sentence is not available under the Code,[20] fixed-length sentences are normally capped at twenty years. The Crown appealed to the Supreme Court of Canada.

Chief Justice Lamer, in a unanimous judgment of the full court, held:

> With the greatest respect, I find no evidence in either the *Code* or the *Corrections Act* [*sic*] that Parliament intended to constrain a trial judge's traditionally broad sentencing discretion through the imposition of a qualified legal ceiling on numerical sentences pegged at 20 years' imprisonment. Rather, in my reading of both statutes, beyond setting statutory maximum and minimum sentences which reflect the relative severity of different offences, Parliament intended to vest trial judges with a wide ambit of authority to impose a sentence which is 'just and appropriate' under the circumstances and which adequately advances the core sentencing objectives of deterrence, denunciation, rehabilitation and the protection of society. Accordingly, in my view, whether or not life imprisonment is available as a maximum sentence in the particular case, there is no pre-set ceiling on fixed-term sentences under the *Code*. (299)

In reaching this conclusion, Lamer C.J.C. emphasized that 'in short, the history, structure and existing practice of the conditional release system collectively indicate that a grant of parole represents *a change in the conditions* under which a judicial sentence must be served, rather than *a reduction* of the judicial sentence itself.'[21] As a result, the offender's original twenty-five-year sentence was restored. It appears to be implicit in the judgment that judges should perform their function according to proper sentencing principles, and that conditional release decision makers should do their job independently.

Communication between Judges and Conditional Release Decision Makers

Notwithstanding the clear distinction in roles emphasized by the Supreme Court of Canada, what happens when a court feels that conditional release decision makers are undermining their sentencing decisions? This was the case in *Oliver* (1997). The offender had been convicted of defrauding her employer; the passing of sentence was suspended and she was placed on probation for three years, in addition to being ordered to make restitution. At this time in Newfoundland, the provincial temporary absence program allowed offenders to be released, sometimes almost immediately, to serve part or all of their sentence in the community. In sentencing Ms Oliver, the trial judge indicated that the appropriate sentence was in fact a custodial term of nine to twelve months. However, he also expressed frustration at what he saw as the practice of correctional authorities immediately releasing offenders if they did not pose a threat to public safety, resulting in some cases in no time being served behind bars. While acknowledging that it was not 'a proper sentencing principle' to take into account what might happen after sentencing, and in particular that it was not appropriate to lengthen the sentence in order to ensure a minimum period of time in custody, the trial judge nonetheless expressed complete frustration:

> So the way I look at it, at this point, it is just a charade and the woman has spent a couple of weeks in custody and as far as I am concerned given everything I know, that is about as much or more than she probably would serve if I had sentenced her to six months last week, given the precedents that have been set where people don't go to jail at all. I do not wish to appear hypocritical. I am tired of trying to fool people. It goes against our professional and personal integrity if the administration of this province or the corrections people are going to be the people that are going to be deciding what jail terms would be. Let the legislation be changed to reflect that. So as far as I am concerned, given all of this, I am not going to sentence her to jail at all. She can walk out of here today. (213)

The Crown appealed. The court of appeal concluded that the trial judge was in error, although it is not clear whether that was because he speculated as to what corrections officials might do, or because he did so based on his personal knowledge of provincial corrections rather than on any evidence before him.

The court acknowledged its previous judgment in *Coffey* (1965), wherein it held that considerations of parole were irrelevant in sentencing. However, the instant case was distinguished in that it involved the provincial temporary absence program, which they held was being administered in a manner not in conformity with the applicable legislation:

> Without question, a sentencing judge should not consider post-sentencing decisions by corrections officials in determining fit sentences, but that pre-supposes that any post-sentencing decision made by corrections officials are properly made within the law and according to established principles. It is inappropriate to adjust sentences on the assumption that they will not be carried out or to foil the impact of programs sanctioned by Parliament or the Legislature. However, by the same token, Corrections Officials must not break the law, in letter or in spirit. If the orders of the courts of this Province are not being carried out it is expected that the Attorney General would ensure that they are, using contempt procedures if necessary. (221)

If the offender could safely be managed in the community, the court of appeal held that information to support that conclusion should be brought before the sentencing court, particularly since the Criminal Code had recently been amended to allow for custodial sentences to be served in the community through conditional sentences. As a result, the court remanded the case for sentencing, requesting that it be provided with an assessment of what risk Ms Oliver might pose to the community, a report from her probation officer as to her performance since the original sentencing, including compliance with the restitution order, a report on the impact of the crime on the victim, and information on community programs for offenders.[22]

Regardless of whether the court of appeal was accurate in holding that the temporary absence program was not operating in compliance with the law, the salient feature of this case was the strength of the court's concern that corrections officials were systematically undermining sentences. Simply cancelling the release program may have abated the court's anger in the short term, but was this a good long-term solution? Where an offender can be managed in the community without risk to the public, shouldn't corrections officials exercise that authority? In many ways, this case illustrates the failure to ensure that courts are provided with detailed information at sentencing, so that a fully informed decision can be made at that point.

Conclusions

Several broad themes emerge from this brief review. First, while their motivation in acting was often prompted by practical concerns relating to costs and overcrowding, the original legislators were committed to the notion that conditional release was an integral, indeed necessary, part of the custodial sentence. It provided incentive for reform while the offender was still behind bars, and aided the successful transition back into the community. Second, while the role of judges in conditional release decision making per se has evolved over the years, there has been a consistent concern that judges should be adequately informed as to correctional and conditional release programs, so that their sentencing decisions can be tailored to individual circumstances. Third, there has been general consensus that while informed as to each other's roles and expectations, judges and conditional release authorities have separate and distinct jobs to do: the former to decide on the appropriate sentence, and the latter to determine the conditions under which that sentence should be served.

In practice, the relationship between sentencing and conditional release has been somewhat less than harmonious. Trial courts have required periodic reminders from appeal courts that the possibility of conditional release is not to be taken into account when sentencing, while appeal courts themselves have carved out exceptions to this rule, including Crown appeals of sentences and the impact of sentences longer than twenty years. At least one appeal court has been highly critical of situations where inmates are being released after serving only a few hours in custody.

So even while appeal courts, and the Supreme Court of Canada, are holding that judges should not take conditional release into account when sentencing, it appears that many judges do so. One of the biggest problems with this practice is the potential for unfairness: a sentencing court cannot know with any certainty whether in fact the offender will be released on temporary absence, parole, or any other form of conditional release. The offender may in fact serve every day of the sentence in custody. One option is simply to abolish conditional release, so that judges will know that a two-year sentence of imprisonment means two years behind bars. However, in the United States, where a package of changes in 1987 severely curtailed the availability of parole, the number of federal inmates has quadrupled between 1980 and 1996, from 24,000 to 106,000.[23] Fifty new federal prisons have been constructed.[24] At the same time, 'academic research has shown little or no correlation between rates of crime and the number of people in prison' (see Donziger (1996), 42).

In Canada, which has maintained its conditional release program, the 'success rates' for penitentiary inmates conditionally released have remained relatively steady,[25] with no increase in overall reported crime rates.[26] Rather than abolish conditional release and run the risk of the same results as in the United States, another option would be to invest resources in promoting better communication and coordination among sentencing authorities, prosecutors, and conditional release decision makers. Judges would still be required to impose the appropriate sentence, based on the offender and the offence, but would have much better information about the treatment programs that might be available, whether those programs are in the institutions or in the community, how correctional authorities view the risk of recidivism posed by the offender and, generally, how the offender's case might be managed. Without open communication about sentencing and correctional objectives in general, or about the risks and needs of the offender in particular cases, the tensions that were articulated in the *Oliver* decision may continue to resonate, even while the players espouse the division of responsibilities confirmed by the Supreme Court of Canada.

ENDNOTES

1 Mary Campbell has worked in the area of corrections for many years. She is a member of the Ontario Bar and teaches sentencing courses at the Faculty of Law, McGill University. She is an editor of *Sentencing Matters*.

2 This history does not purport to be exhaustive, but rather focuses on those aspects which pertain to the relationship between sentencing and conditional release. For a more information, see Cole and Manson (1990), chap. 5.

3 Annual Report of the Inspectors of the Provincial Penitentiary 1839, *Upper Canada Journals of the Legislative Assembly, 1839–40*, Appendix, at 58.

4 Senate *Debates*, 4 July 1899, at 589.

5 House of Commons *Debates*, 5 August 1899, at 9606.

6 Ibid. at 9607, 9728.

7 Ibid.

8 Ibid.

9 House of Commons *Debates*, 24 May 1961, at 5319.

10 *First Annual Report of the National Parole Board for the Calendar Year 1959* (Ottawa, 1959), Appendix 3.

11 House of Commons *Debates*, 10 June 1960, at 5620.

12 House of Commons *Debates*, 30 June 1960, at 5625.

13 At 191.

14 See, for example, *Switlishoff* (1950); *Courtney* (1956); *Holden* (1963); *Heck* (1963); *Moncini* (1975). The same principle was also upheld by the Newfoundland Court of Appeal (*Coffey* (1965)) and the Manitoba Court of Appeal (*Richardson* (1963)).

15 *Meehan* (1989) at 500. A slightly different view of the impact of consecutive sentences was taken by the Alberta Court of Queen's Bench in *Houle* (1993). The court sentenced the offender to fifteen months consecutive to an existing term of

thirty months' imprisonment in order to achieve a global sentence of forty-five months, indicating that the fifteen-month sentence would have been longer were it not for the existing sentence. The judge went on to state clearly that parole eligibility is not an appropriate consideration in sentencing, but that judges should be aware of the implications of multiple sentences.

16 *Cooper* (1997).

17 At 262.

18 At 231.

19 At 435.

20 None of the offences for which M. was convicted carried a maximum punishment of more than fourteen years – see (1994), 28 C.R. (4th) 106 at 124 (Ont. C.A.).

21 At 300 (emphasis in original).

22 Within one week of the court of appeal's judgment, provincial officials cancelled the temporary absence program that allowed for immediate release of offenders sentenced to imprisonment, and subsequently revised their policies to require that all offenders serve at least one-sixth of the sentence before being eligible for release. They also circulated their revised temporary absence policies to judges and Crown attorneys for comment.

23 Bureau of Justice Statistics: Prisoners in 1980 (May 1981); Bureau of Prisons: Monday Morning Highlights (13 January 1997).

24 Bureau of Justice Statistics: Sourcebook of Criminal Justice Statistics 1995 (1996).

25 National Parole Board, 'Performance Monitoring Report 1996/97' (Ottawa, 10 January 1997).

26 Reported crime has in fact declined in the 1990s: see *Canadian Crime Statistics 1996* (Ottawa: Statistics Canada, 1997).

ADDITIONAL READING

Campbell, M., and D. Cole. 1984. Conditional Release Considerations in Sentencing. 42 *Criminal Reports* (3d) 191–206.

Cole, D. and A. Manson. 1990. *Release from Imprisonment: The Law of Sentencing, Parole and Judicial Review.* Scarborough, Ont.: Carswell.

16

Conditional Release from Imprisonment

SANDRA G. LEONARD[1]

As noted in Chapter 1, sentences of imprisonment cannot be fully understood without knowledge of the mechanisms by which inmates spend part of their sentences in the community, under supervision. In this chapter, Sandra Leonard reviews the complex arrangements that regulate these mechanisms. Significant changes have been introduced to the parole process as a result of passage of reform legislation (the Corrections and Conditional Release Act) in 1992.

Introduction: The Statutory Framework

The Division between Federal and Provincial Sentences

In 1867, the British North America Act divided federal power over 'criminal law' and 'penitentiaries' from provincial power over 'the administration of criminal justice' and 'prisons and reformatories.' As a result of the constitutional power over criminal law, the federal government was given the power to control the length and character of the sentence. Thus the federal legislation provides most of the guidance with respect to corrections and conditional release. The Criminal Code of Canada, however, also codified the historical division between the federal penitentiary and provincial reformatory by requiring those serving sentences of two years or more to be housed in the former and those serving less than two years to serve their time in provincial institutions (section 743.1). As a result of this divided custodial responsibility, there are a number of provincial statutes to consider in assessing the differences one day can make in terms of the opportunities for release and the quantity of time ultimately served.

Apart from incarcerating those adults who have received a sentence of less than two years' duration, the province is also responsible for housing those who have been denied bail and are awaiting the hearing of criminal charges, those incarcerated as the result of breaches of provincial highway traffic offences, and those under eighteen. Provincial inmates will often serve their time in detention centres or municipal jails intended for those awaiting charges, rather than in correctional centres, if their sentences are less than ninety days or there is no available bedspace.[2]

Federal

In November 1992 the Corrections and Conditional Release Act[3] (hereafter the CCRA) was proclaimed in force, in an attempt to codify a number of the procedures and policies used by the Correctional Services of Canada and the National Parole Board. It has since been significantly amended at least three times since that date, in order to correct a number of errors and inconsistencies, as well as to fundamentally change release arrangements for certain types of offenders. Part I of the Act adapts the old Penitentiaries Act[4] and deals with the powers of the Correctional Services of Canada regarding the intake, classification, assessment, and housing of prisoners, and any matters under the direct control of the commissioner of corrections. Part II outlines both the structure and procedures of the National Parole Board and its criteria for decision making and the eligibility of applicants to apply for parole, where not specified by the Criminal Code of Canada. Part III speaks to the role of the correctional investigator in dealing with matters arising under Part 1 of the Act.

Attached to the CCRA are two schedules of offences. Schedule I lists violent offences, from assault to both attempt and conspiracy to commit murder. This list contains a variety of sexual offences, including those involving children, and driving and criminal negligence offences in which bodily harm or death ensued. Schedule II provides a list of all drug offences, with the exception of simple possession. Conspiracy to commit all of the drug offences is also included in Schedule II. These Schedules affect the classification of offenders, priority for programming, requests for psychiatric or psychological assessments, and consideration of conditional release. The issue of whether the offender is a first-time, non-violent federal offender is, of course, also important.

The governor-in-council is also empowered to make a number of regulations dealing with time limits, details, and specific procedures. And, to assist the 'institutional heads' and their correctional service staff, the commissioner of corrections publishes 'Commissioner's Directives' aimed at standardizing and explaining the law to its employees and providing more detail.

The Criminal Code of Canada is also relevant; it contains a number of provisions about the parole eligibility of special categories of offenders, such as those found to be dangerous offenders, those serving life sentences (both as a maximum and a minimum penalty), and young offenders who have been convicted and sentenced after transfer to adult court. In addition, section 743.6 of the Code now provides that a court can increase a period of parole ineligibility from one-third to one-half (or ten years, whichever is the lesser) for those sentenced to a penitentiary term for offences found on either Schedule I or Schedule II of the CCRA. Such judicial intervention is to occur where the circumstances of the offence require denunciation or specific deterrence to such a degree that an increase of parole ineligibility is required. There are, however, somewhat conflicting provincial interpretations of when this section should be invoked. In Ontario it was considered an exceptional means to be employed where the Crown satisfies the court, whereas the Alberta Court of Appeal indicates that such application is not limited to special, unusual, or particularly aggravating circumstances, but can only be ordered where the judge is convinced that society's denunciation of the offence will not otherwise be met. In addition, the Criminal Code contains a 'faint hope' clause for anyone serving a life sentence (as long it is for one death, rather than multiple offences) with parole ineligibility more than fifteen years. (This provision is described in greater detail in Chapter 17.) Aside from this provision, the purpose of most of these Criminal Code sections is to restrict the eligibility of certain offenders to apply for conditional release and to ensure that the authority for the decisions in these matters remains with the National Parole Board.

In addition to the CCRA and the Criminal Code, the Prisons and Reformatories Act[5] governs the operation of prisons and reformatories, specifying the transfer and committal of offenders from one province to the next, earned remission, and temporary absences. The Transfers of Offenders Act[6] similarly deals with international transfers both from and to Canada (the latter of which makes up the vast majority of the applications).

Provincial

The CCRA also delegates the National Parole Board's authority to the province, where the province wishes to establish a provincial parole board. With the recent dismantling of the Board of Parole for British Columbia in 1996, however, only Quebec and Ontario retain their own provincial boards. Hence, the power to release prisoners serving less than two years also resides with the National Parole Board in the remaining provinces. There are, however, a number of additional statutes governing the different procedures for provincial corrections, which affect institutionally based grants of conditional release for those serving less than two years. Alberta, British Columbia, Manitoba, New Brunswick, Nova Scotia, and the Yukon all have their own Corrections Acts; Saskatchewan has a Correctional Services Act and Ontario a Ministry of Correctional Services Act; Prince Edward Island's Jails Act still uses the ticket of leave terminology; and Newfoundland has a Prisons Act. Without exception, the provincial legislation covers temporary absences from their institutions. The provincial ministers assigned to handle these areas vary from the solicitor general, attorney general, or Department of Justice for the province, although Saskatchewan legislation names its Executive Council as chief authority. In the province, the Regulations and executive policy memos suggest how the law is to be carried out.

Conditional Release

Although there is insufficient space to adequately cover the classification process and the variety of institutional programming available, it is vital to realize the tremendous importance of the institutional experience in affecting both opportunity for and likelihood of conditional release. This experience is only a partial reflection of the initial statutory categorization of offenders by offence categories, pursuant to the above-mentioned Schedules under the Corrections and Conditional Release Act.

Terminology

Federal

An offender granted an escorted temporary absence is released from the penitentiary for a variety of purposes: medical, administrative, community service, family contact, personal development for rehabilitative purposes, or compassionate reasons, including parental responsibilities. The CCRA stipulates that the time periods may be unlimited for medical reasons and are otherwise permitted up to a maximum of fifteen days (with the commissioner's approval) or five days (with the warden's approval). Escorted temporary absences rarely occur for longer than a day for other than medical reasons, given the usual dependence on staff members and the resulting extra costs for overtime. Escorts may also be citizens authorized to escort by the institutional head. An approval process generally ensures lack of personal connection to the offender, among other criteria.

An unescorted temporary absence permits the offender to be released from the penitentiary for up to seventy-two hours from a minimum security institution or forty-eight hours from a medium security institution per month for the same purposes as available for escorted temporary absences (sections 99, 116). Those classified as maximum security inmates are not entitled to unescorted temporary absences.

Some members of the public have a negative view of conditional release programs such as the escorted or unescorted temporary absences. However, the releases are almost always completed without incident. In the most recent year for which data are currently available (1996/7), Correctional Services of Canada approved 43,666 escorted temporary absences and 5,963 unescorted absences. Of these, only 30 were not completed, for a success rate of 99.9 per cent (Reed and Roberts 1998).

Day parole is defined in subsection 99(1) of the CCRA as 'the authority granted to an offender by the Board or a provincial parole board to be at large during the offender's sentence in order to prepare the offender for full parole or statutory release, the conditions of which require the offender to return to a penitentiary, community-based residential facility or a provincial correctional facility each night, unless otherwise authorized in writing.' Day parole cannot be granted for longer than six months at a time, although it can be renewed.

Full parole means the 'authority granted to an offender by the board or provincial board to be at large during an offender's sentence' (subsection 99(1).

Statutory release is the new name for what was originally called remission or 'time off for good behaviour,' and became mandatory release under revisions to the Parole Act and the Penitentiary Act, in 1970. The CCRA defines statutory release as '...release from imprisonment subject to supervision before the expiration of an offender's sentence, to which an offender is entitled under section 127.' Section 127 sets out a formula for calculations, which essentially entitles a federal offender to release at two-thirds of the sentence, subject to the provisions for detention.

Detention is not formally defined in the CCRA, but it is a procedure which can result in certain offenders spending the remaining third of their sentence in the penitentiary, without the possibility of release.

Provincial

Although the terminology varies from one provincial statute to the next, it is essentially similar to that found in the CCRA, with the following exceptions. The concept of remission has not been abolished for the provinces and in Ontario is governed by the Prisons and Reformatories Act. On the presumptive release date, there is no parole supervision. Releasing authorities such as the Ontario Board of Parole are fond of reminding parole candidates that the earlier release by one-third of a provincial sentence is traded for the extra one-third of supervision received, in contrast to a release on their discharge possible date without any supervision.

All releases except full parole are those pursuant to institutional authority for various types of temporary absences. There is currently no day parole equivalent in Ontario, due to provincial government cuts, which have eliminated community residential facilities for would-be residents. A very limited number of women are being accommodated by the Elizabeth Fry Society, with various women's shelters assisting some provincially sentenced women on extended temporary absences. Generally, electronic monitoring was to have replaced halfway houses, but the eligibility for such programs is often past the eligibility date for full parole, at which point a halfway house is unnecessary. Clearly, electronic monitoring was not brought in to 'enable preparation for full parole,' as in the federal legislation. In addition, electronic monitoring is an option only for non-violent, level one offenders, and the offender qualifies only in the last six months before release. Temporary release is authorized in each province for a variety of purposes, including most commonly the following: (a) to obtain employment; (b) to continue employment; (c) to attend an education institution or vocational training; (d) to provide housekeeping and child/family care services; (e) to seek medical treatment and/or for hospitalization; (f) for compassionate grounds; and (g) for rehabilitative purposes.[7]

A few jurisdictions are now using electronic monitoring for certain offenders on temporary absence. This allows them to be in their home or at their place of employment, wearing an electronic bracelet to ensure they are where they are supposed to be. Given the more invasive and intrusive nature of such monitoring, some provinces stipulate that the 'monitoring is restricted to controlling only behaviour that was directly linked to the offence' (such as the Correctional Services Act).[8]

The Decision Makers

The head of the institution, be it the warden for the penitentiary or superintendent for a correctional centre or reformatory, has authority over his or her institution, subject to these operating statutes, Regulations and any policy directives received from either the commissioner of the Correctional Services of Canada or the Provincial assistant deputy ministers and the provincial ministry of solicitor general and correctional services. With respect to escorted and unescorted temporary absences, again, it is the warden who has authority, unless specifically excluded by the provisions of the Criminal Code and the CCRA, which gives the residual authority to the National Parole Board. Any decision to release a provincial inmate before one-third of his or her sentence has been served is up to either the minster responsible or his or her designated authority, usually the superintendent of the institution (whose wide discretion with respect to level one or Schedule I offenders is severely limited by new policy guidelines). Parole, however, is exclusively the decision of the National Parole Board or its provincial counterpart, where established. Likewise, the conditions of statutory release or the decision to detain federal prisoners remain with the National Parole Board.

In the past there has been a media furore over the composition of parole boards, which reappears during elections and appointment time or whenever a sensational crime has been committed by someone on parole. Board positions are filled by appointment of the governor-in-council, upon recommendation of the minister of the solicitor general. Section 103 of the CCRA indicates that the National Parole Board is to consist of not more than forty-five full-time members and a number of part-time members, who will hold office during good behaviour for periods not exceeding ten years for full-time members and three years for the part-timers. The National Parole Board is separated by region, in accordance with the division established for corrections: Atlantic, Quebec, Ontario, Western, and Pacific.

Section 105 requires the members of the board to be sufficiently diverse in their backgrounds to be able to collectively represent the community and its views. In the Ontario Region, the full-time members were previously teachers, real estate lawyers, social workers, ministers, police officers, wardens, or former parole officers. Some of the present full-time members have previously served on the Ontario Board of Parole and are particularly familiar with provincial institutions from which some federal offenders have unfortunately 'progressed.'

Grounds for Release

The purpose of conditional release, as defined in section 100 of the CCRA, is 'to contribute to the maintenance of a just, peaceful, and safe society by means of decisions on the timing and conditions of release that will best facilitate the rehabilitation of offenders and their reintegration into the community as law-abiding citizens.' On what basis does the board or the institutional head decide to grant any form of conditional release? Section 102 of the legislation sets out the general test. The Board is advised that it may grant parole: 'if in its opinion, the offender will not, by reoffending present an undue risk to society before the expiration according to law of the sentence the offender is serving; and the release of the offender will contribute to the protection of society by facilitating the reintegration of the offender into society as a law-abiding citizen.'

How does the board come to such a decision? It reviews the reports received from the court, from classification, from the institutional or contracted psychologist or psychiatrist, from the police, from institutional program facilitators, and from the community and institutional parole officers. In addition, on grounds of fairness, the applicant is generally permitted an oral hearing. The board's discretion is, however, limited in the taking of decisions involving one category of offender: the accelerated parole release candidates. For these first-time, non-violent federal offenders, the board is directed by subsection 126(2) that it '*shall release*,' upon satisfying itself that there are no reasonable grounds to believe that the offender, if released, will commit an offence involving violence before the expiration of the offender's sentence. (If these concerns exist, a hearing is then scheduled.)

In its exercise of discretion the board must consider that the protection of the public is paramount; it must take all available relevant information into consideration; and it must make the least restrictive decision consistent with protecting society. Provincially, the same legislative criterion applies, although the paperwork on which such decisions are taken is usually less detailed.

Eligibility

Federal

Generally, those serving federal sentences are eligible for escorted temporary absences at any time. In order to be eligible for an unescorted temporary absence the offender must have served one-sixth of his or her total sentence or six months (whichever is the later). Prisoners are eligible for day parole six months before their full parole eligibility date, and for full parole at one-third of their sentence, unless a judge has ordered it increased to one-half, as discussed above. Eligibility dates are, however, no guarantees of release.

A number of exceptions to these general rules should also be noted. The accelerated parole release candidates are now eligible for day parole at one-sixth of their sentence, as was the case for everyone prior to the proclamation of the CCRA on 1 November 1992. The test for release on day parole has also been revised as a result of the recent passage of Bill C-55 sections and is now the same as the test for full parole. Previously, a first-time, non-violent federal offender applying for day parole (the more restrictive form of release) would have to pass the higher threshold of general recidivism than when applying for full parole (less restrictive) later on. In addition, a generally cautious board was directing residency in a community residential facility as a condition of 'full parole,' making such a named release a bit of a misnomer. Where the board has any concerns about violent reoffence after reviewing the APR's file, it is required to hold a hearing on the issue to see if full parole and day parole can still be directed.

Those serving a life sentence (as either minimum or maximum) are not eligible for unescorted temporary absences or day parole until three years prior to the parole eligibility date. For those serving time for first degree murder, this is at the twenty-two year mark, as their full parole ineligibility is twenty-five years. The parole ineligibility for those serving time for second degree murder, may have been set at anywhere between the minimum of ten to the maximum of twenty-five years. For those serving life as a maximum sentence for an offence other than murder, the minimum full parole eligibility is seven years.

Young offenders transferred to adult court and convicted of first or second degree murder are not allowed any form of parole, including unescorted temporary absences or escorted temporary absences for other than medical reasons or to attend judicial proceedings or a coroner's inquest, until they have served four-fifths of their period of parole ineligibility (subsection 746.1(3) of the Criminal Code). For those who were less than sixteen at the time of the offence, the period of parole ineligibility is between five and seven years. For those aged seventeen or eighteen convicted of first degree murder, the period is ten years, while for those of the same age convicted of second degree murder the period is seven years (section 745.1).

Offenders on immigration holds are no longer being granted unescorted temporary absences or day parole. Hence, non-Canadian citizens who have been ordered deported as a result of their criminal record or offence are in a completely separate category. It was no new amendment to the Corrections and Conditional Release Act that effectively wiped out the criteria for parole granting in section 102 of the Act and ignored the guiding principle of 'mak[ing] the least restrictive determination consistent with the protection of society,' or 'ensur[ing] a fair and understandable conditional release process.' This exception to parole ineligibility is the result of the current interpretation of the amendments in Bill C-44 to section 105 of the Immigration Act (IA), proclaimed effective 10 July 1995.

Section 105 of the Immigration Act now reads as follows:

S. 105(1) Notwithstanding the Corrections and Conditional Release Act, the Prisons and Reformatories Act or any act of a provincial legislature, where a warrant has been issued or an order has been made pursuant to subsection 103(1) or (3) with respect to any person who is incarcerated in any place of confinement pursuant to the order of any court or other body, the Deputy Minister may issue an order to the person in charge of the place directing that

(a) the person continue to be detained until the expiration of the sentence to which the person is subject or until the expiration of the sentence or term of confinement as reduced by the operation of any statute or other law or by an act of clemency; and
(b) the person be delivered, at the expiration of the sentence or term of confinement referred to in paragraph (a) to an immigration officer to be taken into custody.

For dangerous offenders sentenced before 1 October 1977 to an indeterminate period of detention, the National Parole Board is required to review their case once every year to see if parole should be granted (subsection 761(2) C.C.C.). For those sentenced after 1 October 1977 but before the most recent amendments to the dangerous offender provisions, parole must be reviewed after three years and thereafter every two years. Those now sentenced as dangerous offenders will have to wait seven years from the date they were first taken into custody for their first review (subsection 761(1)) and are then subject to review every two years. As a result of other changes to the Criminal Code, those deemed to be dangerous offenders will no longer be eligible to receive fixed sentences. Hence their ultimate release is completely dependent on the National Parole Board. Those who are not deemed to be dangerous offenders may however be found to be 'long-term offenders' who will receive a mandatory minimum sentence of two years followed by supervision in the community for up to ten years (subsection 753.1(3) C.C.C.).

Is a hearing a once-only opportunity for release? For those serving longer sentences, the answer is 'not necessarily.' The National Parole Board is currently required to review day parole/full parole cases in which there has been a denial every second year, rather than annually. Anyone serving two years or more and eligible for parole review must now wait another year for the required review, unless the board exercises its discretion to hear the case sooner, as a result of the finding that there has been a significant change in the offender's circumstances since the last review, as confirmed by the institutional parole officer in charge of the individual's case.

The full parole grant rate at the federal level is typically around one-third of all applications. This may come as a surprise to members of the public, as polls have demonstrated that over half the population overestimate the full parole grant rate (see Roberts (1994a), 39). The most recent statistics available at present (for the period 1996/7) show a full parole grant rate of 40 per cent (Reed and Roberts 1998). This is up from 34 per cent in the preceding two years. Most members of the public believe that parolees represent a risk to the community.[9] Reality proves otherwise. Two-thirds of full paroles were completed successfully, with most (71 per cent) failures involving a violation of technical conditions.[10] Less than 2 per cent of paroles were revoked as a result of a fresh criminal charge involving violence.

Provincial

Full parole eligibility is at one-third of the sentence served for all provincial offenders. Where the sentence is longer than six months, there is no need to apply for a hearing; one will be automatically scheduled, unless the inmate prefers to waive it. Statutory release generally occurs at the two-thirds point of the sentence, although a number of provinces stipulate different formulas for calculating remission. Generally, a parole hearing will take place one or two weeks before the eligibility date. Eligibility for other forms of temporary absence are dependent both on the individual provincial regulations and policies, as well as the often enormous discretion left to individual superintendents. Certain policies prevent violent offenders from being allowed out on any form of temporary absence.

The vast majority of inmates released by the provincial parole boards also served the balance of their sentences successfully in the community. The success rate was 85 per cent in Ontario and 73 per cent in Quebec (in 1996/7). The difference in success rates between the two provinces may reflect the fact that the grant rate has tended to be higher in Quebec than in Ontario (70 per cent in Quebec versus 48 per cent in Ontario over the five-year period 1992–7; see Reed and Roberts (1998)).

The Hearing Process

Federal

The CCRA requires the board to review all federal inmates automatically for full parole, and by application for day parole. The only exception is for the accelerated parole review applicants who, in general, should not require a hearing and will be released after a paper review. Some inmates waive their right to a hearing (or postpone it, as more frequently happens, due to the absence of Correctional Services' paperwork to confirm support.)

The hearing generally takes place at the institution in which the applicant is housed. A quorum of two board members attends for regular hearings (or three for lifer, dangerous offender, or detention hearings). Generally, the board also has a hearing assistant, who sets up the tape recorder and ensures that the board members have the necessary paperwork and files, and that all is procedurally correct. The applicant for parole is entitled to have an assistant present, who can be a member of his or her family, a lawyer, a counsellor, or anyone else who is desired to assist and speak on the applicant's behalf. Attempts to compel the board to recognize the right to counsel as part of a Charter-protected liberty interest, even for those serving life or indeterminate sentences, whose only opportunity for release is to satisfy the board, have failed.

The hearing assistant commences the hearing by ensuring that the applicant is ready to proceed. This requires the applicant to have received copies of all of the relevant paperwork on which the board will rely a minimum of fifteen days prior to the hearing date, and to have arranged for an assistant, if desired. The hearing assistant also ensures that the tape is recording the proceedings and that each person who will be speaking has identified themselves on tape. The assistant usually advises of the materials that the board has previously reviewed and will talk to the applicant, to assess the risk to offend and the 'criminogenic factors' which were/are perceived to operate.

The remedy for any new, undisclosed information is an adjournment, as is the request for an assistant. Unfortunately, it is often very difficult for the applicant to realize what material he or she is missing unless (or until) the board specifically refers to it in the midst of the hearing. Applicants often have no idea where a question is coming from, and are not sure whether the board is theorizing or relying on contradictory confidential information or opinion. Many applicants sign the 'sharing of information' form without ever receiving the contents summarized on it, due to case management belief that it is either not necessary or advisable (due to the confidential nature of the reports) to burden the applicant with such paperwork in an institutional setting.

The applicant's case management officer (recently renamed the institutional parole officer) is then asked to summarize the Correctional Services' position by briefly speaking about the offender, the offence, the applicant's institutional behaviour, and plan for release, as well as to provide a recommendation as to whether or not to grant the conditional release requested. As it is now the job of the community parole board to make the written recommendation, this can lead to problems where the institutional case management officer has a conflicting opinion.

At this point, the board asks the applicant a number of questions, many of which may strike the individual as intrusive, compared to the accused and witnesses' protections in a criminal court. Many matters, including old family history, prior charges that were dismissed or withdrawn, prior relationships, and the description of the crime itself are all matters which the board may choose to examine in great detail. Neither the board nor the applicant, however, have the power to subpoena or call witnesses. The applicant will usually be told that only one assistant may speak for him or her, regardless of how many individuals may wish to speak.

At the conclusion of the questioning, the assistant is given an opportunity to speak on the applicant's behalf and the applicant is then granted the 'last word.' The case management officer, applicant, and applicant's assistant leave the room, while the board takes a decision. The board's hearing assistant may help type up the decision, but he or she is not a voting member. Once the decision is made, everyone returns to the room, where the decision is delivered.

As a result of the desire to open up the proceedings and to respect the wishes of victims and their families, the board now permits observers to attend the hearing. Observers generally include victims, victims' families, members of the press, and other interested parties. The board apparently has a negligible screening process, leaving it up to the correctional authorities or the applicant to determine whether such observers should be permitted to attend. Objections may be made on the grounds that the hearing is likely to be disrupted or the ability of the board to make a decision adversely affected by the presence of the observer; that the person's presence is likely to adversely affect those who have provided information to the board, including victims, and members of the victims' families; that the person's presence is likely to affect an appropriate balance between that person and the public's interest in knowing and the effective reintegration of the offender into society; or that the security or good order of the institution in which the hearing is to be held is likely to be adversely affected by the person's presence. Such objections are not necessarily or generally upheld.

The observers are not permitted to speak during the hearing, although frequently victims and families have submitted written victim impact statements prior to the hearing, as an addendum or update to anything that may or may not have been produced in the criminal court. Disruptions may result in the observers being asked to leave, although the standard of what constitutes a disruption appears fairly high, as does the overall tolerance of the board for conceding adverse affect. Limits on numbers present appear to be a concern for space rather than the possible effect on the applicant, although some hearings have occurred in larger institutional locations, such as the chapel, to accommodate victim-observers.

Provincial

Essentially, provincial hearing procedure is much the same as federal procedure, at least as experienced in Ontario. There is no hearing assistant, however, and three members of the board may attend, despite a two-person quorum, thus protecting against a split decision. The biggest difference between provincial and federal parole hearings can be the much more limited disclosure in the former, partly as it is still less common to receive the same amount of paperwork but also because there is a general tendency *not* to provide the inmate with anything generated by the court. Similarly, the fifteen-day rule appears to be rarely applied, perhaps because the hearings occur so much more quickly, given the shorter sentences. Provincial hearings also tend to be briefer, again perhaps as a reflection of frequently less serious matters, shorter sentences, or less material to review with the applicant. Observers appear to be a rare exception, although the issue of victim impact has arisen in a few cases in which it was determined that the board earlier meet with the victim or family of the victim for a prior oral hearing, in the absence of the applicant for parole, and without knowledge or disclosure of what had been said.

Further to a recent amendment of the CCRA, anyone serving a sentence of six months or less is no longer required to be reviewed for parole. It is unclear whether this amendment altering the statutory requirement to review anyone's case upon application will result in no parole for anyone serving a sentence of less than six months, due to time constraints.

Appeals

When the National Parole Board denies a release, appeals can be filed with the Board's Appeal Division in Ottawa within sixty days of the decision. Section 147 of the CCRA states that grounds include: the failure to observe a principle of fundamental justice; an error of law; a breach or failure to apply a policy adopted respecting ethnic, cultural, and linguistic differences, or a failure to respond to the 'special needs of women and aboriginals'; the making of a decision based on erroneous or incomplete information; and the failure to act with appropriate jurisdiction. Judicial review is also an alternative in the Federal Court of Canada. Provincially, the chair of the board can be addressed in writing by the unsuccessful applicant or an assistant to review the parole denial and determine whether the procedural safeguards were applied and the decision fairly taken, while judicial review might be addressed either in Divisional Court (generally too time-consuming) or by prerogative writ in General Division.

Statutory Release

Those who do not receive conditional release on parole can generally look forward to statutory release at the two-thirds point in their sentence. For provincial inmates this means release without any conditions. For federal inmates, however, this release is akin to parole in that there are a number of standard conditions imposed and the individual remains under the supervision of the local parole office. In addition, in the same way that the National Parole Board can impose special conditions particular to the parolee, they can impose special conditions on those receiving statutory release. As the result of a recent amendment, residence may be required in a community correctional centre, a community residential centre, or a psychiatric facility. One would like to think that this may encourage release for those who need the supervision and a place to stay. The more cynical will suggest those who would normally be released on day parole prior to their statutory release will now wait until statutory release, at which point they will be told where they must live.

Suspension and Revocation

Both federally and provincially, a member of the board or designated correctional authority has the ability to suspend parole or statutory release and authorize the apprehension of the offender and his or her recommitment into custody until the suspension is cancelled, the statutory release or parole is terminated or revoked or the sentence of the offender has expired according to law. The grounds for such action are that the offender has breached a condition of parole or statutory release or that it seems necessary and reasonable to suspend the individual in order to prevent an anticipated breach or to protect society. As one of the standard conditions of release is to obey the law and keep the peace, arrest on a criminal charge is considered an obvious breach regardless of the presumption of innocence.

For those who are not sentenced to further incarceration for a further criminal charge, there may be a hearing to decide whether the suspension should be lifted and parole or statutory release reinstated, or whether the release should be terminated or revoked. Where there is a new sentence, revocation occurs on the date the new sentence is imposed, unless the sentence is concurrent and related to a matter that preceded the granting of the conditional release. Termination usually occurs only when the violation alleged was beyond the individual's control. For example, where the only treatment program specified or the particular residence required is no longer in operation this might result in termination, although termination is not a provincial option (see section 45 MCS Reg., R.R.O. 1990 Reg. 779). Revocation means that the person remains in custody, and shall not be released until he or she has served two-thirds of whatever sentence remains.

Anyone who receives a new custodial sentence while on parole or statutory release will find that his or her sentence is no longer calculated in the same way. If a new custodial, consecutive sentence is received, the offender will be required to serve any remaining period until full parole eligibility on the old sentence (or portion of it) as of the date of the new sentence plus the parole ineligibility period of the new sentence, before being considered for further conditional release. If the new sentence is concurrent, the client is not eligible for full parole until the latter of the full parole eligibility dates.

For anyone presently serving a life sentence, the receipt of a further determinative sentence will also result in the offender having to serve the sum of any existing time until full parole eligibility as of the date of the new sentence for the life sentence and the new full parole eligibility of the additional sentence.

Anyone who was eligible for full parole as an accelerated parole review candidate who has day parole revoked before the National Parole Board has done the full parole review is no longer eligible for full parole as an APR.

Detention until Warrant Expiry

While the theory of 'a controlled, graduated return to the community' as discussed in Chapter 17 is still generally employed, this is not an option for those offenders referred for detention. There are now three categories of potential detainees. All are required to be reviewed by the Correctional Services of Canada no later than six months before their statutory release date, unless new information comes to the commissioner's attention during those six months.

The first group consists of those offenders who have been convicted on indictment of an offence found in Schedule I of the CCRA, which caused serious harm or death to another person, if there are reasonable grounds to believe that the offender is likely to commit an offence causing death or serious harm before the expiration of his or her sentence. Serious harm is defined as 'severe physical harm or severe psychological damage.' The absence of a victim impact statement has been filled by the receipt of the prisoner's own counsel's sentencing submissions, conceding trauma or harm to a victim involved under the criteria of 'serious harm' and nothing else. The second group belongs to Schedule I but involves sexual offences with child victims. Here the test is the likelihood of the commission of a sexual offence involving children before the expiry of the existing sentence. It is not necessary to establish that serious harm occurred.

The third group is derived from Schedule II, when the commissioner believes on reasonable grounds that the offender is likely to commit a serious drug offence before the expiration of his or her sentence. Obviously, an addict who has not received substance abuse treatment while incarcerated, or who continued to be involved in the drug trade, may be a prime candidate for such referral for detention, particularly with a record for more than one drug offence. A hearing is then held to determine whether the risk is present in either situation and three board members are required for the quorum.

According to the National Parole Board (NPB) statistics, of the total prison population 'available for detention' the percentage of prisoners actually referred for detention has increased from 4 per cent in 1989/90 to 10 per cent in 1994/5. Of the five regions, both Ontario and the Pacific regions are above the national average. Of cases referred for detention, the average Canadian detention rate was 84 per cent between 1989 and 1995, while the highest average rate of detention took place in the Ontario Region at 87.9 per cent; with the lowest in the Pacific Region at 75 per cent. The Ontario detention rate rose steadily from 73 per cent of all referrals in 1989/90 to a staggering 96 per cent of all referrals in 1993/4 (coincidentally, the same year as the high-profile case of a paedophile hit the press). The rate dropped slightly in 1994/5 to 92 per cent. In 1989/90, 153 prisoners were referred for detention, with 45 per cent of whom were incarcerated in the Ontario Region. This number has steadily increased, with a total of 442 referrals in 1994/5, 166 of whom were from Ontario (more than one-third of all referrals).

Across Canada, if someone is referred for detention, the probability of the offender actually being detained by the NPB until the warrant expiry date is extremely high. Legislation initially passed to deal with a very small portion of the prison population has increasingly widened the net. The types of offences most often referred, in keeping with the new amendments and broader mandate to detain, shows the progression from violent sexual offenders, to often less physically aggressive paedophiles, to offenders who are not serving time for any sexual offences, or for whom there is no evidence of any 'sexual components' to their crime, but who are still on Schedule I.

Beyond Conditional Release and Detention: Long-Term Offenders

On 1 August 1997 the remainder of Bill C-55, dealing with high-risk offenders, was proclaimed in force. Sections of the Criminal Code dealing with dangerous offenders were dramatically altered as another group, the 'long-term offender,' was added to the legislative net and the supervisory capacity of both the courts and community correctional authorities. From the time of sentence until six months thereafter, an assessment may be sought on reasonable grounds to believe the offender may be dangerous or may require long-term supervision. 'Application after sentencing should be made only where notice has been served before the sentencing of the intention to make such application and it is shown that 'relevant information which was not available to the prosecution at the time of sentencing became available in the interim six months' (section 753(2) C.C.C.). The court can impose an order that an offender be supervised for a period not exceeding ten years in the community, after imposing the federal sentence. This order shall be made if the court finds that there is a substantial risk that the offender will reoffend and there is a reasonable possibility of eventual control of the risk in the community. Again, these sections target the sex offender. Substantial risk is found where the offender has been convicted of a sexual offence and a pattern of repetitive behaviour, including the offence for which he or she has been convicted, has shown a likelihood of causing death, injury, severe psychological damage to other persons in the past *or future*!

ENDNOTES

1 Sandra Leonard is a barrister and solicitor who specializes in criminal and correctional law. She was called to the Ontario Bar in 1986 and has been a sole practitioner since 1988. She teaches Bar Admission courses in criminal procedure and is a contributing member of the Criminal Lawyers' Association, the Prison Law Association, and the Canadian Bar Association.

2 Newfoundland, however, still refers to Her Majesty's 'Penitentiary,' although this is where it houses its provincial inmates, pursuant to the Newfoundland Prisons Act, R.S.N. 1990, c. P-21.

3 S.C. 1992, c. 20.

4 R.S.C. 1985, c. P-5.

5 R.S.C. 1985, c. P-20.

6 R.S.C. 1985, c. T-15.

7 The term 'work release' is also used and may apply to inmates working off the institutional grounds by day, but returning to the institution by night, or on weekends only.

8 Statute Sask., c-39.1.

9 In 1982, Doob and Roberts conducted a public survey which found that more than 60 per cent of the sampled public estimated the parole recidivism rate to be between 40 per cent and 100 per cent (see Doob and Roberts (1983)).

10 The success rate of inmates released on day parole is higher still: 82 per cent were completed successfully in 1996/7, with the vast majority of failures involving violation of conditions rather than fresh criminal charges (Reed and Roberts, 1998).

ADDITIONAL READING

Cole, D., and A. Manson. 1990. *Release from Imprisonment: The Law of Sentencing, Parole and Judicial Review.* Scarborough, Ont.: Carswell.

Reed, M., and J. Roberts. 1998. Adult Correctional Services in Canada, 1996–97. *Juristat* 18(3).

17

Sentencing and Early Release Arrangements for Offenders Convicted of Murder[1]

JULIAN V. ROBERTS AND DAVID P. COLE

The murder offences are unique, both in their consequences and in the criminal justice response. This chapter explores the sentencing and early parole arrangements for offenders convicted of murder. We begin by describing the mandatory life sentences for the murder offences. Then we address one of the most controversial issues in the area of parole: the question of conditional release for inmates serving life terms for murder, regulated by section 745.6 of the Criminal Code. This section of the Code has also been reformed recently, by two bills (C-41 and C-45). The nature and the probable impact of these reforms are discussed in this chapter.

Sentencing in Cases of Murder

There are many misperceptions about what actually happens to persons convicted of murder in Canada. Members of the public are under the impression that murderers can only be kept in jail for a few years, that release from jail cannot be prevented, and that once released these presumably dangerous animals are free of any further restrictions on their liberty. Such perceptions are inaccurate.

First, it is frequently overlooked that Parliament decided in 1976 that all adults convicted of murder are to be automatically 'sentenced to imprisonment for life.'[2] That means that the parole authorities have control over the convicted person for the rest of his or her life. They may deem the individual to be so potentially dangerous that every application for release is denied. Even if released on parole, the person may be returned to prison without any new charge being laid or conviction registered. Under Canadian law, a parolee may be reincarcerated upon any breach of a condition of release, or indeed upon a parole supervisor being 'satisfied that it is necessary or reasonable to suspend parole ... in order to prevent a breach of [a] condition or to protect society.'[3] There have been cases of old age pensioners convicted of murder many years previously being returned to penitentiary after decades of successful reintegration in the community because of concerns that their behaviour was deteriorating and that they might become dangerous to others. Another myth about sentencing in cases of murder is that persons convicted of this crime have to serve only a few years in custody. Parliament has created elaborate rules in the Code prohibiting any form of eligibility for conditional release until a specified number of years has been served since the day the person entered custody.

In the first part of this chapter we outline the sentencing arrangements for offenders convicted of murder, beginning with the sentencing of young offenders. In the second part, we explore the provision in the Code that permits life-term prisoners to apply for parole after having served fifteen years of their sentences.

Young Offenders between Sixteen and Eighteen at the Time of the Offence

Although the sentencing of young offenders is not discussed in this text, in certain circumstances young persons fourteen years of age or older at the time of the commission of an offence may be prosecuted as if they were adults. The process is called 'transfer to adult court.' Because young persons charged with homicide are frequently transferred to adult court, a brief discussion of sentencing powers will be useful.

In addition to the requirement that the young person be at least fourteen years of age,[4] the offence with which the young person is charged must be a serious, indictable offence (which murder or manslaughter clearly is). Unlike some American jurisdictions, however, there is no automatic transfer just because these two criteria have been fulfilled. An application must be launched before the youth court, either by the Crown or the defence, to have the young person transferred. Prior to amendments made to the Young Offenders Act in 1996, increasing the available penalties for young persons convicted of homicides in youth court, it was virtually automatic that Crown attorneys would launch applications to transfer young persons charged with murder to adult court. Now that the range of penalties available in youth court has been substantially increased, fewer applications seem to be brought.

If a transfer application is commenced, the Young Offenders Act now specifies different onus provisions, depending on the age of the young person. If the young person charged with murder (or certain other very serious offences) was at least sixteen at the time of the alleged offence, the youth court judge who hears the application is directed that there is a presumption in favour of transfer to adult court. If, on the other hand, the young person was fourteen or fifteen years old at the time, there is no statutory provision in favour of transfer.

The Young Offenders Act and the extensive case law that has developed interpreting its various provisions contain numerous complex factors that must be considered in deciding whether or not a transfer application will be granted. If the application is not granted, the young person is dealt with under that Act. In the interests of space, we have decided not to describe what happens to young persons charged with homicide who are not ordered transferred to adult court, or where an application to transfer a young person to adult court is unsuccessful. What follows considers only the rules that apply where a young person has been ordered transferred to adult court and is subsequently been found guilty of murder or manslaughter.

Where a young person is convicted of first degree murder, the judge has no discretion as to the length of the sentence. Parliament has specified that the young person is to be given a life sentence, with the minimum parole eligibility period set at ten years from the date he or she entered custody.[5] If a transferred sixteen- or seventeen-year-old is convicted of second degree murder, the sentence is similarly life imprisonment, with minimum parole eligibility fixed by Parliament at seven years. In neither case may the judge increase the period of parole ineligibility. The only area in which the judge is allowed some discretion is in deciding where portions of the sentence for first or second degree murder or manslaughter are to be served. Section 16.2 of the Young Offenders Act contains a series of factors that the sentencing judge is required to consider in making this decision, no doubt reflecting parliamentary concern that very young offenders not be sent directly to penitentiary.

Young Offenders over Fourteen but under Sixteen at the Time of the Offence

The statutory scheme for offenders over fourteen but under sixteen years of age is slightly different from the other sentencing provisions we have examined. A life sentence must automatically be imposed upon conviction for either first or second degree murder. However, in considering the appropriate parole ineligibility period for both first and second degree murder,[6] the judge is required to seek the recommendation of the jury, which is told in either case that the potential period of ineligibility varies between a minimum of five years and a maximum of seven years from the date the young person entered custody.[7] The judge may not specify a period of parole ineligibility above or below these limits.

Adult offenders

First Degree Murder

In the case of a person convicted of first degree murder, eligibility for release on full parole[8] is prohibited until the person has served at least twenty-five years in custody. There are a number of types of first degree murder, the most common of which are where a jury is satisfied beyond a reasonable doubt that a murder was 'planned and deliberate,' or where a murder was committed during the course of certain types of other illegal activities, such as a sexual assault or a kidnapping. Then there are 'deemed' first degree murders, where Parliament has decreed that the penalty of parole ineligibility for twenty-five years will apply. These include contract killings; murders of police, prison, or other peace officers; and cases of persons previously convicted of murder who are found guilty of another murder.

Second Degree Murder

A person convicted of second degree murder is also automatically sentenced to a term of life imprisonment. Parole ineligibility in such cases varies. Unless the sentencing judge decides to increase the period of parole ineligibility, Parliament has directed sentencing judges to fix such a period at ten years. In such a case the convicted murderer must serve at least ten years from the time he or she entered custody on the murder charge before becoming eligible for full parole.

The Code also authorizes the sentencing judge to increase a period of parole ineligibility of a person convicted of second degree murder beyond ten years to a maximum of twenty-five years. The judge is required to consider a number of factors in making this determination. First, once the jury has decided that the prisoner is guilty of second degree murder, unlike in other jury trials, it is not discharged at that point in time. Upon hearing the verdict, the trial judge is required to ask the jury whether it has any recommendation to make as to the number of years of parole ineligibility beyond ten and up to twenty-five years. Unlike some American jurisdictions, where the jury hears extensive evidence during the sentencing phase of a murder trial, the Canadian jury does not hear any mitigating or aggravating evidence, nor does it have the benefit of submissions by counsel for the Crown and the defence. The judge cannot provide any guidance beyond reading the section of the Code describing the jury's power to make a recommendation. Although the jury is required to return to the jury room to consider this issue, it is not required to make any recommendation, nor must the jury be unanimous in any recommendation it makes. Some juries make no recommendation, some recommend no increase, and some recommend increases beyond the ten-year minimum. Although the judge is required to consider any recommendation made, he or she is not obligated to follow it. There are many examples of cases in which a sentencing judge has ignored unanimous jury recommendations about the parole eligibility date of the offender.

In determining whether to increase the period of parole ineligibility beyond ten years, the judge is also required to take into account evidence and submissions which the jury has not heard. The case proceeds in the form of a regular sentencing hearing – a presentence report is usually prepared, the written or *viva voce* evidence of mental health professionals may be available, and character evidence may be presented.

Finally, the judge is required to take into account that, whereas broad discretion is reposed in sentencing judges in other types of cases, Parliament has to an extent fettered judges' discretion in this instance. The Criminal Code provides that the judge may increase parole ineligibility of an offender convicted of second degree murder beyond ten years to a maximum of twenty-five years 'having regard to the character of the offender, the nature of the offence and the circumstances regarding its commission.'

Ever since this section was brought into force in 1976, provincial appellate courts have disagreed – on occasion quite sharply – as to how the three factors should be balanced, and how frequently this power should be invoked. According to one view, the sentencing judge should not attempt the impossible, namely to predict the point in the future at which the offender will be rehabilitated. Other courts have held that, at least in particularly horrendous factual situations, repudiation of the offender's behaviour, 'along with that repudiation's concomitants of individual and general deterrence,' may be a sufficient justification for a sentencing judge to increase a period of parole ineligibility.

Ruby (1994) lists a number of factors that have been taken into account by sentencing judges and appellate courts in deciding whether a period of parole ineligibility should be increased beyond the ten-year point. These include disparity between accuseds with regard to their relative degree of responsibility for the killing, whether or not the accused pleaded guilty, youth, the existence and length of a previous criminal record (and the types of offences comprised in any record), brutality in the commission of the offence, elements of planning and deliberation (or, conversely, impulse), motive, vulnerability of the victim, and mental illness of the offender.

The debate between various provincial courts of appeal appears to have been recently foreclosed by the decision of the Supreme Court of Canada in *Shropshire*.[9] In that case judges of the British Columbia Court of Appeal had expressed different views as to whether the power to increase parole ineligibility should be used sparingly. The case involved a plea of guilty to a charge of second degree murder in the killing of one drug dealer by another, apparently motivated by an unpaid drug debt. The trial judge, clearly troubled by the failure of the accused to offer any explanation 'for a random and seemingly senseless killing,' had decided to increase the period of parole ineligibility from ten to twelve years. The majority judges of the British Columbia Court of Appeal considered that the accused's unwillingness to explain himself did not provide evidence that he was exceptionally dangerous, and that the denunciatory aspect of sentencing did not merit an increase in the parole ineligibility period. The Supreme Court of Canada disagreed, holding that section 744 does not require that a sentencing judge find that unusual circumstances exist before parole ineligibility may be increased. According to the court, it was 'proper' for the trial judge to have taken into account the absence of an explanation of attenuating factors.

It therefore appears that so long as the sentencing judge considers all of the factors mentioned in section 745.4, a court of appeal may not interfere, even if this has the effect of making extensions of periods of parole ineligibility more frequent. The Supreme Court of Canada was clear that the power to extend a period of parole ineligibility need not be reserved for highly exceptional circumstances.

A Constitutional Exception? The Case of Robert Latimer

Recently, a Saskatchewan court has considered whether it is constitutionally permitted to reduce the mandatory period of parole ineligibility below ten years. Robert Latimer was convicted by a jury of murdering his severely disabled daughter. The jury appears to have accepted the accused's assertion that he killed his daughter to put her out of her pain and constant suffering.[10] Interviews with some of the jurors after their verdict was rendered indicated that had they known of the mandatory minimum penalty they either would not have voted to find him guilty of murder or would have had extreme difficulty in doing so. When the jury was asked if it wished to make a recommendation as to the appropriate period of parole ineligibility, the jurors voted unanimously to recommend that the accused serve only one year in jail.

In reasons rendered in early December 1997, the trial judge held that in these unique circumstances it would amount to constitutionally impermissible cruel and unusual punishment to impose the ten-year minimum parole ineligibility period on the accused for his act of 'compassionate homicide.'[11] In coming to this conclusion he balanced the personal characteristics of the accused, the gravity of the offence and the circumstances surrounding it, and the effects that the sentence would have on the accused. In addition to the jury recommendation[12] the trial judge had before him evidence of 'an unprecedented public reaction against the severity of the punishment which the law prescribed,' in the form of 'hundreds of letters from all over Canada and beyond protesting the harshness of the mandatory sentence.'

Because the imposition of the minimum mandatory sentence in this 'unique set of facts' would be 'grossly disproportionate in the circumstances,' the trial judge sentenced the accused to a maximum reformatory sentence of two years less one day. Spokespersons for the disabled indicated their outrage with the verdict. As this book goes to press the Crown has indicated that it will seek leave to appeal the sentence to the Saskatchewan Court of Appeal. Regardless of how that court rules, it seems that this complex and controversial issue is likely to be appealed further to the Supreme Court of Canada.

Parole Arrangements for Life Prisoners

The issue of parole for convicted murderers has generated more public debate than perhaps any topic other than capital punishment. As noted earlier in this chapter, although murder carries a mandatory sentence of life imprisonment, this does not necessarily mean that the offender will be imprisoned for life. In fact, almost all inmates serving life terms will eventually be released on parole to serve the remainder of their life sentences in the community, under the supervision of the parole authorities. Life imprisonment then, does not mean natural life in prison, although the sentence does not expire when the inmate leaves the prison. The offender will continue to have to abide by the conditions of parole for the rest of his or her life.

According to section 745.6 of the Code, prisoners sentenced to life imprisonment without eligibility for parole before having served more than fifteen years in prison may apply for a judicial review of their parole eligibility date. This includes all offenders convicted of first degree murder and some of the second degree murder cases. At the fifteen-year mark of the sentence, these prisoners may apply for a jury review of the case, to see if there are grounds to reduce the period of parole ineligibility.

History of the Provision

Section 745.6 was added to the Code when capital punishment was abolished, in 1976. The abolition bill (C-84) contained statutory periods of parole ineligibility, meaning that offenders convicted of first degree murder would have to spend at least twenty-five years in prison before being eligible for full parole.

Offenders convicted of second degree murder would have to serve from ten to twenty-five years (the exact date being at the discretion of the judge) before becoming eligible for parole. The provision allowing for an earlier review was placed in the Code out of recognition of the fact that inmates who have served well over a decade in prison may have changed. Until 1987, section 745.6 attracted almost no attention, since no applications were heard. However, once applications began to be reviewed by juries, the section become possibly the most controversial provision in the Criminal Code. Testimony before the Senate Committee that reviewed the reform bill (see later sections of this chapter) revealed widespread ignorance of the way in which the section functioned.[13] Judicial review of parole eligibility for lifers was the subject of countless newspaper editorials and letters to the editor, as well as a great deal of negative press coverage, in which the term 'loophole for lifers' emerged to describe the provision.[14]

The term 'loophole' has been used throughout the heated debate regarding this section. Describing the provision as an undemocratic loophole is a good example of the rhetoric provoked by this issue. The term is as pejorative as it is inaccurate. After all, the word is usually associated with tax dodges, by which individuals avoid tax by exploiting errors or oversights in the Income Tax Act. Judicial review of parole eligibility is neither undemocratic nor a loophole. It was the product of an amendment to the Code that was debated and eventually passed by the democratic, bicameral Canadian Parliament. If the provision is undemocratic, then any piece of legislation, including a private member's bill to abolish the provision, can be said to be undemocratic.

Results of Applications to Date

Opponents and advocates of section 745.6 have disagreed over the results of applications to date. Several facts are clear. First, only a minority of eligible lifers have applied for a reduction in their parole ineligibility. Why this is so is less clear. Defenders of the provision suggest that inmates see little point in applying for a review, as their chances of a positive response are so low. This seems implausible since results currently indicate that most applications have been successful (although this may change as a result of the reforms introduced in 1997, discussed below). Whatever the reason, the statistics on the outcomes to date should be viewed with this initial degree of selection in mind. Parole Board statistics demonstrate that by the end of 1996 (just prior to passage of the reform bill), sixty-nine applications had been reviewed by juries. Of these, fifty-five, or 80 per cent, had resulted in some reduction in the parole ineligibility period.[15] Of those who had been successful with a jury, almost all had received a positive response on their subsequent application to the Parole Board.

Outcomes of Releases

Statistics of those inmates granted some form of release as of October 1996 reveal the following picture. Of those on day parole, 88 per cent had either completed their day parole period without incident or were still being supervised on day parole. Three out of thirty-two inmates on day parole had had their parole status revoked for violation of conditions; none of these had been charged with a new offence. Of all inmates who were granted a positive jury review and eventually released on full parole, only one had had his parole status revoked for a new crime (armed robbery).[16]

Role of Public Opinion

More than any other area of sentencing or parole, public opinion appears to have played a critical role in the reform of section 745.6. Opponents of judicial review argued that such a provision was contrary to the views of the Canadian public. At first blush, polls would appear to support this interpretation. Although no survey has been conducted specifically on the issue of early parole for inmates serving life for murder, an opinion survey conducted in 1988 found that approximately two-thirds of Canadians were of the view that only certain offenders should be eligible for parole. Of those who held this view, 81 per cent identified murderers as the individual that they had in mind who should never get parole (Roberts (1988a)). However, more than any other issue, judicial review for lifers exposes the weaknesses of measuring public opinion by means of a single question on a survey. If the public are opposed to parole at any point for lifers, they are especially unlikely to favour early parole at the fifteen-year mark. No poll has asked the question directly, but the results of section 745.6 applications prior to the reforms provide considerable insight into the views of the public.

In each case the juries could have granted the application (thereby making the inmate eligible at the fifteen-year mark), rejected the application, or reduced the period of parole ineligibility from twenty-five years to some point between fifteen and twenty-five years. In fact, as noted, in four cases out of five the applicant received some reduction in the portion of the sentence that had to be served prior to parole eligibility. Since juries are composed of members of the community, it seems hard to argue, as some opponents have done, that section 745.6 is against the wishes of the Canadian public. Appearing before the Senate Committee that reviewed Bill C-45 (the bill to reform section 745.6), the Attorney General of Ontario testified that '[t]here is no public support for the legislation.'[17] He then proceeded to note that '79% of the murderers who went before a section 745 jury won some reduction of their sentence.' The relationship between these two assertions was clearly lost on the learned attorney general. Juries are composed of members of the public. If the public were really opposed to parole for lifers, surely they would reject each application with little deliberation. The fact that they responded otherwise suggests that opinion polls do not always tell the full story.

In fact, this provision provides one of the few opportunities for ordinary citizens, who represent the community, to have a direct impact on the sentencing and parole process. As the Canadian Bar Association noted in its brief before the Senate Committee that reviewed the bill to reform section 745.6: 'Section 745.6 provides a unique opportunity for a jury of ordinary citizens, representing the voice and values of the community to be involved in the sentencing process' (Canadian Bar Association 1996, 3). We trust jurors with deciding the outcome of a murder trial, so why should we not allow them some input into the parole eligibility date?

The explanation for the discrepancy between what the public say in response to a poll and what they actually do in court when hearing a section 745.6 application probably lies in the amount of information available. In court, jurors hear a lot of information about the individual inmate and they have a chance to reflect on the merits of the application. When responding to a poll, the public provide an off-the-top-of-the-head reaction, probably with a worst case scenario in mind. Research on public attitudes toward other sentencing issues has repeatedly demonstrated that when the public is given an adequate amount of information about a case, it responds very differently (e.g., Doble and Klein 1989; Doob and Roberts 1988; Zeisel and Gallup 1989).

The statistics on jury decisions to date are also enlightening from another perspective. As noted, if the jurors decide to grant the application and reduce the number of years required to be served prior to parole eligibility, they can pick any date from twenty-five years (minus a day) down to fifteen years (immediate eligibility). Thus the jury can effect a reduction of up to ten years. Results show that juries have been using almost all possible numbers of years reduction, as can be seen by the breakdown of jury decisions in cases of first degree application presented in Table 17.1. In other words, they have been modulating their response to the merits of the individual applications. Since there is clear variability of response, these statistics suggest that juries have been capable of distinguishing applications that merit a reduction from those which require a negative response. In this sense, juries would appear to be applying the law appropriately. After all, the provision was not meant to result in all applications being accepted, or all being rejected. It was designed to serve as a filter, and that is exactly the way in which it was functioning prior to

TABLE 17.1
Results of First Degree Murder Applications

Jury's Decision	% of Applications
Application denied	19
Applicant told can reapply in 4 years	2
Applicant told can reapply in 3 years	2
Parole ineligibility reduced to:	
23 years	2
22 years	2
21 years	2
20 years	13
19 years	10
18 years	6
17 years	6
16 years	4
15 years	31
	100%

passage of the reform bill in early 1997. Exhibit 17.1 (see following page) provides two examples of section 745.6 applications (and the juries' responses) that were heard prior to the amendments (discussed below) being introduced.

Nature of Review

According to section 745.6 of the Code, eligible inmates may make an application for a judicial review after having served fifteen years of their life term in prison. This means that an application is filed with the court, which will then conduct a judicial prescreening. If the judge decides that the individual has a reasonable chance of convincing a jury, the application will proceed.

The legislation directs the jury to consider many aspects of the applicant's profile, specifically:

(a) the character of the applicant,
(b) the applicant's conduct while serving the sentence,
(c) the nature of the offence for which that applicant was convicted,
(d) any information provided by a victim, either at the time of the imposition of the sentence or at the time of the hearing under this subsection, and
(e) such other matters as the judge deems relevant in the circumstances.[18]

EXHIBIT 17.1
Parole for Lifers
(These two applications were heard prior to the reforms to section 745.6 noted in this chapter.)

Application 1

Jean-Louis L. was convicted of second degree murder in Quebec in 1977, with no possibility of parole for twenty-five years. During his incarceration, Mr L., now forty-two, worked on numerous inmate committees. His institutional record was outstanding. Ten witnesses were called to testify on his behalf at the judicial review hearing, including five correctional officers, a psychiatrist, two psychologists, a character witness, and a criminologist. The Crown called one psychologist to give evidence against the application.

Parole eligibility reduced from twenty-five years to fifteen years.

Application 2

Jon R. was sentenced to three life terms for murdering his wife and children in 1976. In 1995, after spending seventeen years in prison, he applied for a review of his parole eligibility date. A parole officer described Mr R. as an ideal prisoner who has been receiving day passes without incident for the previous ten years. The author of his parole eligibility report wrote that he had been a 'virtually perfect institutional citizen' and testified that prison psychologists had no reason to believe that he would be a danger to the public, if released. On the other hand, the Crown attorney in the case noted that while jurors would hear testimony as to Mr R.'s exemplary conduct in prison, they should not lose sight of the original offence, for which the offender still shows no remorse.

Application denied.

One of the essential documents in any such hearing is an agreed statement of facts summarizing the circumstances surrounding the commission of the offence for which the inmate is serving a life term. This is intended to give the jury (in the event that the applicant succeeds in passing beyond the judicial prescreening) an idea of the nature of the offence. The second critical document is a 'parole eligibility report,' which is prepared by Correctional Service of Canada personnel. This report is intended to be a 'comprehensive and factual summary of information relevant to parole eligibility, including the applicant's criminal, social and institutional history' (Correctional Services of Canada 1991). It draws upon psychological assessments, reports of institutional conduct and the inmate's personal development over the preceding fifteen years. In addition to these documents, the jury may hear testimony from individuals familiar with the applicant. Witnesses may appear on behalf of the applicant or the Crown attorney, who usually (but not always) opposes the application.

The wording of section 745.6 makes it clear that juries can consider a wide range of factors in coming to their decision. The words 'such other matters as the judge deems relevant in the circumstances'[19] accord considerable discretion to the judge, and this may play a role in the variable grant rates across Canada. The success rate of applicants in Quebec has been much higher than in other provinces. Over 90 per cent of applications in Quebec have received a positive response from juries, while in Ontario the success rate was closer to 50 per cent.[20] Jurors, Crown attorneys and possibly judges may be more sympathetic to lifers in the Province of Quebec. The result, however, is the same: disparity of treatment in terms of time served.

Options of the Jury

According to subsections 745.6(4) and (5), the jury can reduce the parole ineligibility from twenty-five to some lesser number of years; terminate the ineligibility, thus giving the inmate the right to make an immediate application to the National Parole Board; or leave the parole ineligibility untouched. In the event that the jury votes to reject the application for a reduction in parole ineligibility, it may set another date at which a subsequent application will be made, although there is a minimum two-year waiting period for subsequent applications.

In the event that the jury makes the applicant immediately eligible to apply for parole, he or she will have to proceed through a prerelease process, which includes escorted temporary absences, unescorted temporary absences, and day parole, before being allowed to live in the community on full parole. This process of graduated release takes approximately two to three years.

Reforming Judicial Review

Two reform initiatives have changed the way in which parole applications are conducted. First, Bill C-41 gave the families of victims a greater voice at judicial review hearings: a victim impact statement will now be entered as evidence. Prior to this reform, such information was admitted at the discretion of the court. The federal justice minister also sought the cooperation of his provincial counterparts, asking them to issue instructions to Crown attorneys that victims' families be advised of section 745.6 at the time of sentencing in all murder cases. In this way, the possible impact of the provision on any life sentence imposed would be known to these families, and would not come as a shock fifteen years later.

Origin of Bill C-45

In 1996, after having served fifteen years in prison, Clifford Olson made his application for early parole under section 745.6 of the Code. This application outraged the country and gave fresh impetus to the movement to abolish section 745.6. The section, and in particular Olson's application, became a topic in the 1997 federal election, with two parties – the Reform Party and the Conservative Party – promising to abolish the mechanism if they were elected to office. The federal government was under considerable pressure to abolish section 745.6. At the same time, a much smaller and less vocal constituency argued that the section was working well and should not be amended, let alone abolished.

The federal justice minister was confronted with two opposing constituencies. On one side were organizations like the Canadian Police Association, which demanded the complete repeal of the judicial review provision.[21] On the other hand, defenders of section 745.6 – such as the Canadian Bar Association – argued that only the exceptional applicants who merit such consideration are likely to benefit. Accordingly, they supported retention of the status quo. In the end, Justice Minister Rock opted for a middle ground between retention of the status quo and complete abolition of early parole for inmates serving life terms for murder. He introduced a reform bill (C-45)[22] which, although it preserved the provision, made three principal changes to section 745.6 that will probably reduce the number of successful applicants. After considerable debate in the House of Commons and the Senate, the bill to reform parole arrangements for lifers became law in December 1996 and was brought into force in January 1997.

Multiple and Serial Murderers No Longer Eligible for a Review

Offenders convicted of multiple murders, including serial murders, are no longer eligible for a parole review. This change is unlikely to have much impact, since there are few cases involving multiple victims. As well, these cases were never likely to receive a positive response from jurors, even under the old arrangements. This reform does raise the issue of crime seriousness and culpability. It assumes that all persons convicted of more than one murder are, a priori, more culpable and/or more dangerous than persons convicted of a single murder. This may be an oversimplification. Consider a case of double murder in which a man takes the life of his wife and child. Sentenced for first degree murder, he will be unable to apply for a judicial review of his parole ineligibility and will serve the entire twenty-five years before being eligible to apply for parole. On the other hand, a contract killer convicted of a single premeditated murder for money, also sentenced for first degree murder, will be eligible to make an application under section 745.6 after fifteen years. If his application is successful, he may serve nine years less in prison than the offender in the first case. Would we regard him as less blameworthy, or less dangerous than the other offender?

A Superior Court Judge Now Screens All Applications

Under the old rules, inmates proceeded directly to a jury hearing; according to the new rules, inmates will now have to convince a superior court judge that their application has a reasonable prospect of success. The inmate will submit affidavit evidence to a judge, who will determine, on a balance of probabilities whether the applicant would have a reasonable chance of success before a jury empanelled for a section 745.6 hearing. This threshold of success may be too high. An alternative suggestion made by the Canadian Bar Association was to have the judge determine whether the application has 'no prospect of success,' in which case it would not be allowed to proceed. The higher threshold contained in section 745.6 may mean that fewer applications will proceed to review by a jury. This mechanism is designed to prevent offenders such as Clifford Olson from having an automatic review. The Department of Justice argued that this amendment would prevent the system from wasting precious resources on frivolous applications, while at the same time permitting those with merit to proceed.

It is hard to gauge the effect of this reform on the success rate of future applications. Clearly, this amendment to the rules will prevent cases without any possibility of success from proceeding. However, it is also possible that judicial perceptions will differ from those held by the community. Some of the successful applications to date may well have looked, at the time, as being unlikely to succeed. In addition to suppressing applications without merit, the prescreening mechanism may also prevent some meritorious applications from advancing.[23] Of course, it can also be argued that once a case passes the prescreening stage, it may have a better chance of succeeding than in the past. The fact that a judge has given his or her 'approval' of the application may send a message to the jury that this particular application has sufficient merit to warrant a reduction. Finally, an additional concern raised by the introduction of judicial screening of applications relates to regional disparity. Judges in some provinces may have higher thresholds, and this would lead to disparity in the success rates of applications.

The Jury Must be Unanimous

Another amendment is likely to have a greater impact than the other two on the success of subsequent applications. Prior to passage of Bill C-45, applicants had to convince only two-thirds of the jury. This was a departure from the standard jury arrangement in a criminal trial, in which all members of the jury must agree on a verdict. Under the new rules, the jury must be unanimous before the applicant (the inmate seeking early parole) will be able to make an application to the parole board. The threshold for a successful application has been raised significantly. Henceforth, a single juror will suffice to block an application for early parole.

Retrospectivity of Provisions

The shift to unanimity and the judicial 'screening' of applications are retrospective in nature. That is, they apply not only to people currently being sentenced to life for murder, but also to people already serving life terms for murders committed years ago (provided that they had not already brought their section 745.6 applications before the amendments came into force). Consider the case of an individual who has spent fourteen years in prison for murder, preparing for a judicial review application. Now the rules have changed. The sentencing arrangements in place when he or she entered custody no longer apply. It might be argued that this constitutes a violation of fundamental justice, and as such could in the future furnish the grounds for a Charter challenge. The Canadian Bar Association, which represents over 34,000 jurists in Canada, was strongly opposed to the reform bill for this reason (among others – see Canadian Bar Association (1996)).

Conclusions

The consequence of the amendments made by Bill C-45 is the following. Henceforth, an applicant seeking early parole will have to pass a three-stage test. First, he or she will have to convince a judge that the application has a reasonable chance of success with a jury that must reach a unanimous decision before granting the applicant the right to apply for parole. Where the judge allows an application to be made, the applicant will then have to convince *all* the members of a jury that he or she deserves the right to make an early application for parole. Finally, the applicant will have to convince the National Parole Board that release on parole is not likely to endanger public safety. There are therefore three stages, involving the judiciary, the public (through the jury), and the National Parole Board, respectively. The principal effect of the reform bill will be, for better or worse, to make the faint hope clause much fainter.

ENDNOTES

1 The authors would like to express their gratitude to Mr Howard Bebbington for his careful review of an earlier draft of portions of this chapter.
2 The same principle of a life sentence being imposed upon conviction for murder applied before 1976 to those convicted of non-capital murder and those convicted of capital murder whose execution was suspended by the federal cabinet. The last executions in Canada took place in 1962.
3 Corrections and Conditional Release Act, s. 135(1).
4 Parliamentarians claim to have detected considerable public pressure to reduce the age below fourteen years, as well as generally to reduce the age of criminal responsibility to ten years. This may be reflected in future amendments to the legislative provisions.
5 S. 745.1(b).
6 Although in practice it would be almost unheard of for a judge to decline to specify the length of the parole ineligibility period, the Code is clear that in such circumstances the minimum period of parole eligibility – five years – is to apply. This seems to be a delicate way for Parliament to order a presumption in favour of the minimum penalty without expressly saying so.
7 Section 746.1(3) of the Code specifies that eligibility for unescorted temporary absences and day parole arise once the young person has served four-fifths of the period of the parole ineligibility period.
8 Section 747 provides that eligibility for lesser forms of unescorted release arise when the prisoner convicted of first degree murder has served twenty-two years.
9 *R. v. Shropshire* (1995), 102 C.C.C. (3d) 103.
10 As jurors are not allowed to disclose the contents of their deliberations, it is not known for certain what motivated their verdict.
11 This term does not exist in Canadian law. Since the release of this controversial verdict there has been considerable public discussion as to whether such a category should be created by legislation.
12 One of the reasons juries are not told of the consequences that would necessarily or likely flow from their verdict is that in earlier periods of history juries would sometimes shrink from returning guilty verdicts, especially if death sentences were

involved. Although it is not known for certain, the recommendation may well be unique in Canadian law.

13 For example, when he testified before the Senate Committee, the attorney general of Ontario stated that 'ten or fifteen years later [after the original trial] we will have another jury change the decision that the first jury made. That is what we are doing here. That is what section 745.6 does.' Mr Harnick seems unaware that the application takes place more than fifteen years after the offender was first taken into custody for the offence. He also seems to subscribe to the view that juries in a s. 745.6 hearing are changing the verdict. They are not. They are not even changing the sentence, which remains at life imprisonment.

14 For example, the *Toronto Sun* ran an article on 20 September 1992 under the headline 'Killers going free.' The article noted that 'dozens of the most savage murderers in Canada will gain freedom in coming years.'

15 Statistics provided by Corrections Branch, Ministry Secretariat, 1996.

16 Statistics provided by the National Parole Board.

17 Transcript of Senate Committee hearings, 28 November 1996.

18 Criminal Code, s. 745.6(2).

19 S. 745.6(2)(e).

20 National Parole Board Judicial Review Report, 28 October 1996. A private member's bill (C-234), which called for the complete abolition of s. 745.6, had also been introduced in Parliament.

21 Bill C-45, An Act to amend the Criminal Code (judicial review of parole ineligibility) and another Act, S.C. 1996, c. 34.

22 Against this it can be argued that the statutory right of appeal will ensure no unwarranted variation in judicial behaviour in the screening process.

23 This raises the question of prehearing bias on the part of potential jurors. If the majority of the public is opposed to this provision, then some potential jurors may not be disinterested with respect to the two parties, the applicant and the Crown. If this is the case, we shall see more 'challenge for cause' motions, as defence counsel attempt to ensure that their clients receive a fair hearing.

ADDITIONAL READING

Canadian Bar Association. 1996. *Submission on Bill C-45, Criminal Code Amendments. Judicial Review of Parole Ineligibility*. Ottawa: Canadian Bar Association.

Grant, I. 1997. Sentencing for Murder in Canada. *Federal Sentencing Reporter* 9:266–72.

O'Reilly-Fleming, T. 1991. The Injustice of Judicial Review: Vaillancourt Reconsidered. *Canadian Journal of Criminology* 33:163–70.

18

Sentencing Alternatives

JONATHAN RUDIN[1]

Interest in alternatives to the current sentencing arrangements can be found in many constituencies. People interested in reducing the negative effects of criminal justice processing (and, in particular, the effects of incarceration) have long advocated alternative strategies, particularly for non-violent offenders. As well, there has been a growing acceptance that the high cost of processing cases through the conventional sentencing system means that alternatives are a necessity, rather than a useful option. In this chapter, Jonathan Rudin describes the alternatives that currently exist in Canada.

Introduction

Since the late 1980s and early 1990s, increased interest has been expressed in sentencing alternatives. This interest has come from a variety of sources and is motivated by a number of different factors. In this chapter, some of the major reasons for the current interest in sentencing alternatives will be described. The chapter concludes with an examination of two alternative sentencing projects that appear to fall outside of the theoretical constructs advanced: sentencing circles and family group conferencing.

Why the Increased Attention on Sentencing Alternatives?

The term 'sentencing alternatives' describes a wide variety of approaches, which are often based on very different philosophical grounds and meant to address different practical concerns. Sentencing alternatives can either supplement the range of options available to a judge when sentencing an offender or remove the need for judicial action altogether. Particular alternatives have specific advocates, depending on the rationale for the alternative.

Sentencing alternatives, particularly those that do not involve the court, have been promoted quite aggressively in recent years by provincial attorneys general and by local Crown attorneys. One of the major reasons for the increasingly widespread support of alternatives among these players in the justice system is the growing backlog of cases in many provincial courts. As police lay more and more charges, and as acts which, fifteen or twenty years ago, might have been dealt with by noncriminal sanctions are increasingly brought before the courts for adjudication and disposition, there is concern that the justice system may be unable to deal with the increased volume. In our current judicial environment, alternatives that can free up court time have attracted considerable interest.

On a completely different front, certain individuals and organizations have become increasingly frustrated with the ability of the justice system to address the real needs of offenders, victims, and communities. This constituency is very diverse and includes Aboriginal organizations, faith groups, victims' rights groups, and others who are unhappy with the criminal justice system as currently structured. They are concerned about the ineffectiveness of Canada's criminal justice system to prevent crime, as noted in earlier chapters of this book, and, in particular, there is considerable disillusionment with imprisonment as a penal sanction.

There are several significant problems with reliance on incarceration as a sentencing option. First, it provides only a very temporary solution. The offender will inevitably be released and while society may enjoy a respite while he or she is behind bars, recidivism rates show that incarceration does very little to prevent a recurrence of criminal behaviour. As well, the progressive nature of punishment often leads to the imprisonment of people who pose little threat to society. For example, people who are repeatedly arrested for engaging in prostitution-related acts will eventually face jail sentences. Such sentences do little to deter the behaviour in question; they simply keep the offender off the streets for a period of time. If the criminal activity for which the person is jailed is victimless, it is not clear how incarceration serves any particular societal goal.

A popular assumption is that incarceration protects society against the violent offender. Jails are seen as places to which only the worst members of society are sent. In reality, the overwhelming majority of people sent to jail pose little or no physical threat to anyone. In Ontario, in the 1995/6 fiscal year, 39,121 people were sentenced to correctional facilities. Of that number, slightly less than 12 per cent could be said to have been jailed for violent offences (violent offences being robbery, major assault, sexual assault, sexual abuse, attempted murder, homicide, and kidnapping). None of the six offences for which people were most likely to be sent to a correctional facility in Ontario could be classed as seriously violent offences. The following six offences were responsible for over 54 per cent of admissions: break and enter (15 per cent); impaired driving (9 per cent); fine default (9 per cent); simple assault (8 per cent); fraud (7 per cent); and theft (7 per cent) (Ontario, Admissions to Corrections 1997).

Two crucial facts must be kept in mind when incarceration as a punishment option is discussed: incarceration is expensive and it is counter-productive. Overall, the cost per inmate per year varies from approximately $50,000 to $70,000. But apart from the fiscal costs, incarceration has very real human costs as well. If incarceration, although it did not reduce recidivism, had an otherwise neutral effect on inmates, it could be argued that, while expensive, at least it kept some people off the streets and made the lives of those not imprisoned somewhat safer. However, imprisonment not only fails to prevent inmates from turning to crime again when released, it has exactly the opposite effect.

Survival in prison requires the individual to adapt to life as an inmate. Such adaptation, vital to survival while in prison, does nothing to help the offender readjust to society upon release. What one learns in prison is how to be a prisoner, and the skills acquired will not prove to be of any positive assistance outside the jail environment. Imprisonment, rather than preventing recidivism, actually serves to promote it. Davis writes: 'The prison exists as a necessary ultimate sanction in the effort to limit hurtful or intolerable behaviour prohibited by law. But, by its very nature, it tends to ensure that those subject to this sanction are increasingly likely to become constant repeaters of such prohibited behaviour' (Davis 1976, 367–8).

Essentially, time spent in prison is wasted time. Prison is not able to make inmates better people. In fact, it accomplishes the reverse: prison dehumanizes people and makes them less able to function effectively and positively in society. It is significant that among the greatest crusaders for reform of the prison system are those who have worked most closely within that system. Finally, imprisonment, as the most severe punishment option available to the court, is applied disproportionately to certain portions of the population. It is now common knowledge that the prison population in Canada is made up primarily of the poor, the uneducated, visible minorities, and Aboriginal Canadians.

Theoretical Frameworks

Sentencing alternatives can be examined from at least two perspectives: by seeing who has control over the creation of the alternative sentence or by looking at whether the program focuses on offences or on offenders and victims. There is considerable overlap between these perspectives.

If we look at the issue of control as a continuum, at one end are those programs in which the Crown controls the development and disposition of the alternative sentence; at the other end are programs in which the community controls the process. In the middle are programs referred to as 'brokered' programs. Programs in which the Crown controls the alternative sentencing process tend to be offence based, while programs in which the community controls the process are usually offender based. In the middle of this continuum, once again, are 'brokered' programs.

Crown-Controlled, Offence-Based Programs

Most offences prosecuted through the criminal courts do not involve serious personal injury or significant damage to property. All criminal charges that come before the courts however, are dealt with in the same manner. In the cases of minor offences, this process often seems excessive. Is it really necessary to bring the full weight of the system to bear on a first offender who has taken a five-dollar item from a department store? In response to this perceived misallocation of resources, provinces have established diversion programs for young offenders and adult first offenders charged with minor criminal offences. These programs allow selected offenders who accept responsibility for the acts that led to the particular charges they face to have their matter diverted (i.e., removed from the criminal justice process). Offenders who have their cases diverted do not receive a criminal record with respect to the diverted offences.

Diversion is usually accomplished by the offender entering into some form of agreement with the Crown attorney's office. This agreement specifies what actions the offender is required to take. Options usually available to Crown attorneys in developing these dispositions include letters of apology to victims, community service, and/or restitution or charitable donations. In British Columbia, the first province to establish such programs for adults, the province's *Crown Counsel Handbook* describes diversion as follows: 'It must be emphasized that the purpose of diversion is not retribution or, except in an incidental way, deterrence. Diversion should be viewed as a positive and humane alternative which, for some cases, has the potential to provide greater benefit to the offender, the victim and society than would be expected from further processing through the criminal justice system. Diversion programmes, as they operate in B.C., are not viewed as part of the criminal justice system.'

One of the major attractions of diversion programs for court officials is that they assist in clearing clogged courts. This saving in time is accomplished with only very minor cost implications. The theory behind such programs is that, for first offenders charged with minor offences, the reality of a brush with the legal system is, in itself, usually enough to ensure that such behaviour will not be repeated.

While on a conceptual level there is little opposition to such programs, concerns have been raised about the manner in which they are operated. In the case of shoplifting, for example, the goods are generally recovered, eliminating in most cases any need for an order of restitution. As a result, diversion agreements often require the individual to make a charitable donation. Such a requirement leads to a situation of differential impact: requiring a fifty-dollar donation from a person receiving social assistance is proportionately a much larger hardship than requiring the same donation from someone who is employed. There is also the problem of characterizing what is being given as a donation. If an individual is faced with the choice of making a fifty-dollar charitable donation or pleading guilty in court, the 'donation' increasingly resembles the imposition of a fine (Ruby 1993a, 1993b). This is problematic, since there has been no finding of guilt and the decision of the appropriate donation level is up to the Crown, not a judge.

Given the strains on court resources, Crown-controlled diversion programs should be seen as a way of quickly removing minor cases from the courts in a manner that is generally acceptable to all parties. As noted above, the program is not retributive nor is it designed to function as a deterrent. To the extent that the offender can meet his or her agreement by making a donation to a charitable organization, the program cannot really be seen as rehabilitative either. Essentially, what the program does is give first offenders a break. What they do with that break is totally up to them.

State-operated diversion programs are offence based. In an offence-based system, the assumption is that resources of the court and of the other players in the justice system should be placed where most needed. That need is best assessed by the nature of the offence committed. As a result, Crown-controlled diversion programs operate on a fairly organized and routinized basis. In general, first offenders charged with victimless offences – such as theft under $5,000, mischief under $5,000, joyriding, etc. – are automatically accepted into the program. Given that the purpose of the program is to take these individuals out of the system as quickly and as expeditiously as possible, the easier it is for Crown attorneys to determine who qualifies for the program, the more quickly diversion requests can be processed.

The corollary to diversion is that Crown attention may now be placed in a more focused manner on those offenders seen as deserving that attention. Those individuals are also, once again, determined primarily on an offence basis. Those charged with serious offences, where victims may be involved, become the centre of Crown activity.

Community-Controlled, Offender-Based Programs

Community-based approaches to alternative sentencing generally proceed from a very different starting point and thus result in very different programs. These programs are usually grounded on the principles of restorative justice.

Restorative Justice

The principles underlying restorative justice have been described in various ways. For the Justice Fellowship, an organization with a mandate to promote restorative justice approaches, the paradigm has three fundamental principles:

1 Crime results in injuries to victims, communities, and offenders; therefore the criminal justice process must repair those injuries.
2 Not only government, but victims, offenders, and communities should be actively involved in the criminal justice process at the earliest point and to the maximum extent possible.
3 In promoting justice, the government is responsible for preserving order, and the community is responsible for establishing peace. (Van Ness et al. 1989, 22–4)

Essentially, restorative justice aims to relocate the practice of justice in the community. The retributive justice system, the system in place in Western society, removes the offender from the community and deals with him or her in isolation. In many cases, victims are not aware of what has happened. Even where victim impact statements are prepared and filed with the court, the depth of feeling that the offence has generated is rarely understood. Victims also do not have an opportunity in the current system to tell the offender directly what his or her actions have done to them. Nor do they have the chance to hear the offender explain why they were singled out.

The restorative justice concept recognizes that crime has a very real impact on the victim and also on the community at large. In recognition of this, the concept allows parties affected by the crime to address their feelings directly to the offender as part of a healing process. This opportunity to tell their side of the story allows victims, as McCord (1993) puts it, to get on with life. The theory also sees the offender as a member of the community as well, and thus as a person who should see and understand the nature of the hurt and harm he or she has caused. Restorative justice programs provide the offender with the opportunity to put matters right and to turn or return to being a productive member of the community. The theory holds that this type of justice can restore victims, offenders, and the community to a healthier and more whole way of life.

While the current restorative justice movement is only about twenty years old, the concept has deep historical roots. Restorative justice has much in common with Aboriginal concepts of justice, and restorative justice principles can be found explicitly in many ancient legal codes, ranging from the Sumerian Code of Ur-Nammu (2050 BC), to the Babylonian Code of Hammurabi (1700 BC) to the earliest surviving record of Germanic law, the Lex Salica (496 AD). The concept is also found in many pre-colonial African tribes (Van Ness et al. 1989).

Restorative Justice Programs

The restorative justice movement emphasizes the development of functional programs that can serve as examples of how the principles of the theory work in practice. The key to most restorative justice initiatives is a meeting between the victim and the offender. The meeting allows both parties to gain a better understanding of what occurred at the time the crime was committed, and what the consequences of that action have been for both parties. The meeting is also an opportunity to allow the parties to work toward a resolution of the matter.

Ultimately, the hope is that the matter can be resolved to the satisfaction of both victim and offender, both of whom can then get on with their lives and put the past behind them. In some programs these meeting are referred to as victim–offender reconciliations (VORPs), while other programs describe themselves as mediation. The terminology is not as significant as the common theoretical underpinnings.

These meetings occur only after discussions with each of the parties have been held by a neutral third party. The victim–offender meeting takes place only in the presence of one or more trained mediators. Victim–offender meetings can take place at any point during the criminal justice process: meetings have been held after findings of guilt, in order to determine the amount of restitution, and there are even some programs in which meetings take place with offenders serving time in prison for their violent offences. As real sentencing alternatives, these projects are best undertaken as diversion-type programs.

The idea that victims and offenders can meet to discuss what has transpired between them and work out an agreement as to how to resolve matters might appear utopian, but experience demonstrates that this is what occurs the majority of times in which a meeting takes place. For the process to work, people cannot be coerced into participating. Thus if the victim does not wish to meet the offender, the process cannot proceed.

Umbreit and Coates (1992) conducted a study involving juvenile offenders, interviewing people who participated in victim-offender meetings, those who were referred to programs but declined to participate, and others who had not been referred to the program at all. The major findings of the study are described below:

1 Crime victims who participate in face-to-face mediation sessions with their juvenile offender are significantly more likely to be satisfied with the way in which their case was handled by the juvenile justice system than similar victims who did not participate in mediation.
2 Crime victims who participate in face-to-face mediation sessions with their juvenile offender are significantly more likely to have experienced fairness in the manner in which their case was handled by the juvenile justice system than similar victims who did not participate in mediation.
3 Juvenile offenders who participate in face-to-face mediation sessions with the person they victimized are significantly more likely to have experienced fairness in the manner in which their case was handled by the juvenile justice system than similar offenders who did not participate in mediation.
4 Juvenile offenders who negotiate a restitution plan in a face-to-face mediation session with the person they victimized are significantly more likely to successfully complete their restitution obligation than similar offenders who were ordered to pay restitution, with no mediation involved (Umbreit and Coates 1992).

These findings suggest that victim-offender reconciliation sessions are not only more likely to result in offenders complying with orders for restitution, but that victims find the process itself fairer and more satisfying than participating in the traditional court system. The study also found that while the idea of negotiating restitution was important to nine of ten victims prior to entering mediation, actually receiving the restitution was only important to seven of ten after the mediation: 'The opportunity to directly participate in an interpersonal problem solving process to establish a fair restitution plan was more important to victims than actually receiving the agreed upon restitution' (Umbreit and Coates 1992, 5).

VORP and mediation programs offer a significant alternative to the manner in which the current criminal justice system deals with charges. The Umbreit and Coates study suggests that these programs are better able to respond to the needs of both victims and offenders than the traditional court process. At the same time, it must be noted that the restorative justice model, as it is currently constructed, does have significant limitations.

The biggest difficulty with restorative justice programs is that they require the victim and the offender to agree to participate in the process. This presents a number of problems. For one thing, there is not always an identifiable victim for every criminal offence. For example, it is difficult to find a victim in the case of a person charged with drug possession. Nor is there an identifiable victim in prostitution-related matters. It seems odd that people charged with anti-social behaviour, such as assault, can have their charges taken out of the criminal justice system for resolution in another forum, while those who have the misfortune of committing a crime without a victim do not have this option. Since repeated drug or prostitution-related charges can lead to terms of imprisonment and since imprisonment rarely has any impact on the behaviour of people charged with these types of offences and, finally, since those charged with these offences are generally the poor, visible minorities, and Aboriginal people, this exclusion often leaves out those offenders who might benefit the most from an alternative to the current system.

Even where a victim can be identified, restorative justice programs only proceed with cases where both the victim and offender are willing to participate. In practice, almost half of the cases that are amenable to mediation or reconciliation actually go forward. The main reason for a case's failure to proceed to a victim-offender meeting is reluctance on the part of the victim. This reluctance is often based on misinformation about the actual workings of the justice system and, in particular, on the victim's desire to see the offender go to jail, even when that is not a likely outcome. A victim's unrealistic hope for a punitive outcome can prevent a matter from being mediated.

While it is understandable that the mediation model requires two willing parties, it is unfortunate that offenders who are willing to participate in the process and who might benefit from it may be prevented from doing so because of prejudices or unrealistic expectations on the part of victims. It is not clear why the nature and quality of the justice that is meted out by the criminal justice system should be dependent on the character and attitude of the victim, particularly in cases where the Crown has determined that public safety concerns would not require a jail sentence in any event.

The current restriction on eligibility to those who are unlikely to receive jail sentences, a common restriction on consent to diversion by Crown attorneys, can also be problematic. It can be argued that those who have been to jail on more than one occasion and yet repeatedly reoffend stand as a testimony to the futility of incarceration as a societal response. It might be thought that another approach could be tried, at least once, in such cases. The fact that imprisonment is relied upon disproportionately for the poor, visible minorities, and Aboriginal people means that they are most likely the ones who will be prevented from entering alternative programs – due as much to the propensity of the criminal justice system to punish them more harshly than other offenders, than to any recurring problems they might have with the law.

In order that restorative justice programs be truly accessible to all who might benefit from them, it is important that such programs be available to all members of the community. This raises the issue of offenders who speak languages other than those which are readily available through court services.

Even where both parties are comfortable speaking a common language, cultural differences can make mediation very difficult. The mediator, who may not be familiar with either of the cultures represented at the mediation, must be particularly concerned not to allow prejudices or stereotypes of what constitutes proper behaviour to influence his or her actions. Mediators must therefore understand cross-cultural issues and be sensitive to them. Cultural attitudes may not always be immediately obvious or expressly declared. Often it is the unstated assumptions and attitudes on the part of the participants or the mediator that prevent a successful resolution of the matter at hand.

While such situations call for trained mediators who can follow the underlying dynamics of a situation, the mediator must not necessarily come from the racial, cultural, or ethnic group that is represented at the mediation. Discussion with members of five communities that formed the basis of a study in Vancouver by the University of Victoria on dispute resolution indicated that 'in-group' mediators were not necessarily preferable nor did they do a better job than those from outside the participants' community or communities (Duryea and Grundison 1993).

Aboriginal Justice Programs

Any study of alternatives to current criminal justice system models must seriously examine the variety of initiatives undertaken by Aboriginal communities across Canada. The Aboriginal experience with developing criminal justice initiatives provides examples of how the criminal justice system can be altered to meet the needs of a distinct Canadian community. The Royal Commission on Aboriginal Peoples' report on justice, *Bridging the Cultural Divide* (1996), provides many examples of such initiatives.

Aboriginal justice initiatives have emerged as community-specific responses to problems with the justice system. The range of Aboriginal justice initiatives varies with the needs and resources of each community. Some responses involve Aboriginal input into the sentencing process. This is most often accomplished through the operation of sentencing circles, which will be discussed in more detail later. Aboriginal communities have also developed diversion programs based on restorative justice concepts. Aboriginal diversion programs differ in some significant respects from the VORPs and mediation programs described above.

Aboriginal Legal Services of Toronto's Community Council program is the longest-running Aboriginal diversion program in Canada, having heard its first case in March 1992. The Community Council provides a good example of the similarities and differences between the Aboriginal diversion model and that of other restorative justice programs.

As with other diversion programs, the Community Council deals only with offenders who are prepared to acknowledge responsibility for the offence (or a lesser offence) with which they have been charged. Unlike many other diversion programs, no offences are inherently ineligible for diversion and individuals with prior criminal records (including previous custodial sentences) are not only eligible for the program, but are one of the target groups. To date, approximately 80 per cent of those diverted to the program have a previous criminal record and over 50 per cent have served time in jail.

Unlike other restorative justice programs, victim participation in the process, while desirable, is not a prerequisite. Where the offence involves personal injury, victim consent is sought. Consent is occasionally sought in property offences, but that is more the exception than the rule. It has been found that most victims consent to the diversion when informed about the program. Victims do not usually attend council hearings, although they are explicitly invited. In those cases where the victim does attend, there is usually an ongoing relationship of some kind between the parties (i.e., friendship, family ties, employment). As with other diversion programs, consent must be obtained from the local Crown attorney before diversion can take place.

Community Council members are volunteers. There are currently twenty-seven Council members, ranging in age from their late twenties to their sixties. Their occupations range from social worker to cab driver. The goal of a council hearing is to have the offender accept responsibility for what he or she has done and then take the steps necessary to begin healing. It is during the healing process that the individual learns how to make the life changes necessary to ensure that he or she is no longer before the courts. Healing cannot occur until the person accepts responsibility for his or her actions.

Three to four council members attend each hearing and participate by asking questions of the parties (offenders, victims, family members, etc.) and sharing their opinions and life experiences. Once the council members feel that they have gleaned all they can from the parties, they decide on a disposition of the matter. All council decisions are arrived at by consensus. Thus, unlike mediation or VORPs, council members take an active role in shaping the disposition of a case, rather than brokering an agreement between the affected parties. After the decision has been finalized, the offender returns to the room and has an opportunity to review the decision. If he or she does not agree with the decision, further discussion ensues until all parties feel that a satisfactory decision has been reached. If a victim is present at the hearing, he or she will be asked to speak to the council as well. The victim has the choice of speaking to council members with or without the offender present. The victim is also invited back to the hearing room to hear the council's decision.

Council decisions usually require the offender to do a number of things. Some are directly tied to making that individual understand the consequences of his or her actions – for instance, the offender may be required to write a letter of apology. Others deal more directly with those issues that have led the person into conflict with the law: the offender may be made to seek counselling for alcohol and/or drug dependencies, for example. Still other parts of council decisions are designed to accomplish both goals. Community service orders, for instance, impress upon the individual that his or her actions require that something be given back to the community, but they are also designed to help integrate or reintegrate the offender into the Aboriginal community. Community service orders allow the offender to see positive Aboriginal role models.

One of the major issues facing many of those coming before the council relates to negative self-image. Such a self-image often stems from the overt and systemic discrimination faced by Aboriginal people in Canada. Over 40 per cent of those who have come before the council have been adopted or spent time in foster care. It is significant that approximately 60 per cent of those diverted to the council are not very aware of the range of programs and services available to Aboriginal people in Toronto.

Unlike state-controlled diversion programs, the Community Council is an offender-based program. As a result, the focus of the council hearing is on the individual and his or her needs. The fact that the offence that brought the individual to the council may appear to be a minor one does not mean that the case requires any less attention or is any less important than one in which the individual has committed a more serious offence.

Brokered Programs

Given the narrow range of offences and offenders eligible for diversion under Crown-controlled programs, police and Crown attorneys are now turning to outside agencies to assist with the diversion of offenders who might require more assistance than they can and should provide themselves, but who, nevertheless, are not perceived to present a threat to society at large and thus might otherwise be eligible for diversion. Programs that respond to this need are referred to as brokered programs.

In a brokered program the police (in a pre-charge system) or the Crown (in a post-charge system) determine that the services of an outside agency are needed to construct an alternative disposition. In these cases, the accused is referred to a staff person or volunteer with the outside agency (usually a non-profit agency) who will interview the accused and perhaps the victim, if there is one, and come up with a disposition for the matter. For example, the agency staff person or volunteer may recommend that the accused perform a certain number of community service hours, take anger management classes, or any other appropriate action. If the accused successfully completes this disposition then, in a pre-charge model, the police are informed of the accused's successful completion and charges are not laid. In a post-charge model a note is sent to the Crown, who will withdraw or stay the charges against the accused. One of the advantages of reliance on community-based agencies is that they are better able than police or Crown attorneys to determine what might be in the best interests of the accused and the victim; they will also have the necessary contacts to assist the accused in meeting the terms of the disposition.

Net-Widening

Ironically, the increased use of alternatives to the current sanction-based orientation of the criminal justice system has led to the imprisonment of people who would not have been jailed had such options not existed. This phenomenon is known as net-widening. In order to prevent the occurrence of this unintended consequence, the scope and nature of alternatives must be carefully thought out to ensure that they serve the purpose for which they were designed.

The Justice Fellowship in Washington, D.C., provides an example of how the misuse of discretion by prosecutors where restorative justice programs are in place can lead to expanded rather than lessened state controls over an individual: '... to develop credibility a community-based diversion program may agree to accept referrals of minor offenses from the local court. The court ends up referring cases that are so minor they would have been dismissed otherwise. The problem is magnified when offenders who fail to comply with the reconciliation agreement are then brought back before the judge and sentenced to jail or prison. The unintended effect of this program, designed to be an alternative to prison, may actually be that more offenders are locked up (Van Ness et al. 1989, 41–2).

Net-widening occurs because judges and Crown attorneys realize that the current punishment-based system is not effective in either changing behaviour or making people take responsibility for their actions. Thus, in cases where judges may otherwise simply order a conditional or absolute discharge or a term of probation, additional terms are added for the offender's 'benefit.' Cases in which the Crown would otherwise simply withdraw the charge are diverted to programs that might teach offenders more about the consequences of their actions. Failure to adhere to the conditions attached can lead to the offender being charged with failure to comply with probation (if the conditions are imposed during sentencing) or put the Crown and judge in the position where they feel a custodial sentence must be imposed, because, by failing to follow through with the diversion plan, the individual has demonstrated incorrigibility. How the offender benefits from a jail sentence in these circumstances is not at all clear.

The problem of net-widening is real. One response to the issue is to ensure that alternative programs are seen as true alternatives and cannot simply be grafted onto existing sentencing options. Overall, both Crown-controlled and community-controlled programs should examine their potential for net-widening very carefully prior to implementation to ensure that they end up being part of the solution, not another part of the problem.

What Is Community?

As noted earlier in this chapter, community-developed alternative sentencing initiatives tend to be offender-based programs. What all these programs, of whatever type, have in common, is that they respond to the needs of a particular community. The term 'community' can be defined in many different ways. There are geographic communities, such as streets, neighbourhoods, and cities; religious communities; cultural communities; racial or ethnic communities; communities identified by demographic features, such as age; communities based on sexual orientation and any number of other identifying features. In urban centres it is not unusual to find people identifying themselves as belonging to a number of different communities. The fact that people choose to identify themselves in different ways at different times to different people should not be seen as fatal to the development of community-based alternatives. Rather, this multiplicity of communities allows for the development of a wide array of responses.

The key objective of offender-based programs is the reintegration of the offender into the community and restoration of harmony and balance. Allied with this concept is the realization that the community itself must take some responsibility in assisting the reintegrative and restorative process. Which particular community or communities are involved in this reintegration and restoration is not nearly as important as the fact that it takes place.

Where the goal of a program is to reintegrate a person into a community, the community must have a meaningful role in the development of the program in order for it to succeed. This may well mean that a variety of programs will be developed by communities. Such diversity is not a problem. Rather, it reflects the level of comfort that particular communities have with taking some control over the management of the justice system. If the community is given the opportunity to take some control over the justice system, it must have the right to set out the scope of its involvement.

Community input and control means allowing the community itself to determine its interest in participating in alternative sentencing projects and to decide the extent of such a project. In most cases community control is largely dependent upon meaningful consultation. The importance of consultation cannot be stressed too much; without a proper grounding of community support innovative programs will not succeed.

This point was emphasized in an independent evaluation of the Community Council program outlined earlier. Referring to the need for project development, the evaluators stated: 'Community involvement takes time; it follows the adage, "go slow to go fast." Unless the community is given the required amount of time to take ownership of the program, it may well fail entirely or fail to represent the wishes and objectives of the community' (Moyer and Axon 1993, 23).

Community input and control can threaten some people. For one thing, community control can mean a loss of power to police, judges, lawyers, and bureaucrats. Occasionally, this concern over loss of control leads to a process of what sociologists might call 'elite accommodation.' In such a process, proponents of reform within the justice system approach those community leaders they trust and give to them the right and responsibility of developing and delivering alternative programs. However well-meaning this process is, it rarely works. Even if the individuals chosen are respected in the community, their lack of an express mandate from the community to develop such a program will usually result in the failure of the program itself. This experience has already occurred in a number of Aboriginal justice initiatives.

Concepts of culture and of justice are not static; they evolve over time and place. Aboriginal justice initiatives today do not simply resurrect the manner in which justice was done prior to contact with Europeans, because the reality of the Aboriginal experience has been forever altered by the fact of contact and its repercussions. The manner in which these changes have been felt in Aboriginal communities has also varied. Initiatives in a large metropolitan area such as Toronto reflect the particular needs of that community, while initiatives on Northern reserves will reflect those particular realities. In this light, the term 'culturally appropriate' refers to the current socio-political and cultural realities faced by members of particular racial, ethnic, and cultural groups in specific locations.

Given this expanded definition, it is clear that the development of justice alternatives by, for example, racial or ethnic minorities will involve more than simply importing procedures or processes that were in place in their countries of origin. The study by the University of Victoria of five communities in Vancouver found that: '[p]articipants generally agreed that immigrants' traditional conflict resolution methods did not work well for them in Canada. The complexity of hybrid culture and influence of Canadian values were factors influencing the usefulness of traditional methods. Some variables, such as gender or length of time in Canada, were said to affect the use of traditional ways' (Duryea and Grundison 1993, 196).

It cannot be assumed that all members of a particular minority community have the same needs or wants or that one program will be able to serve everyone's needs. In many cases, the manner in which the dominant society identifies members of racial or ethnic minority groups may well not conform to the way in which the individual members of that group perceive themselves. For example, the University of Victoria study found that while the dominant society believed in the existence of a homogenous Latin American community in Vancouver, members of that community identified themselves on other bases, for example, by country of origin.

Programs that seek to be culturally appropriate may well have to take into account the length of time people have spent in Canada, specific countries of origin, mother tongue, religion, and other factors. Recognizing diversity within racial and ethnic minority communities should not, however, be seen as detrimental to the development of alternative sentencing programs. If communities are given adequate time and resources to consult and discuss matters, consensus will likely be reached regarding which projects are appropriate for which members of the community, at which time.

Sentencing Circles

The remoteness of many Aboriginal communities means that they do not see a judge for months on end. When the judge finally arrives, he or she is part of an entourage that flies into the community for a day or two to dispense justice. Accompanying the judge on this excursion will be the Crown attorney, defence counsel, and other relevant parties. The idea that a judge and Crown and defence counsel, none of whom live remotely near the communities they are visiting or possess more than a passing knowledge or acquaintance of the community and who, in most cases, are neither Aboriginal nor speak the language of the community, can achieve any sort of meaningful judgment in any particular case is a fine example of Western legal conceit.

What makes the situation facing the court officials even more problematic is that the offence that is the subject of the hearing may well have taken place three to six months ago. Given the proximity of the parties to each other and the need to find a way of co-existing pending the arrival of the justice system, the community often manages to find a mutually satisfactory way of dealing with the matter before the court flies in. In some cases, not only has a solution been worked out, but the offending party may have done all that the community feels is required before the case is heard.

These realities have led a number of judges working in remote communities to look for more meaningful ways of dispensing justice. Judges Lillies and Stuart in the Yukon have been pioneers in these quests. In seeking alternatives, these judges looked to the communities themselves. Discussions with community leaders and elders led to a decision to return, in a fashion, to the manner in which justice was done prior to the imposition of the Western legal system. The return to more traditional responses led to an opening up of the sentencing process to greater community input. Essentially, the sentencing process was broadened to actively and publicly seek the input and advice of elders, clan leaders, and community members. This objective was accomplished in a variety of ways. In some cases, elders' panels were set up to sit with the judge and advise him or her on sentencing issues; in other cases, the community was invited to sit together to discuss sentencing options in a sentencing circle.

The purpose of these innovations is to provide the court with meaningful input from those people who know and understand the offender and who are most directly affected by his or her conduct. Those who best understand the causes of a person's criminality will likely be able to provide real insight into the way in which the individual's behaviour can be changed. In addition, the offender will probably respond more deeply to concerns and suggestions expressed by members of his or her community than to a judge who is removed in every way from the offender's world. Sentencing circles and/or elders' panels have attracted a great deal of interest from the Canadian judiciary. While the program is viewed as an Aboriginal initiative, some judges see a role for such programs in cases involving non-Aboriginal offenders. At least one sentencing circle has been held in Canada for a non-Aboriginal offender.

Sentencing circles appear to fall outside of the theoretical framework proposed earlier. Since the circle is directed, controlled, and initiated by the judge, it appears to be state controlled. At the same time, however, the circles involve a significant amount of community input and, by their nature, focus primarily on the offender, rather than on the offence. From all reports to date, sentencing circles and elders' panels appear to perform a useful but limited role. Determinations of guilt and innocence are still made by the court and the final sentencing remains a matter to be resolved by the judge in the particular case. The judge is under no obligation in any program to follow the suggestions of the sentencing circle. Sentencing guidelines and maximums enshrined in the Criminal Code take precedence over any suggestions from the community. In addition to the supervisory role played by the trial judge, sentencing decisions are also subject to review by courts of appeal.

From a practical perspective, one of the drawbacks of this approach is that sentencing circles invite a significant amount of community input in a relatively unstructured setting and with regard to a wide variety of offences. From the perspective of those concerned with addressing court backlogs, sentencing circles are part of the problem, not the solution. For a judge, a sentencing that might take at most fifteen to twenty minutes of court time, if done through the traditional method of submission from counsel, might take hours when done in a circle. While this might make for a meaningful process for all involved, it also takes up a great deal of court time. In particular, where circles are held for offences for which a minimal custodial sentence might be applied in any event, the time required can be seen as problematic from a cost-benefit point of view, in terms of the court's needs to process offenders. This concern over the use of court time has ultimately restricted the ability of sentencing circles to be used in a wide variety of settings.

One of the strengths of circles is that they draw upon a wide range of community members. On the other hand, since the circle is a court process, the determination of who will sit in the circle is ultimately made by the judge. Where the judge is unfamiliar with the dynamics of a particular community, this can prove problematic. Legitimate concerns have been raised, primarily by Aboriginal women's organizations, about the use of circles in small Aboriginal communities, particularly for offences of violence against women. If the judge is not aware of the political and cultural dynamics at play in the community – and judges are often unaware of such things in communities they may visit only once a month or less – then the selection of those who are to sit in the circle and the process itself can cause real harm to the victim of the offence, leaving her in a worse position than if resort had been made to the traditional court process.

While sentencing circles involve a significantly larger number of people in the sentencing process than do many other alternative programs, they ultimately remain, as part of the court process, under the control and jurisdiction of the judiciary. This has led to various attempts by courts to set guidelines with respect to the circumstances under which it is or is not appropriate to hold a circle. The setting of such guidelines is a very difficult endeavour; because judges can easily end up establishing criteria that appear to be 'common sense,' but which might well exclude those most in need of access to alternative sentencing programs.

This situation, if it has not yet occurred, is in danger of occurring in Saskatchewan. In the case of *R v. Joseyounen* (1995),[2] Judge Fafard set out seven criteria to be used in determining whether or not a sentencing circle was appropriate. The reasoning in *Joseyounen* has been approved in a number of other cases and it appears to have received tacit, if not explicit, approval from the Saskatchewan Court of Appeal in the case of *R. v. Morin.*[3]

The most problematic criterion in *Joseyounen* is the second, namely, that 'the accused must have deep roots in the community in which the circle is held and from which the participants are drawn.' On first reading, this requirement would appear simply to be common sense. If a person does not have roots in his or her community, how can it be expected that the response of the community to the actions of that individual will have any significant impact? If the offender in question is not grounded in the community, he or she will feel little or no pressure to accept the support of those in the circle. There will be few consequences if the offender drifts away from a community of which he or she was never a part. Finally, there may well be a concern about the willingness or the ability of the community to respond to the needs of a person who is not a member.

The experience of the Community Council program in Toronto counters these assumptions. As noted earlier, at least 40 per cent of those people participating in the Community Council project have been adopted or in were foster care. Where the placements were to non-Aboriginal homes, the individuals were raised with little or no sense of Aboriginal identity. Overall, over 60 per cent of those participating in the Community Council program have virtually no contact with the Aboriginal community in Toronto and indeed, for many of them, no contact with Aboriginal communities anywhere.

It is precisely such individuals who are most in need of links with the Aboriginal community. Without these links, many, if not most, of these offenders will continue to offend and be subject to greater and greater punishment. It is those individuals who have become estranged or were never part of the Aboriginal community who most need access to alternatives that allow them to connect with their community. Establishing barriers to exclude them from access to such alternatives is writing these offenders a one-way ticket to the penitentiary.

Family Group Conferencing

Another sentencing alternative program that does not obviously fit within the theoretical constructs developed earlier is family group conferencing. Family group conferencing, which can refer to a wide range of activities, is used here in the way that it has come to be known in Canada, as based on a model developed in New Zealand and Australia, in particular, in New South Wales.

Family group conferences have been used primarily with young offenders. In the program many, if not all, affected parties, including the offender, the victim, the offender's family, the victim's family, teachers, social workers, investigating police officers, etc., meet together in an attempt to develop a response to the offending behaviour. The Australian model is referred to as a police-driven model. Police are responsible for the holding of the conferences and are essentially the ones who run them. In this regard, the initiative resembles sentencing circles in that it appears to be an offender-based program within a state-controlled process.

There has been a great deal of interest in family group conferencing in Canada. Much of that interest has been manifested by individuals taking training in how to deliver the Australian model. Similar programs have been in place in Canada for years. Many of these innovative alternative sentencing programs have been developed in communities where the police, often the RCMP, have worked hand in hand with community members to explore new ways of meaningfully addressing the root causes of criminal behaviour.

There is nothing inherently wrong with a police-driven model, as long as it is understood that, in some cases, the fact that the conference is run by a police officer may cause offenders with a distrust of the police, warranted or unwarranted, to be unwilling participants. There is nothing inherently wrong with family participation in the conference, as long as it is understood that the presence of an abusive parent in the same room as their child, the offender, will not lead to any frank discussion of the problems causing the criminal behaviour. Alternative sentencing programs that wish to look at the causes of offending behaviour must always keep in mind that it is not the form but the content of the program that will make it a success.

Insistence that a program must 'look' a certain way or include certain people by virtue of their status relationship in particular roles will ultimately result in the failure of the program to respond to the needs of a community. No matter how well-meaning, police officers, or anyone else for that matter, cannot grant input to a community but restrict that input to determining how best to implement a pre-established model. If a program is truly to address community needs, time must be taken to determine what those needs are and how the community wishes them to be addressed.

The extent to which family group conferencing has had an impact on reducing reliance on incarceration in Australia and New Zealand has mistakenly led people to believe the process itself is chiefly responsible for these changes. It is not the particular program that is somehow special, it is the fact that those governments, Crown attorneys, police, and communities have agreed that alternatives must play a significant role in the criminal justice system, that resources have been put into these programs, and that the focus has shifted away from incarceration.

If similar commitments were made in Canada, similar results would ensue. Without those commitments those results will not be achieved. There are many exciting, innovative alternative sentencing programs in Canada. Many of them are on the verge of closing because there is no commitment to support them on an ongoing basis. We must steer away from thinking that establishing alternative sentencing programs is just a question of importing the right process from somewhere else. Without genuine institutional commitment and support – at both the political and community level – alternative sentencing programs will fail. They will be seen as a 'flavour of the week' solution, an historical anomaly – and that would be a real tragedy.

Conclusions

There is no doubt that the use of sentencing alternatives in Canada will continue to increase. Whether there will be room both for programs that seek to reduce court backlogs and programs that seek to restore harmony and functioning to victims, offenders, and the community is open to debate. In some cases, programs can be developed that address both concerns; in many cases, this will not be possible. One of the critical issues will continue to be access to resources. Crown-controlled programs are designed to be quick, easy to administer, and inexpensive. Community-controlled programs, by their very nature, may take time to resolve matters and will probably require additional resources, both in terms of volunteers and the dollars required to operate and administer programs. There is no single, perfect model; there is no reason to believe that Crown-controlled programs are inherently better or worse than community-controlled or brokered programs. What must always be kept in mind is that programs should only be measured against the goals and objectives that they can reasonably achieve. In considering the need for sentencing alternatives it is important to begin by examining the purposes for which alternatives are being sought. Once this is clear, programs that respond to these needs can be developed.

ENDNOTES

1 Jonathan Rudin is Program Director of Aboriginal Legal Services in Toronto. He has written extensively in the area of alternative justice.

2 [1995] 6 W.W.R. 438 (Sask. Q.B.).

3 (1996), 101 C.C.C. (3d) 124 (Sask. C.A.).

ADDITIONAL READING

R. v. Moses, 11 C.R. (4th) 357 (Y.T. Terr. Ct.).

Umbreit, M., and R. Coates. 1992. The Impact of Mediating Victim-Offender Conflict: An Analysis of Programs in Three States. *Juvenile and Family Court Journal* 43, no. 1, 21–9.

19

Federal Sentencing in America

SHEREEN H. BENZVY MILLER[1]

In order to give the reader an idea of sentencing in other jurisdictions, this chapter presents an analysis of sentencing in the United States. Unlike Canada and other common law countries, many American states use a sentencing grid to determine the nature and severity of the sanction to be applied in any particular case. This resolves some problems and creates others. Shereen Benzvy Miller examines the advantages and disadvantages of the grid approach to sentencing. The focus is upon the sentencing grid used at the federal level, but many of the issues are common to the statewide guideline systems.

Introduction

The principal difference between Canada and the United States with regard to sentencing concerns the degree of guidance provided to judges. In Canada, judges rely upon precedents from case law and appellate decisions to guide them in their sentencing decisions. In the United States, judges in many states[2] and at the federal level are bound by a two-dimensional sentencing table, the format of which resembles a mileage grid.

Sentencing grids emerged in the 1970s as a result of a search for explicit rules for sentencing when the problem of unwarranted disparity became too obvious to ignore. Standards and guidelines of various types were explored and discussed in many jurisdictions, as part of the evolution of sentencing practices. These explorations were undertaken in response to problems associated primarily with the unfettered discretion of judges. Historically, broad discretion (thought to be an essential element of the rehabilitative ideology) had been given to judges to allow them to tailor penalties to the treatment needs of individual offenders. In the preguideline era, sentencing parameters involving minimum and maximum sentences for some offences provided the only guidance available to judges. In this context, individual judges had little idea if a particular sentence resembled another for a similar offence. Since there were no definitions of a norm, judges were free to apply their own standards to each case without worrying about the relative severity of the sentence imposed and without explaining their choices to the court or to their colleagues. Under a guideline system, judges would be expected to choose a sentence within a guideline range and would have to justify any deviation from that range. Another problem that plagued the sentencing process was the discrepancy between the sentence imposed in court and time actually served in prison. Interventions by correctional policies and parole authorities created seemingly greater disparities in sentencing and less transparency in the system.

In the 1980s, public disenchantment with the sentencing process grew. Simultaneously, state legislatures and Congress became increasingly eager to take control of the crime problem by 'getting tough' on offenders. The ensuing debate spawned various proposals for guideline systems, from voluntary guidelines that have no enforcement mechanisms and are generally developed by committees of judges, to presumptive guidelines, which are prescriptive rather than descriptive and are also enforceable. Central to the reform initiative was the concept of 'truth in sentencing.'

Within the context of formalized guidelines, certain variations in dispositions would be permissible when rationally based and relevant to the distinctive characteristics of the offender and the offence, so long as reasons for the variation were provided. Under a presumptive sentencing system, judges would follow explicit rules governing every departure from the norm. In this way, variation could be closely monitored for consistency and fairness over time.

Truth in sentencing, or real-time sentencing, was introduced into the debate as the only way to ensure fairness and equity. As a result, the legitimacy of parole was called into question. Several states took action and established sentencing commissions. Minnesota and Washington State were among the first to develop sentencing guidelines. To illustrate the way in which grid-style sentencing works, this chapter will focus primarily on the federal sentencing guidelines.

Federal Sentencing Reform

After much research and debate, Congress decided that the unfettered sentencing discretion accorded federal trial judges needed to be structured. In 1984 the United States Sentencing Commission (USSC) was created by the Sentencing

Reform Act. This permanent commission, established as an independent agency within the judicial branch, was charged with formulating national sentencing guidelines to define the parameters that federal trial judges would follow in their sentencing decisions. The guidelines were to cover all federal crimes, including many federal regulatory and white-collar crimes and a large number of drug crimes. While the development, monitoring, and amendment of the guidelines is the centrepiece of the agency's work, the USSC also provides training, conducts research on sentencing-related issues, and serves as an information resource for Congress and criminal justice practitioners, as well as the general public. In addition to creating the Sentencing Commission, the Sentencing Reform Act abolished parole for offenders sentenced under the guidelines so that the sentence served would more closely resemble the sentence imposed in court.[3]

Following much public consultation, the USSC submitted its first set of guidelines and policy statements to Congress in April 1987. The work was clearly designed to meet the 'get tough on criminals' political agenda of the time, as well as to abolish unwarranted disparity and the unfettered discretion of judges. The proposed sentencing guidelines took effect in November 1987 and apply to all offences committed on or after that date. The guidelines drastically altered the work of judges, prosecutors, police, and defence attorneys in the federal judicial system. The five most important innovations introduced by the guidelines are: (a) structured judicial discretion; (b) appellate review of sentences; (c) a requirement for reasons for sentence stated on the record; (d) introduction of determinate or 'real-time' sentencing; and (e) a requirement that defendants pay supervision and imprisonment costs.

The Guidelines

Presumptive guidelines link the severity of sentences directly to the seriousness of the crimes for which they are imposed. Theoretically, they can modify sentencing practices so that available prison capacity is generally reserved for the more serious and habitual offenders, and they are intended to ensure that sanctions are applied more uniformly and equitably.

According to the USSC's own description, the sentencing guidelines established by the commission are designed to:[4]

- incorporate the four purposes of sentencing, namely: just punishment, deterrence, incapacitation, and rehabilitation;
- provide certainty and fairness in meeting the purposes of sentencing by avoiding unwarranted disparity among offenders with similar characteristics

convicted of similar criminal conduct, while permitting sufficient judicial flexibility to take into account relevant aggravating and mitigating factors; and to

- reflect, to the extent possible, advancement in the knowledge of human behaviour as it relates to the criminal justice process.

How Do the Federal Guidelines Work?

In developing the guidelines, the USSC was instructed to consider community views of the gravity of offences. The guidelines take into account the specific counts on which the defendant is convicted and the actual nature of the criminal conduct, by assigning a base level (a number) that serves as a starting point in assessing the seriousness of an offence. These numeric values are found in a two-dimensional grid called the Federal Sentencing Table (see Table 19.1). The base offence level can be increased or decreased to reflect the circumstances of the particular case. The factors that modify the base offence level ('specific offence characteristics') are enumerated in the guidelines.

A base offence level, modified by specific offence characteristics and general adjustments, forms one axis of the grid used to determine sentencing ranges. The sentencing table's offence axis extends from Level 1 (least serious) to Level 43 (most serious). The other axis reflects the defendant's criminal history as reflected in one of six categories (Category I – Category VI).

The point at which the offence level and criminal history category intersect on the Sentencing Table's 258-cell grid determines an offender's guideline range. In order to allow some flexibility, the top of each guideline range exceeds the bottom by at least six months or 25 per cent, whichever is greater. In most cases, the judge must choose a sentence from within the guideline range unless the court identifies a factor that the USSC failed to consider, which should result in a different sentence. However, the judge must in all cases give reasons for sentence. Sentences that depart from the guideline range are subject to review by courts of appeal for 'reasonableness,' and all sentences can be reviewed for incorrect guideline application or sentences imposed in violation of law.

The Sentencing Table set out in the Guidelines Manual is used to determine the guideline range of sentence. The offence levels (1–43) are broken down into four zones (A–D), which define the sentencing options by delineating ranges in which the judge may impose partial imprisonment or nonimprisonment sentences, as outlined. The types of sentencing options available depend on the zone in which the defendant falls.

The specific options available under the guidelines are as follows:

TABLE 19.1
Federal Sentencing Table
(in months of imprisonment)

		Criminal History Category (Criminal History Points)					
	Offense Level	I (0 or 1)	II (2 or 3)	III (4, 5, 6)	IV (7, 8, 9)	V (10, 11, 12)	VI (13 or more)
Zone A	1	0–6	0–6	0–6	0–6	0–6	0–6
	2	0–6	0–6	0–6	0–6	0–6	1–7
	3	0–6	0–6	0–6	0–6	2–8	3–9
	4	0–6	0–6	0–6	2–8	4–10	6–12
	5	0–6	0–6	1–7	4–10	6–12	9–15
	6	0–6	1–7	2–8	6–12	9–15	12–18
	7	0–6	2–8	4–10	8–14	12–18	15–21
	8	0–6	4–10	6–12	10–16	15–21	18–24
Zone B	9	4–10	6–12	8–14	12–18	18–24	21–27
	10	6–12	8–14	10–16	15–21	21–27	24–30
Zone C	11	8–14	10–16	12–18	18–24	24–30	27–33
	12	10–16	12–18	15–21	21–27	27–33	30–37
Zone D	13	12–18	15–21	18–24	24–30	30–37	33–41
	14	15–21	18–24	21–27	27–33	33–41	37–46
	15	18–24	21–27	24–30	30–37	37–46	41–51
	16	21–27	24–30	27–33	33–41	41–51	46–57
	17	24–30	27–33	30–37	37–46	46–57	51–63
	18	27–33	30–37	33–41	41–51	51–63	57–71
	19	30–37	33–41	37–46	46–57	57–71	63–78
	20	33–41	37–46	41–51	51–63	63–78	70–87
	21	37–46	41–51	46–57	57–71	70–87	77–96
	22	41–51	46–57	51–63	63–78	77–96	84–105
	23	46–57	51–63	57–71	70–87	84–105	92–115
	24	51–63	57–71	63–78	77–96	92–115	100–125
	25	57–71	63–78	70–87	84–105	100–125	110–137
	26	63–78	70–87	78–97	92–115	110–137	120–150
	27	70–87	78–97	87–108	100–125	120–150	130–162
	28	78–97	87–108	97–121	110–137	130–162	140–175
	29	87–108	97–121	108–135	121–151	140–175	151–188
	30	97–121	108–135	121–151	135–168	151–188	168–210

TABLE 19.1 *(continued)*
Federal Sentencing Table
(in months of imprisonment)

Offense Level	Criminal History Category (Criminal History Points) I (0 or 1)	II (2 or 3)	III (4, 5, 6)	IV (7, 8, 9)	V (10, 11, 12)	VI (13 or more)
31	108–135	121–151	135–168	151–188	168–210	188–235
32	121–151	135–168	151–188	168–210	188–235	210–262
33	135–168	151–188	168–210	188–235	210–262	235–293
34	151–188	168–210	188–235	210–262	235–293	262–327
35	168–210	188–235	210–262	235–293	262–327	292–365
36	188–235	210–262	235–293	262–327	292–365	324–405
37	210–262	235–293	262–237	292–365	324–405	360–life
38	235–293	262–327	292–365	324–405	360–life	360–life
39	262–327	292–365	324–405	360–life	360–life	360–life
40	292–365	324–405	360–life	360–life	360–life	360–life
41	324–405	360–life	360–life	360–life	360–life	360–life
42	360–life	360–life	360–life	360–life	360–life	360–life
43	life	life	life	life	life	life

November 1, 1997

Zone A (Offenders with sentencing ranges of zero to six months):
(a) straight probation;
(b) probation with confinement conditions (intermittent confinement, community confinement, or home detention);
(c) imprisonment; and
(d) a fine as sole sanction.

Zone B (Offenders with minimum terms of at least one but not more than six months):
(a) probation plus a condition that substitutes intermittent confinement, community confinement, or home detention for imprisonment;
(b) imprisonment of at least one month plus supervised release with a condition that substitutes community confinement or home detention for imprisonment; or
(c) imprisonment.

Zone C (Offenders with minimum terms of at least eight, nine, or ten months):
(a) imprisonment of at least one-half of the minimum term plus supervised release with a condition that substitutes community confinement or home detention for imprisonment; or
(b) imprisonment.
Zone D (Offenders with minimum terms of twelve months or more):
(a) imprisonment.

Each sentencing option is defined in detail in the guidelines manual.

The best way to understand the mechanical workings of the guidelines is to follow a hypothetical offender through the sentencing process. Consider the case of a woman who plans the murder of her husband. To this end, she approaches someone reputed to have ties with the underworld. He in turn contacts the police, who set up a sting operation to entrap her. She is arrested after paying the first instalment of the $20,000 to an undercover officer, charged with and subsequently convicted of 'conspiracy and solicitation to commit murder.'

In order to calculate her sentence under the guidelines, the judge must examine the offender's 'relevant conduct' to determine her base level. The judge then adjusts that figure based on certain factors: victim-related adjustments[5] (if the victim's wrongful conduct contributed significantly to provoking the offence behaviour, the court may reduce the sentence below the guideline range to reflect the nature and circumstances of the offence, but for the most part upward departures related to the victim's vulnerability or the official position of the victim are examined), and the offender's role in the offence (whether she obstructed justice and whether she accepted responsibility for her actions). The judge then calculates the offender's criminal history level. (See Roberts (1994b) for further information on the role of criminal history in the federal guidelines.)

The Offence

A judge must start the search with the statutory offence of conviction. A list of federal offences with the corresponding guideline provisions appears in the appendix of the sentencing guidelines. After locating the applicable guideline, the judge uses the conviction-offence conduct and all other acts deemed relevant to calculate a base offence level.

In order to determine how to sentence within the guidelines, the judge must turn to Chapter 2 of the Guideline Manual, which is divided into parts according to offence type. The first line of the relevant part sets the 'base offence level' at 28 before describing 'specific offence characteristics' as follows:

'(1) If the offence involved the offer or the receipt of anything of pecuniary value for undertaking the murder, increase by 4 levels.'

This raises our defendant's score to 32. At a base level of 32, this defendant will be presumed to receive a prison sentence between 121 and 151 months. In general, with the exception of the criminal record, the individual characteristics of the offender are not relevant to sentence calculation under the guidelines.

The Offender

There are six principal rules with annotated commentary and several policy statements that direct the court in calculation of criminal history scores. Criminal history includes six categories that cover the continuum from first offender, with zero or one point, to offenders with thirteen or more points. Points are awarded based on the number and duration of previous carceral sentences. (It is worth noting that state-level guideline systems, such as those used by Minnesota, Oregon, and Pennsylvania, use prior convictions as the determinant for criminal history calculations.)

To calculate a 'criminal history score' for our offender, the judge will examine her criminal convictions going back as far as fifteen years. She will be assigned three points for each previous sentence over thirteen months, two points for each sentence between two and thirteen months, and one point for any other sentence. In addition, two points are added if the current offence occurred within two years of the offender's release from prison or while she was under other correctional supervision. It should be noted that the federal guidelines include no mitigation of sentence for defendants who lead conviction-free lives for a sustained period of time (see Roberts (1994b)). So far, our defendant will be sentenced somewhere on Level 32 of the grid. But, depending on her previous criminal history, her sentence will be increased from the 121-month base. If she has been in prison twice before, the presumptive sentence would be between 151 and 188 months.

Another element introduced by the USSC Guidelines is that this offender would not simply be sentenced for the offence she was convicted of at trial (or pleaded guilty to), but for the 'actual offence behavior,' which the USSC refers to as 'relevant conduct.'[6] In determining the relevant facts, sentencing judges are not restricted to information that would be admissible at trial.[7] Any information, including hearsay evidence, may be considered, so long as it is deemed to be reliable. This means that, even if she was acquitted of obstruction of justice charges for destroying evidence, for example, the court may well increase her sentence based on the preponderance of related evidence submitted at trial, or even on evidence not considered appropriate for inclusion in trial testimony. The defendant might enter into a plea agreement for one offence and then learn that she will be sentenced to another one entirely.

Departures[8]

Because no system should be so inflexible that judges cannot take into account glaringly important details, like the fact that our defendant's husband beat her mercilessly for years, or that she acted in response to real fears that her husband was planning to kill their six-year-old daughter, the USSC incorporated the concept of 'departures from the range.'

The scheme allows downward adjustments to be made to the offence level for 'acceptance of responsibility' and 'providing substantial assistance to the government,' as well as upward adjustments related to the vulnerability of the victim, the offender's role in the offence, and obstruction of justice. None of these are relevant to our offender. Our offender's sound employment record and extensive community work and the effects of the carceral sentence on her young dependents are factors that the judge is expressly forbidden from taking into account.

No guideline system can encompass every permutation and distinction presented by the infinite combination of factors in the universe of potential cases. Some compromises must be made between the goal of reducing or eliminating unwarranted disparity and individualizing sentences for unusual cases.[9] To this end, the USSC has explicit policy statements to regulate departures.

The USSC maintains that, properly understood and used, a court's departure authority is a critical component in the successful implementation of the guideline system. While departures are recognized by the statute and the guidelines as necessary and appropriate in certain cases, they are clearly intended to be the exceptions. The court may depart from guideline-specified sentences only when it finds 'an aggravating or mitigating circumstance of a kind, or to a degree, not adequately taken into consideration by the Sentencing Commission in formulating the guidelines that should result in a sentence' that is outside the guideline range. In all cases, judges must provide the reasons for sentence. Sentences outside the guideline range are subject to appellate review.

Let us return to the case of the defendant who was planning to her kill her husband. If the facts revealed, for example, that the defendant possessed a high-capacity, semi-automatic weapon, an upward departure may be warranted. The policy statement clearly stipulates that the extent of any increase should depend upon the degree to which the nature of the weapon increased the likelihood of death or injury in the circumstances of the particular case.[10] A number of offender characteristics that judges have traditionally examined in sentencing have been specifically excluded as 'ordinarily not relevant' for purposes of departure or 'whose consideration is precluded with respect to any aspect of sentencing decision.' These include socio-economic status, race, sex, creed, drug and alcohol dependence, economic duress, educational level of the defendant, vocational skills, employment record, family ties and responsibility, or ties to the community. Clearly the emphasis is on sentencing based on harm occasioned by the offence, not on offender characteristics.

Many departure models exist that are less restrictive than the federal provisions. Some state guideline systems allow for departures for 'substantial' or compelling reasons. Some allow durational departures (changing the length of sentence), others allow dispositional departures (changing the nature of the sentence from imprisonment to probation, for example). The North Carolina guidelines do not permit standard departures, while Pennsylvania's system severely restricts appellate review of the court's decision to depart. Some states, like Washington, even have a 'first time offender waiver provision' that gives the court broad discretion to sentence outside the sentencing range if the defendant has no prior felony convictions and the defendant's current offence is not a violent offence.[11]

Theoretically, the federal guidelines are not intended to be as binding as mandatory sentences but departures from the ranges are strictly regulated by the guidelines. And as it stands now, the departure provisions are such that the guidelines are, in practice, more mandatory than presumptive.

How the USSC Views Its Own Guideline System

The USSC is charged with the ongoing responsibility of evaluating the effects of the sentencing guidelines on the criminal justice system, recommending to Congress appropriate modifications of substantive criminal law and sentencing procedures, and establishing a research and development program on sentencing issues. According to research conducted by the U.S. Department of Justice (see Parent, Dunworth, McDonald, and Rhodes 1996), the impact of the sentencing guidelines has generally been favourable. By 1996, nine states had implemented sentencing guidelines and eight others had them under development. Four states continued to use voluntary sentencing guidelines.

The U.S. Department of Justice's research indicates that presumptive guidelines have been effective in increasing sentencing uniformity and proportionality. Racial, ethnic, and gender differences in sentencing have generally declined, although even the USSC admits that the congressionally imposed mandatory minimums for crack cocaine sentences have disproportionately affected

African-Americans.[12] The stated goals of reducing sentence lengths for property offenders and increasing them for violent offenders were met, as was the goal of increasing the use of imprisonment generally and decreasing the use of probation.

The same research shows that the impact of the sentencing guidelines on criminal justice operations has also been generally positive. By definition, a system of determinate sentences reallocates the sentencing power shared by legislature and prosecutor. Prosecutorial powers to select charges and plea bargain remain. Selecting the initial charge takes on a new importance in a system in which parole is removed and judges' powers are curtailed, because these become price-fixing mechanisms in a system where the charge at conviction determines the sentence. Prosecutors, who now determine the charge that is brought, are able, in so doing, to determine the sentences imposed. Some critics argue that this simply shifts the disparity and injustices to an earlier point in the process, making the problem less visible and the system less accountable (see Berlin (1993)). For this reason, the USSC included detailed provisions concerning review of all plea agreements by the court. In contrast to what some observers expected from a presumed loss of prosecutors' flexibility, the incidence of plea bargaining did not decline. The USSC admits that, not unexpectedly, the guidelines have modestly increased court workload, reviews have added to the workload of appellate courts, and the number of sentencing appeals has risen substantially. Also, imprisonment rates have increased substantially under the sentencing guidelines.

Criticisms of the Guidelines

Hostile and widespread reaction to the guidelines was quick and a majority of criminal justice professionals remain highly critical. (For an in-depth critique of the federal guidelines, see Doob (1995b); Tonry (1993)). In fact, many lawyers and judges and some prosecutors continue to resent and resist the severe punishments meted out under the guidelines. Several problems have been identified.

Disparity

Narrowing the discretion of judges was intended to create a sentencing system that is more just, both to individual offenders and to society, because it metes out similar punishments for similar crimes and makes punishment more certain and more credible. Has it succeeded in this respect? The USSC claims that disparity has been reduced, but its critics are adamant that pre- and postguideline sentencing practices were so different and based on such different principles and models that they cannot be compared. The commission and its critics cannot even agree on a definition of what constitutes unwarranted disparity in sentencing (Doob 1995b, 235).

Be that as it may, one critic explains how the guidelines have actually created unforeseen disparities by focusing on the amount of harm done rather than on the individual offender's degree of culpability (Berlin 1993). Offenders who have inflicted comparable harms may differ significantly in culpability. By depriving judges of their ability to consider all offender characteristics, the guidelines have actually created some anomalous results.[13]

Further, the USSC has been criticized for a cursory and mechanical handling of mitigating factors (Frankel 1992). Some critics have urged the USSC to adopt a 'guided discretion model,' which would specify offence level reductions for various mitigating reasons.[14] This would allow judges to consider a greater range of factors (such as poverty and family instability) as mitigating factors and thereby help to reduce racial disparities.

Criminal History

These provisions have been criticized for the following deficiencies (Roberts 1994b, 29): They reach too far back into the defendant's past; provide too many justifications for departures that exceed the 'statute of limitations'; fail to distinguish between prior criminal conduct of variable seriousness; fail to distinguish between defendants of variable recidivism risk; provide a definition of 'career criminal' that is too broad; fail to acknowledge the importance of a conviction-free period in the defendant's past; and fail adequately to take into account the relationship between the nature of the prior conviction and the nature of the current offence. By increasing sentence length on the basis of the number of previous terms of imprisonment, the criminal history provisions in the USSC guidelines have dramatically elevated incarceration rates and sentence lengths.

Shifting Discretion from Judges to Other Actors in the System

Research indicates that officials make earlier and more selective arrest, charging, and diversion decisions (Tonry 1987). They also tend to bargain less and to bring more cases to trial. Criminal justice officials, including police, lawyers, and judges, exercise discretion to avoid application of laws they consider unduly harsh, thereby negating the certainty and predictability of these laws.

According to research completed by the U.S. Department of Justice (Parent et al. 1996), mandatory sentencing has had an impact on crime and the institutions that service the criminal justice system: while sentencing laws may disrupt established plea-bargaining patterns by preventing prosecutors from offering short prison terms in exchange for a guilty plea, they can now shift strategies and bargain on charges rather than on sentences, making the process less visible.

Impact on Prison Population

While mandatory sentencing laws do not increase the probability of imprisonment, sentences do become longer and more severe. They also run the risk of seeming arbitrary and overly punitive for marginal offenders.[15] State law enforcement officers and prosecutors often pass prosecutions from state to federal courts in order to take advantage of the tougher, mandatory prison terms. This has created a substantial shift in the population of the Federal Bureau of Prisons. In 1985, 46 per cent of the population was confined on narcotics offences. This figure had risen to 61 per cent by 1990. In federal courts, first-time offenders are more likely to receive sentences of imprisonment, female offenders are sentenced to sanctions of incarceration at much higher rates, and convicted offenders serve much longer terms of confinement (McDonald 1992).

At the state level, research has been conducted to see whether states with sentencing guideline systems have better managed their prison populations. The findings indicate that sentencing guidelines by themselves are not a sufficient regulating device for controlling prison crowding. The national trend is an increase in incarceration rates. The impact on the growth of prison population due to harsher laws and increased federalization of criminal sanctions has been dramatic and will continue for the foreseeable future.

Over-Emphasis on Imprisonment

Numerical guidelines in general and the USSC guidelines, as well, tend to concentrate on the sentence length (time incarcerated) rather than on the type of penalty (Clarkson and Morgan 1994). No guidelines make an alternative to imprisonment the presumptive sentence.

Conclusion

While the notion that a democratically elected legislature should be capable of establishing sentences for crimes has a certain appeal, presumptive sentencing is not a panacea for problems in the area of sentencing. It leaves many issues unresolved, is capable of abuse through circumvention, and it even creates certain problems of its own. With respect to the American experience, sentencing guidelines have been successful in some states, such as Minnesota, in reducing disparity and increasing proportionality in sentencing practices. But for many observers, the federal sentencing guidelines are a failure and should be radically revised or repealed.

However, in the current political climate, the United States Sentencing Commission and its guidelines have become deeply entrenched in the fabric of the federal criminal justice system. Though some are of the opinion that the federal guidelines do more harm than good (e.g., von Hirsch and Greene (1993)), the full impact of the guidelines remains hard to measure. The guidelines have changed the very purpose of and premises upon which sentencing is based – from rehabilitation to punishment. That the guidelines have a serious impact on prison populations is clear. Whether they are helping to win the war against crime is, however, much less obvious.

ENDNOTES

1 Shereen H. Benzvy Miller is a lawyer who is currently working as a special adviser to the Correctional Operations and Programs Sector of the Correctional Service of Canada. She previously worked for the Department of Justice Canada and the Canadian Sentencing Commission.

2 Nineteen states now have guideline systems in place and a further seven are either considering or actively developing them (see Wees (1996)).

3 Under the law, inmates may still earn up to fifty-four days' credit a year for good behaviour.

4 28 U.S.C. 991 (b) (2).

5 See the Guidelines Manual 1995, 5K2.10.

6 U.S. Sentencing Commission 1992a, #1B1.3.

7 18 U.S.C. 3661.

8 The USSC monitors and analyses all departures in order to refine the guidelines over time. In 1991, approximately 81 per cent of cases were sentenced within the applicable guideline range. By 1994, the percentage had dropped to 72 per cent. The vast majority of departures from sentencing guidelines are for defendant assistance to the government.

9 Among states with sentencing guidelines, only North Carolina, Tennessee, and West Virginia do not allow judges to depart from the established sentence ranges.

10 See the Guidelines Manual 1995, 5K2.17. High-Capacity, Semi-automatic Firearms (Policy Statement).

11 Simplification Draft Paper: Departures and Offender Characteristics, United States Sentencing Commission 1997.

12 The congressionally imposed mandatory minimum sentences for crack cocaine

have resulted in substantially longer sentences for African-Americans. This is largely because those convicted of crack trafficking in the federal courts are disproportionately African-American, while those convicted of trafficking in powdered cocaine are mostly white and Hispanic. In fact, in April 1997 the USSC recommended to Congress that the mandatory minimums for powder and crack cocaine be revised to bring them closer together. Previously, for example, possession of 5 grams of crack and 500 grams of powder cocaine resulted in a mandatory minimum sentence of five years' imprisonment. The recommendations to increase the penalties for powder cocaine and decrease the penalties for crack cocaine are, at the time of writing, in the hands of Congress.

13 A good example of this can be found in cases related to sentencing for possession of LSD. The guidelines make the weight of the 'mixture or substance' containing LSD the measure for sentence. As a result, courts have held that the total weight of the drug and the blotter paper, sugar cube, or gelatin capsules it is in must be included. Consequently, a dealer who chooses to sell LSD in sugar cubes will be punished more severely than one who chooses to sell LSD in its pure form, without chemically bonding it to anything, even if both were in possession of the same number of grams of LSD.

14 For example, if poverty, family instability, and other social phenomena were allowed to mitigate the sentence, racial disparities might be lessened under the guidelines.

15 Whatever the cause, the fact remains that between 1980 and 1989 the number of inmates serving prison sentences in the U.S increased by 123 per cent. See United States Department of Justice, Bureau of Justice Statistics (1990).

ADDITIONAL READING

Doob, A. 1995. The United States Sentencing Commission Guidelines: If You Don't Know Where You Are Going, You Might Not Get There. In C. Clarkson and R. Morgan, eds., *The Politics of Sentencing Reform.* Oxford: Clarendon Press.

Miller, M. 1995. Rehabilitating the Federal Sentencing Guidelines. *Judicature* 78, no. 4, 180–8.

Tonry, M. 1993. The Failure of the U.S. Sentencing Commission's Guidelines. *Crime and Delinquency* 39:131–49.

20

Sentencing Reform: Ten Years after the Canadian Sentencing Commission

JEAN-PAUL BRODEUR[1]

This chapter surveys legislation relating to sentencing proposed since the 1987 report of the Canadian Sentencing Commission. The legislation reviewed is classified in several different categories: ad hoc legislation amending the Criminal Code; legislation pertaining to the reintroduction of mandatory minimum penalties; the expansion of indeterminate sentencing; and the curtailment of parole; the creation of new legal provisions against criminal organization offences; and the sentencing reform bill (C-41). Brodeur then examines the impact of these laws on the use of imprisonment. Finally, he compares the content of the legislation examined with the recommendations of the CSC and concludes that, with very few exceptions, the legal developments to date tend to contradict what was proposed by the CSC.

Introduction

Ten years have passed since the report of the Canadian Sentencing Commission (CSC) was published in 1987. This is accordingly a good time to assess developments in sentencing since the publication of that report, which recommended a comprehensive reform of the sentencing process in Canada. I will begin by reviewing the relevant legislation enacted over the past decade and then discuss the principal consequences of this legislation on corrections. The chapter concludes by examining the extent to which these legislative initiatives are consistent with the recommendations of the CSC and those of other bodies, such as the Daubney Committee, which published a review of sentencing and parole in 1988.

Legislation

This section deals only with legislation that has been enacted; legislative proposals are not included. After its release, the CSC report was immediately followed by extensive consultations, which generated further reports (Daubney Committee 1988; Canada 1990).[2] The minister of justice also published a paper in a scholarly journal, outlining the sentencing reform that she contemplated (Campbell 1990). These reports (as well the minister's article) were originally consistent with the CSC's recommendations, with a notable exception in that the government rejected the commission's recommendation to abolish full parole. However, federal support for such key recommendations as sentencing guidelines and the creation of a permanent sentencing commission subsequently began to dwindle. Bill C-90, which received first reading in June 1992, was the Conservative government's last hurrah in terms of sentencing. Bill C-90 died on the order paper and the government was defeated in the 1993 election. The bill was later resurrected as Bill C-41 by the new Liberal government. I refer only briefly to Bill C-41 in this chapter, as it is examined in more detail by other contributors to this volume.

From 1987 to the end of April 1997, some thirty-six bills were passed by Parliament. Twenty-two of these amended the Criminal Code; most had a direct impact on sentencing. Fourteen other bills amended other federal statutes, such as the Young Offenders Act (YOA), the Coastal Fisheries Act, the Explosives Act, and so forth.[3] This discussion is limited to the most significant legislation; it is not intended to be exhaustive.[4]

Some of the amendments are referred to as 'ad hoc legislation.' By 'ad hoc legislation' I mean the annual process of updating current legislation and creating new law according to the immediate needs of the government. For instance, when the Supreme Court ruled that extreme intoxication was a valid legal defence, the government responded with Bill C-72 (self-induced intoxication)[5] in order to prevent a general recourse to such a defence.[6] Bill C-42, the Criminal Law Amendment Act,[7] and Bill C-17, the Criminal Law Improvement Act, are prime examples of this process. Since it is triggered every year, we cannot review every amendment and will discuss only the most significant statutes.

Principal Trends

The principal trend in amendments to the criminal law made since 1987 is toward an increase in the use of punishment. This tendency is exemplified in the case of arson, among many other instances, for which the maximum penalty was raised from fourteen years to life imprisonment (Bill C-53).[8] Increased punitiveness is particularly obvious in the case of sexual offences (Bill C-15[9] – anal intercourse, bestiality, and sexual offences against persons under fourteen years of age; Bill C-128[10] – child pornography; Bill C-27[11] – sexual tourism), where new offences were created and the severity of penalties for existing offences was increased. New offences were also created in relation to the Health of Animals Act (Bill C-66)[12] and the Plant Protection Act (Bill C-67)[13] against selling contaminated animals or plants. No law was enacted to decrease the severity of punishments, with the exception of the redefinition of indictable offences as hybrid offences, allowing for sentencing on summary conviction, which carries a more lenient maximum penalty.

Penal Structure

The amendments discussed so far concern single offences, such as arson or anal intercourse. However, other statutes were much broader in their scope. The most important of these was Bill C-61[14] on the Proceeds of Crime. This statute is the Canadian equivalent of the high-profile American Racketeer Influenced and Corrupt Organizations Act (RICO). It creates a new offence – laundering the proceeds of crime (section 462.31) – which is defined in relation to an open schedule of 'enterprise crime offences' that now includes more than twenty offences. This new offence is punishable by a maximum of ten years' imprisonment. More importantly, however, this statute allows the forfeiture of the proceeds of the enterprise crime offences. The interesting point about this statute is that it is underused by the police who, at the same time, stridently demanded more 'tools' in their battle against organized crime.[15] As we shall see, they were granted their wish, despite their failure to use the full range of instruments already available to them.

Changes of Direction

Although these amendments were also made on an ad hoc basis, they imply more than merely adding a new offence or changing the maximum penalty for existing crimes. Because of their comprehensive character, these modifications are similar to the penal structure discussed above. However, they are even more significant in that they represent a change of direction with regard to previous thinking and legislation.

The Young Offenders Act

When it was first adopted in 1984, the YOA embodied the following principles: crime prevention is essential to the protection of society; young persons should generally not be held accountable for their behaviour in the same manner as adults, and, perhaps most importantly, the protection of society is best served by the rehabilitation of young offenders. These principles remain part of the Act (see the Declaration of Principle at section 3). They were initially applied, among other things, by limiting the length of custodial sentences for young persons to five years,[16] even for the most serious offences, such as homicide, and also by making the transfer of young offenders to adult courts an exceptional measure. The YOA embodied a presumption against such transfers: the onus of satisfying the court of the necessity of proceeding against a young person in an adult court rested with the prosecution.

Despite the fact that lip service continues to be paid to the principles originally underlying the YOA, Bill C-37[17] drastically changed their application. Not only was the maximum possible length of custody raised to ten years,[18] but the presumption against transferring young offenders to adult courts was reversed. Following the amendments to the YOA, every young person charged with murder (first or second degree), attempted murder, manslaughter, or aggravated sexual assault is to be tried in adult court unless an application is made that the case should be dealt with in youth court.[19] Most importantly, the onus of satisfying the court now rests with the young accused, who must apply to remain in youth court.[20]

Bill C-8

The most significant legislation in this category, however, is Bill C-8 (1996).[21] As stated in the preamble of the bill, its purpose is to achieve a new consolidation of all the offences related to drugs, according to the different international covenants to which Canada is a party. Whether all of the provisions of Bill C-8 were consequent upon the signing by Canada of these covenants is unclear. But this bill marked a profound departure from previous Canadian thinking in penology. This law created new offences – obtaining a medical prescription for controlled substances under false pretences (maximum penalty, seven years) or laundering the proceeds of drug offences (maximum penalty, ten years) – and it increased the penalties for drug offences or maintained the punitive *status quo*. More importantly, however, Bill C-8 broke new ground in sentencing.

In considering the purpose of sentencing, Bill C-8 placed new emphasis on rehabilitation and the treatment of offenders (section 10), similar to what had been stated in Bill C-41 the year before.[22] The difficulty is that the main thrust of the content of Bill C-8 belies its reinstatement of the purpose of sentencing. Whatever the controversies surrounding rehabilitation, it is generally agreed that imprisonment does not foster reintegration into society. Bill C-8 contains a list of aggravating factors in the commission of a drug offence. These aggravating factors belong to different categories and they include the use or threat to use a weapon, the use or threat of violence, the commission of drug offences near a school or a place frequented by persons under eighteen years, and the trafficking of drugs to persons under the age of eighteen; a previous conviction of a designated substance offence;[23] and, finally, using the service of a person under the age of eighteen years in the commission of a drug offence. All of these factors are in addition to the aggravating factors already enumerated in Bill C-41, which is supposed to be the cradle of Canadian sentencing. No mitigating circumstances are enunciated in Bill C-8. The crux of the matter rests in the following subsection of the Act:

> 10 (3) Where, pursuant to subsection (1), the judge is satisfied of the existence of one or more of the aggravating factors enumerated in that subsection, but decides not to sentence the offender to imprisonment, the court shall give reasons for that decision.

This is a legal text of potentially momentous significance. In its report, the CSC urged that sentencing guidelines be developed. In the development of such guidelines, the crucial point is the determination of what is called the 'in/out line,' that is, the point at which an offender should or should not be incarcerated. According to several principles ('the least drastic alternative,' 'restraint,' and so forth), there was, at the time of the writing of the CSC report, a presumption against incarceration. This presumption was embodied in the guidelines proposed by the commission. The idea of sentencing guidelines was rejected by the government after the publication of the CSC report. But in subsection 10(3) of Bill C-8 we are now witnessing not only the embryo of sentencing guidelines but the embodiment in law of a guideline that favours incarceration.

Minimum Penalties

In 1987, the Supreme Court of Canada declared that the seven-year minimum penalty of imprisonment for importing or exporting drugs violated the Charter of Rights (*R. v. Smith*). In its judgment, the Supreme Court referred to the report of the CSC, which had recommended the abolition of minimum penalties. At the time, this ruling by Canada's highest court appeared to be a watershed and in the following years no new mandatory minima were added to the criminal law. This status quo on minimum penalties was drastically broken in 1995, by the Firearms Act (Bill C-68).[24] The initial purpose of this Act was to control the possession of firearms. It generated a furore in rural parts of Canada, particularly in western Canada, where it is customary to own rifles and other firearms. Those who possessed firearms for legal purposes claimed that they were being targeted by the law, despite the fact that they were law-abiding citizens. Gun owners further argued that nothing was being done about the 'real criminals,' who would not in any event register their weapons.

In order to placate the opponents of gun control, the government felt obliged to show that it was tougher on potential criminals than it was on law-abiding citizens. Despite the advice of all the experts, who showed that this measure would dramatically compound the problem of prison overcrowding, the government added to Bill C-68 provisions to the effect that several offences would carry a minimum penalty of four years in a penitentiary if a firearm was used in the commission of the offences. Thus, Bill C-68 attached a minimum penalty of four years in jail to ten offences, when committed with the use of a firearm.[25] Some of these offences, like robbery, occur frequently and are usually committed with a firearm. Other offences may raise embarrassing legal problems, such as causing death by criminal negligence, which is the charge often contemplated by the prosecution in the case of wrongful police shootings.

Although it is too early to tell, there are indications that Bill C-68 may start a new trend toward an increased use of minimum penalties. Bill C-27, which amends the Criminal Code with respect to child prostitution and related offences, created an offence of aggravated procuring, with a minimum penalty of five years' imprisonment, for an offender involved in the prostitution of persons under the age of eighteen.[26]

Indeterminate Sentencing

In contrast to the United States, the Canadian legal tradition has been to steer away from indeterminate sentences. Bill C-55, however, makes it easier to have a person declared a high-risk offender (the opinion of only one psychiatrist will be sufficient to provide a basis for declaring an individual to be a dangerous offender).[27] Prior to the passage of this bill, the advice of at least two psychiatrists was necessary (see subsection 755(1)). The harshness of the indeterminate sentence was greatly increased, as the initial period of parole ineligibility for high-risk offenders was increased from three to seven years.

Furthermore, the enactment of Bill C-55 added a new category of high-risk offender. Upon classification as long-term offenders, certain sex offenders would be subject to up to ten years of supervision in the community, in addition to the custodial sentence imposed for the offence. Finally, a new peace bond provision was created in Part XXVII of the Code, which applies to persons who present a risk of committing a serious personal injury offence.

Conditional Release

Because of its major impact on the manner in which custodial sentences are actually served, conditional release plays a crucial part in sentencing. Beginning in 1992, a series of significant changes was introduced in the parole legislation and related statutes. The most important of these changes was introduced in 1992 by the Corrections and Conditional Release Act.[28] This Act initiated a comprehensive reform of corrections and parole. Limitations on space prevent discussion of more than two of its features, which are crucial to our purpose.

First, there is a contradiction between the statement of the purpose of parole and the declaration of principles that should guide the granting of parole. Section 100 of the Act states that the purpose of *parole* is to contribute to the maintenance of a just, peaceful, and safe society by means of decisions that will best facilitate the rehabilitation of offenders. Such a statement clearly embodies a rationale for decarceration. However, the declaration of principle requires that 'the protection of society be the paramount consideration in the determination of any case' (section 101 of the Act). This principle expresses a rationale for incarceration. For instance, it is exactly the same as the primary principle of *corrections*, as it is stated in section 4 of the same Act ('... that the protection of society be the paramount consideration in the corrections process'). The purpose of corrections is primarily defined as carrying sentences imposed by the court and only secondarily as promoting rehabilitation. Not only does the main principle of parole collide with the statement of its purpose, but it is baffling to find that the process of corrections (custody and supervision) and the process of release from custody should obey the same paramount consideration. That the logic of incarceration will eventually prevail over the logic of release and permeate the whole criminal justice system is already announced by the second crucial feature of this Act. According to it, a court may order that the portion of a custodial sentence to be served before the release of the offender on full parole be raised from one-third to one-half of the sentence (or ten years, whichever is less).

Subsequent events confirm that the 1992 amendments were indeed a bad omen for parole;[29] they also provide some validation to my early prediction that the government's reluctance to follow the recommendation of the CSC to abolish parole was a hollow victory for the advocates of early release and that the years to come would witness the progressive attrition of parole (Brodeur 1990). Up until 1996, offenders convicted of first degree murder were condemned to prison for life and could not apply for parole before having served twenty-five years of their sentence. However, section 745 of the Code allowed them to appear before a jury after fifteen years and ask its permission to apply for parole at this point in their sentence. Bill C-45 introduced several modifications in creating new section 745.6. First, it removed the right of multiple murderers to apply for judicial review. Second, future applications would be subject to a judicial screening of applications. Finally, and perhaps most importantly, juries would henceforth have to be *unanimous* before granting an applicant a reduction in his or her period of parole ineligibility (S.C. 1996, c. 34). Taken together, these reforms will undoubtedly have the effect of reducing the number of lifers who become eligible for parole before the twenty-five-year point in their sentence.[30] (This provision is discussed in Chapter 17 of this book.)

We have already seen that Bill C-55 increased the initial period of parole ineligibility for dangerous offenders from three to seven years and added a new category of high-risk offender (long-term sex offenders) to the Code. The period of up to ten years of supervision in the community added to the sentence of these offenders increases the caseload of already overworked parole officers.

Finally, Bill C-95, enacted against criminal organizations, defines a new offence of 'criminal organization offence' (S.C. 1997, c. 23, s. 11, which modifies section 467 of the Criminal Code). This new offence carries a maximum penalty of fourteen years' incarceration. Section 18 of Bill C-95 specifies that where an offender receives a sentence of imprisonment of more than two years for a criminal organization offence, the court may order that the portion of the sentence that must be served before the offender is eligible for parole is one-half of the sentence or ten years, whichever is less.

Organized Crime

To be convicted of a criminal organization offence, a person must first participate on a general basis in the activities of a criminal organization and second, must be: 'a party to the commission of an indictable offence for the benefit of, at the direction of or in association with the criminal organization for which the maximum punishment is imprisonment for five years or more' (paragraph 467.1(1)(b)).

A close reading of this paragraph reveals that it involves duplicating the same offence for the purpose of punishing it twice. A person first commits an indictable offence punishable by a maximum period of imprisonment of five years or more – such as drug trafficking. Then, if the said offence is committed 'for the benefit of, at the direction of or in association with' a criminal organization, the accused becomes liable for another custodial sentence which, according to paragraph 467.1(2) shall be served consecutively to the punishment imposed for the original offence (drug trafficking). However, it is obvious that the clauses 'for the benefit of,' 'at the direction of,' and 'in association with' express different qualifications of the same act; they do not constitute or refer to another act. With respect to sentencing theory, these clauses define aggravating circumstances rather than a criminal offence per se. In other words, merely acting for the benefit of, at the direction of, or in association with a criminal organization is not by itself a crime unless the said act is itself a crime. Transforming an aggravating factor into a separate offence with its own maximum punishment is highly questionable with respect to the principles of sentencing. It may also be unconstitutional, since it violates the legal rights protected in the Charter (subsection 11(h)).[31]

The Sentencing Bill

Notwithstanding its length, Bill C-41 introduces only two substantial innovations. The first, a statement of the purpose and principles of sentencing, is rather theoretical. Although the sentencing bill succeeds in assigning priority to proportionality among the principles of sentencing, the statement of the purpose of sentencing is convoluted and ultimately self-defeating. It introduces a spurious distinction between the purpose of sentencing and the objectives of criminal sanctions. Although there is a single and fundamental purpose, it is said to be achieved by imposing sanctions that have one or more of a series of seven objectives.[32] The list of objectives provided by Bill C-41 is an inconsistent collection of the utilitarian goals of sentencing (general and specific deterrence, incapacitation, and rehabilitation), denunciation, which is central to the just deserts perspective, and the recently popular goals of providing reparation and promoting responsibility. By providing no hierarchy or priority for these objectives, the sentencing bill falls short of the requirements for a sound sentencing framework, as they were expressed in 1984, when a first sentencing bill (C-19) was debated in the House of Commons. (The statement is discussed at greater length in Chapter 3 of this volume.)

The second innovation introduced by the sentencing bill is the conditional sentence of imprisonment (section 742). On the basis of subsection 742.1, the conditional sentence of imprisonment can be defined as a sentence of imprisonment to be served in the community, which is itself a contradiction in terms. Whatever the merits of the conditional sentence as a practical instrument to relieve the pressure of prison overcrowding, it is uncertain that enshrining an oxymoron in sentencing law will contribute to its clarity and accessibility to the layman. In the Province of Quebec, the media have started to refer derisively to the conditional sentence of imprisonment as a prison sentence which is not a prison sentence.

Consequences

Statistics demonstrate an increase in the use of incarceration in recent years. From 1986 to 1996, the prison population grew by 26 per cent, the largest increase having occurred between 1988 and 1993, when the number of incarcerated persons grew by 39 per cent (Statistics Canada 1997).[33] From 1989 to 1995, the federal prison population increased by 22 per cent and the provincial population by 12 per cent. Particularly distressing is the fact that the number of young offenders in custody increased by 26 per cent from 1986 to 1995 (Statistics Canada 1996b). The rate of incarceration was over 130 persons per 100,000 inhabitants in 1995, up from 116 in 1985. The current rate is closer to 136. With the exception of the U.S., Canada has the highest rate of incarceration among Western-style democracies (Canada, Solicitor General 1996; Canada, Correctional Service 1995). A more useful index is the sentenced incarceration rate. This is the rate of prison admissions expressed as a function of the number of persons charged with an offence. Across Canada, the 1994/5 sentenced incarceration rate was 206 per 100,000 adults, a significant increase from the previous year's rate of 188 per 100,000 (Statistics Canada 1996a, 12). This rate has been steadily increasing since 1990. The sentenced incarceration rate varies considerably from one provincial/territorial jurisdiction to another, suggesting wide disparity in the use of incarceration. The rate of incarceration for young offenders was 219 youths per 100,000 young persons between the age twelve to seventeen (Canada, Correctional Service 1995, 3).

With regard to prison populations, there is a basic distinction to be made between the yearly number of custodial admissions and the daily count of inmates. A decrease or a levelling off of admissions coupled with a growth of the daily count of prisoners is usually explained by an increase in the duration of the custodial sentences imposed by the courts or by changes in the practices relating to conditional release (fewer persons are granted parole, the period of parole ineligibility is increased for more offenders, the number of readmissions of persons breaching their release conditions is greater – all three factors may play at the same time). In 1994/5 and, to a lesser extent, in 1995/6, the number of admissions to custodial facilities decreased, while the daily count of prisoners increased (Statistics Canada 1996a, 1997).

The hypothetical increase in the length of custodial sentences should not blind us to the fact that the average duration of a custodial admission is short. The abuse of short-term incarceration is actually one of the direst problems arising from the application of criminal law. In 1995/6, there were 230,330 provincial admissions, as compared to 4,402 federal ones (Statistics Canada 1997). Of these provincial admissions, slightly less than half (106,467) were admissions to preventive custody. With respect to convicted persons, the typical offender serving a provincial sentence was convicted of a property offence and sentenced to a little more than a month in jail (thirty-three days according to Statistics Canada (1996a), 4). Fine defaulters make up a quarter of sentenced admissions (Statistics Canada (1996a), 4). In the Province of Quebec, persons admitted to prison for defaulting on fines imposed for traffic offences account for 28 per cent of the admissions to custody and for only 3 per cent of the sentences of probation. Violent offences account, by contrast, for 10 per cent of the admissions to custody and 25 per cent of the sentences of probation (Soucy 1996, 2). There is obviously a problem in relation to the imposition of custodial sentences for crimes against property and, most of all, for fine defaulting. Finally, it is worth noting that the number of persons on conditional release has decreased by 8 per cent per year for the last two years for which we have statistics (1994–6; Statistics Canada (1997), 12). Without claiming that incarceration patterns are the direct consequence of the legislative changes just described, I would suggest that there is a degree of correlation between these changes and the growth of incarceration in Canada.

The Canadian Sentencing Commission (CSC)

I shall now examine the extent to which recent legislative developments are consistent with the recommendations of the CSC. For the sake of brevity, I will not review the content of the CSC's report. Instead, I will simply review the findings in the two first sections of this paper and compare them with the CSC's recommendations. First, however, some general observations may be useful.

The CSC's Perspective

The approach taken by the CSC and, with their own stated reservations, by subsequent reports on sentencing (Daubney Committee 1988; Canada 1990) was influenced by the just deserts perspective as initially represented in the work of von Hirsch (1976). The CSC's approach shared some (but not all) of the basic tenets of just deserts sentencing. In consequence, the commission's outlook is much closer to penal retributivism than to utilitarianism. Its approach to sentencing is retrospective: it focuses on the past behaviour of the offender and is highly critical of 'preventive sentencing' based on a probabilistic assessment of the risk that an offender will recidivate (Canadian Sentencing Commission (hereafter CSC) 1987, 139). The CSC also believed that the key notion of proportionality should be interpreted through the lens of moderation in the use of punishment and, most particularly, through restraint in the recourse to incarceration (113). To implement this perspective, the CSC recommended the development of sentencing guidelines (269) and presented a scheme to remedy the problem of imprisonment for fine default (380).

With the possible exception of the priority attributed to the principle of proportionality in Bill C-41 and the conditional sentence of incarceration, perhaps no other development in the last ten years is consistent with the approach described above. The growing restrictions on parole (SC 1992, c. 20; Bills C-45, C-55, C-95, and C-17), the explicit use of high-risk offender classifications to justify indeterminate sentencing (C-55), and the multiplication of preventive orders and bonds to keep the peace (C-55, C-95) all testify to the increasing influence of risk assessment and selective incapacitation in Canadian sentencing practice. No sentencing guidelines have yet been developed, with the exception of the guideline in the new drug legislation according to which a judge has to justify *not* imposing the sentence of incarceration required by the law (C-17, the Criminal Law Improvement Act of 1997). As we have seen, Canada is still a leader in the use of incarceration among Western nations; the recourse to custody has been increasing since 1987, particularly in respect to young offenders; and imprisonment for fine default is as big a problem as it ever was.

Specific Inconsistencies

Integration versus 'Ad Hoc-ery'

The CSC repeatedly stressed the need for an integrated approach to sentencing (CSC 1987, 59 and 161). This meant the formulation of a consistent statement of the purpose and principles of sentencing, the updating of sentencing law according to a policy-making framework consonant with the previous formulation, and the development of sentencing guidelines to remedy unwarranted disparity. But the statement of the purpose of sentencing formulated in Bill C-41 is merely a list of disparate sentencing objectives and falls short of the elementary requirements for consistency. Since 1987 criminal law has been enacted strictly on an ad hoc basis, as it always has been. No sentencing guidelines have been developed, with the exception of one legal constraint on judges, which favours incarceration.

The Return of Minimum Penalties

The CSC adopted a very firm position against mandatory minimum penalties, recommending that they be abolished for all offences except murder and high treason (CSC 1987, 190). It also voiced scepticism about mandatory prohibition orders and recommended further study of them within the sentencing framework that it proposed. As we saw, the Firearms Act added mandatory minima to a spate of offences and Bill C-27 created an offence with a severe mandatory minimum penalty of five years' imprisonment.

The Expansion of Indeterminate Sentencing

The approach taken by the CSC was synonymous with determinate sentencing. In consequence, it recommended nothing less than the repeal of the dangerous offender provisions in the Code (CSC 1987, 213). As noted earlier, the House of Commons recently enacted Bill C-55, which expands the use of indeterminate sentences by facilitating their imposition and making them harsher in their application.

The Attrition of Parole

As is well known, the CSC recommended the abolition of full parole, while retaining other forms of early release (CSC 1987, 237). In my view, this recommendation, although crucial, was superseded by a much more fundamental principle. According to this principle, all changes occurring at the exit of the prison system (early release) must be preceded by or, at the very least, balanced by changes affecting the entrance into it (sentencing) (CSC 1987, 245). Not only did the government change the parole legislation in 1992, before introducing legislation on sentencing (thereby putting the cart before the horse) but, as we saw, the initial bill on sentencing died on the order paper. Bill C-41 came into force only in 1996. In the preceding years, the government repeatedly tinkered with the exit door of the prison system without compensating for this pottering at the front door. This fragmentation of criminal justice without doubt constitutes the most obvious and destructive inconsistency with the Sentencing Commission's recommendations.

Parole Ineligibility for Lifers

The CSC recommended that the court set the date of parole eligibility for persons convicted of first and second degree murder. For first degree murder, the date would be set between a minimum of fifteen years and a maximum of twenty-five years; for second degree murder, it would be set between ten and fifteen years (CSC 1987, 262–3). In contrast, Bill C-45 has tightened considerably the criteria by which life-term inmates may obtain early release on parole.

The Principle of Totality

The CSC recommended that the use of consecutive and concurrent sentences for multiple offences be replaced by the use of the total sentence (CSC 1987, 223). It had previously noted that 'as a general rule, consecutive sentences are imposed for multiple offences which arise out of separate criminal transactions.' (CSC 1987, 220). Despite its lip service to the sentencing principle of totality, Bill C-95 collides head on with this principle by explicitly stating that sentences imposed for multiple offences arising out of a single transaction must be served consecutively.

The overwhelming conclusion of this brief survey is that sentencing has developed in a direction completely at odds with the spirit, content, and recommendations of the Sentencing Commission.

Final Remarks

Why did the Sentencing Commission fail to have more impact? With respect to the report, at least two things went wrong. The first concerns the recommendation to abolish full parole. This was premature and the commission did not pay sufficient heed to the advice offered in von Hirsch and Hanrahan (1979) to proceed cautiously in this matter. This recommendation needlessly transformed potential allies of the report (and of the reform of sentencing) into determined opponents. The second explanation, which is more important, bears on the process followed by the CSC and, more generally, by commissions of inquiries in Canada. A Canadian commission of inquiry, whatever its nature, results in a report, which is subsequently submitted to the government department that sponsored the inquiry. Thereafter, the relationship with the political authority that appointed the commission and holds power over the application of its recommendations is immediately severed. This severance of all links between the government and a commission is usually lethal to the latter's report, as its implementation (or, more accurately, nonimplementation) is left to the bureaucratic machinery of government, which tries to make as few waves as possible. No innovative reform can spring from these quarters.

To broaden the debate beyond the CSC, two comments should be added. First, public opinion underwent a momentous change in the years that followed the publication of the CSC's report. In 1986, at the time of the writing of the report, there was still public acknowledgment of the social bond uniting convicted offenders and the community. Notwithstanding the action of organizations like the Church Council and similar groups, this bond appears to have been thoroughly ruptured. Both serious offenders and persistent petty offenders are now considered as social waste by the community at large. Such a development is nothing short of a moral catastrophe.

Finally, I believe that the most significant development for the future is the privatization of corrections as it is fostered by prison overcrowding and the budgetary crunch over public spending. The effect of this privatization, as it is now manifest in the U.S., is to void the debate over incarceration of any ethical consideration and to make it entirely subservient to cost-benefit reasoning. At the present time, the best way to learn about the future of imprisonment is simply to read the *Wall Street Journal.* The ultimate oxymoron of positivistic thinking, 'value-free justice,' has finally come of age through the obsession with the 'bottom line.'

ENDNOTES

1 Jean-Paul Brodeur is a Professor of Criminology at the University of Montreal. He has published many articles on the topic of sentencing. From 1984 to 1987, he was Research Director of the Canadian Sentencing Commission.
2 Canada (1990) contains three documents. The first, published under the heading of the Government of Canada, is akin to a White Paper on criminal justice (Canada, Government of Canada 1990). It is supported by two longer papers, one of which deals with sentencing (Canada, Department of Justice 1990), the other with corrections (Canada, Solicitor General 1990).
3 I have not systematically reviewed every statute enacted since 1987 to assess whether it contained new provisions on punishment that may affect sentencing. Hence, the number of bills directly or indirectly connected with sentencing may be higher than fourteen.
4 This review does not follow a strictly chronological order. The different legislative initiatives have been categorized according to a logical rather than a chronological sequence. However, within each category, a chronological order is followed, to the extent that this is possible.
5 S.C. 1995, c. 32.
6 The Supreme Court acquitted an offender of the charge of sexual assault because of his alleged extreme intoxication by alcohol (the accused claimed not to have

been conscious of what he was doing; *R. v. Daviault* (1994), 33 C.R. (4th) 165). A consequence of this ruling was that if a person killed a pedestrian while driving his or her car reasonably above the legal limit for drunken driving (.08), he or she would normally have been convicted of dangerous driving, if not of a more serious offence. However, if that person was so inebriated as not to realize that he or she was driving a car, then that offender would have benefited from a legal defence, whatever the harm that resulted from his or her drunken driving.

7 S.C. 1994, c. 44.

8 S.C. 1990, c. 15.

9 S.C. 1987, c. 24.

10 S.C. 1993, c. 46.

11 S.C. 1997, c. 16.

12 S.C. 1990, c. 21 (C.S.L. 1993, H-3.3).

13 S.C. 1990, c. 22 (C.S.L. 1993, P-14.18).

14 S.C. 1988, c. 5 (C.S.L. 1993, P-24.5).

15 In the Province of Quebec, as of 1997, *not a single person* has yet been prosecuted according to the Proceeds of Crime statute, which is perceived by the police as too complex to generate a conviction.

16 Actually, five years minus one day; this determination was made in order to avoid trials by jury, which an offender can request when he or she is charged with an offence punishable by five years' incarceration. When the maximum penalty ceiling in the YOA was changed to ten years in 1995, young offenders had to be provided with the option of choosing a trial by jury.

17 S.C. 1995, c. 19.

18 This is all the more significant in view of the fact that there is no parole in juvenile justice in Canada, the only form of release being temporary. Hence, the young offenders sentenced to custody serve their sentence in 'flat time.' According to Bill C-17 (S.C. 1997, c. 18), young offenders convicted of murder of the first or second degree in adult court must serve four-fifths of their sentence before being eligible for parole.

19 YOA, s. 16(1.01).

20 YOA, s. 16(1.11).

21 S.C. 1996, c. 19.

22 S.C. 1995, c. 22.

23 All drug offences, with the exception of simple possession. The provision includes obtaining drugs from a physician under false pretenses.

24 S.C. 1995, c. 39.

25 The offences are causing death by criminal negligence, manslaughter, attempt to commit murder, causing bodily harm with intent, sexual assault with a weapon, aggravated sexual assault, kidnapping, hostage taking, robbery, and extortion.

26 S.C. 1997, c. 16.

27 S.C. 1997, c. 17.

28 S.C. 1992, c. 20 (C.S.L. 1993, c. C.44.6).

29 The curtailment of full parole effected by the Act of 1992 was enshrined in the sentencing bill of 1995 (C-41; see s. 743.6).

30 Since past experience has shown that the decision to reduce the period of parole ineligibility was reached as a rule only after intense debates, the new unanimity requirement is likely to have an important impact. A single juror will henceforth be sufficient to block an application. Under the previous legislation, only a two-thirds majority was necessary.

31 According to s. 19 of Bill C-95, a person who it is feared on reasonable grounds will commit a criminal organization offence, may be ordered by a provincial court judge to enter into a recognizance to keep the peace and be of good behaviour for one year. A person bound by a recognizance who breaches it is liable to imprisonment not exceeding two years (s. 811 of the Code). It is thus conceivable that a person bound by such a recognizance be sanctioned thrice for the same act (e.g., drug trafficking), that is, once for the offence itself, a second time where the original offence is proven to be a criminal organization offence, and a third time for the breach of recognizance.

32 Section 718(b) combines two different objectives, namely specific and general deterrence.

33 The number of persons under supervision in the community also grew significantly between 1986 and 1996, the overall increase being approximately 50 per cent (Statistics Canada 1997). Up until now, the main form of community sentence is probation. What has been occurring is not only a rise of incarceration but a general increase of the population under penal control.

ADDITIONAL READING

Brodeur, J.-P. 1990. The Attrition of Parole. *Canadian Journal of Criminology* 32:503–10.

Canadian Sentencing Commission. 1987. *Sentencing Reform: A Canadian Approach.* Ottawa: Supply and Services Canada.

House of Commons Standing Committee on Justice and Solicitor General (Daubney Committee). 1988. *Taking Responsibility. The Report of the House of Commons Standing Committee on Justice and Solicitor General on its Review of Sentencing, Conditional Release and Related Aspects of Corrections.* Ottawa: Queen's Printer.

21

Sentencing Reform: Where Are We Now?

ANTHONY N. DOOB[1]

In this concluding chapter, Anthony Doob provides an overview of the issues and themes that have emerged over the previous decade, and discusses the future of sentencing reform in Canada.

Introduction

Sentencing policy in Canada during the last two decades of the twentieth century can be described in two quite different ways. It was a period in which fundamental and irreversible changes were made to the structure of sentencing. At the same time, it can be described as a time in which there was a lot of discussion and legislative activity, although little of substance changed. In this chapter, I will outline why I believe that both of these perspectives are correct. The preceding chapters have accomplished two important tasks: they have provided a picture of the various components of the sentencing process and outlined the wide range of problems with the structure of sentencing that have not yet been adequately addressed. From these chapters, we can detect two major inadequacies: the overall structure of the sentencing system is not yet clear or coherent and the major problems that have been identified with sentencing over the past few decades still exist.

After reviewing these problems – which demonstrate how little has changed in the past few decades – I will outline why I believe nonetheless that there has been a fundamental change in the structure of sentencing. Essentially, I shall argue that this change has emerged because Parliament has unambiguously asserted its responsibility for sentencing.

The Structure of the Sentencing 'System' in Canada Is Still Unclear

Almost every chapter in this book identifies – explicitly or implicitly – significant ambiguities in the way in which sentencing 'policy' is laid out. The most obvious weakness in the sentencing structure in this country relates to the purposes and principles of sentencing. As noted in several chapters, the question of *why* we punish offenders is not clear. We may finally have legislated the principle that the amount of punishment an offender should receive should be roughly (though we do not say 'roughly') proportionate to the harm for which the offender is responsible. However, we then go on to modify the 'principle of proportionality' by listing other factors to be taken into account in sentencing (the aggravating factors in subsection 718.2(a) of the Criminal Code) but, as pointed out earlier in this volume, we do not mention the factor that most frequently collides with proportionality: the criminal record of the offender. And even if we did list an offender's criminal record as an 'aggravating' factor, this would not help very much. If we were told the obvious – that sentences should be harsher for repeat offenders – we would not know how to implement this principle. Does any criminal record 'count'? Does it matter how long ago the previous offence was committed? Does the degree of similarity between the current offence and any previous convictions make a difference? There is a long list of questions that one could ask about how to punish offenders with a criminal history. Unfortunately, no clear policy exists that would provide an unambiguous answer to any of these questions.

The fundamental question of why we punish offenders is not answered by the new sentencing sections of the Criminal Code. Are we punishing people to make the rest of us safe, or are we punishing them for the crimes that they have committed? Parliament's response to this question is not very helpful, since it does not explain how sentencing is supposed to accomplish the vague goals laid out for it. Section 718 of the Code states that '[t]he fundamental purpose of sentencing is to contribute, along with crime prevention initiatives, to respect for the law and the maintenance of a just, peaceful and safe society by imposing just sanctions that have [one or more of the standard purposes of sentencing].'

There are many reasons why we have not made much progress in creating a meaningful sentencing structure.[2] In the first place, as this volume should make abundantly clear, sentencing is inherently a complex problem. And, as an almost ignored area of public policy, it will require the government to make some difficult decisions. The chapters in this book that deal with purposes and principles of sentencing make this clear. In fact, coming to grips with the purpose of sentencing should be expected to be difficult, and it is almost certain to create conflict. Conflict can be productive, even if one knows that, in the end, it is unlikely that everyone can be pleased. But establishing a meaningful compromise on sentencing policy is unlikely to win any politician many votes: difficult compromises on complex issues, where nobody is fully happy, hold little attraction for politicians. Unless a minister of justice were to decide that it is more important to be honest with the public and challenge the view that complex public issues can be reduced to simple political slogans, we are not likely to get far with sentencing policy.

Developing the structure of sentencing policy is not an easy task. It first requires convincing those responsible for sentencing policy that a meaningful structure is necessary. This, in itself, is difficult. The Canadian Sentencing Commission (1987) pointed out that 'individualized sentences' are cherished by many observers of the sentencing process. The theory of individualized sentences is simple: judges look at the 'whole' offence and the 'whole' offender. They consider half a dozen or more possible purposes of sentencing and come to a unique or personal blend 'appropriate' to the case in question. They then take scores of factors into account in trying to accomplish this blend of purposes to finally arrive at the 'right' sentence. The fact that two judges looking at the same case might come up with different sentences is not, in a system of individualized sentencing, a problem.

A judge once asked me to describe the evidence for unwarranted disparity in sentencing. I summarized various kinds of evidence, including a sentencing exercise carried out in the 1980s in which 206 provincial court judges were given the same written cases and asked to indicate what sentences they would impose (Palys and Divorski 1986). The results of that study were simple and predictable: there was enormous variation in the sentences that judges thought were appropriate. For some cases, sentences varied between probation alone and a long prison term. The judge listened to me patiently and then suggested that this was not a problem; in his view, the judges who had recommended these very different sentences might both have been right.

What he meant was that if two judges were able to give sensible explanations for what they had done, and if both had tried to accomplish legally defensible purposes, then both might be seen as having given 'correct' sentences. The fact that I, as an outsider, or the victims as people with special concerns, or the identical offenders who would be serving dramatically different sentences for the identical crimes might see this as a 'problem' was irrelevant. The two sentences were 'right' because each had been 'individualized' in a sensible and thoughtful manner.

The Supreme Court of Canada has described sentencing in Canada as 'profoundly subjective' in nature and, in effect, it has endorsed the view that this subjectivity is to be celebrated rather than challenged. Other jurisdictions have found that sentencing does not have to be 'profoundly subjective'; fortunately, the Supreme Court of Canada did not have to consider that evidence. My guess is that policy makers in Ottawa would have a quick answer for my concern that we should not celebrate unprincipled variation in sentencing. They would respond that legislation now places severe – if not absolute – constraints on the subjectivity of sentencing. If the words 'would appear to some to place' were substituted for 'place' I would agree with them.

Since the proclamation of Bill C-41 in 1996, judges have been directed by Parliament that '[a] sentence should be similar to sentences imposed on similar offenders for similar offences committed in similar circumstances' (subsection 718.2(b) of the Criminal Code). On the surface, this would seem to be a fairly clear direction. But aside from qualifying in the Guinness Book of Records for the law that uses the same adjective ('similar') the most times (four) in one sentence, the unfortunate sentencing judge is not given much direction. Consider the following questions:

- Are these 'similar offences'?
  - (a) A theft of a bicycle from a large multinational discount store.
  - (b) A theft of a bicycle from a destitute fourteen-year-old who uses the bicycle to earn money to help support his unemployed parents.
- Are these 'similar offenders' when deciding whether the offender should be imprisoned?
  - (a) An employed offender with a family to support but no assets other than his future earnings.
  - (b) An unemployed offender with a family to support who is presently supported through General Welfare Assistance and whose family would continue to receive welfare if he were in prison?
- Have these offences been 'committed in similar circumstances'?
  - (a) A sexual assault where a drunk male eighteen-year-old at a party touches a woman's breasts.
  - (b) A sexual assault carried out by a sober male eighteen-year-old who commits the identical physical act at school to show off to his friends?
- Are these 'similar sentences'?
  - (a) A sentence of six months in prison for one of the sexual assaults described in the previous question.
  - (b) A six-month conditional sentence of imprisonment where the judge sentences the eighteen-year-old to six months in prison and then orders that the sentence be served in the community?

These questions are currently raised, but not answered, by the Criminal Code.

Unfortunately, issues surrounding purposes and principles are not the only areas of ambiguity in sentencing in Canada. There is the important and unresolved problem of how we deal with different groups in the sentencing process. The Criminal Code tells judges that 'all available sanctions other than imprisonment that are reasonable in the circumstances should be considered for all offenders, with particular attention to the circumstances of aboriginal offenders' (subsection 718.2(e)). However, the Code is silent on exactly how this is to be operationalized. Furthermore, interestingly enough, given that there is considerable evidence that male motivation for committing certain crimes differs from that of women, no special instruction is given to judges about the special 'circumstances' of female offenders. One could easily argue that female offenders are more in need of special attention, since sentencing them may well have immediate and long-lasting impacts on truly innocent others (cf. Johnston (1995)).

There are other structural matters that clearly disadvantage already disadvantaged groups in the sentencing process – whether they be aboriginal offenders, black offenders, or women. Certain 'neutral'-sounding rules may in fact create structural inequities. An informal rule in a province that says that instead of being sentenced to prison a person might serve a conditional sentence of imprisonment in the community if he or she could be 'electronically monitored' could easily exclude those who do not have stable addresses or telephones. More generally, if the 'sentencing alternatives' are not available in a community, or if the 'sentencing options' are not available to the judge in the community, or, in either case, if the broad characteristics of the offender in terms of class, race, education, or economic situation would disqualify an offender from particular sentencing options, do we have a fair sentencing system? To return to a very specific example, if the offender must have ties to a community in order to be able to take advantage of the existence of 'sentencing circles' (or any other innovation in sentencing), what does this mean for the offender who is simply a visitor in the community? Do visitors automatically deserve harsher sentences than those offenders who have ties to the community?

Parliament's actions in the past few years have not helped to clarify other issues, either. For example, the maximum sentences outlined in the Criminal Code give little, if any, guidance to judges on how to sentence. We have a rather bizarre pattern of maximum penalties in Canada. The fact that breaking into a house is punishable by life in prison and sexual assault with a weapon or causing bodily harm is punishable by a maximum of fourteen years might make members of the public think that housebreaking was a more serious crime than serious sexual assault. I doubt if parliamentarians in the early 1980s, when the sexual assault sections were being debated, would have endorsed such a view.[3]

The two chapters on conditional sentences present additional evidence of the fact that the sentencing structure is rather confusing. A new type of sentence is available to judges, yet even a cursory reading of court of appeal decisions suggests that there is enormous disagreement about when it should be used. Probably the most interesting aspect of the debate over conditional sentences of imprisonment, however, is the fact that it has raised the issue of 'purposes' when imposing sentences. The conditional sentence can easily be seen as incapable of achieving certain purposes of sentencing (especially 'denouncing unlawful conduct') to the same degree as does a conventional prison sentence. Perhaps for the first time, judges are now grappling with the relationship between the purposes of sentencing and the sentence that is handed down, beyond simple consideration of whether a sentence is severe enough to accomplish certain goals. But the problems involved in conditional sentences cannot easily be resolved by judges: clearer guidance from Parliament would constitute a more effective way of dealing with these very real problems.

These are only a few examples of insufficient legislative and judicial guidance on sentencing. We may never have a completely understandable and predictable sentencing system in Canada, but the fact that no system is perfect and that no system will please all groups or individuals does not mean that Canada could not improve its present structure.

The Major Problems That Have Been Identified with Sentencing Still Exist

The Canadian Sentencing Commission (1987) provided a convenient list of the problems that exist with sentencing. I will not repeat that list, but I will discuss a few of the more important problems identified. One has already been mentioned: the lack of clear policy directives from Parliament.

As noted, the maximum penalty structure is often incoherent, and it displays an absence of proportionality. The minimum sentences, too, are clearly problematic. Part of the problem, of course, is the peculiar array of offences that command mandatory minimum sentences. The murder offences carry mandatory minimum penalties, but the single most important mandatory minimum sentence (in terms of the number of people on whom it is imposed) is the minimum sentence for second and subsequent impaired driving convictions. In addition, there were, until recently, only a handful of mostly minor offences to which mandatory minimum sentences were attached.[4] However, new minimum penalties were introduced for a long list of serious offences involving violence where a firearm was involved. Although these offences are clearly serious ones, the introduction of minimum sentences was not predicated on a demonstrated need for a change in sentencing. The impetus was quite explicitly political: the minimum sentences were imposed as part of an extension of firearms controls. All firearms would, eventually, have to be registered and in recompense for this minor inconvenience, the 'bad guys' would get harsher penalties. The government of the day hoped, therefore, to be able to counter the claim that they were punishing only the law-abiding with their gun control legislation.

What was ignored in the debate on these 'firearms' provisions was the fact that the minimum penalties made an already inconsistent sentencing structure even more incoherent. It is noteworthy, for example, that the mandatory minimum sentences were not introduced as part of the sentencing reform bill. If they had been, questions might have been raised about the need for these particular minimum sentences. Does it really make sense to impose a mandatory minimum sentence on someone who uses a firearm to threaten a woman whose breasts he touches, but not on a man who brutally rapes a woman and cuts her face with a knife? These are the kinds of problems that are created when sentencing reform is driven by largely political motives.

In general, few, if any, thoughtful observers have ever been enthusiastic about minimum sentences, for a set of rather simple reasons. The primary concern about minimum sentences is that they create inequities (usually by violating principles of proportionality) without accomplishing anything. The Canadian Sentencing Commission's 1987 report describes these problems in detail. It is unfortunate, but not surprising, that ten years after that report was released we have more, not fewer, mandatory minimums.

Other structural problems with sentencing listed by the Canadian Sentencing Commission continue to exist. The difficulties with early release programs outlined by that commission provide a good example. What may have changed is the acceptance of the fact that early release from prison needs to be understood in the context of sentencing.

Unfortunately, other problems appear to be as serious as they were in the mid-1980s. All indications are that the public is just as upset with sentencing today as it has been in the past. Some have argued that this is not surprising: political leaders and criminal justice officials (e.g., police, attorneys general, Crown attorneys, etc.) repeatedly state or imply that 'tougher' sentencing provisions would make us safer. Those most fearful about crime are, as a result, most critical of the courts and of the police for not keeping them safe (Sprott and Doob 1997). Ministers of justice may occasionally point out that there are severe limits upon the ability of the criminal justice system to do anything about crime. Nevertheless, when they introduce Criminal Code amendments, they often state or imply that the amendments will make Canadians safer. It is, therefore, no wonder that at least three-quarters of Canadians (see Roberts (1994a); Sprott and Doob (1997)) want harsher sentences. If the minister of justice states or implies that a mandatory minimum sentence of four years for a violent offence involving firearms will improve our chances of being safe from these offences, why not have mandatory minimum sentences for all offences, or why not increase the mandatory minimums for these offences? When a judge, or a court of appeal, says that a sentence must be two years 'for reasons of general deterrence,' surely logic would dictate that a four- or five-year sentence would prove even more effective. The problem is that this logic is wrong: reviews of the deterrent impact of harsher penalties (see the Canadian Sentencing Commission 1987) demonstrate quite clearly that harsher penalties will not have an impact, even for offences like tax evasion, where one might expect people to be very thoughtful about risks (see Varma and Doob (1998)).

The chapter on sentencing patterns demonstrates that there are quite large differences across provinces in the way in which offenders are sentenced. This evidence of variation in sentencing may, of course, simply be the tip of the iceberg. It may be that even provinces which would appear to be similar in their sentencing practices for particular offenders may be using quite different factors in determining the sentence. In fact, of course, there is almost no reason to expect that the same case would be sentenced in a similar manner by different judges in this country. Aside from the admonitions that similar cases should be receiving similar sentences and that sentences should be proportional to the harm done, etc., there is no standard against which sentences can be evaluated.

Successive ministers of justice have acknowledged that we imprison too many people in Canada. In 1987, the Canadian Sentencing Commission identified this as one of the most serious problems in the sentencing system. Since that time, our imprisonment rate has gone up, although there are now admonitions in the Criminal Code that 'for all offenders, with particular attention to the circumstances of aboriginal offenders' the judge is to consider 'all available sanctions other than imprisonment that are reasonable in the circumstances' (subsection 718.2(e)). The problem is that the Code provides the judge with little advice as to what to do in particular cases. Indeed, even the 'principle' that sentences should be proportionate to the harm done tells the judge nothing about what the distribution of sentences should look like. More serious, given the rather broad consensus that we would be better off if we imprisoned fewer people, is the fact that the very same Parliament that introduced statements into the Criminal Code supporting this principle also introduced a number of provisions that are likely to increase prison populations and imprison people who would otherwise not be there. The mandatory minimum sentences will certainly have this impact. So, of course, will Canada's first sentencing guideline. The requirement that sentences other than imprisonment be justified by the judge for certain drug offences where aggravating factors exist (Controlled Drugs and Substances Act, subsection 10(3)) is likely to act, in effect, as a presumption in favour of imprisonment. Options other than imprisonment are attractive to government largely because they are likely to cost less. At the same time, the most easily identifiable offender group responsible for a high proportion of federal correctional beds – those serving sentences for murder – had their likely terms of imprisonment changed for reasons that seemed to have nothing whatsoever to do with any reason other than electoral politics. And, even though the government modified section 745 in an attempt to appease right-wing Canadians, the public pressure to repeal section 745.6, the so-called 'faint hope' clause for lifers, persists.

The variation that exists in the sentencing structure across the provinces shows up in quite dramatically different imprisonment rates across the provinces (Sprott and Doob 1998). Given that the number and type of cases brought to court vary across provinces, one might expect a certain amount of variation in imprisonment patterns as well. However, the size and nature of the variation suggests that crime does not account very well for the variation in imprisonment levels. The imprisonment data suggest that it may not be productive to think of 'Canada' as having a single rate of imprisonment. Sprott and Doob show that some provinces (such as Saskatchewan) have imprisonment rates that are twice those of others (e.g., Ontario). Equally dramatic are the differences in where these prisoners find themselves. Quebec and Ontario, for example, have quite similar overall imprisonment rates, but a much higher proportion of Quebec's prisoners are housed at the expense of the federal government than in Ontario. Such variation is the inevitable result of a sentencing system that lacks clear direction.

Part of the reason that major problems with sentencing in Canada continue to exist is that Parliament appears to prefer to make easy decisions that are politically attractive in the short run but which do not address the underlying problems. An obvious example of this is the provision in the Criminal Code allowing victims to make a 'victim impact statement.' At one level, a victim impact statement appears to make enormous sense. The present law highlights the principle that sentences should be proportional to the harm inflicted or threatened. One obvious way of acquiring such information is to allow the victim to present such evidence directly to the court. However, it is not that simple.

Imagine that two 'similar' offenders separately break into my house and my neighbour's house. Each offender steals a few hundred dollars' worth of electronic equipment and each does a few hundred dollars' worth of damage. Nobody likes to have their houses broken into, but research data suggest that the impact on burglary victims can vary considerably. Let us imagine that within a couple of days I have replaced the stolen items, had the damaged door repaired, and have more or less put the burglary out of my mind. My victim impact statement, if the offender happened to be apprehended and convicted, might describe this rather minimal impact. My neighbour, however, might be a different case. The well-being of his family might have been seriously affected by the burglary. One or more of them might now have trouble sleeping. Now fearful of being home alone, they might arrange their lives in complex ways so that they did not have to return home alone at night. They may not have had the cash (or insurance coverage) available to replace their lost items and repair the damage. All in all, the victimization could well have had a devastating impact.

The question that this hypothetical, but not implausible, scenario raises is simple: should one offender be treated leniently while another is punished harshly because he or she, by chance, happened to get a more vulnerable victim? Victims vary enormously in their responses to victimization, and for many crimes offenders do not choose their victims very carefully. The Criminal Code says that the judge, when sentencing 'shall consider any [properly prepared and filed victim impact statement]' (subsection 722(1) of the Criminal Code). Should the judge in the scenario I have just described 'consider' the statements, and then ignore the different impacts? Or should the judge punish my neighbour's offender harshly and let mine off with a 'mere slap on the wrist'?

The extension of victim impact statements into parole hearings can, in a similar way, create mischief. Obviously some victims may be able to provide the parole board with very important information – information, for example, that might help the board to decide whether there was a risk that the offender would reoffend. However, the broadly based views of victims as to whether an offender should be released (independent of the criteria laid out in the legislation for parole decisions) may favour some offenders and disadvantage others not because of what they did in the past or might do in the future but because 'their' victims may happen to have differing views about conditional release from prison.

These, obviously, are not the only problems that still exist in sentencing. Virtually every chapter in this book has described problems that remain adequately to be addressed. When might we expect changes to take place?

The Role of Parliament

In 1987, when the report of the Canadian Sentencing Commission was released, there was some discussion about when sentencing legislation would be implemented. There had been an attempt, in 1984, to introduce sentencing provisions to the Criminal Code, but those died on the order paper when the federal election was called. In 1996, however, sentencing legislation – much of which has been the focus of rather critical comments in this book – came into effect. As many chapters make clear, the problems of sentencing have not been solved by this legislation. However, at one level, an irreversible process has begun: Parliament has unambiguously taken responsibility for sentencing policy in this country. And it will not be able to turn that responsibility back to the courts. The run-up to the spring 1997 election – coming only nine months after the new sentencing provisions of the Criminal Code had come into effect – brought amendments to the new legislation.

In the case of conditional sentences, the legislation was amended to instruct the judge that, when considering whether a sentence of imprisonment should be served in the community, he or she should ensure that a conditional sentence 'would be consistent with the fundamental purpose and principles of sentencing' (subsection 742.1(b)) described in the Criminal Code. Apparently, there was political concern that conditional sentences were being used for violent and sexual offences, despite the fact that, as Justice Rosenberg notes in *Wismayer*,[5] this must have been the original 'intent' of Parliament, since there are provisions related to conditional sentences that concern only violent and/or sexual offences. By attempting to 'fine tune' the provisions for conditional sentences, Parliament, in effect, has taken responsibility for determining when conditional sentencing should be imposed. If Parliament, or Canadians in general, do not like the way in which conditional sentences are being used, it is clear who is to blame: the Parliament of Canada.

There are other areas in which Parliament's responsibility for sentencing policy is even more likely to be made clear. As Roberts and von Hirsch (1995) note, Parliament provided judges with a nonexhaustive list of aggravating factors in sentencing. As if to emphasize its responsibility for sentencing policy, Parliament added the admonishment, as part of the so-called motorcycle gang legislation in the days immediately prior to the calling of the 1997 federal election, that 'evidence that the offence was committed for the benefit of, or at the direction of or in association with a criminal organization' was now to be considered an aggravating factor (subsection 718.2(iv) of the Criminal Code). Having created an initial list of aggravating factors, and subsequently adding to it only months after the first list became law, Parliament has assumed complete responsibility for the determination of what is to be considered an aggravating factor and what is not.

Such decisions are not always easy to make. For example, in the legislation that came into force in 1996, Parliament indicated that 'evidence that the offender, in committing the offence, abused the offender's spouse or child' was an aggravating factor (paragraph 718.2(a)(ii) of the Criminal Code). Although most people would probably agree that family violence is a serious problem, it is remarkable that Parliament was able to decide, apparently without much controversy, that it was a more serious offence to hit one's own spouse than to hit a stranger's spouse and that violence directed at one's own child was automatically more deserving of a harsher sentence than violence directed at a stranger's child.

Roberts and von Hirsch also note that, surprisingly, criminal record does not appear in this list of legislated aggravating factors. One possibility, of course, is that Parliament assumed that judges 'knew' that criminal record was meant to be aggravating and there was no need to legislate it. However, the next time an offender with an extensive criminal record receives an apparently lenient sentence (based more on the offence than on the record), creating public controversy, it would seem to be reasonable for the public to ask Parliament to do something about it. In the past, the minister of justice could suggest that such decisions were within the realm of the trial courts or the courts of appeal. Now such a response simply would not, or should not, suffice.

Similarly, as has been pointed out, Parliament has, for better or worse, created a presumptive sentence in favour of imprisonment for certain drug offences. If an offender so convicted is not imprisoned, would it not be reasonable for the public to demand that Parliament clarifies its intent? More generally, Parliament has said that the severity of sentences *must* be proportionate to the harm done and the degree of responsibility of the offender. When it is shown, as inevitably it will be, that this is not being carried out, can Parliament evade the responsibility of creating a structure to ensure that its intent is carried out?

Conclusions

It is clear that much work remains to be done. With the exception of the legislation that came into place in 1996, changes in sentencing laws have been piecemeal and simplistic. Parliament began to address the complexities of sentencing laws in 1996, but immediately after these changes became part of the Criminal Code, it regressed to its old ways of looking for quick political fixes in the domain of sentencing. Whether we can, in the foreseeable future, expect to see comprehensive and integrated changes in the sentencing structure is hard to predict. Parliament's history in dealing with sentencing does not inspire optimism, however.

The term 'truth in sentencing' has come to mean, in various parts of the world, that the sentence as stated in court should bear a close resemblance to the sentence carried out by the state. If an offender is fined, we should expect that the offender will pay the fine rather than serve a prison term because of an inability to pay. If person is sentenced to twenty-four months in prison, that person should serve either the twenty-four months or a predictable portion of that sentence in prison rather than (as in our legislation at present) anywhere from six months to twenty-four months.

But another aspect of truth in sentencing seems not to be so popular in parliamentary circles. We will never make serious progress in sentencing unless we are truthful about what sentencing can and, more importantly, cannot accomplish. Part of Parliament's problem in approaching sentencing sensibly is that few public officials are willing to state clearly what is undoubtedly true about sentencing: variation in sentencing has little, if any, impact on levels of crime. We might succeed in creating an understandable and defensible structure for sentencing, but this will do nothing to reduce crime (see Doob (1996) for a discussion of this issue).

Debates about sentencing are certain to be controversial and unlikely to lead to unanimous support, even after thorough and thoughtful debate. It is equally likely that some criminal justice decision makers will be less pleased with the outcome than others. Ultimately, it is the Canadian public which suffers from an incoherent sentencing structure and it is the Canadian public which would benefit from a thorough, thoughtful, and honest reappraisal of sentencing in Canada. Such a reappraisal will not be easy, and those in charge of it will have to consider carefully whose interests should be given most weight in determining the policy. In their contribution to this book, Daubney and Parry suggest 'the policy direction ... not to have specific numerical guidelines ... was based on two major findings from consultations: most judges ... did not want guidelines ... [and] provinces, as represented by Crown attorneys ... did not want numerical guidelines ...' This could be stated in a different way: those most in control of sentencing at the moment are least in favour of shifting power and responsibility to others. Should we be surprised?

Those currently controlling the sentencing process might, however, oppose change less if they did not feel that they had to choose between extremes on a single dimension. At the moment, for example, judges may feel that the choice is between 'numerical guidelines that would be constraining on the judiciary' and 'flexibility to address the widely disparate types of cases that appear before the courts,' or between the current Canadian structure and guidelines such as those used in the U.S. federal system. These guidelines are almost uniformly seen as being a disaster, not just because they are directly responsible for enormous increases in prison populations, but also because they lack the flexibility that 'guidelines' are supposed to allow. Numerical guidelines are certainly not the only kind of guideline systems. There are numerous ways in which guidance on sentencing can be given, and the degree to which judges are to be constrained in their sentencing decisions can similarly vary enormously.

In conclusion, then, we face many challenges. The first task is to decide whose challenge sentencing is. We have accomplished that in Canada: Parliament has accepted the challenge. It will be interesting to see how, having taken the first step, Parliament will decide to move.

ENDNOTES

1 Anthony Doob is a Professor of Criminology at the University of Toronto. He has published extensively in the area of sentencing over the past two decades. From 1984 to 1987 he was a commissioner of the Canadian Sentencing Commission.

2 It can be argued that what is 'meaningful' is in the eye of the beholder. I will be using this term in a quite specific way. For a sentencing policy to be meaningful, it must exclude certain possibilities. A meaningful sentencing policy should guide the decision maker on which factors are relevant in the sentencing decision and which are irrelevant and should not be considered. A meaningful policy will not necessarily be seen as good by many or most observers. A policy that said, for example, that all offenders convicted of an offence should receive the same legislated sentence would probably qualify as meaningful. Yet it is unlikely, even for an offence such as theft under $5,000, that such a policy would be acceptable to many people since it would mean that the eighteen-year-old runaway girl escaping sexual and physical abuse at home, who stole a candy bar because she had not eaten in three days, would receive the same sentence as the professional thief who carefully engineered a theft of electronic equipment worth $4,500 from a warehouse in which he was working.

3 More confusing, of course, are the instances where maximum (or minimum) sentences are changed by Parliament. Do such changes mean that there should be a wholesale shift of sentences up or down the severity scale? Parliament, of course, does not have to answer such questions, although it might have been helpful if it did.

4 The Supreme Court of Canada, in 1988, eliminated one very important minimum sentence: the seven-year minimum for importing narcotics. See Roach (1989) for a discussion of this case.

5 *R. V. Wismayer* (1997), 115 C.C.C. (3d) 18 (Ont. C.A.).

References

Aboriginal Legal Services of Toronto. 1991. *Elders and Traditional Teachers Gathering on Birch Island Discussion on the Community Council Aug. 27–30, 1991.* Toronto: Aboriginal Legal Services of Toronto.

Adelberg, E., and C. Currie. 1987. *Too Few To Count: Canadian Women in Conflict with the Law.* Vancouver: Press Gang Publishers.

Advisory Board on Victims Issues. 1991. *Victims of Crime in Ontario – A Vision for the 1990's.* Toronto: Ministry of the Attorney General.

Allen, H. 1987. *Justice Unbalanced: Gender, Psychiatry and Judicial Decisions.* Milton Keyes: Open University Press.

American Psychiatric Association. 1994. *Diagnostic and Statistical Manual of Mental Disorders.* 4th ed. Washington, D.C.: American Psychiatric Association.

Arbour, the Honourable Louise. 1996. *Commission of Inquiry into Certain Events at the Prison for Women in Kingston.* Ottawa: Public Works and Government Services Canada.

Archambault Report (Report of the Royal Commission to Investigate the Penal System of Canada). 1938. Ottawa: King's Printer.

Ashworth, A. 1983. *Sentencing and Penal Policy.* London: Weidenfeld and Nicolson.

– 1992. *Sentencing and Criminal Justice.* London: Weidenfeld and Nicolson.

– 1995. *Sentencing and Criminal Justice.* 2d ed. London: Butterworths.

Attorney General of Canada. 1987. *Federal Government Proposals to Assist Victims of Crime.* Ottawa: Department of Justice Canada.

Beccaria, C. 1764/1963. *On Crimes and Punishments.* New York: Bobbs-Merrill.

Berlin, E. 1993. The Federal Sentencing Guidelines' Failure to Eliminate Sentencing Disparity: Governmental Manipulations before Arrest. *Wisconsin Law Review,* 187–230.

Birkenmayer, A., and S. Besserer. 1997. *Sentencing in Adult Provincial Courts: A Study of Nine Canadian Jurisdictions: 1993 and 1994.* Ottawa: Statistics Canada.

Birkenmayer, A., and J. Roberts. 1997. Sentencing in Adult Provincial Courts. *Juristat*, 17, no. 1.

Bonta, J., C. La Prairie, and S. Wallace-Capretta. 1997. Risk Prediction and Re-Offending: Aboriginal and Non-Aboriginal Offenders. *Canadian Journal of Criminology* 39:127–44.

Bottomley, K., and K. Pease. 1986. *Crime and Punishment: Interpreting the Data.* Milton Keynes: Open University Press.

Boutellier, J. 1996. *Beyond the Criminal Justice Paradox: Alternatives between Law Enforcement and Social Policy.* Chicago: Draft Paper prepared for the American Society of Criminology Meetings.

Braithwaite, J. 1989. *Crime, Shame and Reintegration.* Cambridge: Cambridge University Press.

Brantingham, P. 1985. Sentencing Disparity: An Analysis of Judicial Consistency. *Journal of Quantitative Criminology* 1:281–305.

British Columbia. Ministry of the Attorney General. *Crown Counsel Handbook.* Victoria, B.C.: B.C. Ministry of the Attorney General.

Brodeur, J.-P. 1990. The Attrition of Parole. *Canadian Journal of Criminology* 32:503–10.

Burtch, B., and R.V. Ericson. 1979. *The Silent System: An Inquiry into Prisoners Who Commit Suicide and [an] Annotated Bibliography.* Toronto: Centre of Criminology, University of Toronto.

Campbell, G. 1993. *An Examination of Recidivism in Relation to Offence Histories and Offender Profile.* Ottawa: Statistics Canada.

Campbell, K. 1990. Sentencing Reform in Canada. *Canadian Journal of Criminology*, 32:387–96.

Campbell, M., and D. Cole. 1985. Conditional Release Considerations in Sentencing. 42 *Criminal Reports* (3d) 191–206.

Canada. Correctional Services. 1995. *Basic Facts about Corrections in Canada 1994.* Ottawa: Ministry of the Solicitor General.

Canada. Department of Justice. 1990a. *Directions for Reform: A Framework for Sentencing, Conditional Release and Corrections.* Ottawa: Department of Justice Canada.

– 1990b. *Victim Impact Statement in Canada.* Volume 7: *A Summary of the Findings.* Ottawa: Research Section, Research and Development Directorate.

Canada. Government of Canada. 1982. *Sentencing.* Ottawa: Department of Justice Canada.

– 1990. *A Framework for Sentencing, Corrections and Conditional Release, Directions for Reform.* Ottawa: Minister of Supply and Services Canada.

Canada. Ministry of the Solicitor General. 1990. *Corrections and Conditional Release. Directions for Reform.* Ottawa: Minister of Supply and Services Canada.

– 1996. *Corrections Population Growth.* Ottawa: Solicitor General.

Canadian Bar Association. 1993. *Submission on Bill C-90.* Ottawa: Canadian Bar Association.

– *Submission on Bill C-45. Criminal Code Amendments. Judicial Review of Parole Eligibility.* Ottawa: Canadian Bar Association.

Canadian Centre for Justice Statistics. 1991. *Crime in Aboriginal Communities, Saskatchewan 1989.* Ottawa: Statistics Canada.

– 1993. *Police Reported Aboriginal Crime in Calgary, Regina and Saskatoon.* Ottawa: Statistics Canada.

– 1994. *Canadian Crime Statistics, 1993.* Ottawa: Ministry of Industry, Science and Technology.

– 1996. *Canadian Crime Statistics 1995.* Ottawa: Minister of Industry.

Canadian Sentencing Commission. 1987. *Sentencing Reform: A Canadian Approach.* Ottawa: Supply and Services Canada.

Canfield, C., and L. Drinnan. 1981. *Comparative Statistics: Native and Non-Native Federal Inmates – A Five Year History.* Ottawa: Correctional Services Canada.

Carter, E. 1979. *Police Report to the Civic Authorities of Metropolitan Toronto and Its Citizens.* Toronto: Catholic Archdiocese of Toronto.

[Cawsey Inquiry]. Report of the Task Force on the Criminal Justice System and Its Impact on the Indian and Metis People of Alberta. 1991. *Justice on Trial.* III, Working Papers & Bibliography.

Champion, D. 1994. *Measuring Offender Risk: A Criminal Justice Sourcebook.* Westport, Conn.: Greenwood Press.

Chunn, D., and S. Gavigan. 1995. Women, Crime and Criminal Justice in Canada. In M. Jackson and C. Griffiths, eds., *Canadian Criminology: Perspectives on Crime and Criminality.* Toronto: Harcourt Brace.

Chunn, D., and R. Menzies. 1990. Gender, Madness and Crime: The Reproduction of Patriarchal and Class Relations in a Psychiatric Court Clinic. *Journal of Human Justice* 1:33–54.

Clairmont, D. 1989. *Discrimination in Sentencing: Patterns of Sentencing for Assault Convictions.* Halifax: Royal Commission on the Donald Marshall Jr., Prosecution.

Clairmont, D., W. Barnwell, and A. O'Malley. 1989. *Sentencing Disparity and Race in the Nova Scotia Criminal Justice System.* Halifax: Royal Commission on the Donald Marshall Jr., Prosecution.

Clark, S., and Associates. 1989. *Sentencing Patterns and Sentencing Options Relating to Aboriginal Offenders.* Ottawa: Department of Justice, Policy, Programs and Research Sector.

Clarkson, C., and R. Morgan. 1994. Sentencing Reform: Lessons from Abroad. *European Journal of Crime, Criminal Law and Criminal Justice* 2:105.

Cole, D. 1997. Bill C-41: An Overview and Some Introductory Thoughts. Paper prepared for the annual Canadian Institute for the Administration of Justice Conference, Montreal, 24–26 April 1997.

Cole, D., and A. Manson. 1990. *Release from Imprisonment: The Law of Sentencing, Parole and Judicial Review.* Scarborough, Ont.: Carswell.

Commission on Systemic Racism in the Ontario Criminal Justice System. 1995. *Report of the Ontario Commission on Systemic Racism in the Ontario Criminal Justice System.* Toronto: Queen's Printer for Ontario.

Correctional Service of Canada. 1991. Judicial Review. Information for Staff. Ottawa: Correctional Service of Canada, Offender Management Division.

Corrections and Conditional Release Act, S.C. 1992, c. 20, s. 23.

Cook, D., and B. Hudson. 1993. *Racism and Criminology.* London: Sage.

Cousineau, F. 1988. *Legal Sanctions and Deterrence.* Research Reports of the Canadian Sentencing Commission, Ottawa: Department of Justice Canada.

Criminal Code, R.S.C. 1985, c. C-46.

Cumberland, J., and E. Zamble. 1992. General and Specific Measures of Attitudes toward Early Release of Criminal Offenders. *Canadian Journal of Behavioural Science* 24:442–55.

Daubney Committee. 1988. *Taking Responsibility: The Report of the Standing Committee on Justice and Solicitor General on Its Review of Sentencing, Conditional Release and Related Aspects of Corrections.* Ottawa: Queen's Printer.

Davis, M. 1976. The Prison Dilemma. In W. McGrath, ed., *Crime and Its Treatment in Canada.* 2nd ed., ch. 13. Toronto: Macmillan.

Doble, J., and J. Klein. 1989. *Punishing Criminals: The Public's View. An Alabama Survey.* New York: Edna McConnell Clark Foundation.

Donziger, S. ed., 1996. *The Real War on Crime: The Report of the National Criminal Justice Commission.* New York: HarperCollins.

Doob, A. 1986. *Sentencing Information Systems.* Toronto: Centre of Criminology, University of Toronto.

– 1990. Community Sanctions and Imprisonment: Hoping for a Miracle but Not Bothering Even to Pray for It. *Canadian Journal of Criminology* 32:415–28.

– 1995a. *Race, Bail and Imprisonment.* Toronto: Centre of Criminology, University of Toronto.

– 1995b. The United States Sentencing Commission Guidelines: If You Don't Know Where You Are Going, You Might Not Get There. In C. Clarkson, and R. Morgan. eds., *The Politics of Sentencing Reform.* Oxford: Clarendon Press.

– 1996. *Criminal Justice Reform in a Hostile Climate.* Proceedings of the Canadian Institute for the Administration of Justice Meeting. Montreal: Thenias.

Doob, A., and J. Roberts. 1983. *Sentencing: The Public's View.* Ottawa: Department of Justice Canada.

– 1984. Social Psychology, Social Attitudes and Attitudes toward Sentencing. *Canadian Journal of Behavioural Science* 16:269–80.

– 1988. Public Punitiveness and Public Knowledge of the Facts: Some Canadian Surveys. In N. Walker and M. Hough, eds., *Public Attitudes to Sentencing*. Aldershot: Gower.

Dozois, J., M. Frechette, G. Lemire, A. Normandeau, and P. Carriere. 1989. La détermination de le peine: bilan critique de la Commission Archambault. *Canadian Journal of Criminology* 31:63–80.

Dumont, H. 1993. *Pénologie, Le droit canadien relatif aux peines et aux sentences*. Montreal: Les Éditions Themis.

Duryea, M., and J. Grundison. 1993. *Conflict and Culture: Research in Five Communities in Vancouver, British Columbia*. Victoria, B.C.: University of Victoria Institute for Dispute Resolution.

Dutton, D. 1987. The Criminal Justice Response to Wife Assault. *Law and Human Behavior* 11:189–206.

Equal Opportunity Consultants. 1989. *Perceptions of Racial Minorities Related to the Services of the Ministry of the Attorney General*. Toronto: Ontario Ministry of the Attorney General.

Everson, G. 1919. The Human Element in Justice. *Journal of Criminal Law and Criminology,* 10:90–9.

Fauteux Report. Report of a Committee Appointed to Inquire into the Principles and Procedures Followed in the Remission Service of the Department of Justice of Canada. 1956. Ottawa: Queen's Printer.

Frankel, M. 1992. Sentencing Guidelines: A Need for Creative Collaboration. *Yale Law Journal* 101, no. 8, 2043–51.

Gabor, T. 1990. Looking Back or Moving Forward: Retribution and the Canadian Sentencing Commission's Proposals. *Canadian Journal of Criminology* 32:537–46.

Garland, D. 1990. *Punishment and Modern Society: A Study in Social Theory*. Chicago: University of Chicago Press.

Gaudet, F. 1938. Individual Differences in the Sentencing Tendencies of Judges. *Archives of Psychology* 230:1–57.

Gemmell, J. 1997. The New Conditional Sentencing Regime. *Criminal Law Quarterly* 39:334–62.

Gendreau, P., and C. Goggin. 1997. Correctional Treatment: Accomplishments and Realities. In P. Van Voorhis, M. Braswell, and D. Lester, eds., *Correctional Counselling and Rehabilitation*. Cincinatti: Anderson.

Gerstein, R. (Chair) 1980. *Report of the Task Force on the Racial and Ethnic Implications of Police Hiring, Training, Promotion and Career Development*. Toronto: Ministry of the Solicitor General.

Giliberti, C. 1990a. Study Probes Effectiveness of Victim Impact Statements. *Justice Research Notes* 1:1–8.

– 1990b. *Victim Impact Statements in Canada: A Summary of Findings.* Ottawa: Department of Justice Canada.

Glasbeek, H. 1994. *Police Shootings of Black People in Ontario.* Toronto: Queen's Printer.

Globe and Mail. 1997. White Men's Sentences Draw Scorn of Natives, Women. 31 January, 1–3.

Gordon, D. 1991. *The Justice Juggernaut: Fighting Street Crime, Controlling Citizens.* New Brunswick, N.J.: Rutgers University Press.

Green, A. 1990. Asking for More? References of Unduly Lenient Sentences. *Current Legal Problems* 43:55–75.

Hagan, J. 1975. Law, Order and Sentencing: A Study of Attitude in Action. *Sociometry* 38:375–84.

Hall, D. 1997. Victims' Voices in Criminal Court: The Need for Restraint. In M. Wasik, ed., *The Sentencing Process.* Dartmouth: Aldershot.

Hann, R., and W. Harman. 1993. Predicting Release Risk for Aboriginal Penitentiary Inmates. *User Report Number 21.* Ottawa: Ministry of the Solicitor General.

Hogarth, J. 1971. *Sentencing as a Human Process.* Toronto: University of Toronto Press.

Hood, R. 1992. *Race and Sentencing: A Study of the Crown Court. A Report for the Commission for Racial Equality.* Oxford: Clarendon Press.

Hough, M., and J. Roberts. 1998. *Attitudes to Punishment: Findings from the British Crime Survey.* Home Office Research Study Number 179. London: Home Office.

Indian and Northern Affairs Canada. 1995a. *Indian Register Population by Sex and Residence, 1994.* Ottawa: Department of Indian Affairs and Northern Development, Information Management Branch.

– 1995b. *Basic Departmental Data, 1994.* Ottawa: Department of Indian Affairs and Northern Development, Information Management Branch.

Jackson, M. 1983. *Prisoners of Isolation.* Toronto: University of Toronto Press.

– 1988. *Locking Up Natives in Canada.* Ottawa: A Report of the Canadian Bar Association Committee on Imprisonment and Release.

Johnston, D. 1995. Effects of Parental Incarceration. In K. Gabel and D. Johnston, eds., *Children of Incarcerated Parents.* New York: Lexington.

Jull, K. 1997. The Brave New World of Sentencing: A Principled Approach to Bill C-41 (unpublished manuscript available from the author).

Kaplan, H.I., B.J. Sadock, and J.A. Grebb. 1994. *Kaplan and Sadock's Symposium of Psychiatry.* Baltimore: Williams and Wilkins.

Kershaw, A., and M. Lasovich. 1991. *Rock-a-Bye-Baby: A Death behind Bars.* Toronto: McClelland & Stewart.

Langan, P. 1994. No Racism in the Criminal Justice System. *Public Interest* 117 (Fall): 48–51.

La Prairie, C. 1990. The Role of Sentencing in the Over-Representation of Aboriginal People in Correctional Institutions. *Canadian Journal of Criminology* 32:429–40.

– 1995. *Seen but Not Heard: Native People in the Inner City.* Ottawa: Department of Justice, Canada.

– 1996. *Examining Aboriginal Corrections in Canada.* Ottawa: Ministry of the Solicitor General, Corrections Policy Branch.

– 1997. *The Role of Criminal Justice in the Broader Social Justice Agenda for Aboriginal People in Canada.* Regina: Saskatchewan Justice (unpublished manuscript).

Law Reform Commission of Canada. 1985. *Brief Submitted to the Canadian Sentencing Commission.* Ottawa: Law Reform Commission of Canada.

– 1991. *Aboriginal Peoples and Criminal Justice: Equality, Respect and the Search for Justice.* Ottawa: Law Reform Commission of Canada.

Lee, S. Some Views on the Sentencing Process. Paper prepared for the annual Canadian Institute for the Administration of Justice Conference, Montreal, 24–26 April 1997.

Lewis, S. 1989. *Report to the Premier of Ontario.* Toronto: Queen's Printer for Ontario.

Lipkin, R. 1990. Free Will, Responsibility and the Promise of Forensic Psychiatry. *International Journal of Law and Psychiatry* 13:331–59.

Maclean's. 1995. Crime: The Perception Gap. 2 January, 28–9.

Mann, C. 1993. *Unequal Justice: A Question of Color.* Bloomington: Indiana University Press.

Manson, A. 1996. The Supreme Court Intervenes in Sentencing. 43 *Criminal Reports* (4th) 306–16.

– 1997a. Finding a Place for Conditional Sentences. 3 *Criminal Reports* (5th) 283–300.

– 1997b. McDonnell and the Methodology of Sentencing. 6 *Criminal Reports* (5th) 277–92.

– 1997c. The Appeal of Conditional Sentences of Imprisonment. 10 *Criminal Reports* (5th) 279–90.

– 1998. A Brief Reply to Professors Roberts and von Hirsch. 10 *Criminal Reports* (5th) 232–5.

[Martin Report] Ontario. Ministry of the Attorney General. 1993. *Report of the Attorney General's Advisory Committee on Charge Screening, Disclosure and, Resolution Discussions.* (Chair: G.A. Martin). Toronto: Queen's Printer.

McCaskill, J 1988. *A Study of Needs and Resources Related to Offenders of Native Origin in Manitoba: A Longitudinal Analysis.* Ottawa: Corrections and Planning Branch, Solicitor General Canada.

McCord, D. 1993. In the Name of Justice! *Justice Report* 8, no. 2, 1–6.

McCormick, P. 1993. Sentence Appeals to the Alberta Court of Appeal, 1985–1992: A Statistical Analysis of the Laycraft Court. *Alberta Law Review* 31:624–43.

McDonald, J. 1992. *Federal Sentencing in Transition, 1986–90.* Washington, D.C.: Bureau of Justice Statistics.

McFatter, R. 1978. Sentencing Strategies and Justice: Effects of Punishment Philosophy on Sentencing Decisions. *Journal of Personality and Social Psychology* 36:1490–1500.

Meeker, J., W. Jesilow and J. Aranda. 1992. Bias in Sentencing: A Preliminary Analysis of Community Service Sentences. *Behavioural Sciences and the Law* 10:197–206.

Metro Toronto Task Force on Human Relations (Chair Walter Pitman). 1977. *Now Is Not too Late.* Toronto: Council of Metropolitan Toronto.

Meyer, J., and P. Jesilow. 1997. *'Doing Justice' in the People's Court: Sentencing by Municipal Court Judges.* Albany, N.Y.: State University of New York Press.

Miller, M. 1995. Rehabilitating the Federal Sentencing Guidelines. *Judicature* 78, no. 4, 180–8.

Morris, N., and M. Tonry. 1990. *Between Prison and Probation: Intermediate Punishments in a Rational Sentencing System.* New York: Oxford University Press.

Morrison, P. 1993. *Research File for the Commission on Systemic Racism in the Ontario Criminal Justice System.* Ottawa: Canadian Centre for Justice Statistics.

Moyer, S. 1987. *Homicides Involving Adult Suspects, 1962–1984: A Comparison of Natives and Non-Natives.* Ottawa: Ministry of the Solicitor General.

Moyer, S., and L. Axon. 1993. *An Implementation Evaluation of the Native Community Council Project of Aboriginal Legal Services of Toronto.* Toronto: Ministry of the Attorney General.

Moyer, S., B. Billingsley, F. Kopelman, and C. La Prairie. 1987. *Native and Non-Native Admissions to Federal, Provincial and Territorial Correctional Institutions.* Ottawa: Ministry of the Solicitor General.

Muirhead, G. 1982. *An Analysis of Native Over-Representation in Correctional Institutions in B.C.* Victoria: Ministry of the Attorney General, Corrections Branch.

Nadin-Davis, R., and C. Sproule. 1982. *Canadian Sentencing Digest* (Quantum Service). Toronto: Carswell.

National Crime Prevention Council. 1996. *Evaluating the Effects of Imprisonment.* Ottawa: National Crime Prevention Council.

– 1997. *Incarceration in Canada.* Ottawa: National Crime Prevention Council.

Norris, J. 1996. Sentencing for Second Degree Murder: *Regina v. Shropshire. Canadian Criminal Law Review* 1:199–220.

Nuffield, J. 1996. *Evaluation of the Adult Victim–Offender Mediation, Saskatoon Community Mediation Services.* Regina: Saskatchewan Justice.

Ontario. Legislative Assembly. *Standing Committee on Administration of Justice Report Under Standing Order 125 on the Relationship between Victims of Crime and the Justice System in Ontario: Current Status and Improvements.* 3rd Session, 35th Parliament, 43 Elizabeth II, 1994.

Ontario. Ministry of the Solicitor General and Correctional Services. 1997. *Admissions to Corrections, 1995/96 Fiscal Year.* Toronto.

Ouimet Report (Canadian Committee on Corrections). 1969. *Towards Unity: Criminal Justice and Corrections. Report of the Canadian Committee on Corrections.* Ottawa: Queen's Printer.

Palmer, S. 1994. *Assault Causing Bodily Harm: Analyses of RCMP Data.* Ottawa: Department of Justice Canada, Research and Development Directorate.

Palys, T., and S. Divorski. 1986. Explaining Sentence Disparity. *Canadian Journal of Criminology* 28:347–62.

Parent, D. 1988. *Structuring Criminal Sentences: The Evolution of Minnesota's Sentencing Guidelines.* Toronto: Butterworths.

Parent, D., T. Dunworth, D. McDonald, and W. Rhodes. 1996. Key Legislative Issues in Criminal Justice: Mandatory Sentencing. Washington, D.C.: U.S. Department of Justice, National Institute of Justice, *NIJ Research in Action Series* (NCJ 161839).

– Key Legislative Issues in Criminal Justice: The Impact of Sentencing Guidelines. Washington, D.C.: U.S. Department of Justice, National Institute of Justice, *NIJ Research in Action Series,* November 1996 (NCJ 161837).

Parker, G. 1976. The Law of Probation. In Law Reform Commission of Canada, *Community Participation in Sentencing,* 51–118. Ottawa: Ministry of Supply and Services Canada.

Parliamentary Sub-Committee on the Penitentiary System in Canada. 1977. *Report to Parliament by the Sub-Committee on the Penitentiary System in Canada.* Ottawa: Supply and Services Canada.

Paschalli, M., R. Robert, L. Flewelling, and S. Ennett. 1996. Racial Differences in Violent Behaviour among Young Adults: Moderating and Confounding Effects. University of North Carolina at Chapel Hill, Triangle Research Institute (unpublished report).

Petersilia, J., S. Turner, and J. Peterson. 1986. *Prison v. Probation in California: Implications for Crime and Offender Recidivism.* Santa Monica, Cal.: Rand Corporation.

Pires, A. 1990. Le devoir de punir: le rétributivisme face aux sanctions communautaires. *Canadian Journal of Criminology* 32:441–61.

Prince, N. 1996. Some Comments on the Victim Witness Assistance Program. Paper prepared for the City of Scarborough Solutions for Safety Conference Toronto, 11 November 1996.

Quigley, T. 1996. New Horizons in Sentencing? *Canadian Criminal Law Review* 1:278–91.

– 1997. *Procedure in Canadian Criminal Law.* Scarborough, Ont.: Carswell.

R. v. Alessandro (1995), 28 W.C.B. (2d) 520 (Ont. Gen. Div.).
R. v. Alton (1989), 53 C.C.C. (3d) 252 (Ont. C.A.).
R. v. Askov, [1990] 2 S.C.R. 1119.
R. v. Aylward (1978), 43 C.C.C. (2d) 455 (Ont. C.A.).
R. v. B. (A.J.) (1994), 90 C.C.C. (3d) 211 (Nfld. C.A.).
R. v. Bahari (1994), 78 O.A.C. 397.
R. v. Bailey, [1970] 4 C.C.C. 291 (Ont. C.A.).
R. v. Bezeau (1958), 122 C.C.C. 35 (Ont. C.A.).
R. v. Black (1991), 14 W.C.B. (2d) 98 (Ont. Gen. Div.).
R. v. Blacquiere (1975), 24 C.C.C. (2d) 168 (Ont. C.A.).
R. v. Blue (1989), 101 N.B.R. (2d) 57 (C.A.).
R. v. Boucher (1991), 13 W.C.B. (2d) 638 (Alta. C.A.).
R. v. Brown, Highway, Umpherville (1992), 73 C.C.C. (3d) 242 (Alta. C.A.).
R. v. Cain (1993), 28 B.C.A.C. 105 (B.C.C.A.).
R. v. Careen (1993), 105 Nfld. & P.E.I.R. 263 (Nfld. C.A.).
R. v. Chief (1989), 74 C.R. (3d) 57 (Y.T.C.A.).
R. v. Coffey (1965), 51 M.P.R. 7 (Nfld. C.A.).
R. v. Cooper (1997), 117 C.C.C. (3d) 268 (Ont. C.A).
R. v. Cotton Felts Ltd (1982), 2 C.C.C. (3d) 65 (Ont. C.A.).
R. v. Courtney (1956), 115 C.C.C. 260 (B.C.C.A.).
R. v. Culley (1977), 36 C.C.C. (2d) 433 (Ont. C.A.).
R. v. Currie (1997), 115 C.C.C. (3d) 205 (S.C.C.).
R. v. Dankyi (1993), 86 C.C.C. (3d) 368 (Que. C.A.).
R. v. Daviault (1994), 33 C.R. (4th) 165.
R. v. Doyon (1979) 11 C.R. (3d) 188 (Que. C.A.).
R. v. Dunn (1995), 35 C.R. (4th) 247 (S.C.C.).
R. v. Dyer, [1992] O.J. No. 2890 (Ont. Gen. Div.).
R. v. Elliot (1995), 64 B.C.A.C. 64.
R. v. Farizah (1994), 78 O.A.C. 399.
R. v. Fournier (1988), 84 N.B.R. (2d) 250 (C.A.).
R. v. Friesen (1994) 22 *Weekly Criminal Bulletin* (2d) 593 (B.C.C.A.).
R. v. G. (K.R.) (1991), 68 C.C.C. (3d) 268 (Ont. C.A.).
R. v. Gardiner (1982), 68 C.C.C. (2d) 477 (S.C.C.).
R. v. Gill (1991), 32 M.V.R. (2d) 249 (Ont. Prov. Div.).
R. v. Goulet (1995), 97 C.C.C. (3d) 61 (Ont. C.A.).
R. v. Guida (1989), 51 C.C.C. (3d) 305 (Que. C.A.).
R. v. Hamilton (1986), 30 C.C.C. (3d) 257 (Ont. C.A.).
R. v. Hayes (1996), 105 C.C.C. (3d) 425.
R. v. Heck (1963), 40 C.R. 142 (B.C.C.A.).
R. v. Holden, [1963] 2 C.C.C. 394 (B.C.C.A.).

R. v. Hollinsky (1995), 103 C.C.C. (3d) 472 (Ont. C.A.).
R. v. Houle (1993), 142 A.R. 67 (Q.B.).
R. v. Iwaniw: Overton (1959) 127 C.C.C. 40, adapted from 9 *Halsbury* (2d ed.) 256.
R. v. Jantunen (unreported), Ont. C.A., 4 April 1997.
R. v. Jenks, [1979] 4 W.W.R. 226 (Man. C.A.).
R. v. Joseyounen, [1995] 6 W.W.R. 438 (Sask. Q.B.).
R. v. Katsigiorgis (1987), 39 C.C.C. (3d) 256.
R. v. Keefe (1978), 3 W.C.B. (1978) 38 (Ont. C.A.).
R. v. Kendall (1996), 75 B.C.A.C. 90.
R. v. Kirisit, [1993] O.J. No. 1825 (Ont. C.A.).
R. v. Latimer (1997), 121 C.C.C. (3d) 326 (Sask. Q.B.), reversed [1998] S.J. No. 731 (C.A.).
R. v. Leaming (1992), 17 *Weekly Criminal Bulletin* (2d) 58 (Alta. Prov. Ct.).
R. v. Littlechild, [1993] A.J. No. 408 (Alta. C.A.).
R. v. Loughery (1992), 73 C.C.C. (3d) 411 (Alta. C.A.).
R. v. M. (C.A.) (1996), 46 C.R. (4th) 269 (S.C.C.).
R. v. McDonald (1997), 43 C.R.R. (2d) 328 (Ont. Prov. Div.).
R. v. McDonald (1998), 127 C.C.C. (3d) 57 (Ont. C.A.).
R. v. MacFarlane, [1997] P.E.I.J. No. 25 (P.E.I. Prov. Ct.).
R. v. McDonnell (1997), 114 C.C.C. (3d) 436 (S.C.C.).
R. v. McGillivary (1991), 62 C.C.C. (3d) 407 (Sask. C.A.).
R. v. McGillivray (unreported), Daniel J., Docket # 21054671P1, Calgary, Alberta, 16 September 1992.
R. v. McMillan, [1996] O.J. No. 4804 (Ont. Prov. Div.).
R. v. Meehan (1989), 53 C.C.C. (3d) 496 (Que. C.A.).
R. v. Meilleur (1981), 22 C.R. (3d) 185 (Ont. C.A.).
R. v. Miller (1987), 36 C.C.C. (3d) 100 (Ont. C.A.).
R. v. Mills (1998), 129 C.C. (3d) 313 (B.C.C.A.)
R. v. Moncini (1975), 4 W.W.R. 509 (B.C.C.A.).
R. v. Morales (1992), 17 C.R. (4th) 74 (S.C.C.).
R. v. Morin (1996), 101 C.C.C. (3d) 124 (Sask. C.A.).
R. v. Muise (1994), 94 C.C.C. (3d) 119 (N.S.C.A.).
R. v. Negridge (1980), 54 C.C.C. (2d) 304 (Ont. C.A.).
R. v. Oates (1992), 74 C.C.C. (3d) 360 (Nfld. C.A.).
R. v. Oliver (1997), 147 Nfld. & P.E.I.R. 210 (Nfld. C.A.).
R. v. Palmer and Palmer (1979), 50 C.C.C. (2d) 193 (S.C.C.).
R. v. Pepin (1990), 57 C.C.C. (3d) 355 (N.S.C.A.).
R. v. Pinnock (unreported), released 15 January 1996 (Ont. Prov. Div.).
R. v. Piscione, [1997] O.J. No. 4416 (Ont. Prov. Div.).
R. v. Priest (1996), 110 C.C.C. (3d) 289 (Ont. C.A.).

R. v. Read, [1995] O.J. No. 3962 (Ont. Gen. Div.).

R. v. Rezaie (1996), 31 O.R. (3d) 713 (C.A.).

R. v. Richardson (1963), 40 C.R. 179 (Man. C.A.).

R. v. Roberts [1963] 1 C.C.C. 27 (Ont. C.A.).

R. v. Sanatkar (1981), 64 C.C.C. (2d) 325 (Ont. C.A.).

R. v. Scott (1996), 152 N.S.R. (2d) 93 (N.S.C.A.).

R. v. Sherrin (1985), 38 M.V.R. 62 (B.C.Co.Ct.).

R. v. Shropshire (1996), 43 C.C.C. (4th) 269 (S.C.C.).

R. v. Simmons (1973), 13 C.C.C. (2d) 65 (Ont. C.A.).

R. v. Smith (1987), 34 C.C.C. (3d) 97 (S.C.C.).

R. v. Soucie, [1988] B.C.J. 1776 (B.C.Co.Ct.).

R. v. Spurway (1996), 94 O.A.C. 58.

R. v. Sriskantharanjah (1994), 90 C.C.C. (3d) 559 (Ont. C.A.).

R. v. Stairs (1994), 24 W.C.B. (2d) 92 (Ont. C.A.)

R. v. Stolar (1988), 40 C.C.C. (3d) 1 (S.C.C.).

R. v. Stuckless, [1998] 127, C.C.C. (3d) 225.

R. v. Switlishoff (1950), 97 C.C.C. 132 (B.C.C.A.).

R. v. Thomas (No. 2) (1980), 53 C.C.C. (2d) 285 (B.C.C.A.).

R. v. Thurotte (1971), 5 C.C.C. (2d) 129 (Ont. C.A.).

R. v. Wallner (1998), 44 C.C.C. (3d) 358 (Alta. C.A.).

R. v. Wilmott (1966), [1967] 1 C.C.C. 171 (Ont. C.A.).

R. v. Wust (1998), 125 C.C.C. (3d) 43 (B.C.C.A.).

R. v. Ziatas (1973), 13 C.C.C. (2d) 287 (Ont. C.A.).

R. v. Zurlo (1990), 57 C.C.C. (3d) 407 (leave to appeal to S.C.C. refused 60 C.C.C. (3d) vi).

Reed, M., and J. Roberts. 1998. Adult Correctional Services in Canada, 1996–97. *Juristat* 18(3).

Reiman, J. 1990. *The Rich Get Rich and the Poor Get Prison.* 3rd ed. New York: Macmillan.

Renaud, G. 1996. To Appear before the Court When Required to Do so by the Court: The Impact of Sentencing Reform. Discussion Paper, Ontario Judges Association.

Renner, K., and A. Warner. 1981. The Standard of Social Justice Applied to an Evaluation of Criminal Cases Appearing before the Halifax Courts. *Windsor Yearbook of Access to Justice* 1:62–80.

Report of the Aboriginal Justice Inquiry of Manitoba. 1991. *The Justice System and Aboriginal People, Manitoba: The Public Inquiry into the Administration of Justice and Aboriginal People.* Winnipeg: Queen's Printer.

Research Staff of the Canadian Sentencing Commission. 1988. *Views of Sentencing: A Survey of Judges in Canada.* Research Reports of the Canadian Sentencing Commission. Ottawa: Minister of Supply and Services Canada.

Rice, M. 1994. Fixed-Term Sentences of More Than 20 Years Versus Life Imprisonment. 36 *Criminal Law Quarterly* 474–83.

Roach, K. 1989. Smith and the Supreme Court: Implications for Sentencing Policy and Reform. *Supreme Court Law Review* 11: 433–79.

Roberts, J.V. 1988a. Early Release: What Do the Canadian Public Really Think? *Canadian Journal of Criminology* 30:231–9.

– 1988b. *Empirical Research on Sentencing.* Research Reports of the Canadian Sentencing Commission. Ottawa: Department of Justice Canada.

– 1988c. *Public Opinion and Sentencing: Surveys by the Canadian Sentencing Commission.* Research Reports of the Canadian Sentencing Commission. Ottawa: Department of Justice Canada.

– 1988d. *Sentencing in the Media: A Content Analysis of the English-Language Newspapers in Canada.* Research Reports of the Canadian Sentencing Commission. Ottawa: Department of Justice Canada.

– 1994a. *Public Knowledge of Crime and Justice.* Ottawa: Department of Justice Canada.

– 1994b. The Role of Criminal Record in the Federal Sentencing Guidelines. *Criminal Justice Ethics* 13:21–30.

– 1995a. Judicial Review: Abolition or Reform of Section 745? *Justice Report* 11:14–16.

– 1995b. New Data on Sentencing Trends in Provincial Courts. *Criminal Reports* 34:181–96.

– 1995c. Sentencing, Public Opinion and the News Media. *Revue Générale de Droit* 26:115–25.

– 1995d. *The Influence of Race on Sentencing Patterns in Toronto.* Report for the Commission on Systemic Racism in the Ontario Criminal Justice System. Ottawa: Department of Criminology, University of Ottawa.

– 1996a. Public Opinion, Criminal Record and the Sentencing Process. *American Behavioral Scientist* 39:488–99.

– 1996b. *Disproportionate Harm: An Analysis of Hate Crime Statistics.* Ottawa: Department of Justice Canada.

– 1997a. Criminal Record and the Sentencing Process. In M. Tonry, ed., *Crime and Justice: A Review of Research.* Volume 22. Chicago: University of Chicago Press.

– 1997b. Paying for the Past: The Role of Criminal Record in the Sentencing Process. In M. Tonry, ed., *Crime and Justice: A Review of Research.* Volume 22. Chicago: University of Chicago Press.

– 1997c. Refining the Role of Criminal Record in the Federal Sentencing Guidelines. *Federal Sentencing Reporter* 9:213–15.

– 1997d. The Sword of Damocles: Conditional Sentencing in Canada. *Canadian Criminal Law Review* 2:183–206.

Roberts, J.V., and A. Birkenmayer. 1997. Sentencing in Canada: Recent Statistical Trends. *Canadian Journal of Criminology* 39:459–82.

Roberts, J.V., and A. Doob. 1990. News Media Influences on Public Views of Sentencing. *Law and Human Behavior* 14:451–68.

– 1997. Race, Ethnicity and Criminal Justice. In M. Tonry and R. Hood, eds., *Ethnicity, Crime and Immigration: Comparative and Cross-National Perspectives. Crime and Justice: A Review of Research,* Volume 21. Chicago: Chicago University Press.

Roberts, J.V., and R. Gebotys. 1989. The Purposes of Sentencing: Public Support for Competing Aims. *Behavioural Sciences and the Law* 7:387–402.

Roberts, J.V., and M. Jackson. 1991. Boats against the Current: A Note on the Effects of Imprisonment. *Law and Human Behavior* 15:557–62.

Roberts, J.V., and C. La Prairie. 1996. Circle Sentencing: Some Unanswered Questions. *Criminal Law Quarterly* 39:69–83.

Roberts, J., and L. Stalans. 1997. *Public Opinion, Crime and Criminal Justice.* Boulder, Col.: Westview Press.

Roberts, J.V., and A. von Hirsch. 1992. Sentencing Reform in Canada: Recent Developments. *Revue Générale de Droit* 23:319–55.

– 1995. Statutory Sentencing Reform: The Purpose and Principles of Sentencing, *Criminal Law Quarterly* 35:220–42.

– 1998. Conditional Sentences of Imprisonment and the Fundamental Principle of Proportionality in Sentencing. 10 *Criminal Reports* (5th) 222–31.

Royal Commission on Aboriginal Peoples. 1996. *Bridging the Cultural Divide: A Report on Aboriginal People and Criminal Justice in Canada.* Ottawa: Queen's Printer.

Rubel, H. 1985–6. Victim Participation in Sentencing Proceedings. *Criminal Law Quarterly* 28:226–50.

Ruby, C. 1993a. What Price Justice in Ontario. *Toronto Star,* 28 June, A17.

– 1993b. Diversionary Tale of Salvation through Indulgence. *Toronto Star,* 12 July.

– 1994. *Sentencing.* 4th ed. Toronto: Butterworths.

Rudin, J. 1995. *Issues Related to the Establishment of Native Justice Systems.* Report Submitted to the Aboriginal Justice Directorate. Ottawa: Department of Justice, Canada.

Salhany, R. 1989. *Canadian Criminal Procedure.* 5th ed. Markham, Ont.: Canada Law Book.

Schneider, R. 1996. *Ontario Mental Health Statutes.* Scarborough, Ont.: Carswell.

Shaw, M. 1994. *Ontario Women in Conflict with the Law.* Ontario: Ministry of Correctional Services.

Skurka, S. 1993. Two Scales of Justice: The Victim as Adversary. *Criminal Law Quarterly* 35:334–54.

Smith, D. 1994. Race, Crime and Criminal Justice. In M. Maguire, R. Morgan, and R. Reiner, eds., *The Oxford Handbook of Criminology*. Oxford: Clarendon Press.

Sopinka, J., and M. Gelowitz. 1993. *The Conduct of an Appeal.* Toronto: Butterworths.

Soucy, N. 1996. Le profil de la clientèle des services correctionnels du Québec. *Faits et chiffres, bulletin d'information sur la recherche correctionnelle* 4(3), Quebec: Services correctionnels du Québec.

Sprott, J., and A.N. Doob. 1997. Fear, Victimization, and Attitudes to Sentencing, the Courts, and the Police. *Canadian Journal of Criminology* 39:275–92.

– 1998. Understanding Provincial Variation in Incarceration Rates, *Canadian Journal of Criminology* 40:305–22.

State of Washington Sentencing Guidelines Commission. 1996. *Adult Felony Sentencing.* Oregon: Washington Sentencing Guidelines Commission.

Statistics Canada. 1992. *Aboriginal People's Survey.* Ottawa: Statistics Canada.

– 1993. *The Violence against Women Survey.* The Daily.

– 1996a. Adult Correctional Services in Canada: Highlights for 1994–1995. *Juristat* 16(7). Ottawa: Canadian Centre for Justice Statistics.

– 1996b. The Justice Data Factfinder. *Juristat* 16(9). Ottawa: Canadian Centre for Justice Statistics.

– 1997. Adult Correctional Services In Canada, 1995–1996. *Juristat* 17(4). Ottawa: Canadian Centre for Justice Statistics.

Sutton, L. 1978. *Variations in Federal Criminal Sentences: A Statistical Assessment at the National Level.* Washington, D.C.: U.S. Department of Justice.

Task Force on Federally Sentenced Women. 1990. *Creating Choices: Report of the Task Force on Federally Sentenced Women.* Ottawa: Correctional Services of Canada.

Task Force Report. 1990. *Indian Policing Policy Review.* Ottawa: Indian Affairs and Northern Development.

Thomas, D. 1979. *Principles of Sentencing.* 2nd ed. London: Heinemann.

Tonry, M. 1987. *Sentencing Reform Impacts.* Washington, D.C.: U.S. Department of Justice, National Institute of Justice.

– 1993. The Failure of the U.S. Sentencing Commission's Guidelines. *Crime and Delinquency* 39:131–49.

– 1994. Editorial: Racial Disparities in Courts and Prisons. *Criminal Behaviour and Mental Health* 4:158–62.

– 1995a. *Malign Neglect: Race, Crime and Punishment in America.* New York: Oxford University Press.

– 1995b. Twenty Years of Sentencing Reform: Steps Forward, Steps Backward. *Judicature* 78, no. 4, 169–79.

– 1996. *Sentencing Matters.* New York: Oxford University Press.

Tremblay, P. 1989. Les fondements de la métrique pénale. *Canadian Journal of Criminology* 31:117–44.

Trotter, G. 1996. *R. v. Shropshire*: Sentencing, Murder and the Supreme Court of Canada. 43 *Criminal Reports* (4th) 288–316.

– 1997. The Role of Appellate Courts in the Canadian Sentencing Process. *Federal Sentencing Reporter* 9:262–65.

Turk, A. 1969. *Criminality and the Legal Order*. Chicago: Rand McNally.

Turner, J. 1993. *Sentencing in Adult Provincial Criminal Courts – A Study of Six Canadian Jurisdictions, 1991 and 1992*. Ottawa: Statistics Canada.

Umbreit, M., and R. Coates. 1992. The Impact of Mediating Victim-Offender Conflict: An Analysis of Programs in Three States. *Juvenile and Family Court Journal* 43, no. 1, 21–9.

United States Sentencing Guidelines Commission. 1991. *The Federal Sentencing Guidelines: A Report on the Operation of the Guidelines System and Short-Term Impacts on Disparity in Sentencing, Use of Incarceration, and Prosecutorial Discretion and Plea Bargaining*. Washington, D.C.: United States Sentencing Guidelines Commission.

– 1994a. *Just Punishment: Public Perceptions and the Federal Sentencing Guidelines*. Washington, D.C.: United States Sentencing Guidelines Commission.

– 1994b. *The Federal Sentencing Guidelines*. Washington, D.C.: United States Sentencing Guidelines Commission.

– 1995. *United States Sentencing Commission Guidelines Manual, 1995*. Washington, D.C.: United States Sentencing Guidelines Commission.

– 1996. *An Overview of the United States Sentencing Commission*. Washington, D.C.: United States Sentencing Guidelines Commission.

U.S. v. Armstrong. Brief amicus curiae of former law enforcement officials in support of respondents. 1996. *WL 17132, Sct-Brief*, Publishing Company.

Van Ness, D., D. Carlson, T. Crawford, and K. Strong. 1989. *Restorative Justice – Theory*. Washington, D.C.: Justice Fellowship.

Varma, K., and A. Doob. 1998. Deterring Economic Crimes: The Case of Tax Evasion. *Canadian Journal of Criminology*, forthcoming.

von Hirsch, A. 1976. *Doing Justice: The Choice of Punishments*. New York: Hill and Wang.

– 1985a. Guiding Principles for Sentencing: The Proposed Swedish Law. *Criminal Law Review* 746–54.

– 1985b. *Past or Future Crimes: Deservedness and Dangerousness in the Sentencing of Criminals*. New Brunswick, N.J.: Rutgers University Press.

– 1990. The Politics of 'Just Deserts.' *Canadian Journal of Criminology* 32:397–414.

– 1993. *Censure and Sanctions*. Oxford: Clarendon Press.

von Hirsch, A., and J. Greene. 1993. When Should Reformers Support Creation of Sentencing Guidelines? *Wake Forest Law Review* 28:329–43.

von Hirsch, A., and K. Hanrahan. 1979. *The Question of Parole: Retention, Reform or Abolition?* Cambridge, Mass.: Ballinger.

von Hirsch, A., M. Wasik, and J. Greene. 1989. Punishments in the Community and the Principles of Desert. *Rutgers Law Journal* 10:695–718.

Walker, N. 1985. *Sentencing Theory Law and Practice.* London: Butterworths.

– 1991. *Why Punish?* Oxford: Oxford University Press.

Waller, I. 1988. *The Role of the Victim in the Sentencing Process.* Research Reports of the Canadian Sentencing Commission. Ottawa: Department of Justice Canada.

Wasik, M. 1994. Sentencing Guidelines: The Problem of Conditional Sentences. *Criminal Justice Ethics* (Winter), 50–8.

Wees, G. 1996. Sentencing Guidelines: More States Look to Structured Sentencing to Enhance Equity, Consistency. *Corrections Compendium* 21, no. 7.

Wilbanks, W. 1987. *The Myth of a Racist Criminal Justice System.* Monterey, Cal.: Cole.

Wilde, O. 1981. De Profundis. In R. Aldington and S. Weintraub, eds., *The Portable Oscar Wilde.* Rev. ed. New York: Viking Press.

Wolfgang, M.E., and M. Riedel. 1973. Race, Judicial Discretion and the Death Penalty. *The Annals* 407 (May), 119–33.

Wortley, S., and D. Brownfield. 1996. Race, Police Contact and Perceptions of Criminal Injustice: Results from a Canadian Survey. Chicago: Paper presented at the American Society of Criminology Meetings.

York, P. 1995. *The Aboriginal Federal Offender: A Comparative Analysis between Aboriginal and Non-Aboriginal Offenders.* Ottawa: Correctional Services Canada.

Young, A. 1988. *The Role of an Appellate Court in Developing Sentencing Guidelines.* Research Reports of the Canadian Sentencing Commission. Ottawa: Department of Justice Canada.

– 1993. Two Scales of Justice: A Reply. *Criminal Law Quarterly* 35:355–75.

Zeisel, H., and G. Gallup. 1989. Death Penalty Sentiment in the United States. *Journal of Quantitative Criminology* 5:285–96.